youth specialties

ZONDERVAN.com/
AUTHORTRACKER
follow your favorite authors

ZONDERVAN

Youth Ministry Nuts and Bolts, Revised and Updated

Requests for information should be addressed to:

Zondervan, *Grand Rapids, Michigan 49530*

ISBN 978-0-310-67029-2

Cover design: David Conn
Interior design: SharpSeven Design

Printed in the United States of America

HB 12.05.2019

CONTENTS

FOREWORD

Yesterday, a youth pastor showed up at my office and, with an urgency-laced exasperation, basically unloaded on me. For 45 minutes I heard about how the needs of his kids coupled with the "crazy" expectations of his "church" (and by this he meant almost every person in the church) were killing his ability to do his job. He was tired, lonely, and frustrated. He felt called, but he seemed insecure. He told me he felt like he was "reasonably gifted," yet still felt inadequate. He was "energized" by kids and families, and had never questioned his love for them, but was reeling under the strain of trying to pull off what he now saw as an "impossible" job. He had come to me—a distant friend and his former youth-ministry prof—hoping I could point him toward some level of sanity in a job that had become overwhelming and chaotic.

Before we left for lunch, I handed him the first edition of *Youth Ministry Nuts and Bolts* by Duffy Robbins.

This winsome youth worker had nearly a decade of youth ministry experience, was gifted and relational, possessed an impressive youth ministry library, had attended some seminary and many youth ministry training conferences and seminars, and in general was a confident, gifted servant of Christ. But it became clear to me that, even though he had the pieces to do great youth ministry work, the gifts to serve the body of Christ, and the love for kids and their families, he hadn't found his rhythm in his role and job as a youth worker. He could teach and train on "the essence of the youth ministry task," but he had yet to land on how he could pull together the day-to-day aspects of the ministry he loved in a way that brought the theory into sync with the ongoing needs of the task.

While it is obvious that youth ministry leaders need to be trained to think theologically and to understand developmental and cultural realities, Duffy Robbins's *Youth Ministry Nuts and Bolts* is a resource that every youth ministry leader needs to read and refer to often. This book is especially essential for those who are responsible for making sure the elements of any program are getting covered in a way that ensures that the work is being delivered with integrity, substance, and sustainability.

As I consider the state of youth ministry leadership, I see four broad areas of glaring need—or, at least, areas that can easily get out of balance and wreak havoc with a youth ministry team and program. These are not the only four, and they often overlap, but these seem to be the most significant places where even the best of youth ministry leaders get tripped up:

- Time Management
- Skill Management

- People Management
- Life/Spirit Management

Time Management has to do with not only how we spend our time, but how we arrange and orchestrate our work and time in such a way that we will be able to build an effective and sustainable youth ministry. *Youth Ministry Nuts and Bolts* offers a clear map for determining what it means to think and lead and live in a way that allows for order in the midst of chaos, and health and priorities in the face of multiple expectations.

Skill Management is where we recognize that while we may be good at some things, maybe even very good, each of us lacks the full package of what is needed to even begin to address the needs of today's kids and their families. In *Nuts and Bolts*, Duffy spends a great deal of time on relationships and teamwork. This is not so much a book that is focused on helping you refine specific technical skills that are useful in youth ministry, although you will find dozens of insightful and helpful tips throughout. Instead, this book will help you develop those skills needed to *sustain a youth ministry program*, which requires creating a community of youth ministry stakeholders that includes both parents and other adults.

People Management comes down to the practical theology of the youth worker's job as "the leader" versus the callings and roles of those with whom we work and serve. If, for example, we see parents as obstacles, we will greatly limit the power of partnership that both the Scriptures and research tell us is the primary influence in the lives of youth. When volunteers' gifts are not valued and their voices are not heard, our kids are the losers. Managing people is not about controlling people, but rather about honoring their gifts and contributions, and setting them free.

Life Management reflects how authentically our ministries flow from the center of our lives. Our walk with Christ, the health of our primary relationships, and the integrity of our commitment—all of these have a far more significant impact on ministry (and especially youth ministry) than any program or strategy.

Youth ministry has had lots of heroes, authors, influencers, and guides. We've had great pioneers, who have blazed trails for us and led us into ways of thinking about loving kids for Jesus' sake. We've had prophets, who have spoken into our work and ministries to keep us on a path that honors Christ and the kingdom of God. There are those who have built powerful and successful ministries, many times sustained over years and even decades, who have shown us how well youth ministry can be done. We've had teachers and speakers and writers and presenters who help us to think differently and program creatively and process theologically. And then there is Duffy Robbins—all of these and more.

The best thing about *Youth Ministry Nuts and Bolts* is that Duffy offers what he himself has lived, tested, and taught to thousands of youth workers. For decades he has been recognized as one of the most—if not *the most*—significant leaders in the practice of youth ministry. Duffy is a tireless prophet, pioneer, practitioner, teacher, discipler, and friend to youth workers around the world. This book brings together the "best of Duffy Robbins" in a real-life, straightforward, and fun-to-the-point-of-hilarious way that will bring life and depth and wholeness to every youth worker and any youth ministry program. I have learned most of what I know about youth ministry from Duffy, and I am confident that, as you read this book, it will become much more than just another on the shelf, but a handbook for years to come.

Chap Clark
Professor of Youth, Family, and Culture
Fuller Theological Seminary

ACKNOWLEDGMENTS

Every time I finish a book, I am reminded how much it is like childbirth. There is the conception, and then the anticipation, and the hope, and the pushing, and, as we move closer to the delivery, there are a few shrieks and groans. I have had some wonderful folks helping me through this process and, even though this has been a revision and update of a book that was born a few years ago, it is only by their grace, talent, and skill that you hold this re-born baby in your hands.

Thanks, first of all, to Eastern University for granting me the sabbatical time away from my normal teaching responsibilities so I could work on this project. I must also express my gratitude to my colleagues in the youth ministry program—Darrell Pearson, Calenthia Dowdy, Eduardo Ramirez, and Eric Kraihanzel—for taking up the slack in my absence (um...actually they do this a lot!). Special thanks also to our faithful assistant Linda Hytha for helping me chase down books and quotes and sources. Usually this process involved my being hundreds of miles away and describing over the phone exactly where she would find a particular book, only to have Linda remind me that my bookshelves haven't been that organized in several years (which is true).

I also want to express my gratitude to Thea Lamberson, who has been my teaching assistant during three of her years at Eastern. Not only has her research help been very valuable, but she is the kind of youth ministry major that makes me glad I do what I do. If anyone reading this book is looking for a great youth worker, you should try to hire Thea. And, for those of you reading these words who know high school students who are sharp, passionate about Jesus, and feeling called to youth ministry, we're always looking for more Theas! Contact our admission folks immediately.

Thanks to Jay Howver and the Zondervan/Youth Specialties team for believing in this project. It was Jay's idea to revise and update this book (if you're looking for a villain), an idea that came to him, no doubt, on the strength of the warm and fuzzy memories he had of using this book as a text when he was a youth ministry undergraduate at Judson College several lifetimes ago.

I deeply appreciate the excellent editing work done by Doug Davidson (Proverbs 27:17). Doug is now an old(er) married man with a son in middle-school, but we first met when he was a student worker in my office at Eastern University, where he enthusiastically studied sociology and dreamed about how to make the world a better place. Aside from this book project, I'll bet he's still doing that. (In fact, after editing this book, he may be more committed than ever that something must be done to save the planet.)

Finally, thanks to my wife, Maggie, with whom I have shared an amazing adventure called marriage, so far for 37 years. You are still my best friend and true companion. Thanks for your patience in helping me once again through the birthing process. This time, you did the coaching and I did the screaming. Now that it's in print, enjoy the silence.

SECTION ONE

DESIGN

CHAPTER 1

Getting Them Through the Roof

Some men came, bringing to him a paralyzed man, carried by four of them. Since they could not get him to Jesus because of the crowd, they made an opening in the roof above Jesus by digging through it and then lowered the mat the man was lying on. When Jesus saw their faith, he said to the paralyzed man, "Son, your sins are forgiven."
(Mark 2:3-5)

Let's begin with a mind experiment. Jesus is coming to your town, and you have a dream—a big idea. More than anything, you'd love to arrange for the kids in your youth group to have some face time with this guy! You're convinced that if you could just get your youth to the feet of Jesus, some amazing things would happen.

How cool would it be if he came to your youth group and gave the talk Sunday night? (Can you say, "Powerful testimony"?) Maybe you could snag a picture with him for the website; maybe have him shoot a video plugging the upcoming events ("Hi, I'm the son of God, and I look forward to seeing all of you at the Winter Retreat!"); maybe arrange for him to have a one-on-one encounter with that troublemaker kid. Oh, baby—that would be the best.

But how to pull it off? What could you do?

You know the itinerary: Where Jesus is going to be and when he's going to be there. But so does everybody else in town. The place is going to be jammed. And, of course, there will be security. The disciples will have those cool robes that say "EVENT STAFF," and a few invited guests will have passes that say "ALL ACCESS." But you and your kids would be lucky to get access to the T-shirt table. You don't want to be disrespectful to others who might want to see Jesus, and you're not trying to cause a scene, but this is going to be complicated. *How do you get your group from where they are to where Jesus is?* That's the question.

So how would *you* do it? Before you read any further (even if you know where this is headed, Mr. I-Know-My-Bible-Stories!), take a minute to think about this dilemma. How would you get your group from where *they are* to where *Jesus is*? That's the question.

To make this interesting, why don't you come up with two plans. *The first will be a plan of complete lunacy.* (EXAMPLE: Your youth steal some "EVENT STAFF" robes, then begin circulating through the crowd explaining that this man claiming to be Jesus is an impostor—the real Jesus is in the house next door. Then, as the room empties out, go up to Jesus, apologize for calling him an impostor, and ask him to sign your Bible and pose for a picture with your group. Granted, it's a long shot—but you never know.)

Your second plan needs to be feasible. I'm not saying it has to be fully orthodox. In most cases, when passion and faith come together, creativity is the midwife, and that's when the best ideas get hatched—and those ideas are sometimes a little unorthodox. But it's got to be a realistic possibility. (EXAMPLE: You move as far forward in the crowd as you can, and then, when it's impossible to move any closer, try to disperse the crowd by shouting loudly, "Fire!" or "Lepers coming through!" or—worst-case scenario—"I've got a group of middle school kids here!")

Let's stop here while you think through your options.

PLAN A (Lunacy):

PLAN B (Realistic Lunacy):

GETTING TO THE FEET OF JESUS

It wasn't just a mind experiment on that day about two thousand years ago. It was a very different time—around 30 AD—and a very different place—somewhere in Capernaum—but this was precisely the same dilemma facing a paralyzed man and his friends in the Gospel of Mark.

Jesus is giving his homecoming address at a friend's house in Capernaum (Mark 2:1-12). Hordes of people jam the main room, with hundreds more waiting outside, hoping for a glimpse of this one about whom they've heard such incredible stories and rumors.

The room is hot, the air close, and the crowd is absolutely silent as they strain to catch every word of the Master. Suddenly, those nearest to Jesus feel pieces of roofing falling down, showering them with clods of dirt, twigs, and finally larger slabs of tile. Heads tilt back as the amazed crowd sees a ragged hole open in the ceiling and a mat lowered into the house. The glare of the sunlight shining through the hole obscures the four men as they lower a man suspended on rope and mat so that the paralytic passenger stops just in front of Jesus—a first-century elevator, if you will.

All over the room there is whispering, a sense of shock and nervous excitement. What is this about? What's going on? How will Jesus respond to this shocking intrusion? But Jesus silences the crowd with a strong, clear proclamation. Looking directly into the eyes of the paralyzed man, he proclaims, "Son, your sins are forgiven."

Now the confusion and stunned conversation in the room below is matched by the confusion and stunned conversation up on the roof.

"Did you hear what he said?"

"Yeah, Jesus said his sins are forgiven."

"Well, that's just great. A lot of good that's going to do him. If we went to all this trouble just so Charlie can have a clear conscience [names have been changed to protect the innocent], I'm gonna be ticked off!"

But, then, down below, the Son of Man speaks again. With all the authority of heaven, he calls to the paralyzed man, "Get up, take your mat, and go home." And to everyone's amazement, that's exactly what happens. The man rises, stretches limbs that seem to be awakening from a deep sleep, and then picks up his mat and walks out in full view of everybody.

Meanwhile, up on the roof, four guys are laughing, yelling, and giving one another high fives.

JESUS + PASSION + PLANNING = LIFE CHANGE

Most of us would like to think the hushed mob listening carefully to Jesus' every word is reminiscent of the way the high school youth listened to our talk at the last Sunday night youth meeting. (If I'm honest, when I read about the ceiling damage and the hapless man being lowered from the rooftop, it sounds more like my first youth group lock-in!) But whether we see ourselves in this scene or not, this is a story very close to where most of us do youth ministry, and both the plot and the plan are as recent as this week's calendar. That's because this story is more than an account of divine power—it's a drama of determined friendship. It's a story about four individuals who went to incredible pains to see that their friend got to the feet of Jesus.

Jesus was impressed by their faith. I am, too.

But I'm equally impressed by their ingenuity and determination. Absolutely convinced Jesus could heal their friend, and motivated by authentic compassion for the paralyzed man, they overcame all the logistical, interpersonal, and physical obstacles to get him to Jesus. And that's a key component of this narrative. It wasn't enough that they had faith, or even that Jesus had power. For this healing to take place, these guys had to have a plan. They had to organize and pull off a complex strategy.

MEANWHILE, BACK AT THE YOUTH GROUP

The task faced by those four men on the roof in Mark's narrative is the same task volunteer and professional youth workers face every week. We know these teenagers are needy, and we know Jesus has the power to heal. But how do we help this to happen? What kind of equipment will we need? How do we recruit the personnel required? How do we get everybody working together? How do we fund this little roof-top adventure?

Now, admittedly, these are not the questions most youth ministers get excited about. Florists don't embrace gardening because they like the smell of fertilizer, teachers don't sign on as educators so they can grade papers and keep attendance, and youth workers don't get into youth ministry so they can do administration. But blooming flowers, effective classrooms, and fruitful ministries all require someone doing the dirty work behind the scenes. Those who have a heart for youth ministry have to be prepared to get their hands dirty dealing with budgets, weighing legal issues, working through conflict, recruiting volunteers, doing careful program evaluation, involving parents, laboring over ministry decisions, and pondering the politics of staff relationships. *Nobody gets into youth ministry because they want to think about this stuff. But a lot of people get out of youth ministry because they haven't thought about this stuff.* It's the behind-the-scenes dirty work, week in and week out, that ushers our teenagers into a place where they might have a healing encounter with Jesus.

I wish every book I write could be about seeing youth who were once maimed and paralyzed by sin throw their crutches and hurts away and walk into new lives of wholeness. It's the excitement of being a part of that kind of transformation that motivates otherwise normal adults to tolerate lost sleep, lousy food, low pay (or no pay), loud music (and loud body noises), and little recognition for the privilege of walking alongside teenagers. Sure, there's sacrifice. There's a price to be paid. But that's why we got into youth ministry! We've never gotten over the wonder of being there when a teenager crippled by fear, hurt, anger, insecurity—you name it—discovers that life change comes in the healing forgiveness of Jesus.

It would be more fun to write another one of those books. But this book addresses instead the not-so-glamorous, behind-the-scenes work of youth ministry administration.

Paralyzed people don't get around too well on their own. There have to be people willing to go to the trouble of "carrying." Someone has to lay out a strategy for breaking through interpersonal, logistical, and physical barriers so our youth can actually get to Jesus' feet. We know the kids have a need. We know Jesus has the power. But how do we get through the roof to bring them to Jesus? That's the nuts and bolts of youth ministry.

MINISTRY BEHIND THE SCENES

Although the actual healing of kids may take place at a Sunday night youth meeting, during the fall retreat, or at a Friday night coffeehouse or mid-week club, much of youth ministry happens unnoticed and behind the scenes. The nuts and bolts of youth ministry are those Monday morning staff meetings, Tuesday afternoon planning sessions, and Thursday night team gatherings.

To help yourself think about this in a more concrete way, reread Mark's account (2:1-12) of this miraculous healing. Don't try to read *into* the lines, but use your imagination to read *between* the lines, and make a list of the logistics of the dramatic incident that occurred that day in Capernaum. Use the four categories in the diagram below to help you brainstorm:

Planning What issues would have to be addressed to come up with a plan that would get the paralyzed man to the feet of Jesus?	***Leadership*** What sorts of issues might arise in relation to leadership and interpersonal dynamics?
Team Ministry What questions would have been relevant in terms of how to get the necessary people working together to carry out the plan?	***Equipment*** What considerations would come into play in terms of equipment needed to execute the plan?

Working through the passage, it's pretty clear there were some very real nuts and bolts issues that had to be addressed behind the scenes so the paralyzed man could get to the feet of Jesus. Thinking through our four categories, let's do a simple inventory.

Planning

1. Evaluation. Surely they must have considered some other plans for getting this paralytic into the presence of Jesus. Mark 2:4 suggests they must have at least attempted a more conventional approach at first. Why was the rooftop plan chosen? Why were other plans rejected?

2. Strategizing. They had to think carefully through their strategy. For example, they needed proper information. It would have been really embarrassing if they'd broken through the roof of the wrong house! "Sorry about the ceiling, folks. We're looking for Jesus." Or what if they had broken through the right roof at the wrong spot, say, two feet further back. Jesus would have been right in the middle of his sermon, and a man on a pallet would have landed on his head. Not a pretty picture.

Leadership

1. Leadership Style. How does one motivate a group of people to undertake so bold a plan? And what about the person who hatched this crazy idea—what was it about that person that compelled a group of people to follow this plan? Where would such a plan come from? A dream? A vision? A nightmare? A youth group lock-in?

2. Authority. Someone had to be in charge. Someone had to call the shots. Someone had to organize and tell everyone when to lower and when to stop.

3. Mediation. Was there disagreement over the plan? How was that disagreement worked out? It's likely that a plan this wild met with some initial resistance. It's hard to imagine the friends saying, "Hey, what a great idea! We climb the roof with a paralyzed man, tie his bed to ropes, break through the roof, and drop him down in front of a carpenter!" I would suppose that plan came under a fair amount of criticism at first. Who made the final decision? Did they vote? Did it come down to one person's call? Did they pray about this?!?

Team Ministry

1. Recruitment. Before any healing could take place, someone had to have a vision, a hope that this paralyzed man could—just maybe—get healed if he could somehow get close enough to Jesus. Someone had to believe that strongly enough to recruit people to help, and so motivate them with enough of that same vision that they were willing to take part in a pretty bizarre plan.

2. Screening. Obviously, thoughtful recruitment begins with a basic question: Who should be recruited? It wouldn't do to involve someone who approached the task with the wrong motivation. This would have been, for example, an excellent opportunity for someone harboring a grudge against the paralyzed man to make a nasty scene. Common sense mandates that all the people recruited would have had to be people who genuinely cared about the welfare of the paralyzed man. There was also the question, one supposes, of physical strength. I would hate to be on the pallet being lowered through the roof by four men whose strength only lasted for half the journey. And, how many would be needed to complete the task? Mark tells us there were four men involved. Perhaps they decided one man was needed for each corner of the pallet. Too few might have made the task too difficult; too many could have made the entire roof cave in. Then, Jesus would have had lots of people to heal!

3. Training. There had to be some effort taken to make sure everyone understood the plan and was prepared to do his part. This may not have taken more than a sentence or two, but it surely must have happened. If one team member planned to lower the mat on the count of "three" and the other three began lowering the mat on "two," the result could be a very frightened paralyzed man doing a fly-by as Jesus was teaching in the room below.

4. Teamwork. Finally, it wouldn't be enough to recruit and train four individuals. They would have to work as a team. Just getting the paralyzed man up on the roof would require their strong arms working together. And then, perhaps, someone was responsible for making the opening in the roof while others prepared the man on the mat so he could be lowered safely. It was a small operation, but a challenging one. And the challenges could only be addressed if every member of the team were willing to play his part.

Equipment

1. Procurement. We can assume someone gave some thought to what equipment would be needed. Obviously, there had to be rope, and it had to be long enough. As confusing as the scene was, we can only imagine what it might have been like if there'd been only enough rope to lower the man partway to where Jesus was standing. There, above the crowd, would be a pallet, suspended in mid-air, with a deeply frustrated paralytic cursing his ex-friends on the rooftop. And, of course, they had to get something to pick through the roof. Mark says they "dug" (literally, "made an opening") through it. That suggests some kind of tool or implement with which they could break through the earth-and-tile roof.

2. Money. I don't know. Maybe they had all the rope they needed already. Maybe they didn't need to buy digging tools. Maybe there were no costs for roof repair. But if they didn't have everything they needed, they had to come up with some money to pay for this stuff. Where was the money going to come from? Who was going to keep it once it was collected, and how would they be sure that it was handled properly?

Of course, we don't know how any of these issues were handled because they were all handled behind the scenes. What we hear about and celebrate is that four men lowered a sick friend through the roof, and Jesus forgave his sins and healed his paralysis. But we can be sure of this: Either formally or informally these very questions were dealt with. It may have been done in haste, or they may have spent several days planning it. But none of this wonderful story would have happened if some compassionate people had not taken time to work through the nuts and bolts of their task.

WORD OF WARNING

Let's be clear: Fruitful, effective ministry is about a lot more than good planning and organization. It's true, these four men had to work through organizational and interpersonal details to get their friend to the feet of Jesus. But we wouldn't be reading about this episode if Jesus (and his feet) had not been in that house below. Every new Sunday brings thousands of well-organized, carefully planned worship services around the globe where the music, the pageantry, and the announcements are all very nicely done. But the sad fact is that many of these services result in neither healing nor forgiveness of sin. It is Jesus alone who takes human effort and turns it into life-changing ministry. To paraphrase an essential truth: "Man does not live on administration alone..."

On the other hand we shouldn't be deceived into thinking good planning and organization will quench the work of God's Spirit. One of the first lessons of ministry administration is that the right kind of thorough planning can provide a platform for the right kind of God-inspired spontaneity. The Holy Spirit works when and how he chooses to work. Our intention in this book is simply to reflect on ways of fertilizing and utilizing our resources to set the stage for what God wants to do.

TO THE PROFESSIONAL ROOF WALKER

Some of you, like me, are paid to bring people to the feet of Jesus. When you dream about, strategize, and plan for ministry, you're also earning a living. You're a "professional" youth worker. And that's okay.

I mention this because you probably won't be fully comfortable with a book like this if you're troubled by that word, *professional*. And if we take professional to mean, "working without heart," "slick," "going through the motions," "mailing it in," or "driven by money," it is troubling. But one of the premises of this book is that there is nothing profane about the word professional. At its root, it means "promise"—a promise to be prepared, a promise to responsibly perform our work with excellence, a promise to God and to the people we serve. It's the kind of promise inherent in Paul's exhortation: "Whatever you do, work at it with all your heart, as working for the Lord, not for human masters, since you know that you will receive an inheritance from the Lord as a reward. It is the Lord Christ you are serving" (Colossians 3:23-24). There is nothing profane about a vow before God to do our work the best we can do it.

And yet, having said all that, we need to be on high alert for the temptation to over-professionalize youth ministry. After all, most of us are self-aware enough to recognize how easy it is to fall into the trap of an unholy professionalism—ministry done more out of habit than in response, ministry born less of compassion than of know-how, ministry based more on works of the flesh than fruit of the Spirit. Frankly, a book like this can lead us in that direction. We need to understand right at the beginning that tightening a few nuts and bolts can make us more efficient, but only the Spirit of God can ignite our ministries with that divine Master-work that yields changed lives.

Henri Nouwen does a good job of reminding us that professional training has its place, but that it also brings with it some very real dangers:

> Everywhere Christian leaders...have become increasingly aware of the need for more specific training and formation. This need is realistic, and the desire for more professionalism in the ministry is understandable. But the danger is that instead of becoming free to let the spirit grow, the future minister may entangle himself in the complications of his own assumed competence and use his specialism as an excuse to avoid the much more difficult task of being compassionate...the danger is that his skillful diagnostic eye will become more like an eye for distant and detailed analysis than the eye of a compassionate partner...More training and structure are just as necessary as more bread for the hungry. But just as bread given without love can bring war instead of peace, professionalism without compassion will turn forgiveness into a gimmick, and the kingdom to come into a blindfold.[1]

PROFESSIONALS AND PROFESSIONALISM

Why is this a big deal? Because youth ministry is not a career; it is a calling. The English word *career* comes from the French *carriere*, meaning "a road," or "a highway."[2] Think of someone setting out on a road—map in hand, goal in sight, with stops marked along the way for food, lodging, and fuel. No wonder we often hear the word *career* coupled with the word *track* or *ladder*. Both images suggest a well-marked course, a set itinerary, an expected schedule of travel. The traveler's choices are left solely to the dictates of the map.

A *vocation* or *calling* is different. (See chart on following page.) Derived from the Latin word *vocare*,[3] it points neither to a map nor a guidebook—but to the Guide himself. The emphasis here is not on following a course, but on responding to a voice—no schedule, no itinerary, no well-laid plans. In fact, sometimes it's downright messy and, at least from a human perspective, not very well-ordered. But in the called life, God-ordained always trumps well-ordered. From beginning to end, the key is maintaining an open, intimate relationship with the One who speaks (John 6:28-29). Os Guiness defines *calling* as "the truth that God calls us to himself so decisively that everything we are, everything we do, and everything we have is invested with a special devotion and dynamism lived out *as a response* [emphasis added] to his summons and service."[4]

Career	*Calling (Vocation)*
...lends itself to formulas and blueprints;	...is linked only to a relationship;
...can be pursued with a certain amount of personal detachment—just keep moving forward and stay on track;	...demands our attention, because it's hinged on response;
...requires activity;	...requires stillness and solitude;
...demands professional credentials;	...sees professional credentials as helpful, but the key credentials are an ability to hear and a willingness to respond to the voice of God;
...is defined by what we do;	...is defined by who we are (and Whose we are);
...fosters a growing sense of independence and competence;	...fosters a growing sense of dependence and need;
...is marked by ownership ("I've got to work for what's coming to me");	...is marked by stewardship ("I've got to make good use of what's been given me");
...sees the steps of the journey as less important than the destination;	...understands it is on the journey that vocation is lived out;
...is preoccupied with symbols of accomplishment (titles, office size and location, positions on flow charts, special perks);	...is preoccupied with the One who accompanies us on the journey;
...justifies the means by pointing to the ends;	...understands that the means are the way God accomplishes his ends;
...is predictable;	...is unpredictable;
...is called to a task.	...is called to a Master.

Table: The difference between career and calling

Gordon MacDonald highlights this same distinction by pointing us to the important difference between being called and being driven.[5] He observes that driven people are usually gratified only by the sense of accomplishment. Arrival is everything. You are what you do. The journey is not so much an opportunity for adventure as it is a requirement for advance. Of course, what makes this danger so seductive is that in looking at ministry as a career this way, we gain a sense of identity. It helps us feel a little better about being a "professional" youth pastor.

Little wonder then that John Piper prays, "God, deliver us from the professionalizers." How can we at the same time be professional and "childlike" (Mark 10:15)? How do we professionally "take up the cross" (Luke 9:23)? How can we professionally be "fools for Christ's sake" (1 Corinthians 4:10)? How can we be professionally "compelled by the love of Christ" (2 Corinthians 5:14)? Obviously, it is a matter of the heart (Proverbs 4:23).

It is only an attentive heart that can prevent the slide from "professional" into "professionalism." Cultivating a heart that listens to God is more important than all the topics in this book combined. A well-organized, tightly-administered youth ministry without heart is little more than a well-dressed, nicely preserved corpse. It may "look just like it's alive"—but it's dead.

TO THE VOLUNTEER ROOF WALKER

What about those of you reading this book who do youth ministry as volunteers? What about the plumber from Duluth who just loves Jesus and loves kids, the student intern in the Philadelphia suburbs stretching new ministry muscles, or the Mom in Kansas trying to make a youth group great for her kids? You don't think of yourself as a "professional" youth worker. Are your *promises* any less real?

No—but they are different. The guy who lives two houses down might be a conscientious participant in Neighborhood Watch, but no one on the block expects him to perform like a policeman. He doesn't have that kind of training. In a similar way, the expectations are different for the volunteer youth worker. Your work is vitally important, but you're working the streets under a different set of guidelines. But trained or untrained, paid or unpaid, you still want to do your work for the Lord the best you can do it.

Hopefully, this book will help you do that. In fact, as a volunteer leader it may be even *more necessary* that you learn to do your work efficiently and effectively. Because your youth work doesn't earn a check, you very likely have other competing responsibilities and demands in your week. You can't afford to spend a lot of time exploring extra rooftops and experimenting with ways to get people to the feet of Jesus. Your schedule requires that you place productivity above activity. This book will help you practice that kind of stewardship.

But you should also be warned that there's some risk of discouragement in reading a book like this. A volunteer going through the table of contents could potentially get totally depressed. Chapters on budgeting, dealing with conflict, decision-making, when to leave a ministry—not exactly the stuff you signed up for. But please understand that this book is not intended to help you discover all the things you are *not* doing.

The history of God's work through his people is that God can do much with little. Rather than being intimidated and discouraged by discovering in this book all you *could* be doing, focus on one or two strategies that might help you improve what you are *already* doing. In fact, as a volunteer, some of these issues may not even be a concern for you. Or, if your group is small in number, there are some issues in this book that may not be pertinent to your situation. That's awesome. Be thankful. You can just use this book as a resource for troubleshooting those areas that are presenting some sticky problems. Use it as a manual that will help you avoid time-consuming mistakes, so you can maximize the time you are able to devote to ministry with kids.

THE BOTTOM LINE

When you get to the very heart of it, youth ministry isn't a matter of budgeting, publicizing, and organizing. It's a matter of loving teenagers, spending time with them, and helping them hear and understand the gospel of Christ. And youth workers who are involved in that kind of ministry—be they volunteers or professionals—will see God work, even when all the nuts and bolts aren't tightened down and there are a couple of screws loose.

SECTION TWO
LAYING THE FOUNDATION

CHAPTER 2

Starting with the Heart

And David shepherded them with integrity of heart;
with skillful hands he led them.
(Psalm 78:72)

We begin the task of organizing a youth ministry not by talking about which nuts and bolts need tightening, but by talking about the hand (and heart) turning the wrench. If we don't begin working from the inside out, we're in danger of functioning like the flame of an artificial fireplace—it's quiet; it's clean; there are never ashes or scorch marks; but neither is there ever any warmth or energy. It's a weakness reminiscent of Paul's complaint that people in the last days will have "a form of godliness" but will lack its power (2 Timothy 3:5).

But if we're to talk about hand and heart, flame and heat, we have to think carefully about the distinctive way these two combine in Christian leadership. *Which is more important in youth ministry leadership: being or doing, intention or skill?*

Let's do an experiment: If the continuum below represents Christian (youth ministry) leadership, where on the spectrum below do you think best represents the biblical emphasis on heart and hand? Is it more heart than hand, or is it more hand than heart, or is it an equal blend?

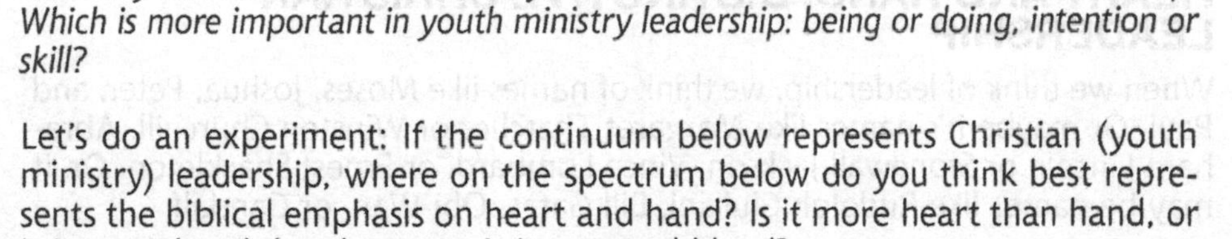

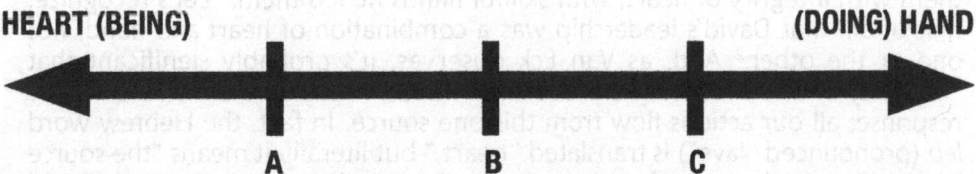

For example, a mark in the A position indicates you believe good leadership is all about intention. In this view the leader is a visionary whose hands-on ability *to do* is not as important as the God-given ability *to see what needs to be done.* The key to good leadership is seeing with the eyes of God and being in tune with the heart of God. If those bases are covered, a good leader can find the right people to actually do the work of God.

A mark in the C position puts the emphasis on the opposite pole. In this view the best leaders lead by doing, by modeling. This is the proverbial hands-on leader, the can-do commander who goes into battle with the troops instead of drawing up strategies back at headquarters. Let someone else dream the big dreams and give the touchy-feely speeches. This leader will be the one at crunch time who can "get 'er done."

A mark in the B position values both heart and hand. Those who look at leadership from this perspective are convinced *being* is at least as important as *doing*, that the doer who acts without heart and conviction is little more than a technician, a survivor whose basic creed is "outwit, outplay, outlast." This perspective recognizes a skilled leader with a bad heart can be a very dangerous leader indeed. On the other hand, the B position is pragmatic enough to say that passion without execution is like a bureaucratic wildfire: It burns bright and draws attention, but it accomplishes little of value. There are those who perform in the game, and there are those who just attract attention by yelling out heartfelt motivational messages. One is a leader; the other is merely a cheerleader. True leadership requires a balance of motivation and execution.

If you haven't already done so, stop and mark the continuum in the spot that best represents your view of leadership.

HEART AND HAND: DISTINCTIVE CHRISTIAN LEADERSHIP

When we think of leadership, we think of names like Moses, Joshua, Peter, and Paul. Or maybe it's names like Margaret Thatcher or Winston Churchill, Abraham Lincoln or Stonewall Jackson, Vince Lombardi or Ernest Shackleton. Or, it may be names like Rudolph Giuliani, Bill Gates, Obi-Wan, or Gandalf.

In her book *Leadership 101*,[1] Denise VanEck helps us consider the importance of both heart and hand by pointing us to Psalm 78:72: "And David shepherded them with integrity of heart; with skillful hands he led them." Let's recognize, first of all, that David's leadership was a combination of heart *and* hand, not one or the other.[2] And, as Van Eck observes, it's probably significant that "integrity of heart" comes before "skillful hands." The heart is the reservoir of response; all our actions flow from this one source. In fact, the Hebrew word *leb* (pronounced "lave") is translated "heart," but literally it means "the source of man," as in the seat of appetites, emotions, and passions. Granted, David had some pretty profound weaknesses in all three categories (appetites, emotions, and passions), but the consistent cry of his heart was a hunger for God.

David's leadership was also marked by "skillful hands." VanEck suggests David's life shows us five essential skills for a godly leader:[3]

1. Listening

2. Communicating

3. Managing Conflict
4. Learning from Failure
5. Raising up Other Leaders

We'll see these five skill areas cropping up again and again throughout this book—so we won't stop to examine each of them now. The point is that David was not just a shepherd in name; he knew the skills of leading a flock. His was a hands-on leadership (in the case of Bathsheba, a little too "hands on"!) that, combined with "integrity of heart," allowed him to shepherd the people of God for more than four decades (1 Chronicles 3:4).

The road to effective leadership and good administration leads through an intersection of faithful heart and skillful hands. Heart without hands lacks muscle and movement.[4] Hands without heart lack reason to move. Youth ministry needs leaders who exercise their skills and spiritual gifts because their hearts are stoked by the grace of Christ.

I used to work with a godly preacher, Roy Putnam, who groomed his staff and congregation with Ephesians 2:8-10:

> For it is by grace you have been saved, through faith—and this not from yourselves, it is the gift of God—not by works, so that no one can boast. For we are God's handiwork, created in Christ Jesus to do good works, which God prepared in advance for us to do.

Dr. Putnam used to say it like this: "Effective ministry comes not just through greater efficiency but through greater *Ephesiancy*."

GIFTED FOR MINISTRY WITH TEENAGERS

J.R.R. Tolkien's *The Fellowship of the Ring* tells of a hobbit named Frodo who receives the mysterious Ring of power and who must journey to almost certain death in Mount Doom to destroy the Ring. The wizard Gandalf, who guides him in his quest, listens as Frodo responds to the weight of his mission:

> "I am not made for perilous quests," cried Frodo. "I wish I had never seen the Ring! Why did it come to me? Why was I chosen?"
>
> "Such questions cannot be answered," said Gandalf. "You may be sure that it was not for any merit that others do not possess; not for power or wisdom, at any rate. But you have been chosen and you must therefore use such strength and heart and wits as you have."

Probably all of us, from the greenest of rookie volunteers to the most sage youth ministry veteran, have wondered on occasion if we are, in fact, suited to this "perilous quest" that is youth ministry. Perhaps, like Frodo, we doubt our capacities to faithfully organize and execute effective ministry. It seems like such a big and difficult task. But, in fact, that kind of humility is probably the one essential for faithful ministry. Youth ministry is not merely a nuts and bolts operation. The difference between efficiency and *Ephesiancy* is God's gracious work in our lives.

SPIRITUAL GIFTS: "STRENGTH AND HEART AND WITS"

The New Testament gives no evidence that the lists of spiritual gifts appearing in 1 Corinthians 12 and Romans 12 are exhaustive. In fact, years of youth ministry experience have convinced me that certain spiritual gifts that never made the Pauline lists are vital in working with teenagers—gifts like creative thinking, problem solving, leading worship, technical know-how, and interpersonal communication. Mike Yaconelli of Youth Specialties liked to say that a number of spiritual gifts have been overlooked and underappreciated when it comes to youth ministry. Perhaps God has given you some of these lesser-known "gifts."

The Gift of Helplessness: Ephesians 2:8-10

Maybe you've never thought of helplessness as a gift—and certainly, in the heat of action, know-how feels more valuable than no-way. But helplessness opens us to new ideas and strategies; it keeps us teachable and moves us to innovation. Veteran youth workers can burn out or become stale when they're not motivated by a helplessness that drives them to go deeper for new strength and to go outside their experience for new ideas.

I'm reminded of my own helplessness when I consider the challenges of youth ministry in this new millennium. There are so many new issues to be addressed, so many new complications to be untangled. When I started out in youth ministry, we rarely encountered issues like self-injury or homosexuality. While families have always been under assault, the deterioration of the very *idea* of family in our culture puts teenagers in a position of risk and instability that is far more serious than three decades ago.

And there's the whole technology piece: Back when I started in youth ministry, none of us had to worry about kids texting their friends during the Bible study, and it never occurred to us that we might someday have to contend with teenagers taking cell phones on the retreat and shooting candid pictures of their friends in the cabin that would get uploaded on the internet. Heck, we never even had to consider the Internet at all! Back then, when grandma said, "Log on," she meant, "I'm cold." Although I consider myself fairly literate when it comes to technology, there are parts of it that make me really uncomfortable. I don't blog. I don't "tweet." My wife and I didn't meet through eHarmony.

The last time I checked my Facebook page there were 275 unanswered messages. (Maybe I'm not checking my page frequently enough?)

And I don't look like a teenager. If I walk into the lunchroom at a local high school, the kids know I'm not one of them. They don't see me seated at a cafeteria table and nudge their neighbors to ask, "Hey, who's the new kid—and what happened to his hair?" I'm around teenagers a lot. I still enjoy it most of the time. But, more and more, it feels like an alien culture.

Yet I've come to understand that this discomfort is good—sort of—because it forces me to focus on the more substantial ministry avenues of caring relationships and creative thinking, and less on the shallow "I can be just like one of the kids" shortcuts that will, in time, turn out to be a dead-end. It reminds me that praying is more important than pranks and caring is more important than coolness. The great danger of long-term youth ministry is that I will rely more on "hands-on skill" and less on "integrity of heart." The gift of helplessness reminds me that my ministry with teenagers must be rooted in the power and grace of God.

The Gift of Truthfulness: Ephesians 4:15, 6:13-14

Having observed Roman soldiers firsthand, the apostle Paul likens the Christian's armor to Roman battle gear. The first piece of armor he mentions is the belt of truth. All other pieces of Roman armor were attached to the girdle-like belt. The soldier tucked his tunic into the belt, and attached his sword to it. He secured his breastplate to the belt to hold it firmly in place. If his belt were not buckled tightly, even the most experienced centurion might trip over his tunic or fall because his breastplate had slipped into shin-guard position.

In our cultural moment when it *seems* like up is down, "truth" is a falsehood, and the only thing absolutely certain is that there are no absolute certainties, youth workers must root their strengths, wits, ideas, and resources in truthfulness. This is a multi-faceted process that begins with knowing the truth (John 17:17; 1 Timothy 1:15), then matures into a commitment to be true to what we know.

Bryan was a volunteer in our youth ministry who possessed few of the traditional skills of gifted youth ministers. He wasn't funny. He couldn't play guitar. He had little public speaking experience. And he didn't have any kind of facial hair—not even a soul-patch. But the way he lived his life made vivid his love for Christ, and that gave him a potent ministry with the kids in our group. They respected his integrity. He walked what he talked. That's truthfulness.

April is a youth pastor who exhibits truthfulness in another way. Even under pressure, even when it may make some of her kids angry, she consistently speaks the truth. That's also truthfulness.

Sometimes, oddly enough, truthfulness is being honest about what we don't know. In the leadership setting, where not knowing can leave a person vulnerable, such truthfulness takes courage. As youth workers, we are especially intimidated when kids ask questions for which we have no answer. We somehow feel that our unanswered questions are making faith less attractive to our youth. But could it be that, in the truthfulness of our questions and the authenticity of our struggles, we make faith even more real to them? We help them understand that faith is not always in the knowing, but in the trusting. (See Hebrews 11:1.)

The Gift of Listening: Ephesians 4:2

Amy sat in my office intense and confused. Over the two years she'd been in my ministry I had developed genuine respect for her as a Christian. Now she was dating a non-Christian, things were getting serious, and he was putting pressure on her to have sex. She had resisted so far. She didn't want to go against God's Word. But she confessed that part of her wanted to have sex with her boyfriend.

I listened to her, nodding occasionally, and asking questions about where God fit in with all of this. After a half-hour we prayed, and she left my office. I felt the encounter had been positive. She had talked freely and I had responded to her struggle with restraint and support. Then it hit me—this eighteen-year-old girl was somebody's daughter. I grimaced at how different my attitude might have been if she had been *my* daughter:

> *Daughter:* Dad, my boyfriend and I are trying to decide whether we should have sex or not. What do you think?
>
> *Me:* I can fix that for you, honey. I'll kill him.

Through the gift of listening, we can offer teenagers the advantage of experienced counsel guided by a heart of concern, without the sometimes-sharp edge of parental over-concern and (sometimes justifiable!) panic.

In John 9 there's an amazing narrative about Jesus healing a man born blind, and it's made all the more amazing by virtue of the method Jesus used: A mud-and-spit concoction smeared on sightless eyes. But this startling episode of healing started simply enough with Jesus' habit of being attentive to need—taking time to look and to listen. Jesus "saw a man blind from birth" (9:1). Had Jesus failed to notice the man's blindness we might have had a completely different story. Suppose Jesus had been less attentive and mistaken the man's affliction for a sore throat. That would have made the mud-and-spit therapy even more awkward than we can assume it already was.

More than thirty years ago, Russell Hale did a massive study of unchurched people in America.[5] He summarized his findings with this insight: "The overwhelming experience my conversations with the unchurched conveyed to me was that those outside the church *want and need to be heard...*" [emphasis added]. Does anyone reading these words suppose it is any different today? Or that it will be any different fifty years from now? What a gift it is to be able to listen, to *really* listen.

Dietrich Bonhoeffer crystalizes the mandate here:

> The first service that one owes to others...consists in listening to them...Many people are looking for an ear that will listen. They do not find it among Christians, because these Christians are talking when they should be listening...Christians have forgotten that the ministry of listening has been committed to them by Him who is Himself the great listener and whose work they would share. We should listen with the ears of God that we may speak the Word of God.[6]

The Gift of Liking Teenagers: Ephesians 1:15-16

As I was preparing to board a recent cross-country flight, I noticed a large crowd of teenagers preparing to take the same flight I was taking. As other adults made the same observation, I felt a wave of sheer dread flooding over them. Businessmen asked if there were later flights. One lady wondered aloud if there was a "no-kids section" on the plane. Others downed a few extra drinks so they wouldn't notice they were on the flight at all. One irate businessman remarked to me with some relief as he took his seat on the plane, "I was afraid they were going to put me up there in that section with all the teenyboppers." I felt like smiling and saying, "Yeah, just sit here next to me. I usually throw up every few minutes when I'm flying, but other than that, I bet it will be pretty quiet back here."

Most adults don't like teenagers at all. Some adults, including some who perhaps do like teenagers, think youth ministry is about adults trying to *act like* teenagers. Youth ministry rooted in either of those attitudes is likely to fail. Teenagers don't need adults who act like teenagers, and they certainly don't need more adults who just don't like teenagers. What they need are adults who don't freak out when *teenagers act like teenagers*. If that's your attitude, teenagers need you, and God can use you, because that's a rare gift.

Maria is an unassuming woman with a heart of gold. She told me the story of how she used to look out on her south-Florida street week after week at the kids hanging out and getting into trouble. People passed by them scornfully like a driver passing by a deep, ugly pothole. Then one day the Lord laid it on her heart to invite those kids to dinner in her home—no catch, no conditions. She has only one rule—and I still smile when I think of her saying this—"We told them they had to leave their weapons outside." That first meal went on to become a weekly tradition of great food spooned up with large servings of love at Maria's house. Those meals opened the door to questions, which opened the door to conversations, which led some of those kids to open the door to Jesus. And, it happened because one woman (with an amazing husband!) exercised her gift of liking teenagers.

The Gift of Nurture: Ephesians 4:11-13

Nikki is a youth worker who is herself just a few years beyond high school. She would be the first to say that her role places her in the front of the room more than she likes. She prefers the small group settings and one-on-one conversations, out of the limelight and away from the platform. But don't mistake her quiet, unassuming style for timidity. Nikki is a velvet-covered brick, soft on the outside, but rock-solid on the inside. And each week she nurtures relationships in her small group of girls—braiding thin lines of friendship into thick cords of caring. Having earned the right to talk with these young women personally about their walks with Christ, she patiently leads them into closer relationships with Jesus. Her eyes light up when she talks about the way God is moving in the lives of these girls.

We can only begin to guess the impact of such gentle gifts. What power there is when someone is willing to labor over one plot of spiritual soil—cultivating, tending, and fertilizing it! It's sometimes dirty work, sometimes beautiful, sometimes about encouragement, sometimes about correction and rebuke, sometimes face to face, sometimes through a short post on Facebook. But through the entire process, Nikki is clear about her goals. She is exercising her gift of nurture, growing teenage girls into young women of God.

The Gift of Affirming: Ephesians 4:15, 29

In a culture that scrawls crude graffiti on the self-images of most teenagers, youth workers offer kids a vision of who they are in Christ. I remember years ago hearing a story about missiologist and international youth ministry expert Paul Borthwick. He'd been asked to speak on the topic of self-image in Soweto, South Africa. His teenage audience had grown up under the oppression of apartheid, having been told from birth that they were nonpersons. Bringing the students back to the heart of the gospel, Borthwick reminded them that self-worth is not calculated by government ruling or media images, but by the God who made each one of them in his image.

We occasionally get so busy managing ongoing youth programs that we forget the power and impact of a simple word of affirmation—especially for the "average" teenager who is constantly being reminded he or she is not smart enough, not athletic enough, and not attractive enough. Writing a quick note to a youth, offering public praise for a job done well, posting a word of encouragement on a Facebook wall—all these actions express affirmation to a teen.

One of the continuing cycles of effective youth ministry begins with affirming teenagers' gifts by identifying the talents they possess, and then discovering ways for them to display those gifts in ministry. We occasionally do that with youth talented in music or public speaking. But what about the kid who is good in photography? Or computers? Or poetry? Or visual art? Can we encourage the teenager with special talents in photography to prepare a special piece that corresponds with the hymns on an upcoming Sunday? Could the student who's great with computers help in a tutoring program or spice up the ministry website? Why not invite that young poet to read her work as part of club or during a worship service or at the coffeehouse?

Helping young people see they are fearfully and wonderfully made by a God who wants to use each of them in unique and practical ways is a profound means of pointing teenagers to their Creator. Affirmation of self-value leads to affirmation of God's goodness which leads to affirmation of faith—and it all begins by exercising the simple gift of affirming.

The Gift of a Sense of Humor: Proverbs 17:22

After thirty years of youth ministry, I'm convinced humor is vital. Having a sense of humor doesn't necessarily mean we must *be* funny; it means we must be able to recognize what *is* funny. It doesn't mean always making people laugh; it means knowing when to laugh. It's a great gift to have the ability to see the humor in everyday life, especially in youth ministry!

Why? Because all youth workers know what it's like to be laughed at when we weren't trying to be funny!

Maybe it was the time we got our words mixed up and what they heard us say was not what we meant to say. (Remember the preacher who meant to say "pitched his tents," but accidentally switched the "en" of "tents" with the "it" of "pitched"?) Maybe it was the game idea that so totally and obviously bombed that the most fun part of the whole activity was when you finally said, "Okay, game over!" Maybe it was the unfortunate timing of the ringing cell phone (or some other unintended sound) right in the middle of the poignant illustration. Maybe it's that physical feature of your body that makes you feel self-conscious around teenagers so you've carefully disguised it by the way you dress and compose yourself, camouflaging it from the teenage snipers in your group who are just waiting for the chance to take a cheap shot, and then you discover that they haven't just *noticed* the asymmetrical placement of your ears, or the relative size of your nose, or the stunning lack of hair on your head, but they have discussed it, and they even have a name for it! We've all had times when we knew—everybody knew—the kids were not laughing *with* us; they were laughing *at* us.

The gift of a sense of humor shows kids we don't take ourselves too seriously. From the teenager's point of view, taking oneself seriously is the most telling trait of terminal adulthood. Losing the ability to laugh at ourselves makes us boring people. But the real dividend of being willing to laugh at ourselves is that we can help teenagers develop that same perspective. Let's be honest: there are few people who take themselves *more* seriously than teenagers. That's why kids who are trying really hard to be cool come off as insufferably boring. My jokes about my bald head help the students I'm speaking with develop a more positive and healthy perspective about their own imperfections.

Sharing a good laugh communicates acceptance. We don't laugh with our enemies. When it comes to communication, humor really is the great global warmer. It is not a gift you will find in any of the New Testament "gift passages," but a sense of humor is a gift indeed.

The Gift of Flexibility: Ephesians 5:15-20

Anyone who has ever driven a church-owned vehicle has learned the importance of flexibility. A few roadside episodes standing next to a broken-down bus remind us of the need to become comfortable with surprises.

Youth ministry is fraught with pitfalls and potential disasters. Sometimes it's the mechanical surprise—a projector bulb that blows just before the presentation; sometimes it's the more human element—you've planned to break the kids into six teams of four, and only ten show up for the meeting. But there are always enough bumps to make the journey interesting. A youth worker who has the gift of flexibility will be able to absorb the shocks with enough finesse to go the distance.

Flexibility is critical not only for prolonging the youth worker's sanity and survival but also for teaching kids a mindset that guards their sanity and survival in an unpredictable world. Teens glimpse our faith in the sovereignty of God most clearly when times are tough. Paul wrote to Timothy, "You... know all about my teaching, my way of life, my purpose, my faith, patience, love, endurance..." (2 Timothy 3:10). And where did Timothy learn these lessons? Paul reminds him in the very next verse: It was through Paul's "persecutions, sufferings—what kinds of things happened to [him] in Antioch, Iconium and Lystra, the persecutions [he] endured." (2 Timothy 3:11). Grace is easy to exhibit when there are no problems. But it's when we're flexible enough to bounce back under negative circumstances that our faith really stands out.

Blessed are the youth workers who stay cool when the bus breaks down, for theirs is the ministry that keeps on rolling.

The Gift of Perseverance: Ephesians 1:17

Perseverance is the gift of God's grace that allows us to hang in with a kid when we might prefer to just hang that kid!

In the first edition of this book, published in 1990, I wrote about a kid named "B.J." That wasn't his real name, of course. But if you were to go back to that first edition of the book, you'd see that I described him as "one of those teenagers that makes career youth workers decide to become senior pastors... talking when he was supposed to be quiet, hushed when he was supposed to be singing, laughing when he was supposed to be sober." I even added what I thought was this clever one liner: "In terms of spiritual potential, anyone who knew him would have guessed that 'B.J.' stood for 'Big Job.'"

Well, a funny thing happened when "B.J.'s" youth worker read that book. He recognized himself in my story, and thought the real "B.J." would be excited to see that he'd been mentioned in the book! Okay, that was a little awkward. But fast forward about six or seven years. By this time, "B.J." has met Christ, completed college, and gone into youth ministry. (This, of course, is the justice of God.) And one day, "B.J.", whose real name is, in fact, *T.J.* Foltz, was doing an event with me. That gave us the chance to have a little conversation about his close brush with fame in the pages of my book, and about how he'd been described in the book as (his words) "a creature distinguishable from an ape only because he had opposable thumbs!"

It was a fun conversation, a little uncomfortable (I was afraid he was going to start beating his chest and peel me like a banana), but it also reminded me of the gift of perseverance. It reminded me of how T.J.'s youth pastor, and other youth ministry mentors after him, had hung in there with T.J.—kept loving him, spending time with him, investing in him, never giving up on him. They were there all those years, through the occasional times of promise and through the frequent occasions of doubt.

Now, two decades since I wrote that first version of this chapter, T.J. and I go to the same church! He's still active in ministry with young people and has an infectious love for Christ. T.J. speaks all over the country to lots of youth groups and camps full of kids who are just like he was (again, the justice of God). We have, on several occasions, shared in ministry together, and it is my great honor to call him a close friend. *But here's the important part:* I couldn't have written that chapter all those years ago, and I wouldn't be able to share this testimony today, if there hadn't been some persevering, caring, tenacious youth workers in T.J.'s life who believed God was writing a bigger story than any of us could imagine.

When it's all said and done, tightening the nuts and bolts of a youth ministry is sometimes more a function of heart than muscle. In those times when a lack of results might tempt us to stop fooling with the nuts altogether and just bolt, it is the gift of perseverance that heartens us and keeps us pressing on.

CHOSEN FOR A PERILOUS QUEST

Are there other gifts that haven't been mentioned here? Of course. God's Spirit continues to move across the church to provide for us the unique gifts we need to build up the body of Christ. This sampling is a simple reminder to all of us that (a) God is the giver of gifts, (b) that all our service grows from a heart moved by grace, and (c) that God has given us these gifts so we can use the strength and heart and wits we have to serve him faithfully. That is the difference between leadership focused on efficiency and leadership focused on Ephesiancy.

A book focused on ministry issues like budgeting, time management, and dealing with staff conflicts can become intolerably stale if it isn't kept fresh by this vision of our calling. Ephesians 1:11-12 reminds us: "In him we were also chosen, having been predestined according to the plan of him who works out everything in conformity with the purpose of his will, in order that we, who were the first to hope in Christ, might be for the praise of his glory."

CHAPTER 3

Excellence in Ministry

Be very careful, then, how you live [and work]—not as unwise but as wise, making the most of every opportunity, because the days are evil.
(Ephesians 5:15-16)

As a college professor my least favorite part of the job is grading. Not only is it difficult when it's done well, but it's also a thankless task. If a student gets a good grade, she won't thank me for it (nor should she) because she feels she's earned it. But if a student gets a bad grade, well, of course, it's totally my fault.

"Duffy, I worked really hard on that paper. Why did you give me an F?"

"Uh...well...because the school doesn't allow me to give Gs."

As you might imagine, these short conversations are highly motivational for both professor and student. But I take great pains in the grading process because I want to approach my work as a professional. The way I see it, I've made some important promises:

- To my students: That I will give them my best effort, even if they don't want it;
- To my school: That I will be conscientious in the execution of my duties;
- To the Lord: That I will do my work as a professor not to help people make good grades but to help them make better disciples.

I could, no doubt, do the task of grading in a less conscientious way. I could give everyone high marks, give each paper minimal attention, or give the papers to my granddaughter to grade. And that might even get higher student evaluations. (I think my granddaughter is fairly lenient, in part because she hasn't actually learned to read). But I can't do that, because *I've made a promise to do my work with excellence*. And while I no doubt fall short of my promise to *do* excellence in every aspect of my work, I don't want to ever get slack about my intention to *pursue* excellence.

Understand, this is not about excellence for the sake of excellence; it's excellence for the sake of Christ. It's understanding the difference between what Eugene Peterson calls "a job" and what he calls "a profession or craft."[1] He defines a *job* as what we do to complete an assignment. It's focused on execution. We learn what is expected by those to whom we're responsible—and we do it. A profession, on the other hand, brings with it an obligation beyond pleasing somebody:

> For physicians it is health (not merely making people feel good); with lawyers, justice (not helping people get their own way); with professors, learning (not merely cramming cranial cavities with information on tap for examinations). And with pastors [Author's note: And youth pastors] it is God (not relieving anxiety, or giving comfort, or running a religious establishment).[2]

This is similar to the distinction researchers like John Kotter have drawn between *leadership* and *management*. Both are important, but they are not the same. Kotter argues that the distinction between leadership and management is crucial for an effective leader. ***Managers:*** (1) Plan and budget, (2) organize and staff for execution, and (3) control resources and solve problems. ***Leaders:*** (1) Establish direction, (2) align people through communication and equip them to pursue the vision, and (3) motivate and inspire those people to maintain the pursuit.[3] Managers get things *done* (sometimes described as *transactional leadership*). Leaders determine what we *must do* (sometimes described as *transformational leadership).*[4] Most of us have known some youth workers and pastors who were good managers but poor leaders, and others who were good leaders but poor managers. Youth workers who see their task as *not just a job but a promise* will take seriously both leadership and management.

Unfortunately, when it comes to excellence, either in leadership or in management, it can be a long journey from *pursuing* to *doing*. The fact that we mean well doesn't guarantee we will manage well. I think we all know that. Whether coordinating the leadership of a 300-member youth group or leading three to five teens in an informal, weekly Bible study, most of us have observed that a church organization does not function automatically. To be all we can be for the glory of Christ, to do the work with excellence, we need to learn how to knit together flowcharts, paid staff, volunteer staff, job descriptions, planning work, and the inspiration of the Spirit so that they fit the tasks to which God has called us. Our opportunities with students are too few, and the time we can devote to ministry is too precious, to waste them with muddled plans, poor communication, and unproductive activity.

THE JOURNEY FROM *PURSUING* TO *DOING*

Very early in my ministry an earnest volunteer leader was both kind enough and bold enough (at the time, it felt more bold than kind!) to share with me just how far I had yet to travel on that journey from *pursuing* excellence to *doing* excellence. As I recall, it wasn't a very pleasant conversation. I don't remember any specifics, but let's just say that if we'd been on Facebook together, I would have "unfriended" him. As part of those conversations, he shared with me a book that had been making the rounds in his corporate office—*In Search of Excellence* by Thomas Peters and Robert Waterman.[5] I admit, books about management and corporate leadership hadn't been very big on my reading list. But this book had a profound impact on the way I think about and carry out the administrative tasks of ministry—and I believe it continues to have significant relevance for youth ministry today.

Waterman and Peters based their findings on some very basic assumptions about people. My thirty-plus years of youth ministry experience have only further convinced me of the validity of these assumptions.

All of us want to think of ourselves as winners. The problem is that most of us are amazingly normal. We win some, and we lose some (I refer you back to my conversation with a student about grades that began this chapter). Wise leaders understand that we respond better when our wins are emphasized more than our losses. We are, in the words of Waterman and Peters, "suckers for a bit of praise."

The imaginative, symbolic right side of the human brain is at least as important as the rational, deductive left side. That means it's often more important to ask, "Does it feel right?" than, "Does it add up?" When I was a young, newly-married husband, if my wife and I were in disagreement over some matter of finance or schedule or household responsibilities around the house, I thought all I needed to do was simply explain the flaw in her logic and she would see the light. I was sure that if I carefully and thoroughly explained to her the defects in her reasoning, then she would brighten up, smile, and say, "You're right; I'm wrong. Let's have sex!" This might surprise you, but that's not what happened (see "we win some, and we lose some"). I would lovingly dismantle her opinions and ideas, carefully showing where her thinking was mistaken. But, then, she would say, "I don't care. I still think you're wrong!" And, of course, being male, I knew what that meant. That meant I should explain everything again, but this time at a higher volume.

What I came to realize in time about human behavior, to paraphrase Blaise Pascal, is that there are reasons beyond reason. And if those reasons are *your* reasons, it doesn't matter whether they seem reasonable to someone else. We may be doing our youth ministry the way they said to do it in seminary or the way that appears most logical to us. But if it doesn't feel right to the ministry team, the youth, and the parents, it probably won't work well. The actual temperature in the room doesn't matter; if people are uncomfortable, there has to be a change in the environment.

God has given us a wonderful capacity to learn and store information. However, most of us find we are better at remembering stories than facts, better at remembering movie plots than sermon outlines. Therefore, it's to everyone's advantage to make plans, strategies, and goals as simple as possible. Elaborate management schemes may work out great on paper, but if we want them to play out in the everyday arena of youth ministry, we should keep the vision and procedures basic. In the words of my friend, Doug Fields, "Clear is always better than cute" (which is, I think, itself kind of a cute expression).

Not long ago, Doug and I co-wrote a book called *Speaking to Teenagers*. As we talked about that book, Doug pointed to six questions Rick Warren always asks himself as he prepares a sermon—questions that help him put clarity before cuteness:

1. What is the most *practical* way to say it?
2. What is the most *positive* way to say it?
3. What is the most *encouraging* way to say it?
4. What is the *simplest* way to say it?
5. What is the most *personal* way to say it?
6. What is the most *interesting* way to say it?

These questions are probably just as relevant when it comes to leading and organizing a group of people.

We respond to external rewards and punishments. I can talk to leaders and students about how God calls us to a mission project so others will experience God's love. The response: Polite enthusiasm. But what really kicks the fundraising campaign into high gear is my offer to reward free youth group T-shirts to the ten teenagers who raise the most support. All of a sudden, we get some forward motion! This is not to say every appeal should be based on bribery and gimmicks. On the other hand, even a small amount of manure, if spread in the right places, can help a fruit tree grow and produce!

People often demonstrate remarkable inner passions and motivations that seed their commitments. Unquestionably, this is part of what Paul is pointing to when he talks about the "fruit of the Spirit," and it's certainly what we mean when we say that ministry starts in the heart. But we should never underestimate the motivational power of the simple pat on the back (or T-shirt, or text, or affirming word). We all like to hear the words, "Job well done!"

People judge our beliefs more by our actions than by our words. If we give lip service to the notion that "every person on this student leadership team is important" but only relinquish responsibility to two or three trusted kids, they'll draw their own conclusions about our truthfulness and their gifts. Sweet talk and kind words are no substitute for concrete action.

People will sacrifice a lot to institutions that will provide meaning for them. As a young college student on staff with Young Life, I spent forty-plus hours a week doing contact work with students through Young Life clubs—even when it meant cutting college classes one or two days a week—all for the exorbitant salary of $60 a month! Why? Well, obviously, it wasn't the money. I'd like to think it was all rooted in my rock-solid commitment to Christ—but there were a lot of different ministries through which I could have served Christ. There had to be more to it than that. I think it came down to this: In the fellowship and work of Young Life, I found deep friendships and a sense of purpose. I felt it was my niche. I belonged there. Their needs and my gifts seemed to mesh. *I didn't just work with Young Life. I became a part of Young Life, and Young Life became a part of me.* If we want to develop youth and volunteers who are committed to our youth ministry, they need to sense that the ministry is committed to them. Don't just call people to a task; call them to a quest, a shared adventure, a "Fellowship of the Ring."

DOES THIS STUFF REALLY MATTER IN YOUTH MINISTRY?

Most of us can see ourselves in the assumptions Waterman and Peters used to approach their management skills research. But how does *In Search of Excellence* parallel our search for excellent youth ministries? This is where it starts to get interesting.

In their research from the business world, Waterman and Peters observed that organizations which function with excellence do it by paying attention to seven common variables, known as The McKinsey 7-S Framework: ***structure, strategy, staff, style, systems, shared values, and skills.*** Let's categorize some typical issues of youth ministry within these variables.

Structure. How will we divide the youth group? Will we use a small group model with the entire group meeting only on occasion? Do we break down the large group by age, by geographical region, by school? When, if ever, is a group too big to be effective? Should we structure our youth program to include early adolescents (grades 5-6) and late adolescents (college-age and post-college)? Or just focus on the more traditional middle school- and high school-age youth? Should we keep those age groups together? Or should they meet separately?

Strategy. Do we use the PDYM approach (See Doug Fields, *Purpose-Driven Youth Ministry*, Zondervan, 1998) or a more contemplative model (See Mark Yaconelli, *Contemplative Youth Ministry*, Zondervan, 2007) or something else? Do we need to do a work project, a Bible study, a prayer warrior weekend, or a Backwards Night?

Staff (and other people). How do we find effective leadership for a growing youth ministry? How can we motivate young people to be involved in leadership? How can we nurture and effectively train the kinds of adult volunteers we need? Do we have a mechanism for engaging youth so they are able to share their gifts and talents in our ministry? Are we meeting teenagers at lots of different places on the spectrum of spiritual commitment? Do we tend to be wired more for outreach or for discipleship? Are we designing programs that invite teenagers from diverse backgrounds and cultures, or do our programs unintentionally (intentionally?) screen out certain youth?

Style. What should be our posture in working with the church board? The pastor? Other staff members? Volunteers? How do we decide what to do and when to do it? Does our leadership and management style encourage others to use their gifts or discourage them from doing so?

Systems. Is there any ongoing evaluation of our ministry? What sort of procedure should we use for budgeting effectively? Have we given careful thought to child protection issues and questions of legal liability? Do we have a procedure for keeping accurate attendance records? What sort of emphasis will we place on our Web presence (Web site, Facebook group)? Do we have a system for follow-up with new Christians, first-time visitors, and regular attenders who have ceased to come?

Shared values. Why do we have a youth ministry? Do we have a clearly stated vision that helps leaders, youth, and parents understand why we do some of the things we do—and why we *don't* do some other things? What do we want youth to look like when they have come through our ministry? If we have to cut back our youth budget, which areas should be cut first? Which areas should be cut last? What are our priorities?

Skills. What are the present and hoped-for strengths of our ministry? What are the strengths and liabilities of our facility? What can our smaller youth group offer to teenagers who could attend two other mega-youth groups in our area? What are some areas in which our youth still lack a biblical understanding of the Christian life? What are some of the resources (off-property, community, school, natural) that we have available because of our specific geographic location?

YOUTH MINISTRY: AN EXCELLENT ADVENTURE

Here's the critical question that confronts us if we take seriously Waterman and Peters's analysis: How can we implement some of these marks of excellence in our ministries with teenagers? Chances are that Waterman and Peters have never done a prayer group chat room or an evangelistic Halo night for video gamers, but some of their writing is relevant to organizing a youth ministry. Drawing from their research of excellent organizations, let's consider four implications for effective youth ministry.

1. Close to the Customer: A Good Youth Ministry Puts People at the Center.

"The good news from the excellent companies," the researchers write, "is the extent to which, and the intensity with which, the customers intrude into every nook and cranny of the business." Regardless of how busy we become, how zealous our vision is, or how demanding our other responsibilities are, we need to remember we cannot have a youth ministry without youth. (Some of us would have to confess that this thought has occurred to us on occasion! "The retreat would have been a blast, but the kids showed up.") For a youth-ministry organization to be excellent, it must cater to the needs of its youth and be sensitive to each teenager's individual well-being. It must put people ahead of programs by accomplishing the following tasks:

Focus on the number of volunteer leaders as much as on the number of youth involved. A good leader-to-youth ratio that allows for full and frequent interaction among kids and leaders is approximately one adult for every ten high school students, and about one adult for every six middle school students. Increasing the number of youth in our group without boosting the leadership roster assures that we will involve more kids than we can care for. This approach, made famous by "The Old Woman Who Lived in a Shoe," makes for great nursery rhymes, but it's not a good way to care for children of God.

Urge volunteer leaders to spend time with the youth outside of organized meetings. Not every adult volunteer can juggle family and job responsibilities to budget in the fifteen hours weekly of informal contact that some para-church ministries ask of their volunteers. The critical emphasis for the volunteer youth worker who wants to stay "close to the customer" is to spend time on a regular basis with some kid apart from the regular meeting, even if it's only 30 minutes a week.

One of the most practical suggestions I've heard in this regard is what Jim Burns calls "The 90-Minute Challenge." It offers a very simple way for volunteers to budget their time with youth apart from the normal ministry meetings that occur each week. And it all boils down to a commitment to invest 90 minutes each week in building relationships with youth-group kids.

The first 60 minutes is spent in one-on-two or one-on-three interaction—maybe it's a small group, maybe it's a Facebook chat, maybe it's a breakfast meeting with some kids, or a pizza after youth group on Sunday night. Then, the remaining 30 minutes is split in half—15 minutes for written communication (anything from texts to e-mail to postcards), and 15 minutes for making two phone calls. Perhaps you send a birthday greeting to a student, or maybe it's a quick note to a kid who wasn't at youth group this week. Maybe you make a follow-up phone call to a youth who gave you a prayer request or give a kid a quick call just to make sure he's going to be at youth group this week. One small-group interaction, three postcards, and two phone calls; and you have personally touched the lives of as many as eight different kids in 90 minutes. That's staying close to the customer.

Survey (informally or systematically) teenagers as well as adult leaders about what activities might be planned, what topics might be studied, and what changes might be made. The survey can be as simple as giving the group a *4321 Survey*: "On a blank sheet of paper, write down four topics you'd like to see the group study, three activities you'd like to see our group do, two ways we could make the group better, and one way you feel you could be better involved in this ministry family." As a youth program becomes larger, it grows both increasingly important and increasingly difficult to get feedback and suggestions from those involved. Waterman and Peters note that one strength of excellent companies was that they had mastered the art of growing big while acting small.

Communicate with your group members on special occasions (birthdays, milestones of spiritual growth, achievements). I discovered early in my own ministry that simply sending a birthday card was a gesture kids notice. More than that, I began to realize this birthday note was one of the most significant notes I could write to that student all year. I could offer words of encouragement and challenge to them in that letter that might not be accepted from me at any other time of the year. It was as if kids perceived their birthdays as appropriate occasions for looking back and looking ahead, for evaluation and challenge.

Now, if these efforts to stay close to the kids in your group sound a little inconvenient, that's because they are. Love, at times, can be very inconvenient. Oswald Chambers said it well:

> What a marvelous illustration fishing is, especially fishing with the net, and Jesus Christ told the disciples He would make them "fishers of men," catchers of men. Unless we have this divine passion for souls burning in us because of our personal love for Jesus Christ, we will quit the work before we are much older. It is an easy business to be a fisherman when you have all the enthusiasm of the catch, everybody then wants to be a fisherman. Just as everybody comes in with the shout and the "Hallelujah" when revival signs are abroad; but God is wanting those who through long nights, through difficult days of spiritual toil, have been trying to let down their nets to catch the fish. Oh, the skill, the patience, the gentleness and the endurance that are needed for this passion for souls; a sense that men are perishing won't do it; only one thing will do it, a blazing, passionate devotion to the Lord Jesus Christ, an all-consuming passion.[6]

2. Autonomy and Entrepreneurship: A Good Youth Ministry Gives Visionary People Freedom to Act.

Based on their research, Waterman and Peters suggested the most discouraging fact of big corporate life was "the loss of what got them [the companies] big in the first place: Innovation."[7] As a company grows, it typically becomes more careful, less willing to take risks. As it becomes less willing to take risks, it becomes less likely to grow. They cite a National Science Foundation study reported in *Inc.*, in which researchers found that "small firms produced about four times as many innovations per research-and-development dollar as medium-sized firms, and about twenty-four times as many as large firms."[8]

One way excellent large companies "act small" is by giving people creative freedom and encouraging entrepreneurship. Workers are invited to think in new ways and to try new approaches. Or, to put it more simply, employees are allowed to act on their ideas without submitting four copies of the proposal to six different people so all the higher-ups can send a memo saying why the suggestion won't work.

When a youth program is small, the leadership is often hungry and desperate, willing to try anything. Sparks fly. Sure, some mistakes are made—but creativity happens, and kids start to get excited. As the group grows, however, the leadership often becomes more conservative, less willing to try new ideas, more conscious of maintaining its high standard than reaching for new goals. This isn't surprising. After all, an idea that bombs with a group of five teenagers is something you laugh about afterwards when everyone goes out for pizza. An idea that bombs with a group of 50 is "a bad night," a rationale for "slowing down," an excuse for a meeting. The price for a strategy of program maintenance is usually loss of innovation. It's the age-old rule: Greater risk means greater potential loss, but also greater potential gain.

A ministry full of encouragement and risk-taking reflects a humble leader. Most of us have seen the poster that identifies the "seven last words of the church": *We've never done it that way before.* One danger of having a successful youth ministry is the tendency to think the way we're doing things is the best way and we have nothing to learn from other ministries. That kind of myopia blinds us to innovations that might strengthen our ministries. An excellent youth ministry has an organizational climate that allows for autonomy and entrepreneurship. We can give people freedom to act in the following ways:

Sow seeds of encouragement. There is no better way to warm up an organizational climate than through encouragement. Seed-sowing phrases sound like this:

- That's a great idea. How could I help you make something like *that* happen?
- I like that idea; tell me more about it.
- What if we could rewrite the script for ______________ (Sunday, Friday, Wednesday) night? What would it look like?
- What are you guys seeing that I'm not seeing?
- You know, (name), you seem to have such a passion for _________. How could we use that as tool for ministry with our kids?

The secret to seed-sowing phrases is an attitude that says, "Try it; it *might* work," rather than, "Do you think we should try it? What if it *doesn't* work?"

Give away ownership. Even when we delegate the responsibility for a project, Bible study, or program to youth or adult volunteers, they often sense that we expect them to do the job our way. We communicate that expectation by taking back the project if they try something different, by ignoring their suggestions, or by "riding in" like the cavalry to rescue them if they encounter difficulty. (After all, we are seminary-trained and, therefore, more experienced and semi-messianic.) The people we work with may comply with our wishes regarding the projects, but by forcing them to do it our way, we short-circuit innovations that might have been sparked if they'd been convinced the assignments were theirs, start to finish. Waterman and Peters describe this as the principle of autonomy (based on the Greek: *auto*=self, *nomos*=rule or law).

If we really want to see something new happen with youth group outreach or worship or cultivation of new members, we need to challenge the kids or adult leaders assigned to these programs to genuinely *own* them. People cannot be creative if they feel us breathing down their necks—if they feel that, just when they're starting to paint, we're going to change the colors or grab the brushes from their hands. It's really tough to work on a car if the owner is still driving it, and it's nearly impossible to be innovative with a program when leadership hasn't really yielded the steering. Ownership encourages innovation.

Don't be afraid to fail. For the youth-ministry volunteer lost in a maze of websites, software, books, discussion guides, game resources, and Bible studies, the possibility of failure stifles innovation. Sure, the game sounds good, but will it work with our kids? What if it doesn't work? *We must be willing to accept some misses if we ever hope to have a big hit.* Failing at something new doesn't mean our students are unreachable or we're incapable. Sometimes the difference between an idea that flies and an idea that crashes is little more than a matter of timing, or location, or group size, or group personality.

Every effective youth minister has times when the game plan has to be changed after the opening whistle. A lot of us don't believe that. We think mistakes don't happen to the really experienced, really good, really talented youth workers who lead seminars and share ideas, because we've never heard them talk about that stuff. Of course, that's because these really experienced, good, talented youth workers couldn't get anyone to come to a workshop called "Ten Worship Ideas that Totally Died." People want to know what works; they're not as keen to hear about all the mediocre ideas that fell between strokes of genius.

Just because you don't hear about the experts' mistakes doesn't mean they don't have them. Those who attempt new things will occasionally fail. Those who never fail never attempt anything.

Allow time for incubation. One reason youth ministers seldom innovate is that they simply don't have time. Most youth workers program to survive, but innovation takes time. People need adequate time to formulate and incubate new ideas; they need to be allowed the luxury of long-term planning.

At one church I served, we sketched out the themes for our Sunday night Breakaways at least nine months in advance—well before we laid out any specific programming for particular evenings. Generally speaking, the specific planning for a Sunday night took place one month prior to the date. At the meeting to plan the October 31 Breakaway, we considered how to develop the "fear" theme we'd chosen to capitalize on for Halloween. In the course of the conversation, someone suggested doing a media presentation of what teenagers fear. Beyond that there was little specific guidance. One of our volunteers, Thom Scott, was pretty good with a camera, so he was assigned to prepare the show. He had one month to complete the job. He eventually produced a remarkably entertaining and creative piece of work, including background music, narration, and humor, all the while involving several of our students in the filming. It was a masterpiece.

Aside from Thom's talent, the two keys to his completing such a blockbuster presentation were *ownership* and *time*. By giving him a month to work on the project and freedom to take it in the direction he felt would be most effective, we showed that we took him and his work seriously. We were saying, "We don't already have in mind some idea we want you to carry out. We trust your ability. We sincerely want you to be innovative, and we know that this takes some time."

Our normal approach to delegation is to say to someone, "We really need you to come up with some wild, creative stuff for an upcoming event. The sky's the limit! It's your baby! Go for your dreams! Anything goes! And...it needs to be ready in seven hours." Not only is this an insult, but it's also an excellent way to stifle innovation.

3. Productivity through People: A Good Youth Ministry Develops and Deploys Workers' Gifts.

It was Elmo "Bud" Zumwalt, chief of U.S. Naval Operations in the early 1970s, who observed, "The Navy assumes that everybody below the rank of commander is immature."[9] Sad to say, sometimes the Lord's army operates the same way, except our version sounds like this: "Everybody below the rank of pastor is unfit for real ministry."

Waterman and Peters consistently found that excellent secular companies develop and utilize the strengths of their employees, treat their people with respect, and take them seriously. But they weren't the first to value such an approach. Before any Wall Street wunderkind articulated the principle of productivity through people, the apostle Paul wrote this:

> So Christ himself gave the apostles, the prophets, the evangelists, the pastors and teachers, to equip his people for works of service, so that the body of Christ may be built up until we all reach unity in the faith and in the knowledge of the Son of God and become mature, attaining to the whole measure of the fullness of Christ. (Ephesians 4:11-13)

We, in the church, talk about the concept of productivity through people. Our Scriptures explicitly state it. But when it comes right down to the way we actually do youth ministry, our instincts often bear testimony to a different doctrine: Productivity through profit ("We need a bigger budget"); productivity through preaching ("We need to give these kids more doctrinal teaching; I'd better take care of it"); or productivity through program ("Only a few kids came to our peer-ministry class and we get huge crowds out for Friday night outreach; we may have to cut the peer-ministry program").

When it comes to productivity through people, Jesus makes it clear, nonparticipation is not an option. In his parable of the talents (Matthew 25:14-30), there are two rather blunt lessons:

(1) God expects everyone to utilize for his kingdom whatever gifts and talents they've been given (v. 29-30);

(2) When those gifts are exercised, there should be appropriate recognition of the efforts made—even when differences in talent produce differences in outcome (v. 23).

How, then, can we massage this principle into the flesh and bones of real-life youth ministry? Maybe the best place to begin is by asking some practical questions:

Do we meet with our student leadership core on a regular basis to get feedback on the program and meet regularly with our adult volunteer team for the same purpose? Or, do we meet with them only occasionally, when we need their blessing on something we already have planned?

Do we treat the volunteers with respect? Or, do we frustrate capable ministers by entrusting them with responsibility for our teenagers, but not the key to the church kitchen?

Do we take seriously the contributions of our leaders? Or, do we require leaders to pay out of their pockets for supplies, food, and retreat registrations—adding a financial expense to the high cost volunteers already pay in terms of time and energy to be involved in youth ministry?

Do we attempt to provide those who teach our youth with the kind of classroom environment and instructional equipment that allows them to do their best? Or, do we communicate that their jobs are unimportant by allowing them to walk into classrooms where basic supplies are lacking and the most up-to-date communication tool is a blackboard that's not been cleaned since the apostolic age?

Are we facilitating the ministries of others by helping youth and adult volunteers discern their gifts and giving them opportunities to test and sharpen those gifts? Or, do we hold to the motto, "If you want it done right, you've got to do it yourself"?

Are we enhancing the morale of our leadership by communicating with words and actions that we take seriously their potential and contributions? Or, do we undermine these people (who hold responsible jobs, create personal momentum, organize their homes, make decisions, and gain the respect of their coworkers on a daily basis) by entrusting them only with the responsibilities of serving food, inflating balloons, and performing police operations?

At the heart of biblical Christianity is our belief in the priesthood of all believers—the notion that all believers, whether adult or adolescent, whether ordained or not ordained, whether paid or volunteer, are capable of and called to ministry. This means we need to structure our youth ministries to discern, develop, and deploy gifted people.

Beyond carefully training leaders and plugging them into slots suited to their gifts, deploying gifted people requires trusting their abilities and ideas—believing that they can make significant contributions. It's not just that we need to learn to trust the people who surround us in ministry (although we do). Even more, we in Christian ministry must also have a bedrock trust in a God who does extraordinary feats through ordinary people. We've got to have a basic belief in the ability of kids and adults to live lives of kingdom significance. For example, consider these:

- Zach, who was not quite a teenager when he did a report for school about slave trading. It started out as normal homework, but in his research he discovered there are still many parts of the world where there is a thriving trade in human trafficking and slavery. And that sparked an outrage in Zach that prompted him to start Loose Change to Loosen Chains (LC2LC), a student-led campaign for elementary to college students to combat modern-day slavery.[10]

- Or Lindsey, whose compassion for her sister with cerebral palsy led her to start a youth group for kids with special needs in her Minnesota community. Friends United meets every Wednesday night in what Lindsey describes as a "peer-to-peer ministry." Her vision was sparked by a desire to bring together her two worlds—her friends at school and people with special needs like her sister, so that together they could discover the love of Jesus.[11]

- Or Austin, who in the spring of 2004 watched a video about children who had lost their parents to AIDS. At the time, he was only

12 years old, but he recognized that these kids were no different from him except for their suffering. And God used that to prompt Austin to do something. Since he loved basketball, he decided to see how much money he could raise by asking people to pledge a certain amount for every free throw he could sink in one day. On World AIDS Day 2004, Austin shot 2,057 free throws and was able to raise almost $3,000. That year, the money was used by World Vision to provide hope to 8 orphan children. Since that first day in the gym, Hoops of Hope participants around the country have raised over $1 million.[12]

- Or the Class of 2009 at Wheaton Christian Academy in Illinois, which raised $14,000 for Opportunity International, an organization specializing in micro-lending to provide small loans allowing people living in poverty around the world to launch their own small businesses.[13]

Stories like these remind us that we underestimate God when we are reluctant to let teenagers lead worship or give testimony simply because we lead or speak better, and that we may be overlooking crucial gifts when we refuse to let adult leaders step forward simply because they don't have as much formal training as we do.

There are so many ways to show that we trust and value the contributions of others. We need to make every effort to enhance among volunteers a sense of team membership, of family. Some youth programs do this with baseball caps or T-shirts that say "Youth Staff." I remember speaking at a camp in upstate New York some years ago where every adult leader at the camp was awarded a special counselor's T-shirt that read

> OSWEGATCHIE STAFF /os-we-GA-chee staf/ n. (Am. Indian: black waters and a bent stick; or long, skinny bacteria) 1: adults running around in the woods acting as if they were teenagers 2: the cause of the disease *Oswegatchicus exhausticum*, characterized by hysteria, exhaustion, hoarse voice, and a fear of bears (see Ursophobia) 3: the group of people allegedly supervising KP, classes, and night activities 4: the Christian servant-leaders of the greatest senior teen camp in the world; syn: see fools for Christ's sake.

It was more than a T-shirt; it was a badge of camaraderie and affirmation. It may have been corny, but it said, "We appreciate you, and we take seriously what God can do through you."

4. Hands-On/Values-Driven: A Good Youth Ministry Makes Its Clear Purpose Known throughout the Organization.

The writer of Proverbs 29:18 puts it this way: "Where there is no vision, the people perish" (KJV). People tire of moving forward when there is no goal ahead. The shape of any excellent organization, whether in business or youth ministry, is determined not by changing circumstances or the ups and downs of passing opinions, but by long-term vision. Waterman and Peters are adamant on this point. "Every excellent company we studied is clear on what it stands for, and takes the process of shaping values seriously. In fact, we wonder whether it is possible to be an excellent company without clarity on values and without having the right sorts of values."[14]

This mark of excellence is the most critical. Without a vision, efforts to stay close to the customer degenerate into a namby-pamby political game of trying to please everybody—and nothing of substance gets accomplished. Autonomy and entrepreneurship become little more than tinkering—an empty drive to perfect technique without any purpose. Productivity through people becomes a confusing chaos in which each person does his or her own thing without any common head to direct the parts of the body.

Thomas J. Watson wrote a book some time ago based on his experiences as a chief executive at IBM. Waterman and Peters draw from that book a lengthy quote that defends the importance of an organization deciding what it stands for:

> One may speculate at length as to the cause of the decline and fall of a corporation. Technology, changing tastes, changing fashions all play a part...No one can dispute their importance. But I question whether they in themselves are decisive. I believe the real difference between success and failure in a corporation can very often be traced to the question of how well the organization brings out the great energies and talents of its people. What does it do to help the people find common cause with each other? And how can it sustain the common cause and sense of this direction through the many changes that take place from one generation to another? Consider any great organization—one that has lasted over the years—I think you will find that it owes it resiliency not to its organization or administrative skills, but to the power of what we call "beliefs" and the appeal these beliefs have for its people. This then is my thesis: I firmly believe that any business, in order to survive and achieve success, must have a sound set of beliefs on which it premises all its actions and policies. Next, I believe that the most important single factor in corporate success will be the faithful adherence to those beliefs. And, finally, I believe if an organization is to meet the challenge of a changing world it must be prepared to change everything about itself except those beliefs as it moves through corporate life. In other words, the basic philosophy, spirit, and drive of an organization have far more to do with its relative achievements than do

> technological or economic resources, organizational structure, innovation, and timing. All these things weigh heavily in success. But they are, I think, transcended by how strongly the people in the organization believe in its basic precepts and how faithfully they carry them out.[15]

Watson's statement is remarkable. Except for a few business terms, and the lack of even one mention of Facebook, NOOMA, or the word *missional*, it could have been a description of the importance of vision as the driving force of youth ministry.

One of the gravest mistakes in modern youth ministry is ministering without a vision or philosophy of youth ministry—being stimulated into action through the latest resource, nudged into submission by some ruling elder, paralyzed into imitation by the latest survey of cultural attitudes, or halted by some bored teenager who doesn't consider the ministry adequately entertaining. There is no shortage of books that define and clarify some sort of youth ministry philosophy. Some use funnels. Some use pyramids. Others use circles. Virtually every geometric shape has been called into service. And yet, defining a philosophy is only the first step. Not only must we have a vision in youth ministry, but we must openly and frequently communicate that vision to everyone involved in the youth program—to the adults involved in leadership, to the youth who attend every week, and to the parents of teenagers involved.

CORRECTING BLURRED VISION

One day when I was in fourth grade, I was clowning around with a buddy and put on his glasses. All of a sudden the world came into focus. It was incredible. The blackboard suddenly made sense. Trees outside had leaves instead of green blobs. Cafeteria signs became clear enough to read. All along I'd assumed everyone saw the world as I did—a little fuzzy, hard to read, tough to understand. It took proper lenses to help me recognize that *I had blurry vision.*

Later in this book, we will address in some detail a process for hammering out and articulating a ministry philosophy (see chapter 5). For now, let's just consider some of the key questions that will help to diagnose blurry vision in a youth ministry program.

What are we here for? Pose this question to the volunteer leaders, the pastor, the parents of youth in the program, and the youth themselves. Ask them to write out specific examples that demonstrate what they think you are trying to accomplish in the youth program. Much church conflict is rooted in the simple fact that the people involved haven't agreed on an articulated common goal.

I remember a time when, after I explained the vision for our youth ministry to our congregation's council on ministries, the whole room erupted into applause. Since spontaneous applause was not a common feature of our all-day meetings, I was a little taken aback. But I think the enthusiasm was a product of two things: (1) Our board was excited to see the youth ministry had a clear vision about which *we* were passionate; and (2) I think it helped our board gain clarity about a vision *they* could embrace, about which *they* could be passionate. These faithful congregational workers, church leaders, and sincere Christians had been working with a blurred sense of purpose. But a simple, succinct statement of both vision and plan helped them regain their focus.

What do others see? If someone were to observe your youth program for a one-month period, what would they observe about the values that drive your group? What might people observe about your group's values if they were part of a leadership planning session? How about if they witnessed a game night? Your website? Your Facebook group? A retreat? A parents' meeting? A fundraiser? We communicate our values most accurately when we are not intentionally doing so.

How do we make decisions? The criteria we use to evaluate our ministries reveal our values. What do we really mean when we say last night's youth program really "worked"? Do we mean it got a laugh, it drew a crowd, the kids got really quiet, it was really edgy, everybody liked it, it made three kids cry, it was cool? How do we decide to do what we decide to do? It is in those decisions that our real values and intentions come to light.

Often when I am consulting with a church, I will observe that the ministry's authentic values are exposed when a decision is made to cut or discontinue something (or not to). Did we drop the discipleship program because "there weren't enough kids involved"? Did we stop talking about that topic because "we got a lot flak from the kids"? Did we cease the outreach program because "it drew the wrong kinds of kids"? Jesus said, "For where your treasure is, there your heart will be also" (Matthew 6:21). Watch how your program allocates funding (or cuts off funding) and you'll get a glimpse of where the heart of your ministry is.

How precious are our methods? Listen to the discussions in planning sessions or staff and committee meetings. Is *how* more important than *why*? Ministries in which techniques and methodologies are precious are seldom guided by vision.

Are we taking our pulse every year? Frequent checks alert us early to inaccurate and unclear vision. We need to schedule periodic meetings with our various youth ministry constituencies—youth, parents, ministry leaders, and congregational leaders—to inform them about our vision.

We need to consistently preach our vision, model our vision, remind ourselves of that vision as we plan, and make it known unashamedly to our leaders, our youth, and their parents. Does your youth ministry have a clear, written vision statement? The first question you need to ask is not, "Will it work?" or, "Can we do it?" but, "How does it help us reach our goal?" and, "Does it fit our vision?" This is the mark of an excellent ministry.

LEADERSHIP STYLE

Close to the Customer, Autonomy and Entrepreneurship, Productivity through People, and *Hands-On/Value-Driven*—all four are critical to an excellent youth ministry. But the conversation between these four areas of emphasis will take on different accents depending on one's individual leadership voice. Bernard Swain refers to this as leadership *style*, defining it as "the complex and varying patterns of behavior and relationship among ministerial leaders and between these leaders and other people."[16] Based on his research and consultation with a wide range of congregational and denominational bodies, Swain defines four leadership styles, each based on a unique *recipe* combining four ingredients (in different measures): Degree and locus of authority, division of labor, delegation of responsibility, and joint performance. We see his description of the four styles in the diagram on the pages that follow.

While most leaders function in one style most of the time, the most effective leaders will likely operate within two or more of these styles depending on the circumstances. The key question for leaders is not, "Which style-type is the will of God?" but rather, "How can we build a recipe for a leadership style that best fits our strengths, mission, and ministry context while incorporating the marks of excellent ministry?" Give these charts a careful look before you leave this chapter.

A DESIRE FOR EXCELLENCE

To be sure, our vision and mandate as ministers of the gospel take us into realms that cannot be touched by secular business consultants. Ours is a realm in which the report of the prophet carries more weight than the actual profit report. However, the development of excellence is worth our time—even if it requires listening to the counsel of two high-powered business types. We are working with precious human lives, helping teenagers grow into the image of Jesus. We are serving Christ, his Excellency, and he desires and deserves our best.

Swain's Four Leadership Styles

SOVEREIGN

Description	***EXAMPLE:*** Youth leader who pretty much operates as the "youth ministry guru in residence," and sees adult staff or interns as drones who do the "grunt work." • centralized authority; • not necessarily negative, just marked by hierarchal structure.
Values	• someone *must* lead so there will be a sense of order; • professionalism: getting the job done *right;* • playing one's role without disrupting the system; • accountability for one's area of authority; • uniformity.
Features	• authority is not shared or divided with anyone else, i.e. "The buck stops here"; • decision-making is highly centralized.
Relationships	• relationships are based primarily on authority (rank and position); • volunteers and staff depend on the "paid youth worker"; • peerage is rare; people do not relate to each other as equals; • relationships based on institutional role rather than personal character.
Strengths	• efficiency; simplifies decision-making; • economical; gets work done with minimal investment of time and energy; • provides control and structure; • takes personality out of the equation (it doesn't really); but this leadership style says, "We do it my way because I'm the Youth Pastor—not necessarily because you like me."
Weaknesses	• most people have a natural mistrust for authority; • provides a very weak base of delegation and synergy; • discourages initiative and entrepreneurship; • comes across as elitist and dictatorial; • discourages Body life.

PARALLEL

Description	***EXAMPLE:*** Youth worker who functions alongside a team of volunteers, some who teach Sunday school, some who do midweek programming, etc., but makes no real effort to conjoin and coordinate everyone's efforts. • authority is vested in a team of people who work alongside each other, but *not* necessarily *with* each other; • the team members understand their job, and individually, each of them does what's needed to accomplish the task.
Values	• high value on division of labor, and personal responsibility; • high value placed on personal autonomy; • values diversity: people doing their specific jobs in their personal ways.
Features	• allows energy to be focused on task rather than side issues of authority and obedience; • real delegation, as opposed to sovereign style that only delegates the work, not the planning and method; • in pure parallel style, there is no one person in authority; • self-reliance.
Relationships	• peerage or equality is created—in a strange way—by the fact that people are doing their own pieces of the project, so everyone is equally alone in his/her work, even though all are working on the same project; • generates independence; • requires little or no trust between leader and co-leaders, volunteers.
Strengths	• it's simple—lean and mean, not a lot of boxes and flowcharts; • keeps too many cooks from "spoiling the broth"; • working alone allows people to work without distraction; • neutralizes negative vibes regarding authority.
Weaknesses	• lack of communication; • isolation can make people afraid to make decisions —don't want to go out on a limb by themselves; • loses benefits of collaboration; • eliminating authority creates a body with no head.

MUTUAL

Description	***EXAMPLE:*** Youth leader who wants to discern the gifts of others on the team so those gifts can be developed and deployed in a united effort. • team of people is involved at all levels: planning, executing, and evaluating.
Values	• stress on sharing: feelings, thoughts, ideas, and the work itself; • autonomy is absorbed in group identity; • stress on integration and fitting in with team.
Features	• consensus is big part of decision-making process; • lots of interaction with others.
Relationships	• interdependence; • authority is shared; • trust is very important, not just for character, but also for teammates' ability to do the job.
Strengths	• keeps one from being the "Lone Ranger"; • overcomes isolation; • creates greater synergy: more people with more ideas mixing together in more ways; • most people enjoy the interaction with other people.
Weaknesses	• as go the relationships, so goes the work; • expends a lot of resources just to build the team, before ever thinking about the youth program; • complicates decision-making process. ("A camel is a horse designed by a committee.")

SEMIMUTUAL

Description	***EXAMPLE:*** Youth leader who has co-responsibility for youth group, alongside a team or committee—which *shares equal authority* and equal accountability for the ministry. • a hybrid of mutual and parallel; • sort of like relationship between youth pastor and youth leadership team—they work together but one or the other is probably in charge.
Values	• a division of labor (as with parallel style) but not as pronounced and complete; • some joint accountability, but still the emphasis is on autonomy.
Features	• consensus about goals and objectives is more important than any one job; • no joint responsibility for performance: One or the other does the job; • there is interaction but it's not ongoing.
Relationships	• moderate level of trust; • can be stressful because of energy required to maintain balance in relationship; • authority is vaguely defined: Is the youth committee working *with* the youth pastor, or is the youth pastor working *for* the committee—or is it something else altogether?
Strengths	• provides checks and balances; • perhaps, of all the leadership styles, this one most accurately reflects the way youth workers and committees actually function together.
Weaknesses	• tougher to integrate planning and performance because it's not clear who plans and who performs; • provides neither the clear authority of sovereign style nor the relationships and peerage of the mutuality style.

CHAPTER 4

Getting It Done in Time: Mission Impossible?

One who is slack in his work is a close
relative of one who destroys.
(Proverbs 18:9)

No doubt you've heard the story—I don't know its source[1]—about the man who'd experienced some sort of industrial accident at work and, in the process of trying to get compensation from his insurance company, had been asked to provide a fuller explanation of his misfortune. What follows is the letter he wrote in response:

> Dear Sirs:
>
> I am responding to your request for additional information. In block number three of your accident reporting form, I had originally written "poor planning" as the cause of my accident. You said in your letter that I should explain more fully, and I trust the following details will be sufficient.
>
> I am a bricklayer by trade and on the day of my accident I was working alone on the roof of a six-story building. When I completed my work I discovered that I had about six hundred pounds of bricks left over. Rather than carry the bricks by hand, I decided to lower them in a barrel which, fortunately, was attached to the side of the building at the sixth floor.
>
> Securing the rope at ground level, I went up to the sixth floor and swung the barrel out and loaded the bricks into it. Then I went to the ground and untied the rope. And I held it tightly to insure a slow descent.
>
> You will note in block number seven of your accident reporting form that my weight is listed as 137 pounds. Due to my surprise at being jerked so suddenly off the ground, I lost my presence of mind and forgot to let go of the rope. Needless to say, I proceeded up the side of the building at a rather rapid rate.
>
> In the vicinity of the third floor I met the barrel coming down, and this will explain the fractured skull and broken collarbone. Slowed

> only slightly, I continued my rapid ascent, not stopping until the fingers of my right hand were two knuckles deep inside the pulley.
>
> Fortunately, by this time, I had regained my presence of mind and was able to hold tightly to the rope in spite of the intense pain. At approximately the same time however, the barrel of bricks hit the ground. That made the bottom fall out of the barrel.
>
> Devoid of the weight of the bricks, the barrel now weighed some 50 pounds. I refer you again to my weight in block number seven. As you might imagine, I began a rapid descent down the side of the building.
>
> In the vicinity of the third floor I met the barrel coming up. This accounts for the two broken ankles and lacerations on the legs and lower body. The encounter with the barrel slowed me only slightly—but not enough to significantly lessen my injuries when I fell onto the pile of bricks. Fortunately, only three vertebrae were cracked.
>
> I am sorry to report, however, that as I lay there on those bricks—in pain, unable to stand, watching the barrel six floors above me, I again lost my presence of mind...and I let go of the rope.

A lot of painful episodes begin with "poor planning"—and they don't all involve brick and mortar. Early in my ministry, I witnessed what I fear were the early stages in this same kind of slow-motion disaster. Back in those days, when I went to speak for a church or youth group, I would bunk in the youth worker's home to help shave expenses. Most of the time, my visits were congenial and comfortable enough. But sometimes I had a front-row seat at various forms of life and ministry dysfunction.

Over the course of our week together, I watched Terry with a combination of pity and awe. I remember one night when he staggered into the bedroom of his small apartment at about 2 a.m. It was the third night in a row Terry had been out late with some of his kids. I awoke just long enough to thank the Lord that Terry wasn't married, or I might have been a firsthand witness to a domestic assault.

I could hardly believe it when he woke me up at six(!) the next morning to tell me where to find breakfast supplies in the kitchen. He whispered that he was on his way to the church to get everything set up for the youth group activity later that day. It was just the kind of rude awakening that would eventually convince me that staying in hotels was a really good idea, even if it added a little to the expense. I don't remember precisely what I whispered back to him at that hour, but I think the sentence may have included the word *homicide.*

What struck me about that episode was that Terry was absolutely sold out on giving his life to teenagers—loving them creatively, intensely, and personally—sprinting through his schedule at a breakneck pace that took him over a nineteen-hour obstacle course every day. It seemed sad that someone so in love with Jesus and with kids might, within five to ten years, end up sick, burned-out, divorced—or all of the above. But I'd seen it happen too many times to other well-intentioned youth pastors.

POOR PLANNING AND GOOD SELF-MANAGEMENT

Bricklayers and youth workers who labor under the weight of heavy loads and poor planning don't need to hear easy answers. Cute slogans and quick-fix plans only add to our stresses. For example, consider this hot tip from chain-store expert (!) Godfrey M. Lebhar: If we reduce our sleep time by two hours a night, devote at least one hour a day less to mealtime chatter, friendly conversation, and leisure activities, and recover an additional hour of work by moving closer to the workplace, thereby reducing the time spent commuting, we could add five and a half years of usable time to our lives![2]

In his book *The Tyranny of Time,* Robert Banks observes that most of what we read about time management, even from Christian writers, emphasizes a view of time that underlines urgency: Time is fleeting, and we must grab from it what we can before it's gone.[3] But Banks points out that Scripture never encourages a busy use of time at all, but challenges us to discern appropriate timing.[4] The apostle Paul puts it this way:

> Be very careful, then, how you live—not as unwise but as wise, making the most of every opportunity, because the days are evil. Therefore do not be foolish, but understand what the Lord's will is. (Ephesians 5:15-17)

The key here is discernment and stewardship.

Practicing Discernment: "...not as unwise but as wise..." (Ephesians 5:15)

When we're overly concerned about how much time we're spending, we'll be overly concerned about time running out—and that leads to pointless, feverish activity (See Philippians 4:6). Wise youth workers practice the discipline of discernment with regard to their time.

Most of us are locked into one of two basic approaches to time. Christian management consultant Fred Smith describes the two approaches this way:

> One is the technological: Minutes as units. The other is the philosophical: Minutes as meaning. It's possible to grasp the technological view so tightly that you end up with no meaning. Technology should always be the servant of philosophy. Too often people don't know the difference between a fast track and a frantic track.[5]

And the frantic track almost always leads to poor planning.

There are two factors that make us vulnerable to this frantic pace—two factors especially prominent among youth workers.

1. Vanity. We want to feel important, necessary.[6] In Eugene Peterson's words, "We don't like being wallflowers at the world's party."[7] So we say "yes" when we should say "no." It's not enough to lead a Young Life club, serve as a youth pastor, or volunteer with the youth group. There must be something beyond the pastoral tasks that gives us importance. We fill our Day-Timers and Blackberries with appointments and activities so there can be no question that God really needs us and kids really need us and "doggone it, people like us." We seek validation by seeking invitations to speak outside of our normal sphere of ministry, or by pursuing opportunities to write, or by participating on boards and commissions. All of these are valid and important opportunities, but they are, nonetheless, opportunities that consume us with activity and take us away from our central task of discipling the same group of kids week after week.

2. Slothfulness. Just as dangerous, but perhaps a little more insidious, is our tendency toward what the Scripture calls *slothfulness* (See Proverbs 18:9; Ecclesiastes 10:18). A *sloth* is a tropical mammal that lives much of its life hanging upside down from tree branches. On the rare occasion each day when it descends from the tree, it crawls along at a blistering ten feet per minute, which means it would take a sloth just under nine hours to run a kick-off all the way down a football field. Most notable is the sloth's reputation for sluggishness and inactivity. Building no nests and seeking no shelter, even for its young, the sloth prefers to sleep, typically anywhere from 15 to 22 hours a day. When the sloth finally awakens in late afternoon, it's only to eat whatever leaves may be close at hand. Finally, true to its reputation for slow movement, a sloth defecates only once every three to fourteen days (and then, only when it's raining).[8]

It may strike some as ironic that slothfulness would be identified as a cause of busyness. And yet, as C.S. Lewis was fond of pointing out, lazy people often work the hardest. When we don't do the hard work of setting goals and priorities, saying "yes" to some activities and "no" to others, the task is left to other people. And when that happens, we find ourselves frantic and weary, seeking to serve the many last-minute masters who make demands on our time.

Slothfulness then, as John Ortberg reminds us, isn't the absence of activity. It is "the failure to do what needs to be done when it needs to be done."[9] We end up like the kamikaze pilot who flew 17 missions—he was extremely busy, but he wasn't doing what he supposed to do when he was supposed to do it. That is why slothful people are often consumed by increasing activity coupled with diminishing contentment. Frederick Buechner says this:

> "A slothful man...may be a very busy man. He is a man who goes through the motions, who flies on automatic pilot. Like a man with a bad head cold, he has mostly lost his sense of taste and smell. He

> knows something's wrong with him, but not enough to do anything about it. Other people come and go, but through glazed eyes he hardly notices them. He is letting things run their course. He is getting through his life..."[10]

As youth workers who face constant and unending demands in our work with teenagers, we need to reshape our thinking and practice discernment about personal management. The frantic youth worker is often a blur of busyness, always going somewhere and late for the next place, multitasking with the ever-present Blackberry or iPhone, playing catch-up and praying someone will cancel an appointment. Smith sums up the principle: "Opportunity is *not* a mandate *to do*." We have only so many fingers to plug the holes in the dike.

Of course, there are those who will say, "I'd rather burn out than rust out." I suppose if I had to choose between only those two options, I would agree. But are those our only two options—"burn out" or "rust out"? What about "time out"? What about "plan out"? (And, for those of you who came of age in the 60s, what about "far out"?) Donald Bloesch is right when he says that in modern Christianity "busyness is the new holiness."[11] Lack of time has become a badge of spirituality. John Wesley wrote, "Though I am always in haste, I am never in a hurry because I never undertake more work than I can go through with calmness of spirit."

According to the gospel writers, Jesus was determined and single-minded, but he never seemed to be in a hurry. Even in those situations when haste might have seemed appropriate (the death of his friend Lazarus, for instance), Jesus took his time. He had three years to establish the kingdom, three years to recruit and train his disciples, three years to prepare for the redemption of all creation, and yet he never seemed to feel the pressure of time.

I'm convinced one of the keys to discernment with regard to our time is learning to convincingly and graciously use the word *no.* Doug Fields, who is as good at saying "no" as anybody I've ever met, reminds us we aren't really serious about what we say "yes" to unless we are willing to protect it by saying "no" to other things.[12] Marlene Wilson, in her book *Survival Skills for Managers*, says it well: "The true meaning of a leader is not what he or she does, but what he or she decides to leave undone."[13]

Discernment of time begins with living on purpose—being fully present in the moment, instead of being stressed out about the next moment: In other words, "not as unwise but as wise."

Practicing Stewardship: "...making the most of every opportunity..." (Ephesians 5:16)

No less important than the discipline of discernment is the discipline of stewardship—making the most of every opportunity. Marlene Wilson reminds us how easy it is to misuse our time because of misunderstandings about the way our time is spent. She refers to these misunderstandings as paradoxes in time management.[14]

The open-door paradox. We youth workers practice an open-door policy that says to the students in the youth group, "I am available anytime if you need to talk." That means we always have students hanging around in our office. Our intentions are good, but paradoxically, students who really need to talk about their problems are embarrassed to bring them forward in a place crawling with other kids. Consequently, they may never get to discuss the problems with us at all. We have discouraged the very thing we hoped to accomplish.

Tyranny-of-the-urgent paradox. Youth ministers tend to scamper around putting out fires instead of doing the kind of long-range planning effective ministry requires. The result is that long-range planning is neglected, thereby ensuring future crises and more fires to fight. Moral to the story: Busyness is *not* next to godliness.

Cluttered-desk paradox. We leave items on our desk so we won't forget them. But as the pile of important materials mounts up, the items on the desk get lost or misplaced, and we forget them altogether. Or occasionally a critical note resurfaces as the pile changes shape, reminding us that we need to act on an important matter, and that matter of urgency distracts us from what we were originally doing.

High tech/low efficiency paradox. We try to save time by sending a text message, but because we can use only a limited number of characters, the abbreviated message requires further elaboration, which leads to additional texts, which take longer—and it's all less clear than a simple phone call would have been.

Delegation paradox. We don't bring on new leaders (adults or youth) because we don't have time to train them. But if we spent the time in recruitment, training, and delegation, we would have far more time in the long run.

Virtual communication paradox. Everyday we have more tools and technologies that allow us to communicate, but the maintenance of these tools (checking e-mails, being preoccupied with incoming texts while meeting with someone else, combing through spam, obsessing over a Twitter message, surfing the Web) often distracts us from quality face-to-face interaction. Technologies designed to facilitate communication end up impeding it.

Each of these myths cripples our stewardship of time and leads us to misuse the time we have. But these are blunders made through wrong thinking. Sometimes our worst misuses of time are the simple result of *not* thinking at all. The greatest single mismanagement of our time is rooted in inadequate self-discipline, which manifests itself in a number of ways:

Double-mindedness. We waste time thinking about the next project while we're working on this project, and thereby take twice the time to complete this project.

Distraction. If I were in an addicts' support group, I would have to introduce myself by saying, "My name is Duffy Robbins, and I am a browser." I browse bookstores, hardware stores, library bookshelves, fascinating Web sites, even my own files. And it's all interesting stuff! But my lack of discipline and abundance of curiosity can turn a quick trip to the store into an extended trip to Vanity Fair. I begin by doing a Google search on the words *sloth* and *defecate,* and I end up wandering off into Web articles about how screech owls bring blind snakes to their nests to help kill parasites. It makes me fun at parties, but it squanders needed prep time.

Compulsive behaviors. Sometimes we waste time adding unnecessary touches. How much do you really need to Photoshop that background slide? And what about the flyer for the winter camp: Is it really necessary for the production to merit an art award in the category of "Composition, Art Work, Creativity, Profundity, Social Consciousness, and Hilarity"? It's a flyer, for heaven's sake!

And then, there are the e-compulsions. Do you really need to respond to every post on Facebook? Is it really essential to check your e-mail every five minutes? What would be the cost to the kingdom if you just turned off the Blackberry or iPod for the entire mealtime? And, okay, fine, you're on Twitter—but does the world really need to know about the rash on the back of your left thigh? Beware the compulsion that distracts you from your commission.

Socializing. Youth workers are sociable people. We like to talk and visit, even when we have other work that deserves our attention. I used to work in a ministry in which the normal routine for the morning was an extended coffee break. And there was an unspoken assumption that anyone who passed on the coffee break in favor of doing necessary work was angry or upset about something. None of us intended to be shirking our duties, but the breaks got longer and longer. (We finally had to limit the coffee break to 45 minutes because it was interfering with our lunch hour.)

Poor organization. For decades, there were rumors in the neighborhood about the two reclusive brothers who made their home in the Harlem brownstone on Fifth Avenue in New York City. Homer Collyer and his brother, Langley, obsessively collected newspapers, books, furniture, musical instruments, and many other items, with booby traps set up in corridors and doorways around their house to protect against intruders. When police finally found their dead bodies in March 1947, the corpses were surrounded by over 130 tons of rubbish and filth they had gathered over several decades.[15]

A scenic tour through the canyons of books, gear, resources, and empty Red Bull cans in the average youth worker's office suggests that some of us suffer from *Collyer Syndrome*. One study concluded that the typical American spends an average of one year of his or her life looking for lost objects. For youth workers, it may be more than that. We waste a lot of time trying to find "that study we did two years ago," "the letter we wrote to the deacons last quarter," "the original install disk," or "the small child that wandered in from the nursery." A little better organization could allow us to invest that time more profitably.[16]

Procrastination. This should probably have been mentioned much earlier in the chapter, because it may be the biggest time-waster. The great thing about procrastination is that it isn't as clear-cut as blatant postponement of a task. Procrastination allows us to avoid something by doing *something!* And we can be very creative. We procrastinate by over-researching, over-praying, over-waiting-on-God. Procrastination is an especially attractive option when we don't want to complete the task anyway. How often do we procrastinate and put off a task because we consider it a waste of time when the greater waste of time occurs simply because we don't just plunge in and get the job done?

Indecision. Sometimes, the more we desire to be sensitive to God's leading, the slower we are to follow it. Bill was a younger youth minister friend who was so zealous in his waiting on God that he never did anything. I used to jokingly tell him, "I think God is the one waiting on you." He loved Christ, and he loved the ministry; but he was so fearful of making a wrong decision that he never made any decisions. This tendency cost him several significant ministry opportunities before he learned to start moving. Faithfulness is not waiting until everything is clear and absolutely certain. Faith is acting on what we know and trusting God to help us with what we don't know and might face. It's easier to steer a *moving* vehicle.

The momentum of the culture pushes us to move faster, do more, make it happen, and multitask. The momentum of the gospel spurs us to move with intention, to focus on being as well as doing, to do all we do with excellence as serving the Lord. To use Paul's words, we should be "making the most of every opportunity."

FIRST THINGS FIRST

Practically speaking, that kind of stewardship begins by setting firm priorities. As we've already observed, it's tough to say "no" until we've determined to what or to whom we will say "yes." Our willingness to set firm priorities and to stick with an action plan that gives those priorities expression is one of the toughest tests of leadership. As Alec MacKenzie says,

> One of the measures of a manager is his/her ability to distinguish the important from the urgent, to refuse to be tyrannized by the urgent, to refuse to be managed by the crisis. They must forget the unnecessary and ignore the irrelevant.[17]

The difficulty of sticking with priorities confronted me in my first youth ministry position. At the interview I said I felt called to disciple students—and that this would determine the way I programmed for the youth ministry. Everyone agreed with this policy—until I cut the traditional summer camp the students went to every year in favor of some activities that would better achieve our primary purpose of discipleship. The retreat was a nice idea, but it didn't fit our immediate goals and objectives concerning discipleship. While I wanted to take advantage of some summer-camp ministry, I was not prepared to spend budgeted money on that particular site, with the traditional group of students who took part in that particular retreat.

The three-day blizzard of phone calls and complaints was uncomfortable, to say the least. People were happy for me to have objectives and goals, as long as they didn't interfere with the way they'd always done things. But I came out of the experience with no permanent scars and one valuable lesson: Any time we take a stand for something, we can almost guarantee we will be standing on somebody's foot. If we take priorities and goals seriously, we should be prepared for a few screams and gasps. Our willingness to set priorities grows out of a confidence in who we are called to be and what we believe God has called us to do.

TIME TO MAKE CHANGES AND CHANGES TO MAKE TIME

When priorities are set, then it becomes a matter of walking through a management process that includes these things:

- identifying goals,
- organizing the goals into key areas,
- establishing clear objectives,
- developing a plan of action,
- setting priorities, and
- making a "To Do" list.

Let's use the following case study to find out what this looks like in a youth ministry context.

> Jim and Sally are the loving parents of twenty-two kids—two of them by birth, ages three and five, the other twenty by "adoption," ages twelve to eighteen. Jim and Sally are the volunteer youth leaders at Christ Community Church. Jim is an electrician by trade and runs his own business. Sally is not employed outside the home, but caring for two young children keeps her pretty well occupied.

This is their third year with the youth group, and it has been their most satisfying and productive year yet. The group is growing in breadth and in depth. In fact, that's part of the problem. Some students are asking if Jim and Sally would be willing to have an extra weekly discipleship group in their home. This would be in addition to teaching the weekly Sunday night youth group and Sunday school lesson. Jim's career is demanding, and he doesn't know if he can afford another night with the youth group every week. As the children get older, Sally is more concerned that the family has adequate time together.

They're not at the point of panic—not by a long shot. But they have discussed the busyness that seems to keep them ever on the run, and they're concerned that they're just holding on now with little prospect that it's going to get much better. They are excited about what God is doing with the youth group. They have no desire to end their involvement there. But they're feeling stressed about how to manage it all.

Step One: Identify Goals

Jim and Sally begin to take control of their time by separately writing down some of their goals. They divide them into three categories: Goals for the family, goals for the ministry, and goals for Jim's business. After discussing their individual goals, they agree on some mutual goals. For the sake of example, we will chart their goals in the areas of family and ministry only.

Goals:

Family

Maintain our strong marriage and family life.

Increase our time for family activities involving both children.

Make sure we *both* have adequate time to stay healthy—physically, emotionally, and spiritually.

Youth Ministry

Continue our current level of youth group involvement.

Continue to see the youth group grow numerically and mobilize the students to do outreach at the high school.

Nurture the spiritual growth of those youth who are seeking discipleship.

Step Two: Organize Goals into Key Areas

Their next step is to organize their various goals into key areas so that they can establish objectives—specific actions that are steps toward the goals.

Key Areas:

Family

Time as a family

Exercise

Hobbies

Church/spiritual growth

Fellowship

Youth Ministry

Better youth-ministry training

More adult leadership in the youth program

Added time for discipleship of interested teenagers

Step Three: Establish Clear Objectives

Having developed from their goals some clear statements of need, Jim and Sally are ready to talk about specific objectives. It's critical that the objectives be measurable, achievable within the allotted time period, and compatible with the other goals.

Objectives:

Family

1. Hold at least four evenings a week for time at home as a family.

2. Save two Saturdays a month for family activities.

3. Walk, jog, or swim at least three times a week.

4. Sally will continue to pursue her crafts, Jim his fishing.

5. Attend church consistently, read one good Christian book a month, and attend one retreat just for our growth as Christians.

6. Go out to dinner with adult friends once every two weeks.

Youth Ministry

1. Attend at least two youth-ministry training workshops or seminars.

2. Draw up a job description to use for recruiting some more leaders.

3. Investigate what kinds of curricula are available for discipling students.

4. Set aside one breakfast per week for discipleship group—6:30 to 8:00 on Wednesday mornings.

5. Cancel Sunday night youth group every eighth Sunday night.

6. Recruit another couple to take primary responsibility for youth Sunday school class.

7. Twice a year, hold leadership training for more mature youth group kids (four-week series) culminating with an overnight retreat.

Step Four: Develop an Action Plan

By defining specific objectives, Jim and Sally are saying, "We won't do everything; we won't allow our goals to be crowded out by the urgencies that press in on us everyday. Instead, we'll do only the objectives we listed, because we believe reining ourselves in will help us to meet the family and youth-ministry goals on which we've agreed."

Taking each of the objectives one at a time, Jim and Sally now plot out a strategy that allows them to fulfill their objectives. This action plan involves bite-sized chunks. The bigger the plan, the less likely it is to be carried out.

Action Plan:

Objective:

To attend at least two youth-ministry training workshops or seminars

Who: Jim and Sally will both go

When: Within next six months

How: Sally will investigate by getting info online; Sally will handle registration, etc.

Cost: About $200

Step Five: Set Priorities

After Jim and Sally have worked through their action plan, they go back over the list of objectives and decide which is most important. Since they can't do everything right now, they discuss what would be the *best* investment of their time right now. Going back through the list, Jim and Sally agree their first priority with the youth group is setting up the Wednesday morning discipleship group. They decide to take action on the plans that will open up some time for that. As a family they decide to spend fewer nights out with the youth group. Feeling their next critical need is for additional leadership, they decide to begin pursuing that goal as well.

Step Six: Make a "To Do" List

Based on their chosen priorities, Jim and Sally are now ready to put together a "To Do" list that will help them take action on their plan. Since they have decided to move forward with the Wednesday morning discipleship group, Sally prepares the week's "To Do" list with that objective in mind.

Things to Do:

Go online and find material we can use for discipleship

Prepare hand-out flyer and put notice on Facebook group announcing the new Wednesday morning meeting

Let's observe that this week's "To Do" list doesn't accomplish everything. It doesn't even address all their priorities. But this is, after all, just one week. What it does do is mark some specific baby steps forward that Jim and Sally can take. Too many times we forget that even the longest journey begins with just such small steps. And, in postponing any forward motion until we can take giant steps, we never begin the journey at all.

Remember the proverbial question: "How does one eat an elephant?" Answer: "One bite at a time." Jim and Sally have taken some important steps here: (1) They've divided their priorities into bite-sized chunks. (2) They've decided not to bite off more than they can chew.

THE BEST LAID PLANS...

It was the Prussian military analyst Carl von Clausewitz who wrote: "The great uncertainty of all data in war is a peculiar difficulty, because all action must, to a certain extent, be planned in a mere twilight, which in addition not infrequently—like the effect of a fog or moonshine—gives to things exaggerated dimensions and unnatural appearance."[18] Although Clausewitz was writing about the confusion of armed warfare, he might well have written the same about the hand-to-hand intensity of a youth pastor's weekly schedule. Why does it feel like we work harder and still lose ground? Where does the time go? Is our enemy the clock—or are we really in conflict with ourselves? Even the best laid plans of organization and personal management seem to get torpedoed in the dust and smoke of the average week.

Time management experts suggest one of the best ways to get a good view of our own ministry is by doing a survey of how time is used in a normal weekly schedule. It's a simple (although tedious) process of recording in 15-minute segments exactly how a week is spent. The discipline of writing our activities out helps us discern what could be done, what should be done, what must be done, and what should be left undone. Alec MacKenzie helps us to understand the importance of this kind of personal research and accountability:

> The time inventory, or log, is necessary because the painful task of changing our habits requires far more conviction that we can build from learning about the experience of others. We need the amazing revelation of the great portions of time we are wasting to provide the determination to manage ourselves more effectively in this respect...we think our time wasters are primarily external forces until we see a picture of ourselves...One surprise will be that time is generally wasted in the same way every day and another surprise is the small fraction of the day that is free and uncommitted.[19]

Whether you do a thorough inventory or not, most of us recognize that the biggest battles we fight in personal management are over the little everyday issues of life. As we finish out this chapter, let's look at some of the landmines and booby traps that blow up the weekly schedule.

Mail. Did you know you spend approximately eight months of your life just opening junk mail? That is the estimate of one consulting firm. Forget about spam and e-mails for a minute. We're just talking about the stuff the post office delivers—the deluge of mailings that promise the "latest", "best," and "blessed" resources. One youth minister told me she's reluctant to toss any of it because—who knows?—she could be ditching *the* idea or *the* resource that will help her students find Christ. I know what she means. I used to have this recurring dream that I was standing before the throne of God, and he was asking, "Why did you throw away all those inspiring ideas I sent your way?"

But it's not just junk mail that creates problems. Our tendency is to read mail as soon as it arrives on our desks, even if we are in the middle of other projects. This forces us to read through the mail at least twice—once out of curiosity and once to actually respond. We should try to handle mail items just once. Except for correspondence that can't be answered immediately, a good rule of thumb is to open the mail only when you are able to answer it, and answer it as soon as you open it.

With e-mail, Facebook, IM, and text messages, the problem is even more intense. The very nature of these delivery systems seems to demand an immediate response, which means the first key is to decide you won't let the technology determine your schedule. Set your Facebook settings so you appear offline. Don't feel compelled to answer every message when it arrives. The second key is resisting the thought that you are being bombarded with so many important messages that the Internet will crash unless you check them frequently. Rather than checking your e-mail as soon as you arrive at the office, and then every two minutes throughout the day, work on another project first. Gain some momentum in your day. Then, when you need a break, check e-mail, Facebook, etc.

Meetings. Apparently, Christians like to have meetings. "Wherever two or three are gathered, someone will convene a meeting." A quick skim through the New Testament shows only two real business meetings—one described in Acts 1:12-26 and a second in Acts 15:1-29. Reading these two passages, we might reasonably conclude that Scripture suggests only two situations in which a meeting is called for: When we need to replace an apostle and when we need to discuss circumcision.

Why do we meet so much? Partly from a fear of making our own decisions. Although Scripture says there is wisdom in the counsel of many, often we meet not to make a better decision, but so others will share the blame if we make a poor or unpopular decision.

In his book *Death by Meeting*, Patrick Lencioni suggests two reasons why meetings are tedious and boring:[20]

1. *They lack drama (or conflict)*. People generally find movies more interesting than meetings. Why? Because movies tell a story. They engage us with drama. *Solution:* Lencioni suggests, "Leaders must look for legitimate reasons to provoke and uncover relevant, constructive ideological conflict [in meetings]. By doing so, they'll keep people engaged which leads to more passionate discussions, and ultimately to better decisions."

2. *They lack contextual structure*. If a staff meets every week, the purpose for each meeting may feel unclear. Is it for getting updates and coordinating calendars? That doesn't need to happen in a face-to-face meeting. Is it for long-range planning? That requires more time than is available in a weekly staff gathering. Is it for fellowship? Let's meet at Starbucks! *Solution:* Lencioni suggests that wise leaders plan different types of meetings so participants better understand the expectations. He proposes four types of meetings, depending, of course, on the organization: The Daily Check-In, more like a huddle than

a meeting (about 5 minutes in length); The Weekly Tactical, where tactical issues and progress reports are discussed with what Lencioni calls *disciplined spontaneity* (60-90 minutes); The Monthly Strategic, where the team considers challenges and opportunities (2-4 hours); and The Quarterly Off-Site Review, a comprehensive review of strategy, dreaming, and big-picture issues (1-2 days). Obviously, this is neither a thorough review of Lencioni's plan nor a thorough endorsement. The necessity of all four types of meetings will vary depending on the ministry landscape. But the idea of providing context for a meeting is critical. Otherwise, says Lencioni, "the participants have a hard time figuring out whether they're supposed to be debating, voting, brainstorming, weighing in, or just listening." And that's when people begin to wonder, "Was this meeting just a waste of time?"

Mealtime Appointments. We often use an hour at lunch discussing matters that could have been dealt with in 20 minutes, not because we want to be thorough but because we want to try and enjoy lunch. I'm a big fan of breakfast meetings, and—now that I think about it—of food, in general. But I'm careful not to let a 20-minute appointment take an hour because of a shared meal.

Civic "Duties." Beware the civic dinner circuit, where we're invited to offer an opening prayer and then keep our mouths shut. Early in my ministry, I was flattered by invitations to be guest pray-er at the Rotary Luncheon or the Christian Women's Club. While the gesture was well meant, these activities were so time-consuming that I almost had to change my job title to Minister of Mealtimes. Of course, there will be those occasions for the strategic cameo (such as praying at a school sports event, speaking at the women's tea, or making a presentation at a civic luncheon), but Eugene Peterson's complaint has a lot of merit:

> One of the indignities to which pastors [and occasionally youth ministers] are regularly subjected is to be approached as a group of people are gathering for a meeting or a meal with the request, "Reverend, get things started for us with a little prayer, will ya?" I am not prescribing rudeness: The bellow does not have to be audible. I am insisting that the pastor who in indolence or ignorance is politely compliant with requests from congregation and community for cut-flower prayers forfeits his or her calling. Most of the people we meet inside and outside the church think that prayers are necessary, but harmless, starting pistols that shoot blanks and get things going. It is an outrage and a blasphemy when pastors adjust their practice of prayer to accommodate these inanities."[21]

Commuting/Driving. Most youth workers spend a lot of time driving around. We get to choose whether that time is pain or gain. One youth volunteer told me he never goes on any errand alone. He always takes one of the kids from his group. "I get more youth ministry done that way," he claims, "and it allows me to spend time with students." Or keep some good teaching podcasts in the car to make your time on the road work for you and not against you.

Waiting. We can turn everyday frustration into a pleasant surprise of added time by planning to make waiting work for us. I make it a habit to always have with me some reading material (magazine, book, e-book), no matter how short the trip. And then, if I'm stuck in traffic, waiting in line, or delayed at an appointment, I can whip out *National Review*, *Christianity Today*, or C.S. Lewis and take in an article or chapter I've been wanting to read. Blackberry and iPhone people, God bless 'em, tell me they use "waiting time" as a time to check and answer e-mail. If it's a long wait, I've been known to pull out my iPod and catch a podcast of *This American Life* or listen to a downloaded audio book.

TIMELY TRUTH

The remaining chapters in this book will offer lots of practical guidance in youth ministry behind the scenes. But we need to be clear early on: *There is no management more important than personal management*.

The following extreme paraphrase of a familiar proverb reminds us that effective personal and ministry management is a sacred responsibility:

> I passed by the church of a sluggard, by the youth group of a man without sense; and lo, the kids were facing some thorny issues; their hearts were tied and tangled with all kinds of worldly concerns, and the sense of community in the group had broken down altogether. Then, I saw and considered it; I looked and received instruction. "A little wastefulness, a little disorganization, a little mismanagement, and a little pride, and a youth ministry will be greatly impoverished, robbed of potential as an armed man robs his victims." (Proverbs 24:30-34, NRSV: New Robbins Standard Version)

CHAPTER 5

Visioneering

The simple believe anything, but the
prudent give thought to their steps.
(Proverbs 14:15)

Let's begin with a question of imagination. Imagine you are three to five years into the future, and your ministry is becoming all you have hoped and prayed it would be. It's not perfect, but it's excellent (see chapter 3). Here's the question: *What five to ten descriptive terms (or phrases) might help someone picture your ministry?* Or, to put it another way, what five to ten adjectives would you like people to use to characterize your youth ministry?

Circle your choices from the list below, or feel free to add you own:

Bible-based	edgy	missional	best-paying
creative	contemplative	fun	diverse
socially active	open-minded	awesome worship	charismatic
connected to denomination	provocative	non-traditional	traditional
smoke-free	theologically deep	seeker-sensitive	unpredictable
liberal	for people who don't like church	dynamic	large
small	experiential	looking for a new youth pastor	relational
pastor-pleasing	impressive	tech-savvy	budget-conscious
relaxed	liturgical	postmodern	outreach-oriented
inclusive	family-based	smoke-filled	cool
great food	mostly for "church kids"	mullet-friendly	emergent
cozy	small-group-based	active	student-led

What we're talking about here is a basic question: What do you want your ministry to look like? And when we talk about what a ministry *looks* like, we're talking about *vision*.

BEGINNING WITH THE END IN MIND

Earlier in this book (chapter 3), we talked about how to diagnose a blurry ministry vision. What we didn't address was how to correct a blurry ministry vision.

Suppose I'm just starting out in ministry, or I've been in ministry for awhile but I simply haven't given much thought to the question of vision or ministry philosophy. How do I begin to hammer out my own philosophy of ministry? How do I go about understanding and defining my own ministry vision?

In the early years of my ministry, I didn't take much time for questions of vision. Who has time to think about vision? My long-term goal for the youth group was to pull off the next meeting without embarrassing myself, burning down the church, or humiliating my family. It's hard to dream about what your ministry will look like three years from now when you're laying awake thinking about next Sunday night. Like most rookie youth workers, my ministry philosophy was summarized in the battle cry: "Ready!...Fire!...Aim!"

But over time, I began to ask bigger questions. What was the *real* source of joy and satisfaction in my ministry? Would the short-term goals that occupied me now be big enough to sustain me long-term in youth ministry? What was I *really* accomplishing when I left my wife and children at home on Friday nights so I could spend the evening with somebody else's kids?

Don't get me wrong. I loved the youth in our group. We had some super times, and our group was growing larger. The parents were supportive, and the congregation was impressed. The journey was a blast, the scenery was beautiful, and the company was great. But deep down I knew something: We were making great time, yet had no real sense of where we were going.

In my conversations with youth workers I often hear this same haunting sense of confusion. It's born of our intuitive recognition that forward progress is good only if we're headed in the right direction! And in youth ministry, it's easy to function without direction, perhaps for a very long time, and sometimes with a fair amount of "success." But if we're to be true to our calling, if we value building disciples over building programs, then we have to give some thought to the development of a ministry philosophy. We have to talk about *vision*.

As I mentioned in chapter 3, there are several excellent books that suggest various philosophies of youth ministry.[1] My point in this book is not to suggest what your youth ministry philosophy should be, or even to describe my own philosophy of youth ministry.[2] *My intention in this book is to help you think through the nuts and bolts of forging and articulating your own youth ministry philosophy.* You might think this seems like a needless academic exercise, especially if you're a volunteer, or if your group is relatively small, or if the needs are obvious and urgent. After all, when Jesus is in the house and there are paralytics to heal, what is there to talk about? But, again, it comes down to a simple idea: Are youth workers called to be chaperones or shepherds? If we're called to be shepherds, we better think about where we're leading the sheep!

FOUNDATIONS OF A MINISTRY PHILOSOPHY

In *Education in the Truth*, Christian educator Norman DeJong proposes a ladder of issues (Figure 5-1) that are critical in forging a philosophy of ministry.[3]

Starting at the base of DeJong's ladder and climbing upward, we encounter the following crucial elements:

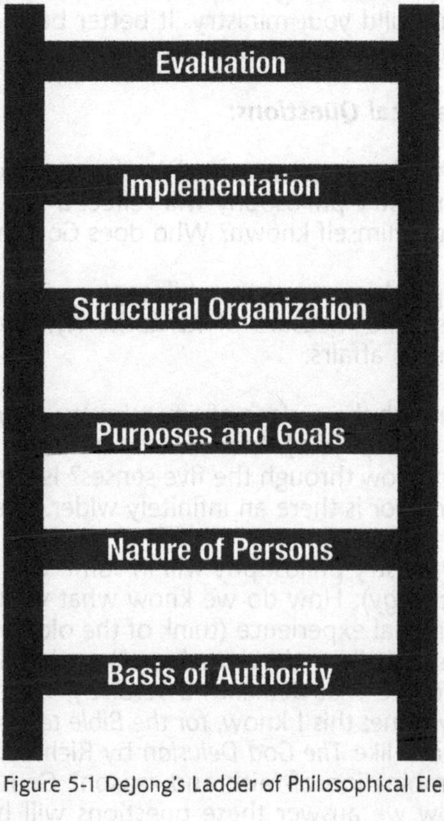

Figure 5-1 DeJong's Ladder of Philosophical Elements

1. ***Basis of Authority.*** What is the source of authority for the ministry philosophy?

2. ***Nature of Persons.*** What does it mean to be human, and how does this understanding of full humanity shape a ministry philosophy?

3. ***Purposes and Goals.*** This is the all-important question of destination. Where should this journey take us?

4. ***Structural Organization.*** Regardless of scenery, popularity, or degree of difficulty, which road is most likely to take us where we need to go? What will we need to successfully complete the journey?

5. ***Implementation.*** This is utilizing the resources God has provided, material and human, to step out in pursuit of the goal.

6. *Evaluation.* This is the pattern of stopping periodically to look again at the map and measure the progress of the ministry against the goals of the ministry.

Let's take a more thorough look at each rung of the ladder.

Rung 1: Basis of Authority

We can't play a game if we haven't decided which rule book defines boundaries, goals, and fouls. And so it is in youth ministry. We have to begin by asking, *What is the basis of authority for our ministry philosophy?* Do we base our ministry philosophy on congregational preferences and traditions, on the felt needs of the teenagers, on the opinions of youth ministry experts, on the gospel according to Oprah? We're talking here about the foundation on which you build your ministry. It better be rock-solid because there will be storms, and it will be tested (Matthew 7:24-27).

Practical Questions:

While it may go unstated (and sometimes, unfortunately, even unconsidered), a ministry philosophy will reflect *a view of God*. Who is God? How does God make himself known? Who does God show himself to be?

Implied in a ministry philosophy will be one's *view of Scripture*—its truthfulness, the measure of its authority, and its relevance to speak to everyday human affairs.

Beneath the surface of any ministry philosophy is also *an understanding of reality (metaphysics)*. Is this world all there is? Is there a reality beyond what we can know through the five senses? Is there only the dimension of time that we know, or is there an infinitely wider, deeper dimension called eternity?

A ministry philosophy will in some way even reflect *a view of knowledge (epistemology)*: How do we know what we think we know? Do we know through personal experience (think of the old hymn lyric, "You ask me how I know He lives; *He lives within my heart*"), rational logic (think of Josh McDowell's book *Evidence That Demands a Verdict*[4]), Bible teaching (think of the classic, "Jesus loves me; this I know, *for the Bible tells me so*"), scientific verification (consider books like *The God Delusion* by Richard Dawkins[5]), or do we know through a combination of faith and reason? Or is there some other means altogether? How we answer these questions will have huge implications for everything from how we try to help teenagers experience God, to how we teach teenagers about God, to how we talk about God and the Christian faith.

Most, if not all, of these questions have probably already been hammered out by your local church or ministry board and are clarified in founding documents. But we all know these documents and statements can grow stale. It might be worth a review, a read-through with the pastor, or a short-term series of once-a-month dinner conversations about "what we believe." Small fissures in these basic foundations can lead to major fractures on the staff, on the team, or in the ministry.

Rung 2: Nature of Persons

Teenagers are pulled in lots of directions by people who want them to be responsible, tolerant, great-looking, athletic, "well-rounded" people who get straight As and "make their parents proud." But how much of that picture is framed by the culture and how much is framed by the Word of God? And if our intent is to make God and his Word the source of authority, what kind of people are we trying to build? What does it mean to be fully human, and how does this understanding of full humanity shape a ministry philosophy?

Practical Questions:

Among the questions implicit in our understanding of personhood will be questions about *how people learn*—questions that shape the way we communicate biblical truth to our students:

How do teenagers mature and develop into persons who are mature and whole—and, what does whole personhood look like in the life of an adolescent?

Do we have different goals and expectations for early, middle, and late adolescents?

What is the role of family in building healthy, whole persons, and is that vital role reflected in the way we do youth ministry?

Rung 3: Purposes and Goals

Jesus clearly calls us to think about end-goals. (See Luke 14:28-29.) Before we begin to build, we need to ask, "Why does this ministry exist?" and "Where should this journey take us?" This is the language of goals and purposes.

For example, most of us have heard someone describe a youth group as "really, really active." And, very likely, when we heard it, we took it to be a good thing. But is it really? Nowhere in Scripture are we called to be *active*; we're called to be *productive*. When Jesus gave his disciples their final words of instruction (John 13-17), he gave them a very clear statement of purpose: "You did not choose me, but I chose you and appointed you so that you might go and bear fruit—fruit that will last" (John 15:16). It was a reminder of a principle he had often stated: "Each tree is recognized by its own fruit" (Luke 6:44).

Jesus didn't say a tree would be known by how large it is (*"Look at all the kids coming to youth group!"*), or by the variety of its fruit (*"Look at all the different programs we have!"*), or by whether folks admire the gardener who planted the tree (*"Look how cool our youth pastor is!"*), or by whether the landscaping was new and edgy (*"Look how innovative and cutting edge our ministry is!"*), or by how neat and clean the tree was (*"Look how clean we've kept the carpet in the youth room!"*). Jesus said it all comes down to the end-product—the quality of the fruit.

In the face of busy schedules, eager teenagers, and expectant parents, we can easily fall into "program planning mode," feeling pressure to "do something" to get the youth group "active." Too many sincere youth workers, paid and volunteer, burn out of youth ministry because their working assumption is "Something must be done! This is something; therefore, it must be done!" We throw activities and ideas at the wall, hoping something will stick, without ever asking what we're trying to do. Developing a program without defining a purpose is like planning a surgery without diagnosing the disease.

Practical Questions:

Begin with *rationale:* Why should the church have a youth ministry? Some say the very idea of youth ministry is unbiblical.[6] Is that true? Why is youth ministry important, and how does it fit into the overall mission of the church?

Which values (community, creativity, contemplation, fun, digestion of biblical truth, etc.) will shape our processes and structures?

Do we have a clear sense of where we want this ministry to go?

What three to five short sentences would best articulate our *goals*? What is it we're trying to accomplish? Why do we say "yes" to some ideas and "no" to others? Or why do we have such a hard time saying "no" to *any* new idea?

In *Purpose-Driven Youth Ministry,* Doug Fields explains this all-important step: "Once you communicate God's purpose for your ministry, you won't have to ask the *why* question again. The new question will be *how*: How do we accomplish what God has called us to do? The *why* must be answered before the *how* can make sense to others."[7]

Rung 4: Structural Organization

Let's say some friends value very much the time they have together, and they want to nurture their relationships with one another, and together grow in their relationships with God. (These are *purpose and goal* statements). But, how to do that best? Do they take a road trip? Do they move in together? Or, do they meet for breakfast once at week at Denny's for a Grand Slam Friendship Jam? These are what might be described as structural questions. How do we create a structure that will help us to get from where we are to where we want to go?

Guiding the process here for a youth ministry is this basic question: How can our articulated values (creative, edgy, fun, etc.) be massaged into the flesh and tissue of our ongoing ministry programs and practices?

Practical Questions:

What sort of meetings (weekly, monthly, coed, single-gender, parent-involvement) might we incorporate into our ministry environment to prepare the soil to grow the kind of Christians we want to grow?

What kinds of realities will we need to consider in terms of the socioeconomic context in which we're doing ministry?

It is at this point that a philosophy of youth ministry will manifest some understanding of leadership and leadership roles. What is the relationship between a youth leader and her volunteer staff, any potential student leaders, or even her other colleagues on staff who might not be directly involved in the youth ministry? What style of leadership best reflects this understanding?

What facilities are available to us, and how can we make the best use of those facilities?

Rung 5: Implementation

This is exactly what it sounds like. We actually make use of the resources we have to do what we believe God has called us to do. This is where we add sweat and effort to vision and prayer. Really, at this point, it's not so much a matter of practical questions; it's more a matter of putting into practice the answers to questions we've already answered. It's time to create a ministry plan and begin following that plan. This includes all of the specific elements of the program (Sunday night meeting, drop-in center, tutoring ministry, worship time, online presence, backpacking trip, etc.), as well as systems of planning, resourcing, staffing, publicizing, and evaluating.

Rung 6: Evaluation

The author of Proverbs writes, "The wisdom of the prudent is to give thought to their ways, but the folly of fools is deception." It's at this point that we stop and ask ourselves: Is what we have done what we intended to do? If not, why not? What can we do better?

Practical Questions:

We'll give specific attention to the practical questions of evaluation in chapter 12.

BOTTOM LINE: BIG DREAMS ARE SHAPED BY BIG QUESTIONS

DeJong's ladder reminds us that every ministry activity (whether it be a Sunday night program, a Tuesday afternoon small group, a game of Whackyball, a skit, a Bible study, an online chat room, a retreat, or a leadership recruitment effort) is a reflection of a youth ministry *program*. And every programming model is rooted in a ministry *purpose* (or lack of purpose). And every ministry purpose (knowingly or not) reflects a basic understanding of *what it means to be called human* and *what it means to be called the people of God*. And every notion of what it means to be fully human is anchored in some understanding of *ultimate truth* (or authority). That means every *what, how, who, why,* and *when* of a local youth ministry is born of a ministry philosophy.

This ministry philosophy may be clearly defined or it may simply be a set of unstated assumptions that tints all facets of the ministry. But every youth ministry reflects a philosophy that speaks to the six key issues DeJong raises—whether anyone is aware of it or not.

Someone might say, "Why go to all the effort to hammer out a philosophy of ministry when we already know our mission is to help kids get to know Jesus?" Because whether you describe your ministry as *traditional, biblical, cutting-edge, multiethnic, emergent, student-led, extreme, new, contemplative, Sonlife, Young Life, WyldLife, family-based, Jesus-focused, seeker-sensitive, purpose-driven, Youth Specialties-centered, Group-oriented, or Harry Potter-inclusive*—attention or inattention to these six issues will likely mean the difference between a foundation that sustains effective youth ministry and a foundation that crumbles.

And there are ample collapses to prove this point.

What's more, we *don't* "all know our mission is to help kids grow in Jesus." And, even if we agree that "our mission is to help kids grow in Jesus," there can be a lot of confusion and disagreement about what that means. And, when we try to build a ministry on that confusion, it's the Babel story all over again: Miscommunication and conflict, and the building stops.

In *Leadership's* study of pastors "forced out" of their positions, "pastors indicated that conflicting visions for the church was their greatest source of tension and the top reason they were terminated or forced to resign."[8] Based on countless conversations with youth workers over the years, I'm convinced the same is true of youth pastors.

If this still seems overly complicated, it might be helpful if we shuck it all down to five basic questions at the heart of any realistic youth ministry philosophy. If you begin by answering these basic questions prayerfully and thoughtfully, you will have established at least some fundamental foundations on which to build your ministry.[9]

1. ***Focus:*** Who is being served by this ministry? What is the ultimate purpose?

2. ***Attitude:*** How does one view those being targeted and served? What are their needs?

3. ***Motivation:*** What is one hoping to accomplish with these people? What is the dream or vision that motivates the work?

4. ***Values:*** What values will be cultivated in the process of pursuing this vision?

5. ***Authority:*** On what basis have you answered these questions? Is it based on denominational guidelines? What the kids want? What the parents want? What the Bible teaches? The prayer of Jabez? Why have you answered these questions the way you have?

Digging through some of these basic questions and thinking about them carefully in light of both biblical teaching and what we know about adolescent development is the first step of excavation. It prepares the ground for developing a philosophy of ministry on which you can build a strong program.

DEVELOPING A PHILOSOPHY OF MINISTRY

Let's assume you've done the initial spadework. You've given some careful consideration to the relevant questions. Now you're ready to build your own philosophy of ministry. The task of forging that ministry philosophy can be encompassed in a four-phase process, what Aubrey Malphurs describes using *"foundational ministry concepts"*[10] (Figure 5-2):

- ***PHASE ONE: Mission.*** The WHY? question; Why does the ministry exist?

- ***PHASE TWO: Core Values.*** The HOW? question; How will the ministry conduct its mission?

- ***PHASE THREE: Vision.*** The WHAT IF? question; a mental picture of what this organization or ministry should look like;

- ***PHASE FOUR: Strategy.*** The WHAT NOW? question; How can we accomplish this mission?

Carefully and prayerfully thinking through these four concepts is essential to developing a personal or corporate philosophy of youth ministry.

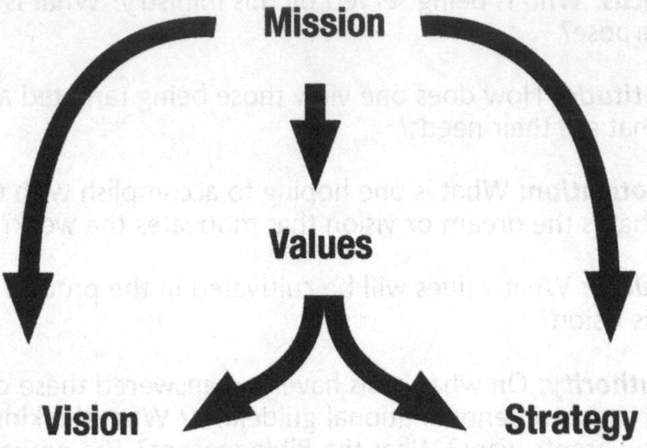

Figure 5-2 Four phases of developing a ministry philosophy: "Foundational ministry concepts"(Malphurs)

Phase One: MISSION. Getting a Fix on the Ministry Purpose

A mission statement is a statement of a ministry's purpose that is broad enough to encompass all that ministry defines as its mission, but brief enough to state in a sentence why this ministry exists.[11]

Typically, a mission statement combines a verb and one or more infinitives in a statement that is compelling, concise, meaningful, and action-oriented.[12] For those who are grammar impaired, here is a list of sample infinitives:[13]

to assist	to create	to craft	to convert
to prepare	to train	to raise up	to incite
to proclaim	to reach	to develop	to empower
to energize	to challenge	to equip	to connect
to establish	to help	to lead	to produce
to promote	to provide	to share	to nurture

To get an idea of what a mission statement might look like, consider these examples:[14]

- **Crossroads Church**: Our youth ministry mission is to win lost teenagers and enable them to become growing and fruitful followers of Christ.

- "The purpose of **Wooddale Church** is to honor God by making more disciples for Jesus Christ.
- **The Salvation Army**: Our mission is to make citizens out of the rejected.
- **Saddleback Church Youth Ministry:** Our youth ministry exists to REACH non-believing students, to CONNECT them with other Christians, to help them GROW in their faith, and to challenge the growing to DISCOVER their ministry and HONOR God with their life.
- **Eastern University:** Eastern University exists to equip students to engage and live the whole gospel for the whole world in diverse vocations and locations.
- **Chick-fil-a:** Our corporate purpose is to glorify God by being a faithful steward to all that is entrusted to us [and] to have a positive influence on all who come in contact with Chick-fil-a. (And they make a darn good chicken sandwich!)
- **The U.S. Marine Corps:** Our mission is to attack the enemy and defeat him.[15]

It may be that your church or parent organization already has a mission statement, and your ministry's mission statement will simply be an adoption or rewording of that statement. If you are starting the process from scratch, here are some suggestions:

1. *Pray about who should be involved in the process.* The group might include youth ministry staff (volunteer and/or paid), parents, youth, and church elders. Don't make the group so big that it impedes focus and discussion, but, neither should it be so small that the process yields a statement that cannot be embraced by those in the ministry.

2. *Remember to do the foundational work first.* Don't begin the process by just inviting input from the group. The more careful the excavation (using DeJong's ladder and the five fundamental questions articulated in the previous section), the more certain the foundation.

3. *Resist the temptation to stand for everything.* Yes, there are many good ways your ministry might serve the kingdom, but be concise. There may even be some political pressures here. Experience has proven the simple truth that an organization that stands for everything stands for nothing.

4. *Don't try to begin with a statement.* Begin with the infinitives. You might offer the group a sample list as we've done here, or invite them to brainstorm some suggestions.

5. *If you're working with a larger group, it might be wise to do some of the initial discussion in smaller groups that report back to the larger group.* The more input people have in the process, the more likely they are to embrace the finished product.

6. *Aim for consensus.* This mission statement is too important to settle for the support of a simple majority. While it may not be possible, make it your intention to aim for consensus.

7. *Don't rush the process.* The mission statement is the heartbeat that feeds pulse and life to the ministry philosophy. It's worth taking the time to get it right.

Phase Two: CORE VALUES. Guidelines for the Venture

Core values are an organization's (or person's) "foundational set of convictions on which it premises all of its actions and policies."[16]

The second phase of developing a sound ministry philosophy is the clarification of Core Values, the priorities that undergird every facet and every enterprise of the ministry. Malphurs has pointed out that Acts 2:42-47 suggests that the first-century church in Jerusalem was shaped by at least six core values:[17]

Core Values of the Jerusalem Church, Jerusalem, Israel

1. Apostolic teaching (Acts 2:42-43).
2. Fellowship (Acts 2:42).
3. Prayer (Acts 2:42).
4. Community (Acts 2:44-46).
5. Worship (Acts 2:47).
6. Acts of mercy and proclamation (Acts 2:43, 45).

Core values impact goal-setting, team-building, program execution, resource allocation (people and money), decision-making, and more. One of the best ways to define core values is simply by thinking through a response to this question: "What five to fifteen adjectives would you like to see people use in characterizing your ministry?"[18] Most ministries will have several core values, but often there is one overriding value that adds a particular texture to the whole ministry portrait. For example, in the statement of Core Values for the student ministry at Saddleback Church (Orange County, CA) there is a clear emphasis on relationships:

Relational approach

Encouragement

Laughter

Acceptance

Transparency

Involvement of students

Outreach orientation

Numerical growth

Spiritual growth

Home-like feeling

Intimacy

Professionalism

Strategic follow-up[19]

The defining of core values can be done in a group setting, applying many of the same suggestions offered above for the mission statement. Again, don't rush this process. These core values will have a fundamental impact on your youth ministry environment. The table that follows on the next pages illustrates how a ministry's focus on a particular core value (or "unifying value") can flavor every other aspect of that ministry (Figure 5-3).[20]

Type of Youth Ministry	***Unifying Value***	***Role of Youth Pastor***	***Role of Youth***	***Key Emphasis***
The KING JAMES Youth Group	Knowledge	Teacher	Student	To Know
The OUTREACH Youth Group	Evangelism	Evangelist	Recruiter	To Save
The BOOT CAMP Youth Group	Missions	Prophet	Agents of change	To Serve
The EXPE-RIENTIAL Youth Group	Experience	Facilitator	Participants	To Feel
The FAMILY REUNION Youth Group	Loyalty	"Parent"	"Siblings"	To Belong
The LIFE DEVELOP-MENT Youth Group	Character	Trainer	Learner	To Be
The SPRING BREAK Youth Group	Strong Program	Ringmaster	Consumer	To Be Active

Figure 5-3 Youth Ministry Values Impact Youth Group Programming

Type of Youth Ministry	***Typical Tool***	***Desired Result***	***Source of Legitimacy***	***Positive Trait***
The KING JAMES Youth Group	Bible study	Informed Christians	Emphasis on Truth	Knowl-edge of Bible
The OUTREACH Youth Group	Mid-week outreach meeting	New believers	Results	Heart for lost
The BOOT CAMP Youth Group	Work project	Students with social conscience	Cause	Compas-sion for oppressed
The EXPE-RIENTIAL Youth Group	Worship, candles, music	Feelings	Spirit	Vitality
The FAMILY REUNION Youth Group	Sharing groups	Secure Christians	Roots	Identity
The LIFE DEVELOP-MENT Youth Group	Accountabil-ity groups	Disciple	Changed lives	Growth
The SPRING BREAK Youth Group	Games	Partici-pants	Increased attendance	Enticing

Figure 5-3 Youth Ministry Values Impact Youth Group Programming

Phase Three: VISION. Imagining the End of the Journey

A vision statement is a word picture of what the ministry or organization will look like as the mission is achieved. It should be a statement that is clear enough and provides enough of a sense of urgency that others will hear it, understand it, and be enticed to embrace the same dream.

The third phase of the process of developing a youth ministry philosophy involves defining a clear vision. Is this just a rehashing of purpose or mission? It shouldn't be. Mission and vision are two ways of thinking about the same purpose. *One is a statement, the other is more of a snapshot.* One is rooted in the head, the other is rooted in the heart. One is informational, the other is inspirational. Malphurs draws sharp distinctions between the two (Figure 5-4).[21]

	MISSION	***VISION***
Definition:	Statement	Snapshot
Application:	Planning	Communication
Length:	Short	Long
Purpose:	Informs	Inspires
Activity:	Doing	Seeing
Source:	Head	Heart
Order:	First	Second
Focus:	Broad	Narrow
Effect:	Clarifies	Challenges
Development:	Deductive (Taught)	Inductive (Caught)

(Figure 5-4) Mission and Vision: How do they differ?

When I'm asked what major principle I would convey to someone just starting out in youth ministry, I find myself consistently coming back to the vision question: Do you have a dream for what God has called you to do with students? To be sure, we need to be clear on *mission*. But, to remain passionate, we need to be vivid in our *vision*. This is absolutely essential for someone who wants to stay fresh and enthusiastic about youth ministry over the long haul. Most of the time, what we hear described as "burnout"—when people run out of steam—is more likely "blur-out"—when people are without a clear vision in ministry and simply don't have anything to get "steamed up" about!

In putting together a vision statement, the principle task through prayer and brainstorming is to consider, *What will this mission look like when it is fleshed out in this ministry?* Here are some questions to guide your thinking:

- *Is our vision clear enough to be grasped and owned by people both within and outside the ministry?* Will this help others in the congregation embrace the dream of this youth ministry? Will this help potential supporters understand and buy into the vision of this youth ministry?

- *Does it offer a clear challenge?* Have we embraced a vision that is big enough to inspire, or have we shrunk our dreams to fit what would probably happen anyway?

- *Does it offer a picture?* Peer evangelism is a concept; teenagers sharing their faith with friends is a picture. Christian community is a concept; youth meeting in covenant groups on a weekly basis, committed to sharing faith and life—that's a picture. Servanthood is a concept; young people willing to give a week of their summer vacations to serve God in a work project is a picture. Outreach is a concept; unchurched kids who feel welcomed and embraced by the church is a picture. People are much more willing to sacrifice for a dream than a concept.

- *Is it future-oriented?* Does the vision describe where the ministry is, or where the ministry is going? Position informs; direction inspires.

- *Is this vision feasible?* Will our students buy into this vision? Will the parents? The church board?

- *Is there firm commitment to this vision?* If a vision is big enough to inspire, it won't be reached without effort. Is there a clear resolve to make this vision a reality? Followers are galvanized by a leader committed to going somewhere.

Phase Four: STRATEGY. Getting From Here to There

Strategy is the plan for accomplishment. It is process-oriented: How will we get from where we are to where we believe God is calling us to be?

Finally, after establishing clear notions about what the ministry should look like and where the ministry should go, it is time to put brush to canvas, and shovel to dirt. This is the place where we begin to think in terms of ministry models and strategies. It is here that we move to hands-on ministry planning:

- Programming components: Will our ministry environment include small groups, Sunday night meetings, mid-week gatherings, a breakfast club?
- Resource allocations: Do we spend the money on a missions trip, a half-pipe for skateboarders, a winter outreach, or a fall leadership weekend? Do we upgrade the website or invest in A/V upgrades for the youth room? How do we best use the leaders we have?
- Ministry activities: How do we schedule an average month of programming? Will we do outreach every week, once a month, or only during certain "seasons" of our youth ministry year?
- Program structure: Will middle school and high school students meet together? How will we coordinate the various components of the program so that there is coherency? (We don't want to plan a huge Sunday school outreach on the same weekend as the Discipleship Retreat.)

A WORD OF WARNING

Given the pressures of juggling ministry, family, and work, there will always be a very real temptation to shortcut this process of developing a clear philosophy of ministry. That would be a mistake. There is a related temptation to take a new route simply because it *is* new—and this, too, is a wrong-headed notion. Handy shortcuts to the wrong destination are a waste of time and resources.

A "handsome, strong-faced" man who was "quick and intelligent of speech," Lansford Hastings was an opportunist and political adventurer who in the mid-1840s endeared himself to immigrants along the Oregon Trail by offering them a shortcut through the Rocky Mountains. "There is a nigher route," he promised, "and it is no use to take so much of a roundabout course."[22]

The promise of what became known as the Hastings Cutoff captured the attention of George Donner and his party of 20 wagons and 73 people. Donner's group welcomed the opportunity to shave as much as a month off what would already be a grueling journey.

Unfortunately, the promise was empty. What was advertised as a cutoff ended up being a dangerously difficult trail that led through salt deserts and rugged mountain passes. Three months into their journey, exhausted and near starvation, the party stopped to rest only three miles from the summit of the Sierra Nevadas on November 1, 1846. It was a deadly delay. The snow that fell that night and the days thereafter made progress even more difficult. By the time the Donner Party realized they were caught in winter's trap, their temporary camp was surrounded by nine feet of snow. It was the beginning of a nightmare that involved horrific hardship, cannibalism, and unimaginable grief as one after another of the party died.

I apologize if this sounds overly dramatic. I don't really think cannibalism is a threat to your ministry. But the story of the Donner Party offers a metaphor for those of us pursuing the adventure of youth ministry. The easiest route is not necessarily the best route, and going the right direction on the wrong map can have serious consequences. Take the time to think prayerfully about your own philosophy of ministry.

Don't trade away productivity for activity. You were never called to build programs; you were called to build disciples.

SECTION THREE

CONSTRUCTION

CHAPTER 6

Making Decisions without Making Enemies

Trust in the Lord with all your heart and lean not on your own understanding; in all your ways submit to him, and he will make your paths straight.
(Proverbs 3:5-6)

Peter and Erin had been working with the youth ministry at Third Church for almost five years. Because of their seniority, they were widely recognized within the congregation and among the group of eight volunteer leaders as the couple in charge of the youth ministry. When plans went well, the credit eventually trickled back to them. When there were problems, the blame usually found them as well. Despite their status as volunteers, they were clearly in charge.

In a December meeting, the youth ministry team discussed plans for the upcoming summer. The youth group traditionally had a full summer program, and Peter and Erin liked to stake down some of the important dates in December. The progress, however, slowed when the agenda pointed the group to something called *IZ2C* (Eyes to See), a one-week combination mission trip-Vacation Bible School-arts fair done annually as part of a youth ministry outreach they'd developed called *Thou Art...*

Thou Art... was an innovative notion that had evolved over the years into a unique and creative ministry of visual art, dance, drama, and music. The core of the ministry was a simple idea birthed by Katie Barton, the mother of two youth group kids. She had said, "God is a creative God, so let's design a program that helps our youth celebrate and magnify God through creativity." It began as a sacred dance team that occasionally performed in worship services. But over the years it had morphed into a drama team, a musical worship team, and a growing new group of teenagers who were interested in visual art (painting, murals, collages, graffiti, and digital photography). Under Katie's leadership, *Thou Art...* was reaching out to a whole different group of kids from their other efforts, providing a place where those young people could exercise their gifts in unique ways.

Thou Art... wasn't for everybody, but it had become a valuable part of the church's ministry to teenagers. And the centerpiece of the program was this annual week-long trip called *IZ2C*. The hosting church, typically in a low-income urban area, served as a ministry base. During the course of the week, *Thou Art...* students would enjoy their downtime by taking in two or three area art institutions (museums, theater, etc.), and use those visits as a basis for their discussions about faith, art, and life. It was a pretty cool context for building relationships with students in a way that allowed them to exercise their gifts in ministry. For the students in *Thou Art...*, the *IZ2C* tour was a highlight of the year—no question about it. That trip was the dangling carrot that energized the group and gave them something to prep for and dream about throughout the year.

The questions at the meeting surrounded the timing of the tour. In past years the schedule of *IZ2C* had sometimes conflicted with the schedule of the youth program, but Peter, Erin, and Katie had always worked something out. But this year there appeared to be the seeds of a major standoff. Katie insisted that the *IZ2C* tour needed to happen during June. Too many churches shut down or drastically cut back their programs in July and August, making it almost impossible for Katie to line up a good host church. Congregations seemed to want to dial back their programming in the late summer months, and that diminished what Katie and her team could offer.

Peter explained to the rest of the youth ministry team that this was the precise reason he'd always appreciated *IZ2C* being scheduled during the month of July. It never interfered with the traditional dates of youth camp during the third week of June. "It's hard to catch many students in town during July," he told them, "and during the month of August, the students who *are* in town are tied up with band camp, cheerleader camp, or football camp." Peter couldn't see changing the dates of the youth camp schedule so that *IZ2C* could be shifted to June, especially since *Thou Art...* didn't involve the whole youth group.

Ron and Terry sided with Peter. They'd already made family vacation plans based on the normal June camp week, and it would be very difficult to change them now.

Dave and Maggie were fairly open either way, although their 15-year-old, Sadie, was a member of the *Thou Art...* team, and should there be a conflict of dates, it would land them in a dilemma.

Linda, a young woman who had been working with the group for about a year, was open to both positions, but she'd already proposed a more traditional student work project this year rather than the normal camp week. She felt they needed to inspire the students to authentic servanthood, and that meant giving kids "a chance to get their hands dirty."

Here were eight sincere people, all committed to ministry with teenagers, and all willing to give up some of their summer vacation time to the youth program. There were no hard feelings—not yet. These people were good friends and they cared about one another. But a decision had to be made, and relatively soon. How could these folks on the ministry team make these decisions without making enemies?

AN OCCUPATIONAL HAZARD OF LEADERSHIP

Making decisions is the loneliest, the most exciting, and the most critical part of leadership—all at the same time. When we begin talking about decision-making, we can start with these premises:

- ***Every effective leader will eventually make some hard choices.***
- ***Genuinely hard choices will inevitably disappoint somebody.*** While we're always looking for "win-win" solutions, it's impossible to give both parties their way if the preference of one party negates the preference of the other party.
- ***No one is always right.*** Therefore we must be humble in our decision making, and make use of the counsel of others whenever possible—not for protection against blame, but for guidance.
- ***Anyone in a position that involves making a lot of decisions will eventually make some that are less-than-great.*** That is the price we pay for being human. The appropriate response to that reality is to ask forgiveness of God, any offended constituency, and ourselves, and then learn from our errors (never waste a mistake) and move on. The good news is that God is a redeemer; he makes the crooked way straight.

Just because we're working in ministry with others who share a common vision and a love for Christ is no guarantee we'll agree on every issue. In fact, that is the splendor of the church of Christ—we can have remarkable diversity and still cling to a basic unity in Jesus. Our call as a church is not uniformity, but unity. Organizing everybody to walk in lockstep may be more efficient, but it's not at all *Ephesiant.* As the apostle Paul put it:

> Be completely humble and gentle; be patient, bearing with one another in love. Make every effort to keep the unity of the Spirit through the bond of peace. There is one body and one Spirit, just as you were called to one hope when you were called; one Lord, one faith, one baptism; one God and Father of all, who is over all and through all and in all. (Ephesians 4:2-6)

THE PROFILE OF PROBLEM-SOLVING: TWO KEY FEATURES

Because every issue looks different, every decision looks different. But there are two key features in the profile of every good decision.

FEATURE 1: Effective problem-solving requires a balance of creativity and discernment.

In youth ministry we face dilemmas that require decisive action. Some are as simple as what theme to use for the next game night or which movie to show at the lock-in. Others are more complex: How will we lay out the summer youth program schedule? How will we deal with the discipline problems of the two tenth-grade girls? How will we allot the youth budget? Will we allow Steve to stay on the youth-ministry team if he and Sherry get a divorce? Bobby is vocal about the fact that he's gay, and some of the parents are concerned about their kids being in the same cabin with him at camp. Will there be any accommodations made to alleviate the fears of these parents?

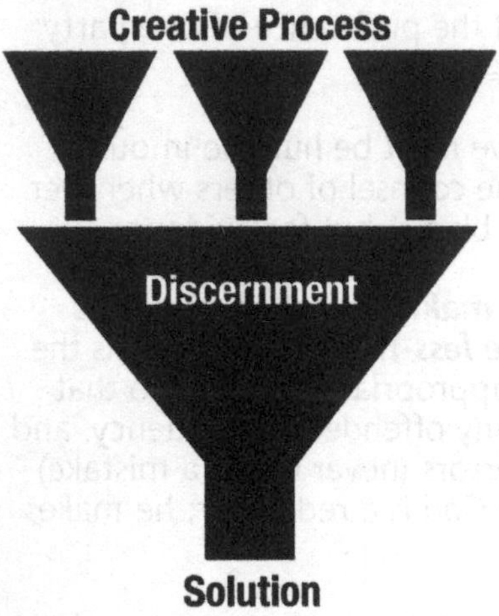

Figure 6-1

Whether simple or complex, every decision has two stages: creativity (getting input about what *might* be done) and judgment (deciding what *should* be done). Both elements are critical. Creativity is like a gold rush miner directing the streams of runoff from several sources into one spillway. Judgment is when the miner uses a pan to sift through the ore to find the real gold. The more streams he draws from, the more likely he is to find his treasure (Figure 6-1). On the other hand, if he keeps everything that runs down the spillway, he'll end up with tons of mush.

While every decision-making process needs both creativity and judgment, the balance between the two differs depending on the decision. Let's consider three scenarios:

Scenario 1: Go for the Gusto?

The degrees of creativity and judgment required depend on the decisions that need to be made. If we need to get a log from Point A to Point B, it doesn't really matter much how we do it. We might even allow two small children to try to carry it. They may try several different ways of moving the log, but since the risk of failure is not so severe, we let them try virtually whatever they will. We're not sure if they can pull it off, but there's little harm in letting them give it a shot.

Likewise, in youth ministry, if the decision we're making is not so serious, we may decide to put more weight on the creativity side of the equation (Figure 6-2). The stakes for failure are no big deal, so we allow ourselves the freedom of extra innovation. If we're planning a lock-in, for example, we don't have a heavy agenda for the evening. As long as we maintain a wholesome Christian environment where we can be with students, we're not that uptight about the programming. This is, after all, a lock-in; it's not confirmation class.

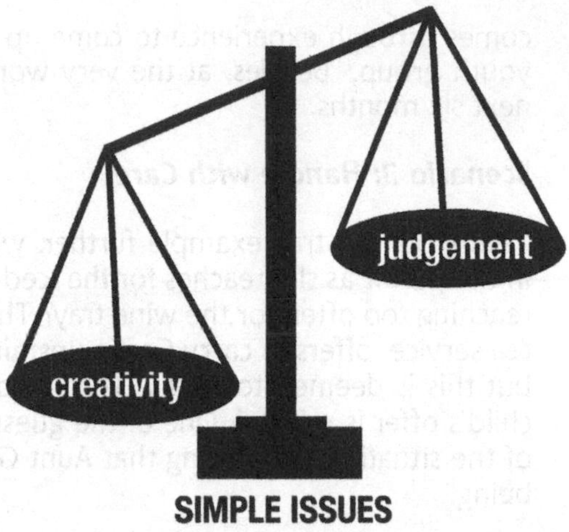

Figure 6-2

So we may allow some teens from our group to plan the entire event. Maybe we give them a few guidelines, and then say, "It's your call. All decisions are up to you." We're willing to allow for more creativity in a situation like this, even if a little mush gets mixed in with the runoff. As long as the youth stay within the prescribed guidelines, the consequences of poor decisions will not be that costly.

Scenario 2: Creativity and Judgment

But what if our decision is about how to carry a tray full of iced tea glasses across the room to the guests in the den? This operation is a bit more delicate than dragging logs around. We may be more cautious this time (Figure 6-3). There is less room for experimentation here, and the consequences of a wrong approach will be more messy. Suppose there's a spill. The stain on the carpet won't be the end of the world, but it will be small consolation to the hosts to say that they may see the face of Jesus if they stare at the stain long enough.

Using judgment, we decide to allow one of the children to carry the tray if he will accept help from one of the adult guests. The child still gets practice carrying the tray (innovation or creativity), but in judgment we've added the steadiness of an older hand.

A lot of the short-term programming decisions in youth ministry require a similar blend of creativity and judgment: What topics will we study in Bible study? What activities will we plan for the next six months? We need to allow the teenagers in our group to bear the weight of responsibility. That's the way they learn. The youth add creativity and freshness to our more mature steadiness. And while they may make choices on the basis of personal likes and dislikes, we exercise judgment that

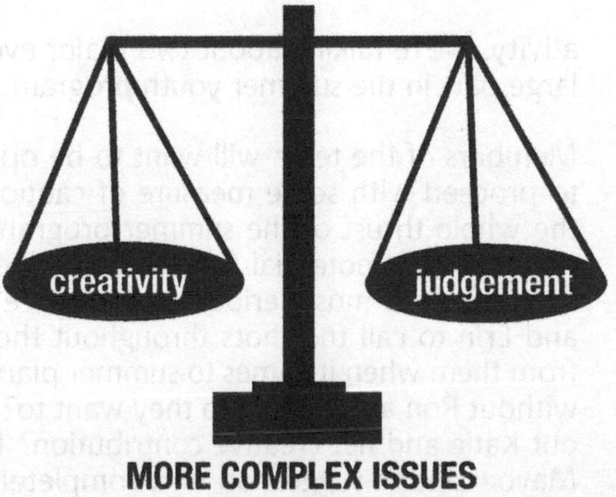

Figure 6-3

comes through experience to come up with a plan that is best for the whole youth group.[1] Besides, at the very worst, their decisions will affect only the next six months.

Scenario 3: Handle with Care

Taking our tea-tray example further, what happens if Aunt Gertie passes out in the parlor as she reaches for the iced-tea tray—perhaps because she's been reaching too often for the wine tray? The child, fresh from his victory with the tea service, offers to carry Gertie upstairs with the help of his adult teammate, but this is deemed too risky. This is no time for creativity and learning. The child's offer is refused. One of the guests, a doctor, steps in and takes control of the situation, suggesting that Aunt Gertie not be moved at all for the time being.

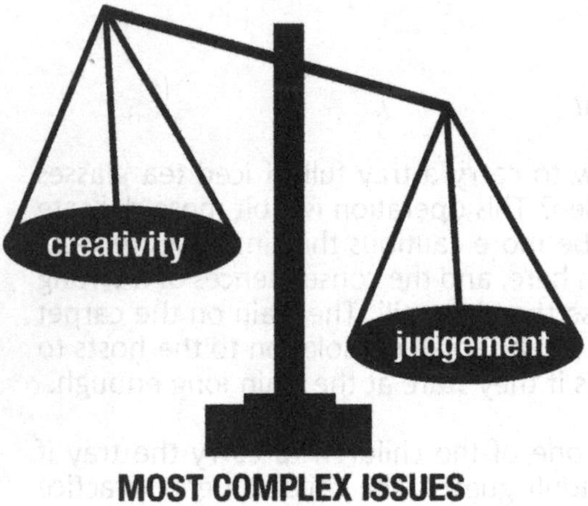

Figure 6-4

At times in our youth ministries, lives are at stake, and wrong decisions will have serious consequences. Will the group proceed with the planned ski trip even though the highway patrol says the weather is unsafe for driving? Will we allow John to continue working with the youth group even though he admits to being arrested for molestation? In these cases the equation will be weighted far more on the side of judgment (Figure 6-4).

The question of the summer youth program calendar and when to schedule the *IZ2C* trip is probably a scenario in which judgment will weigh a bit more heavily than creativity. We're talking about two major events that have traditionally played a large part in the summer youth program.

Members of the team will want to be open to new ideas, but they will want to proceed with some measure of caution. Their decision will directly affect the whole thrust of the summer program, and—perhaps even more importantly—it has potential for disrupting the unity of the leadership team. That would be the most serious consequence of all. Is it fair to encourage Peter and Erin to call the shots throughout the year and then yank that authority from them when it comes to summer planning? Can they pull off a July retreat without Ron and Terry? Do they want to? What about a summer retreat without Katie and her creative contribution? No one would look forward to that. Maybe Linda's suggestion of a completely different kind of summer event is worth considering.

Surely there are issues more serious than laying out a youth program's summer plans. There's room for some creativity here. On the other hand, any issue that involves this many valued volunteers is more than just a calendar question. In that sense, the group will want to move forward carefully. Good decision-making requires discerning the appropriate blend of creativity and judgment for a particular decision.

FEATURE 2: Effective problem-solving requires a willingness to consider different types of solutions.

In the kind of situation presented to us by our case study, obviously, the hope would be to find some kind of win-win solution. But suppose that's not possible? Is the only alternative a win-lose decision? Even for the "winning" side, that could ultimately prove to be a losing proposition. These people need one another, they work well as a team, and they value very much the unique contribution each individual makes to the youth program. No one wants anybody to walk away from this meeting feeling like they "lost." But are there other options?

Consultant Robert Moskowitz suggests that there are four basic types of solutions to any kind of problem, and that understanding these four types of solutions can help expand our problem-solving and decision-making equipment.[2] Let's explore briefly each approach:

Type A Solution

Let's say I have a cold—complete with postnasal drip, itchy-watery eyes, sneezing, runny nose, and sore throat. So I take Sudafed. That takes care of the postnasal drip, the itchy-watery eyes, sneezing, and runny nose. But, alas, it does not take care of the sore throat, *and* it makes me drowsy and hoarse. It's not a very satisfactory way of dealing with my distress. But it does deal, at least temporarily, with some of my symptoms.

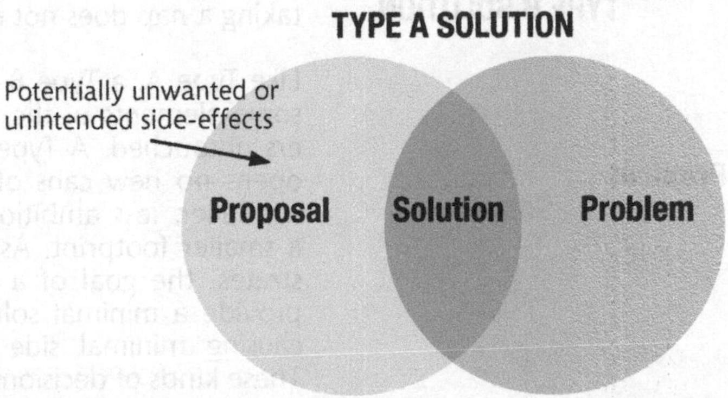

Figure 6-5

The most common approach to decision-making is the Type A solution. As the diagram (Figure 6-5) indicates, a Type A solution solves some aspects of the problem. That's good. But, as the diagram also makes clear, it leaves other aspects of the problem untouched. That's not so good—and, specifically, it's probably not good enough for a decision like this one. It would leave too many people dissatisfied. Plus, as the diagram indicates, it may result in unintended and unwanted side effects.

In the end, the youth leaders at Third Church may have to settle for this kind of decision, but that's not what they're hoping for.

Suppose, for instance, that the group were to embrace Linda's suggestion, taking the entirely new approach of a week-long work project. It would offer some appeasement to Katie as well as to Peter and Erin. Because a smaller group of students is likely to be interested in such a trip, Katie would not feel as if the *IZ2C* tour is threatened by massive camp participation. At the same time, this would still allow Peter and Erin to offer the group a major June event. Linda's suggestion would also take care of Ron and Terry's scheduling problems. So it would resolve some of the problems.

On the other hand, it would resolve *only* some of the problems. It would still preclude the *Thou Art...* kids from being involved in the work project. And it would disappoint all the students who love summer camp but are not interested in doing a work project. After all, the June summer camp is a tradition in this church! This decision might arouse the ire of a whole new core of people who believe they are facing the prospect of a summer with neither an *IZ2C* tour nor the traditional camp week.

Type B Solution

Let's go back to my cold, postnasal drip, itchy-watery eyes, sneezing, runny nose, and sore throat. A Type B solution would be to buy Kleenex and get some sleep. That resolves very few of my symptoms, but it doesn't make me hoarse, and happily, I discover that, unlike Sudafed, taking a nap does not make me sleepy.

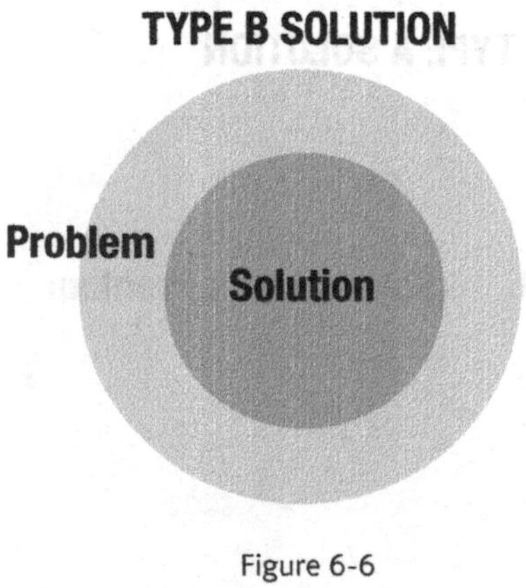

Figure 6-6

Like Type A, a Type B solution resolves only some elements of the problem, leaving others untouched. A Type B solution, however, opens no new cans of worms. It's typically a smaller, less ambitious plan, but it leaves a smaller footprint. As the diagram demonstrates, the goal of a Type B solution is to provide a minimal solution in the hopes of causing minimal side effects (Figure 6-6). These kinds of decisions tend to be more reasoned and less bold.

A Type B solution to our case study is to run both the *IZ2C* tour and the summer camp simultaneously. Katie would have her way with the tour schedule, and Peter and Erin could schedule the retreat for the usual June dates. This would help Ron and Terry, who have been holding these dates in anticipation of the normal summer schedule.

But this solution would *not* resolve Dave and Maggie's dilemma. Ashley will still have to decide which event she is going to participate in, and that will put them on the spot. What if their daughter doesn't go to the summer camp? Should they go as leaders anyway? And—probably the biggest concern—what about all the other students who have traditionally been involved in both the *IZ2C* tour *and* summer camp? They still have one or the other, but they no longer have both. This solution brings added problems for them. And it doesn't address Linda's suggestion of the mission project.

Type C Solution

Still suffering the effects of a bad head cold, I resort to a Type C solution. After my nap, I take Tavist-D in the place of Sudafed. That seems to make me less drowsy and less hoarse. To deal with my sore throat, I begin chain-chewing Hall's Menthol Drops—which offers some relief without making me drowsy and hoarse (but it does give me awful "medicine breath").

A Type C solution is really two or more Type A solutions brought together and applied simultaneously (Figure 6-7). The good part of a Type C solution is that it may solve all or most aspects of the problem. It's a bold plan. The bad part is that it usually brings unwanted side effects. Think: Using a bazooka to kill a housefly...and firing it twice.

Meanwhile, back at Third Church, Dave and Maggie suggest that perhaps all three events could be offered. The *IZ2C* tour could be scheduled for the earlier part of June, during which time the youth group would also sponsor a weeklong work camp. And then, youth camp would be during the

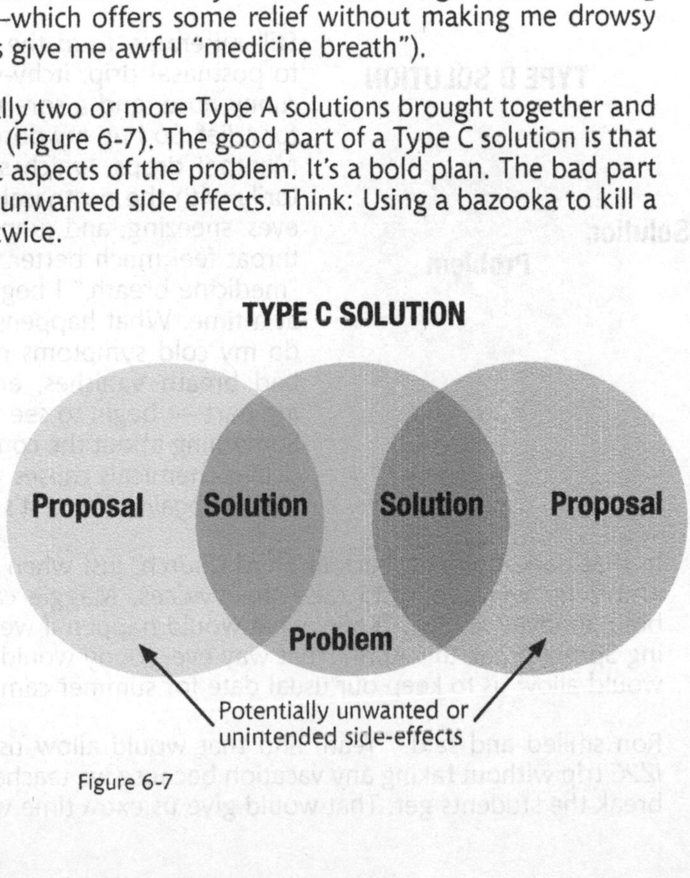

Figure 6-7

traditional week in late June. That would please everybody—at least partially.

Peter's response was almost immediate. "Yeah, but what about the extra money for three trips? We just don't have it in the budget. And what are we going to do about leadership for three events? I can't take any more time away from work. I'm already giving up one week of vacation for camp. Does that mean I have to take another week off for the work camp? And if Erin and I aren't there, Katie's with the *Thou Art...* kids, are you guys willing to put the work camp together without us?"

The room was quiet. Tension was beginning to build. People began to look uncomfortably at the floor when, all of a sudden, they all shouted at the same time, "What we need is a Type D solution!"

Type D Solution

A Type-D solution is a total solution that deals with all aspects of the problem, and may even provide some added benefits and side effects no one thought about (Figure 6-8).

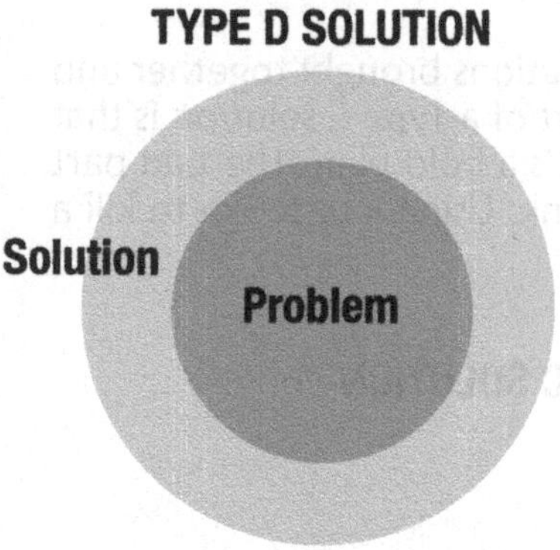

Figure 6-8

Still miserable from the bad cold that has led to postnasal drip, itchy-watery eyes, sneezing, runny nose, and a sore throat, I am desperate for relief. So I up my dose of Tavist-D and Hall's Menthol drops, which seems to deal satisfactorily with the postnasal drip, the itchy-watery eyes, sneezing, and runny nose, and makes my throat feel much better. And, to deal with the "medicine breath," I begin popping ten Altoids at a time. What happens is amazing: Not only do my cold symptoms remain at bay, but my bad breath vanishes, and—this is the amazing part—I begin to see my hair growing back! Something about the combination of these particular chemicals causes what scientists refer to as *The Rogaine Effect*! It's a miracle!

In that dark moment, back at Third Church, just when it appeared that Katie and Peter were going to raise their voices, Maggie came up with a pretty bold, innovative idea. "Katie, what would happen if we did the *IZ2C* tour during Spring break this April? That way everybody would still be around, and it would allow us to keep our usual date for summer camp."

Ron smiled and said, "Yeah, and that would allow us to chaperone on the *IZ2C* trip without taking any vacation because we teachers get the same Easter break the students get. That would give us extra time with the group!"

Peter, looking around at the others said, "I like it. That would allow Erin and me to take some time off from the youth group during Easter week. We've always wanted to do that but felt we had to be here to do something with the kids."

And Linda, ever buoyant, said, "Yeah, and that would open up some time later in the summer if we wanted to try some sort of mission project!"

And a mighty wind filled the room and tongues of fire appeared above their heads as they began to speak in other tongues...

Beyond Cold Symptoms and Concentric Circles

In Never Never Land, every problem has a Type D solution. Too bad more of us don't serve the First Church of Never Never Land. Unfortunately, defining different kinds of solutions is much easier than finding them. Typically, ministry teams get bogged down in the decision-making process because those involved have preconceived notions of what a solution looks like. We spend all our time and energy looking for an elusive Type D solution when we might be able to break the decision gridlock by understanding that solutions don't always look the same way. When a planning meeting seems hopelessly snagged on some issue, we may be able to craft a compromise proposal simply by playing out how the issues might look if we sought a solution other than the "perfect" one. Effective problem-solving requires a willingness to consider different types of solutions even if they may not be the perfect solution.

DECIDING HOW TO DECIDE

In the case history of Third Church, the leadership team escaped into decision-making nirvana through a process of consensus. While this is an effective and satisfying way to reach a group decision, it is not always the best way. Nor will it always work. Difficult decisions may require us to choose among several good ideas, or settle for the best of a few unattractive options. We're looking for a solution that gives us the maximum amount of benefit with the minimum amount of negative side effects. Type D solutions are not always available to us in youth ministry. If they were, we would all be well liked by everyone, we'd never face criticism or have to make tough choices, and there really would be such a thing as *The Rogaine Effect*.

In his article "Four Ways to Make Group Decisions," Em Griffin outlines five criteria for evaluating the methods we use to make group decisions:[3]

- *Time.* Will the process allow us to reach a decision in a reasonable amount of time?

- *Commitment.* Will the decision-making process encourage our team to own and support the decision?
    - *Learning.* Can we learn through the process of making this decision?
    - *Attractiveness.* Does the process build the morale of our group?
    - *Quality.* Will this process yield the best possible decision?

Obviously, somewhere in the alchemy of this process we're searching for the will of God. So when we speak about the *best possible decision,* we're not talking necessarily about the decision most profitable, most relevant, most edgy, or most popular. As believers, our assumption is that the best possible decision is faithfulness. So we're seeking discernment—what is the most faithful decision in this context?

For most of us, that discernment doesn't come through burning bushes or hand-written messages on the youth room wall. So we need a practical process for working that out with a team of people. We want to make the best possible decision in the timeliest fashion with the least amount of animosity in a way that is likeliest to maintain strong group unity and team spirit.

CHOOSING BETWEEN GOOD IDEAS

Consider the following case study adapted from a situation that occurred with a youth ministry in the Northeast. First Church received an anonymous gift of $1,000. The donor stipulated that the money be used *in direct ministry with the teenagers*, and that it be used *within six months*, not sit in some account for several years. No problem, right?

Wrong. When the chairperson of the youth committee made her announcement, all seven strong-minded leaders offered different ideas about how the money could be used to the glory of God. Sarah, the chairperson, spoke first, recommending the purchase of *youth ministry resources*: A set of drama books, an amazing book about speaking to teenagers, several discussion-starter DVDs, a DVD seminar that would help the team deal with kids in crisis, and few hundred dollars' worth of various source materials. "There's a lot of stuff out there that will help this ministry for years to come, but we just haven't had the money to put into resources until now."

That prompted Jim to speak: "Do we want to invest money in books or in people? Why don't we use it to *send one of our students to the mission field this summer* with Youth With A Mission? We can pay for almost all the expenses with a gift that size."

Guy spoke next. "We saw God use that weekend backpacking trip last summer to change kids. With $1000 we could *upgrade the youth group's gear supply*."

Stan wanted to use the money to provide *scholarships* for some students who would not be able to afford the summer camp.

Bill felt strongly that the *church bus needed overhauling*. (He was usually the one driving it.)

Cindy thought new *presentation software* would give a face-lift to the teaching and worship graphics. No one could deny that her expertise in computer technology had helped the youth group on several fronts (and fonts!).

Pat, whose teenaged son was in the youth group, listened to all the ideas before she suggested, "I think we ought to *let the kids decide* what to do with the money. After all, it was given to the youth group, not the leadership committee."

Murmurs and mumbles circulated around the room. Seven different suggestions had been made, and at least one leader favored each of them. This was not going to be an easy decision. How should they proceed?

DECISION-MAKING STRATEGIES

We want to make decisions without making enemies (if possible) and, hopefully, without making bad decisions. God has provided the group of caring adults at First Church an opportunity—not just to allocate funds, but to learn, to share, to seek God together, and to experience God in their midst. How might they best resolve the question of how this generous gift will be allocated? Em Griffin suggests that, essentially, there are four strategies they could use for coming to a group decision.[4] They could vote; they could appoint an expert; they could use the Delphi method; or they could seek consensus.

Let's consider each strategy:

Voting

Sarah could lead the entire group to discuss the various options as presented by their advocates and then take a vote on the matter. It would be relatively quick, and it's certainly an approach with which everyone is familiar. Because there are so many options on the table, she might find it worthwhile to canvass the group with two ballots, the first ballot sifting out the three favorite options of the group, and the second ballot voting among those three for the final project to be chosen. Since Sarah's deadline is six months away, she may encourage a more informed decision by allowing people a week or two to research the options before coming back to the group for a vote. But voting works best if the chairperson sets a time limit for discussion, and then calls for the question. We've all been in meetings where the discussion was allowed to go on and on interminably to where the only unanimous vote was to adjourn the meeting and let everybody out of the room!

It almost seems un-American to challenge voting as the best way for a committee to make its decisions, but the question is worth considering. "One person, one vote" sounds good in principle, but there is a downside. Let's see how voting stacks up against each of the five criteria.

Quality. Using Griffin's criteria of evaluation, the first consideration is quality. Will the voting process help the youth committee make the best possible decision? Maybe yes. Maybe no. To begin with, we're all aware that the majority is not always right. One lesson of the Holocaust is that the majority may have the might, but that doesn't render them right. If the U.S. Supreme Court, using democratic principles, renders a judgment that runs counter to biblical teaching, does that make it right? According to majority rule, it does. But the verdict of Scripture is that it does not.

On the other hand, if we suppose the youth ministry team includes nine Spirit-led Christians sincerely seeking the will of God, we might reasonably assume the decision chosen by the majority will give us our best chance of discerning the mind of God. One individual might be fooled into a wrong decision, but as Scripture reminds us, there is a greater wisdom in the counsel of many (Proverbs 24:6).

Plus, our chances of a high-quality decision are increased by the amount of discussion involved in this method. Each person will be attempting to hype his or her idea. That will assure that each suggestion gets ample exposure before the group. And, just as the process underlines the strengths of good ideas, ideas that are not as strong will have the weaknesses exposed. This should improve the quality of the decision as well.

Time. One attractive part of putting the question to a vote is that the process doesn't have to take that long. Voting can be a relatively quick way for a committee to reach a decision. Unfortunately, the quicker the process, the lower the chances of a high-quality decision. For that reason, Sarah prefers to let everyone have his or her say on all the issues before any final vote. But, again, she has to be deliberate about this process.

Commitment. One of the downsides of the voting process is the risk of winding up with a decision that 49 percent of the people on the team don't like. The whole committee is going to have to live with this decision. If people feel they've been steamrolled into a decision with which they're uncomfortable, they aren't going to support it. There are some issues where full support isn't as important. And, of course, the best decision isn't always the one that makes everybody happy. Skilled leaders understand that a "best" decision that causes mutiny may not be as good as a "second-best" decision that keeps the crew in line and on the boat. Sarah can't afford to have Cindy hurt and angry and feeling her gifts and opinions aren't valued. Bill is going to have to drive those kids to the summer camp. Camp scholarship money won't be worth much if Bill refuses to drive the group on a bus he feels is in disrepair. The group's commitment to the final decision is going to depend on how clearly and fairly everyone feels their input was received.

Learning. Whether the group learns anything in the voting process will depend on how the process is handled. If it's just a matter of getting seven options on the table, and then, as quickly as possible, getting six of those options off the table, that probably won't be very enlightening. But a robust period of discussion and honest well-moderated debate could yield a process that allows people to learn about issues and about one another. Most folks will find that valuable, and it facilitates the kind of "iron sharpening iron" (Proverbs 27:17) process Scripture points us to in the community of faith.

Attractiveness to the Group. One of the biggest problems with voting is that it breeds winners and losers. As our national political process demonstrates, the debate leading up to the vote can be pretty rough and tumble. What good is it to have a really good decision made by a group of people who are no longer talking to each other? Voting can be a good way for people to win battles and lose wars. We can alleviate some of the divisiveness of a vote by allowing more than one round of balloting. That way, as the choices are narrowed down, it's possible that my opponent in the first ballot can become my ally by the final ballot.

Appointing an Expert

Sarah suggested that maybe the group should seek to get some advice from someone with professional youth ministry experience. After all, this was a lot of money, and none of them professed to have any real expertise in youth ministry. Chap Fields, the youth pastor at Fullerback Community Church, had given them some good counsel on a few other occasions. Maybe this was another time when it would be wise to call on his experience for help.

Quality. Depends on the expert, doesn't it? There's the old joke that expert comes from two words: *ex*, meaning *has-been*, and *spurt*, meaning *drip under pressure*. We've already noted the dangers of taking shortcuts based on the word of supposed experts. (See Lansford Hastings, chapter 5.) On the other hand, for a group of people traveling unfamiliar ground, a wise guide is a most welcome gift indeed. The moral to the story here is simple: If a consultant is to be chosen, choose carefully—consider the consultant's track record and don't too quickly allow your questions, opinions, and experiences to be drowned out. You may or may not be a youth ministry expert (whatever that means!), but you are likely more of an expert about your group and its needs than someone from the outside.

Time. One immediate benefit of bringing in an expert is that it could save a lot of time. It doesn't take any genius to compute that nine people meeting twice for three hours each adds up to 54 hours of time invested in the decision. An expert like Chap Fields could do some pretty thorough investigation of the situation and give the committee a recommendation in less than a fourth of that time.

Commitment to Solution. Will the group be committed to Chap's suggestion? Maybe—or maybe not. Even if the entire committee trusts Chap's expertise, some individuals may feel he cannot fully appreciate their viewpoints. Someone may well raise the question Stan raised, "What does Chap Fields know about our youth program that we don't know? Plus, I've heard that he thinks mission trips are a waste of money for students under the age of 17. I don't know if we can trust this guy." Bill doesn't believe anyone but him fully appreciates the risk of driving the bus in its current condition. For him, it's not a question of expertise, but of necessity.

Learning. Another knock on appointing an expert is that the group isn't likely to benefit from the learning that comes through debate. The expert comes, sees, and decides. He hands down the oracle, the group stamps it, and then the one who best understands the decision (the expert) leaves. Not much learning in that process.

Attractiveness to Group. In terms of *esprit de corps*, appointing an expert may be a good move. This process, at least, eliminates the divisive debate that comes along with the voting. Once the group has decided to rely on the expert, the burden of judgment is on someone else's shoulders. This takes some of the emotional charge out of the decision.

The Delphi Technique

The strength of the first two approaches is also the weakness of the first two approaches: Each of them lacks precision. Both of these approaches take seven different ideas and virtually wipe six of them off the table with a single swoop—either through a vote or an expert's verdict. These two approaches lack the finesse of allowing committee members to say, "I like this idea best of all (because it's mine), but if I were to choose other options I could get excited about, it would be these."

This Delphi approach to decision-making is essentially what happens when the judges average their scores for an Olympic figure skater. Using our case study of the $1,000 designated gift, it would work like this: The chairperson instructs committee members to vote on each of the seven ideas suggested, *ranking their preferences for each idea beginning with one for highest preference and seven for their lowest preference.*

Consider the chart that follows:

Ideas	Sarah	Jim	Guy	Stan	Bill	Cindy	Pat
Purchase resources (Sarah)	1	7	4	3	4	4	4
Missions scholarship (Jim)	3	1	3	2	6	7	6
Backpacking gear (Guy)	4	3	1	4	7	3	2
Retreat scholarship (Stan)	5	2	2	1	3	5	3
Overhaul church bus (Bill)	2	4	5	5	1	2	5
Computer upgrades (Cindy)	6	6	6	6	5	1	7
Let the kids vote (Pat)	7	5	7	7	2	6	1

Then, Sarah takes this information and gives the voting totals to the youth committee without identifying who voted for what.

Ideas	TOTAL	Ranking
Purchase resources (Sarah)	27	4
Missions scholarship (Jim)	28	5

Backpacking gear (Guy)	24	2/3
Retreat scholarship (Stan)	21	1
Overhaul church bus (Bill)	24	2/3
Computer upgrades (Cindy)	37	7
Let the kids vote (Pat)	35	6

It was obvious after the first ballot that the committee was not eager to turn the decision over to the kids in the youth group. Equally obvious is that computer upgrades Cindy desires are going to have to wait—the committee wasn't convinced the technology was worth the cost.

Having cut the list down to five choices, the group then moves through the ranking process again. On the second ballot, a clear preference might emerge. If not, the committee can eliminate one or two more preferences and then vote again by ranking the remaining three. After moving through the cycle three times, it should be possible for the group to come up with a final decision based on the preference with the lowest total. That preference with the lowest total represents the idea that people either preferred or were most willing to embrace.

Quality. The Delphi method brings with it the same quality assurances voting does. But it has the added advantage of giving everyone a chance to vote their opinions in a more precise way. Instead of having each person vote only his or her "favorite idea," the Delphi method gives everyone a chance to assess the value of *all the ideas* on the table with one ballot. Granted, when the numbers are tabulated, there may the need for a second ballot to choose between the top two favorite options. But, this approach allows the benefit of considering several ideas, which hopefully will improve the quality of the final proposed course of action.

Time. The Delphi method quickly narrows down a long list of options without wasting a lot of time on unpopular ideas. That's a plus. On the other hand, to really narrow down a long list of options may mean the committee must cast more than one ballot. And the nature of the Delphi ballots means it will take a little longer to tabulate a final result than a straight up or down majority vote.

Commitment. Here's the real weakness of the Delphi approach. It is quite possible that the group could end up making a decision that no one is totally excited about. In other words, the group could wind up making a decision that was everybody's number two choice, and no one's number one choice. For example, according to our chart, the number-one option in our case study is *using the money to underwrite retreat scholarships*. But go back and look at the chart of voting results. That was the first choice of only one person (Stan). It was the fifth choice of two people, and the third choice of two people. In other words, at least half the people ranked this choice no higher than their third preference. But, because the aggregate scores for that choice were the lowest, the committee chose an option most of them weren't very excited about. That's not the kind of outcome that evokes group ownership of the final decision.

Learning. Again, this really depends on how the process is handled. If discussion is given to each of the ideas, then the group can learn from the process. On the other hand, if the Delphi approach is used intentionally to get several less popular ideas off of the table quickly, then obviously, not much is learned about the ideas that were quickly dismissed.

Attractiveness. Typically, the decision reached through this method is one nobody really hates. That's good. Unfortunately, it may also be a decision nobody really loves either (except, in this case, Stan!). It will be hard to really build group morale on the foundation of this kind of decision.

Consensus

The last method the youth committee could use to reach a decision about allocating the special gift is to seek consensus—a process that involves discussing the matter until all the parties can come to some agreement on what should be done. Consensus is probably the decision-making process that most closely approximates the way we are told to function as Christ's body. But it is also the toughest way of all to decide an issue. As the parody of the old hymn reminds us, "To dwell above with saints we love, O that will be glory. But to dwell below with saints we know; that's another story!"

The group must keep in mind that the ultimate question they are addressing is not "Which way is easiest?" or "What will make Bill happy?" but "What does God want?" In a meeting of Christians, presumably when we work through difficult decisions, we are seeking to know the mind of God.

To reach consensus, we must keep in mind at least these five guidelines:

1. Announce the intention right from the start. Let everyone know we do not plan to move ahead on a matter until we are in relative agreement on how to proceed. Tell the committee, "This is too important to move ahead with only a simple majority."

2. *Be prepared to take time to process.* Consensus does not cater to someone looking for a quick decision or someone impatient with process. This approach takes a lot of time.

3. *Encourage open expressions.* People have to feel free to disagree or the consensus will yield a false representation of what the committee agrees upon.

4. *The chair must not mistake silence for agreement.* The chair must make sure all voices are heard, staying on the lookout for the person who sits in quiet discontent until five minutes after the meeting is over and then complains that no one cared what she thought.

5. *Consensus is not the same as 100 percent agreement.* It is an agreement among group members that they have arrived at the best solution possible, given the many opinions involved.

While consensus is difficult to reach, it generally produces a decision that ranks very high in four of the five criteria we've considered. Consensus results in a *high-quality* decision that tends to be *attractive* to the entire group. After hammering out this consensus, the group will be *committed* to follow through, and the give and take of open discussion will encourage *learning*. The only drawback to consensus is the large expenditure of *time*. Consensus doesn't allow microwave decisions. It is a marinate, roast, and simmer approach.

Why Four Methods?

Different youth ministry situations call for different decision-making methods. Choosing a teaching curriculum, for example, requires a method that engenders commitment. People need to be excited about what they're going to be teaching. That probably means a rejection of the Delphi approach. It wouldn't do to choose a curriculum just because most people don't hate it. For that same reason, voting is only moderately helpful for a decision like curriculum choice. You don't really want your team teaching a topic that only 51 percent feel is important. Neither is this probably the best time to play "Ask the Expert." It's probably more important that our teachers feel good about what they are teaching than that the curriculum meets the approval of an expert who won't be there in the classroom trenches. So, in the case of this specific decision, we may work for consensus.

On the other hand, if we have several ideas on the table for the fall calendar, none of the ideas is really awful, and no one is strongly attached to any one idea, we can quickly narrow our list of options and make choices using the Delphi method. Speed is more important than a precise group decision that everyone feels good about. Good decision-making utilizes different types of strategies for different types of decisions.

BEWARE OF *GROUPTHINK*

We close this chapter with a word of warning: Beware of *groupthink*. Irving Janis coined this term to describe what happens when well-meaning people hide their true feelings from the group in order to maintain the appearance of group unity and cohesiveness.[5]

As Janis points out, the classic example of *groupthink* was the Bay of Pigs invasion of Cuba ordered by President John F. Kennedy in April 1961. The plan was that a small band of Cuban exiles would secretly land on a beachhead in the Bay of Pigs. From there they would launch an offensive with the aim of overthrowing the government of Fidel Castro. To be sure, Castro's Communist regime was marked by a brutal dictatorship that imprisoned dissenters and impoverished the population of Cuba. But the plan, ill-conceived and executed without conviction, was nothing less than a total rout. Within three days, the ragtag band of would-be conquerors had been overcome, and their secret mission directly traced to an embarrassed U.S. government. Later Kennedy said, "It was the perfect failure. How could I have been so stupid as to let them go ahead?"

In the postmortem discussions of the incident, virtually everyone, including Kennedy himself, agreed that the decision to launch the initiative came out of a White House leadership team marked by several factors that made *groupthink* probable:

- The group had a highly directive and charismatic leader (Kennedy).
- Group members shared (and highly valued) a strong sense of *esprit de corps* (a sense of *group-ness*) that encouraged them to make decisions as a group they would not have made as individuals.
- There was social pressure on all group members to conform to the wishes of the leader.
- The group had a strong inherent belief in its own morality and had an equally strong inherent belief that its opposition (Fidel Castro) was inept, wrong, and weak.

We can see quite easily how this same pattern of *groupthink* could easily happen in the church setting, particularly in the context of a youth ministry team where we value group unity and share a strong sense of mission. It's true, our bad decisions in youth ministry seldom lead to international incidents, but we make some costly mistakes because of *groupthink*.

I made one of my most memorable mistakes in youth ministry at my first full-time position. Young and eager for direction, I highly valued the few strong supporters I had on the youth committee. The unity of that group was so important to me that it clouded my judgment on a key decision involving one high school girl named Mary.

Having only been in this position for a few months, I was approached by some of my strongest and most trusted adult leaders. They recommended that Mary not be allowed to go on an upcoming out-of-the-country trip. They explained that, because I was new, I had no way of knowing about Mary's moral reputation and her penchant for extracurricular activities on retreats. They had seen the group grow much since my arrival, and they felt Mary's participation in the mission project might hurt our newfound momentum.

It all made perfect sense—at the time. We talked about it, agreed on it, and I called Mary. What seemed like a good group decision turned out to be a fiasco. Mary cried on the phone for about 30 minutes until her dad took over. His portion of the phone call alternated between extreme anger and occasional crying. By the time Mary's mom was on the phone, crying and screaming, I was beginning to wish I were floating somewhere in the Bay of Pigs.

Mary's parents phoned around to share their story with their close friends at the church, and my Bay of Pigs became a can of worms. By the next day, everything broke loose, and I was thinking maybe there'd been a change in God's will for my life. Perhaps I was being called to work in another church, maybe one just off the coast of Cuba.

As I look back on that decision, I can excuse it, in part, because of my youth and inexperience. But in retrospect, I can also see that it was a decision we came to as a group that none of us probably would have made individually. It was a bad decision born of textbook *groupthink*.

We are especially susceptible to *groupthink* in the Christian community because we tend to think of conflict as negative. Sometimes, however, conflict can be greatly used by God. We must not allow our strong desire for unity in Christ to override our willingness to wrestle through a tough decision. *Groupthink* is partially born of the notion that love is always "nice"—and we've been taught that, if we can't say something nice, we shouldn't say anything. While the Scripture never teaches that kind of "sloppy agape," many have been misled to believe voicing an opposing view in a meeting or planning session is a sign of a divisive spirit.

All this is muddled even further by the mistaken but popular notion that genuine trust in God relieves us from having to exercise our own critical judgment. If we are being led by the Spirit, the thinking goes, we can trust that all of our decisions initiate from God's guidance. But the heart is deceitful. John the Elder consistently encouraged the leadership in his churches to "test the spirits" to see if they were of God (1 John 4:1-6).

PREVENTING *GROUPTHINK*

Recognizing some of the causes of *groupthink* is one of the best ways to prevent it. But there are concrete steps we can take to ensure that team decisions are sound and not just the result of *groupthink:*

1. Assign to one person in the group the role of critical evaluator. One pastor told me that, in an attempt to keep himself and his staff honest in meetings, each meeting he appoints a different staff member to play the role of the devil's advocate. This person is responsible for asking the hard questions and questioning the easy assumptions. It's an important ministry role for any functioning group.

2. Periodically divide the decision-making group into subgroups that meet separately under different moderators and then come back together to share input. This exercise reduces the chances that group pressure will overly influence the decision-making process. In the smaller group setting, and under the leadership of a different chair, group members feel a bit more at ease about speaking what they believe.

3. On a regular basis invite outsiders to your meetings. Some youth workers invite parents to sit in on planning meetings so they can give the ministry team a reality check. Others invite the pastor, a member of the church, or even some of the kids. Outsiders don't have the same bias toward group unity. This gives them the freedom to voice opposition when it needs to be spoken.

4. Require group leaders to withhold opinions and preferences until the group has a chance to hear from others. This diminishes the chances that the group will be overly influenced by the opinions of leaders.

CHOOSE YOU THIS DAY

This has been a lengthy chapter, in part, because decision-making is so central to effective leadership. As youth leaders, we face numerous choices—some pleasant, some not so pleasant; some easy, some not so easy. The mark of effective leadership is not always making right decisions; it is making thoughtful, faithful decisions.

An effective leader uses all possible resources to come to the best possible decision and arrives at that decision in a way that utilizes and affirms the roles of others in the body of Christ. That takes creativity, judgment, and courage. But most of all, it takes confidence in the God who promises: "I will instruct you and teach you in the way you should go; I will counsel you with my loving eye on you...Many are the woes of the wicked, but the Lord's unfailing love surrounds those who trust in him" (Psalm 32:8,10).

CHAPTER 7

Blessed Be the Tie: Staff Relationships

"...locusts have no king, yet they advance together in ranks..."
(Proverbs 30:27)

I suppose it seems a bit odd that we would begin a chapter on staff relationships by using a verse that references locusts. It may feel a little unkind to draw a connection between your colleagues on the ministry staff and legendary pests who can gnaw through an entire field of corn in a single day so that it's left completely barren. But what I'm celebrating here, along with the writer of Proverbs, is not a swarming, rampaging grasshopper, but the fact that *even small creatures, when they act together, can accomplish big things.*

One of the most prominent books in the world of corporate leadership over the last decade was Jim Collins's classic, *Good to Great.*[1] At the core of that book was a very basic idea which Collins articulated in an October 2001 article in *Fast Company*[2]:

> Good-to-great leaders understand three simple truths. First, if you begin with "who," you can more easily adapt to a fast-changing world. If people get on your bus because of where they think it's going, you'll be in trouble when you get 10 miles down the road and discover that you need to change direction because the world has changed. But if people board the bus principally because of all the other great people on the bus, you'll be much faster and smarter in responding to changing conditions. Second, if you have the right people on your bus, you don't need to worry about motivating them. The right people are self-motivated: Nothing beats being part of a team that is expected to produce great results. And third, if you have the wrong people on the bus, nothing else matters. You may be headed in the right direction, but you still won't achieve greatness. Great vision with mediocre people still produces mediocre results.

Collins believes the key to any effective organization is almost always getting the right people on the bus. He reminds us that effective ministry begins with people who are going somewhere together. Although I think he overstates the case a bit,[3] there's no question that the people who are on the bus with us will have a big impact on the success of any ministry journey and our ability to enjoy it. This emphasis on the importance of a quality team is a thoroughly biblical idea. And it points us to the issue of staff relationships.

How many times in Scripture do we read about teams of people working together and walking together, sometimes so closely that their names almost become one: Moses and Aaron; Moses and Joshua; Elijah and Elisha; Peter, James, and John; Aquila and Priscilla; Paul and Timothy; Peter and Paul; Peter, Paul, and Mary; Simon and Garfunkel? The psalmist was right: "How good and pleasant it is when God's people live together in unity!" (Ps. 133:1). There's nothing quite like the camaraderie and community of joining together with like-minded men and women who share a vision for ministry. That's the upside of working on a cohesive, effective staff.

On the other hand, few elements in ministry are more nagging, draining, and frustrating than negative staff relationships. Trust me, I used to ride a bus every day to get to school, and, with all due respect to Jim Collins, there were times it could get pretty ugly—not because the wrong people were on the bus, but because the people assigned to that bus (the *right* people) could be mean, selfish, immature, and unruly. Like it or not, we all had to ride together, every day.

If you're a youth worker, whether you serve in a local church setting or in some sort of parachurch ministry, you've probably experienced both the good and bad sides of this journey. And you likely would agree that *who* is on the bus with you can make all the difference between whether it's a great ride or a bad trip. Consider this observation from researcher Karen Jones, drawing from a cross-denominational survey of over 2,000 youth workers: "The relationship between the youth minister and the senior pastor is one of the most critically important measures of a ministry climate; it has the power to impact a young youth minister's success like nothing else."[4]

Staying with the bus analogy, think about it this way: It doesn't matter if the scenery outside the bus window is beautiful, if you're enthusiastic about where the bus is headed, whether the bus is making good time, or even whether the vehicle is operating well and running smoothly; if the relational climate inside the bus is bad, it can negatively impact every other facet of the trip. And the reverse is also true: Maybe the scenery is quite plain, the destination not very alluring, and the bus well behind schedule and showing symptoms of severe engine failure. If the relationships on the bus are positive, that can make almost every other facet of the trip tolerable, and perhaps even fun. So it is with staff relationships in a ministry.

In the survey by Jones and her colleagues, roughly three quarters of the youth workers disagreed, to some extent, with the statement, "Conflicts with coworkers hinder my ministry." That's the good news. But just over one of four agreed that conflict with coworkers was a hindrance.[5] So, clearly staff relationships are a sensitive issue with a lot of youth workers. In fact, in Len Kageler's fascinating survey of youth ministers who were fired from their positions, when respondents were asked to choose up to three reasons (from a list of ten) for their dismissal, "Conflict with the Pastor and/or Church Leadership" was named by 94 percent of those who were fired. Of those who left voluntarily because of burnout, 44 percent named the senior pastor's being "hard to get along with"—the number one reason cited.[6] As Collins put it, "Nothing beats being part of a team that is expected to produce great results, [but], if you have the wrong people on the bus, nothing else matters...Great vision with mediocre people still produces mediocre results."

In chapters 10 and 11 of this book, we'll address questions related to working with volunteers and developing a volunteer ministry team. But in this chapter we want to focus on relationships with our colleagues on paid staff: How do we nurture healthy relationships with the people—right or wrong—who are on our bus?

LIKE IT OR NOT, WE'RE A TEAM

Let's begin with three basic facts about staff relationships:

Fact 1: *If we're feeling frustrated about staff relationships, any initiative for improvement will probably have to come from our end of the equation, not from the top person or the senior pastor.*

According to author Kenneth Mitchell, the senior minister usually grades the quality of staff relationships more highly than do other members of the same staff.[7] In one sample of 88 churches, Mitchell found that while 61.2 percent of the senior pastors graded the staff relationships as "basically good," 74 percent of the assistant pastors on the same staffs rated their relationships with the other ministers as "basically poor." When asked to assess the quality of staff relationships in their churches on a scale of one to five, 95 of 136 assistant pastors gave a grade of one or two. When the senior pastors on the same staff were asked for their assessment, however, 42 of the 80 senior pastors rated their staff relationships as a grade of four or five.

In other words, if we're waiting until the pastor realizes something's wrong, we may be waiting a long time. It's not that senior pastors don't care.[8] But imagine building a human pyramid four or five levels high. If one were to ask the pyramid participants, "How long can you stay together like this?" it would likely be the people on the top of the pyramid who would be most optimistic. The people on the bottom of the pile are the ones feeling the pain. Suggestions about "ways we could reshuffle the structure" may need to come from the bottom up.

Fact 2: *By virtue of our position, youth workers may be perceived by colleagues as the stereotypical rookies, short-term young people hoping to learn the ropes of ministry so that they can move on up to more weighty, long-term positions.* One study observed that nearly a third of all associate ministers are in their first pastoral position, are involved in an internship program, and/or are under 32 years of age.[9] Even if a youth worker has a seminary education, ten years of ministry experience, and is over 35, she may still be treated as if she's just gotten out of college, with no graduate degree, no experience, and no long-term commitment to youth ministry.

Fact 3: *The more we enjoy our coworkers, the more likely we are to enjoy our work.* While the research is limited, the studies that have been done over the years demonstrate conclusively that there is a direct correlation between healthy staff relationships and youth worker job satisfaction.[10]

MODELS OF STAFF RELATIONSHIPS

The staff of Grace Church is top-notch: Professional people who play out their roles on the ministry team with commendable commitment and a sense of excellence. Known for its strong pulpit ministry and varied programs for all ages, the church is growing and the ministry flourishing. From all appearances, Grace Church is an oasis of vibrant ministry. And in many ways that's true. But for the youth pastor who needs or enjoys close working relationships shaped by a sense of community and mutuality, Grace Church can be more of a desert than an oasis—a wasteland of organizational charts, interoffice memos, and staff meetings that are 98 percent business and less than 2 percent nurture.

Bannerside Presbyterian Church is almost the exact opposite. To begin with, the staff is much smaller, and the organizational chart is something someone drew up on a napkin one night after the staff had eaten dinner together. Off hours, the staff gets together for recreation—some of them play basketball together, others enjoy cutting firewood, but they often spend time together in some kind of fellowship. Staff meetings, held during the daily morning coffee break, are an informal mixture of ministry business, personal sharing, and chit-chat.

Grace and Bannerside represent the two predominant models of staff relationships that youth workers are likely to experience: The functional model and the fellowship (or family) model. Let's take a look at the strengths and weaknesses of each.

Functional Model: The Church as Corporation

At Grace Church, staff relationships are determined primarily by the functions different individuals have within the church. Everyone from the senior pastor to the youth pastor has a role to play, and the lines dividing jobs are clearly drawn. Members of the staff are courteous to one another and willing to work together, but typically are uninvolved with each other at a deep relational level.

The major advantage of shaping staff relationships on the functional model is that it is more efficient, particularly in a large church with a large staff where the emphasis may need to be on accountability rather than community. Obviously, the two are not mutually exclusive, but the larger the staff, the more important it becomes to make sure responsibility is owned by individuals and not by the group. The reason for this is simple enough: When the game is tennis, and the partners are playing in a doubles match, game strategy can be based on knowing the instincts and tendencies of one's partner. Quick communication in the spur of the moment is adequate to coordinate the movements of two people. But when the game is football, and the team posts eleven players on the field simultaneously, players are assigned a position and *defined by that position*. Plans are more elaborate and the *x*'s and *o*'s must be clearly drawn up in advance. There may be a great sense of camaraderie on the team, but if everybody is responsible for every task, some tasks will get missed. The emphasis is on function, not fellowship.

The functional model is most effective when each staff member has a clear and explicit job description. Just as "good fences make good neighbors," clear delineations of responsibility can prevent the kind of turf battles that break down staff relationships. Typically, this model is best led by a strong, directive, hard-working senior pastor who can manage a staff of people working in different areas while moving them toward a common goal.

The disadvantage of more clearly defined boundaries is that those clear lines often provoke the border wars they are intended to prevent. That's why, again, a strong senior minister or supervisor is so essential, because he or she can prevent staff members from building their own little fiefdoms. If the senior pastor is detached, preoccupied, disinterested, or weak, the staffers may busily develop their own pet projects and neglect working for unity in the overall ministry of the church.

The staff that operates along functional lines is usually operating a ministry organized by specific programs and policies as opposed to a ministry based on personalities or areas of giftedness. In other words, the youth pastor would typically be responsible for all areas of youth ministry—and only areas of youth ministry. It doesn't matter that the youth worker is also a good preacher; that's not the purpose for which he was hired. The youth minister who is gifted musically and wants to start a youth choir will have to negotiate the idea with the music director, or her efforts might be construed as trespassing on the music director's turf.

When staff relationships are functional, staff members generally work with a committee that supports their specific area of responsibility. The children's minister, for instance, works with the children's committee, the youth minister with the youth committee, and so on. Staff members develop their own support constituencies through these committees. The difficulty is that when staff members leave for a new position at another church or agency, their committees and the constituencies they represent can lose their voice until the staff member is replaced.

One advantage of the clearly defined responsibilities in the functional model is that it's easier for new staff members to move in and begin their work. For the coach to replace his running back is a matter of recruitment; the running back must learn the new system, but his adjustment to the system is largely based on performance. But what if that coach had to replace a family member? That would be a process far more complex—perhaps even impossible. He's not just looking for someone who can perform certain tasks or play out a specific role; he's looking for someone with whom he shares affection and chemistry and a variety of other personality intangibles that don't show up in the stats.

That explains why it's often easier for a new staff member to get up and running in a functional system rather than a family system. In a functional system, most of the networks and functional lines are above ground, and one doesn't have to navigate through a maze of underground, informal relational networks. The formal structures of the functional system help assure that the appropriate people are involved in the appropriate decisions.

The biggest flaw of the functional model of staff relationships is that it tends to breed little long-term tenure, particularly among people who have grown up in an era that so emphasizes the importance of relationships. Walking out of an organizational role is much easier than walking out on relationships. We build loyalty not by giving out job descriptions and offices, but by giving ourselves.

Fellowship Model: One Big, Happy Family

The five staff members at Bannerside Presbyterian Church are not only coworkers, they are close friends. It's not that they're working without job descriptions; it's that they approach their work the way a family approaches weekly life together: Everyone works together to do what must be done. If that means the youth minister needs to help with hospital visitation, it's no more a big problem than when the family member who usually takes out the garbage gets pressed for time and asks another family member to care for this chore.

An advantage of the fellowship model of staff relationships is that work is more fun when we're working with friends. We trust other members of the staff to defend us if our work is attacked. We trust them to direct critics to come and speak to us personally, rather than allowing them to stew behind our backs. We're also not as likely to concern ourselves with turf battles and power struggles. If we are members of a family, what's good for you is what's good for me (at least in theory!). Plus, the fellowship model tends to breed staff loyalty and longer tenures of commitment. People can walk into and out of functional positions without a lot of emotion, but when it comes to walking out on family, the cords are tougher to sever.

So why doesn't every staff operate this way? Who would pass up a chance to work with the Walton family? Because the reality doesn't always live up to the ideal. Sometimes it's strictly because of staff size. I spoke with a youth minister recently who is serving at a church in Colorado on a staff that numbers 35 people. Frankly, this makes it hard to genuinely flesh out the fellowship model. A household of 35 is a complex family to manage! Like in a family, if the staff isn't intentional about nurturing relationships and cultivating community, it simply won't happen.

An additional significant dynamic of the fellowship model of staff relationships is that broken or strained relationships can impair the function of the ministry. Unlike the functional model where "getting the job done" carries staff members through tense relationships, a fellowship model can wither or flourish with people's sense of connectedness. Imagine a spouse complaining, "Honey, it feels like we're growing apart; we're not communicating," only to be told in response, "Look, what's the big deal? Meals are being served, bills are being paid, and the children are doing well in school." If the locus of the union is a relationship, a breach in the way staff relate to one another can mean a breach in the way they operate as a staff team together.

Another problem encountered in a fellowship model of staff relationships is that the close-knit feel that retains employees also tends to make it difficult for new staff members to feel accepted. What feels like a family to those on the inside can feel like a clique to those on the outside. That's the nature of family connections. We don't get that uptight about a new mailman or a new paperboy, but we're apt to be a little more cautious about accepting someone who wants to be a member of the family. The loyalty nurtured by the fellowship model can also nurture insularity.

BREAKDOWN ON THE BUS

Neither of the two basic staff models is immune from relational breakdowns. As long as human beings are involved, there will be the potential for blowups, blow-outs, and unintended retirements. After all, this is not just any bus; this is a *church* bus (the very icon of a vehicle under stress). We'll talk in a later chapter about dealing with conflict, but for now, let's look at a few issues that can let the air out of the tires and puncture good staff relationships.

Poor Hearing (Due to Poor Speaking)

In the Monday morning staff meeting, the senior pastor, Darrell Ramirez, makes an off-handed comment to the youth pastor, Eric Dowdy, "Hey, that was quite a presentation the kids did in the service yesterday morning. Next time, give me a heads up when you're going to slip into your *'youth pastor mode.'* That gives me a chance to get the congregation ready."

It was a simple exchange; it might even have been an attempt at a little *Senior Pastor* humor. But what Eric heard from his pastor neither amused nor affirmed him. In fact, what he heard in the senior pastor's comment was a message of disrespect—not just that Sunday morning's youth group presentation was

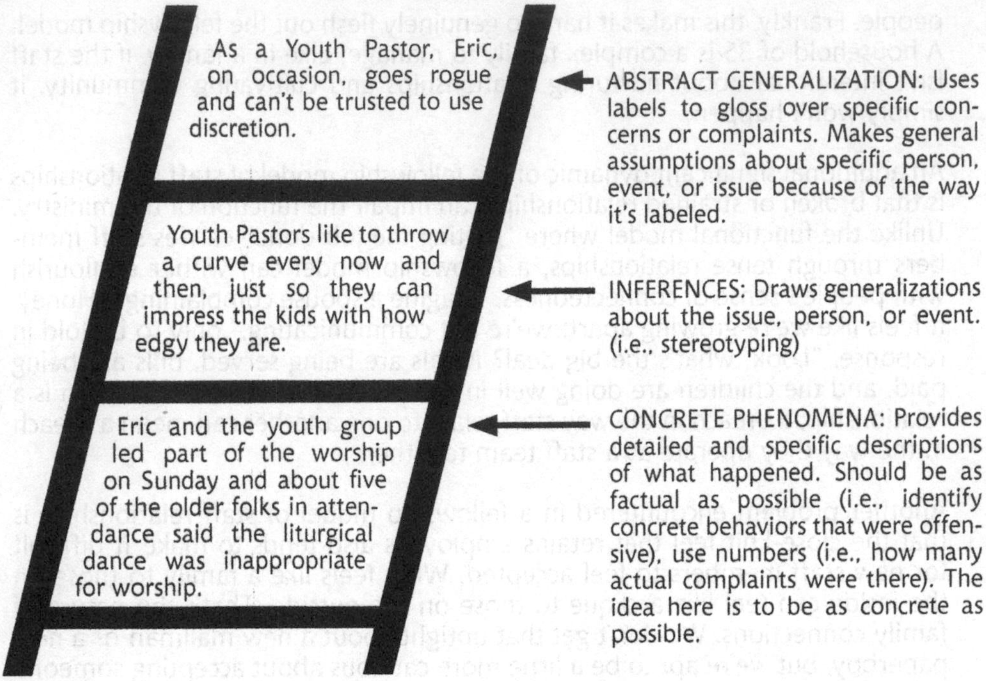
As a Youth Pastor, Eric, on occasion, goes rogue and can't be trusted to use discretion.
ABSTRACT GENERALIZATION: Uses labels to gloss over specific concerns or complaints. Makes general assumptions about specific person, event, or issue because of the way it's labeled.
Youth Pastors like to throw a curve every now and then, just so they can impress the kids with how edgy they are.
INFERENCES: Draws generalizations about the issue, person, or event. (i.e., stereotyping)
Eric and the youth group led part of the worship on Sunday and about five of the older folks in attendance said the liturgical dance was inappropriate for worship.
CONCRETE PHENOMENA: Provides detailed and specific descriptions of what happened. Should be as factual as possible (i.e., identify concrete behaviors that were offensive), use numbers (i.e., how many actual complaints were there). The idea here is to be as concrete as possible.
Figure 7-1

bizarre, but that youth pastors probably shouldn't be allowed near a pulpit without a chaperone. Needless to say, it brought some tension to the bus. What happened?

It was the renowned linguist S. I. Hayakawa who noted that the way we use language can have a huge impact on our relationships with other people. If we want to nurture strong relationships, we must not communicate in ways that demean people or put them on the defensive. *The key here is to select language that is appropriately clear and direct for the situation.* Hayakawa described this as a Ladder of Abstraction (Figure 7-1).

CONCRETE PHENOMENON: Pastor Ramirez wasn't specific in his comments about the Sunday morning worship. Was this criticism? Humor? Awe? Bewilderment? Amusement? He wasn't concrete enough in his communication for Eric to know. And, if the comment was intended to be critical, what precisely was the nature of the criticism? The fact was that several of the older parishioners had been uncomfortable with the liturgical dance the youth had performed in worship. But because that wasn't made clear, Eric didn't know if the pastor was referring to his sermon, to the fact that he wasn't wearing a tie, to the way the kids used Facebook as part of their presentation, or to the liturgical dance. Had Pastor Ramirez wanted to motivate Eric, and give him actionable intelligence, he should have been concrete and specific in his remarks. Instead, his abstract remark served no positive purpose, and very likely will have a negative impact on their relationship.

INFERENCE: Pastor Ramirez's comment suggests that he believes all youth pastors are loose cannons—non-conformist types who have little regard for ritual or propriety. No doubt, there are many youth pastors who would proudly claim those descriptors. But it is unfair to stereotype all youthworkers as loose cannons or non-conformist because they color outside the lines on occasion, or to assume they reject all rituals because they critique some of them.

ABSTRACT GENERALIZATION: Because Eric is a youth pastor, and Pastor Ramirez associates certain traits with that role, the pastor makes certain assumptions about the way Eric operates. It might even be that Pastor Ramirez is reluctant to articulate the specific complaint about the worship service because he assumes Eric, as a youth pastor, is a non-conformist and wouldn't respond well to criticism or coaching, and probably can be corrected only in terms of sarcasm.

Now, before all the youth workers reading this book robe themselves in garments of righteous indignation, let's remember that this kind of miscommunication works both ways. We are quick to form assumptions and unhelpful generalizations of our own: About senior pastors, coworkers, parents, church boards, older people, and, of course, any guy who does not have a shaved head and a soul patch. And, it is often out of those assumptions that we respond to the abstract comments of others, which begins a new ladder of abstraction (Figure 7-2).

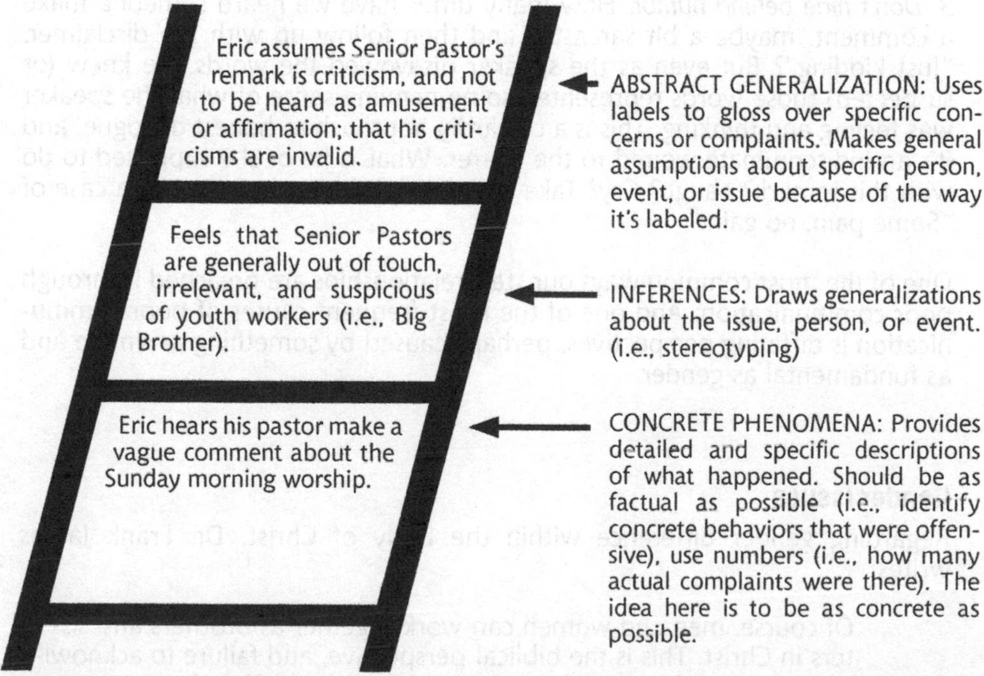
Eric assumes Senior Pastor's remark is criticism, and not to be heard as amusement or affirmation; that his criticisms are invalid.
ABSTRACT GENERALIZATION: Uses labels to gloss over specific concerns or complaints. Makes general assumptions about specific person, event, or issue because of the way it's labeled.
Feels that Senior Pastors are generally out of touch, irrelevant, and suspicious of youth workers (i.e., Big Brother).
INFERENCES: Draws generalizations about the issue, person, or event. (i.e., stereotyping)
Eric hears his pastor make a vague comment about the Sunday morning worship.
CONCRETE PHENOMENA: Provides detailed and specific descriptions of what happened. Should be as factual as possible (i.e., identify concrete behaviors that were offensive), use numbers (i.e., how many actual complaints were there). The idea here is to be as concrete as possible.

Figure 7-2

How do we remedy the miscommunication so that we can maintain strong staff relationships?

1. Be clear and concrete in communication. Avoid drive-by criticism or ambush conversations where clarity is almost impossible. If you have affirmation to offer, offer it; if you have criticism, offer it. But try to be as concrete as possible so that translation by the other party is accurate. Rather than say to your senior pastor, "I love it when you get all *Prayer of Jabez* on us...," it would be more concrete and specific to say, "I appreciate the way you were willing to be aggressive about the budget for the youth building addition."

2. Don't be too electronic. In our love affair with e-mail and texting, we've forgotten the significance of Marshall McLuhan's maxim, "The medium is the message."[11] What that means in simplest terms is that our words don't stand alone. The medium through which we communicate a message is, itself, a part of the message. Someone who chooses to communicate by means of smoke signals is, by default, limiting the kinds of topics they can communicate about and the depth of the dialogue. The medium isn't neutral; it actually shapes the message. Which means that when we communicate through texting, or even through e-mail, it shapes the very nature of *what* we communicate. Just because you can save time by texting a message to a staff colleague doesn't mean you should. Face-to-face interaction (think: Word become flesh) is the best way to communicate certain ideas. Electronic messages may be more efficient, but they aren't always more *Ephesiant*.

3. Don't hide behind humor. How many times have we heard someone make a comment, maybe a bit sarcastic, and then follow up with the disclaimer, "Just kidding"? But even as the speaker disavowed the words, we knew (or suspected) those words represented some genuine sense of what the speaker was feeling and thinking. This is a cowardly approach to honest dialogue, and it's an indiscriminate wound to the hearer. What is he or she supposed to do with this remark? Laugh? Cry? Take it seriously? Apologize? Here is a case of "Some pain, no gain."

One of the most common ways our staff relationships are breached is through poor communication. And one of the most frequent causes of poor communication is differing perspectives, perhaps caused by something as simple and as fundamental as gender.

Gender Issues

Regarding gender difference within the body of Christ, Dr. Frank James writes:

> Of course, men and women can work together as brothers and sisters in Christ. This is the biblical perspective, and failure to acknowledge this is a denial of the redemptive power of Christ's work in

our lives. However, this is a fallen world and there is such a thing as sibling rivalry. Male-female relationships are caught in the "already-not-yet"—already redeemed but not yet fully sanctified.[12]

In a research project conducted by Dr. Joye Baker at Dallas Theological Seminary, 377 female seminary graduates were asked to identify their most difficult challenges in ministry leadership. The specific question was, "How can the seminary best prepare women students to meet these challenges?" Their responses were noteworthy:

- "Prepare men and women to more successfully minister together" (24 percent).

- "Help men value and respect women in ministry" (18 percent).[13]

In terms of staff relationships, gender issues play out in a wide range of ways, some of them fairly uncomfortable to talk about: Disrespect of the opposite gender, stereotyping roles ("We really value Kelley on our youth staff; if we didn't have her on our team I don't know where we'd be in doing housing for the retreats and stuff like that!"), inappropriate relationships, and professional jealousy among others. There isn't space in a book like this to address all these issues. But there's no question that some of these issues come into play when a ministry staff sets men and women working together.

When we think of gender differences in ministry, there are the obvious conclusions to which we usually jump. It's been said that men are less verbal than women, that women can multitask better than men, and that men tend to be more focused on getting things done while women tend to be more focused on nurturing relationships. There may be an element of truth to some of these stereotypes, but more often than not they are based on faulty assumptions. The debate about gender differences has fervent proponents on both sides of the issue: Some say that there are no differences beyond anatomy, while others say there are real and significant differences in the way men and women approach their work. I'm convinced that the research supports the latter conclusion.

Consider these sample findings catalogued in the excellent book, *Mixed Ministry: Working Together as Brothers and Sisters in an Oversexed Society*:[14]

1. Girls' hearing is substantially more sensitive than boys', especially in the 1,000-to 4,000-Hz range, and these differences increase with age. Women probably hear better than men.

2. Women typically navigate using landmarks while men are more likely to use absolute directions like north and south.

3. Boys and girls assess risk differently, with boys more likely to report feeling exhilarated by the possibility of danger, whereas girls are far more likely to report feeling fearful. Boys systemati-

cally overestimated their own ability while girls were more likely to underestimate their abilities.

4. Boys fight 20 times as often as girls do, but after fighting boys usually end up better friends and are more likely to play together. Girls seldom fight, but when they do bad feelings last.
5. Women tend to make moral decisions on the basis of who it might help and who it might hurt. Men tend to make moral decisions on the basis of right and wrong, regardless of how it impacts others.

Again, I don't suppose it's possible in this space to address all gender issues in detail. What I do propose is that we recognize that men and women bring different gifts to a church staff, and that we need both the gifts men bring and the gifts women bring. It is significant that when Paul needs someone to deliver his letter to the church in Rome, arguably one of the most important documents in the corpus of Christian literature, his emissary is a woman:

> I commend to you our sister Phoebe, a deacon of the church in Cenchreae. I ask you to receive her in the Lord in a way worthy of his people and to give her any help she may need from you, for she has been the benefactor of many people, including me. (Romans 16:1-2)

That's a pretty strong reference letter, but it also illustrates the fact that women played a vital role in the New Testament church.

As important as this is, honesty demands that we consider other dynamics in this exchange. We must recognize that, because we are fallen creatures, these potentially very helpful relationships can also be potentially harmful relationships, relationships scarred by bias, harassment, and inappropriate sexual conduct. We must take that reality seriously and take care to protect one another. The biblical mandate and the most practical way to respond to this reality is that men and women should treat each other as brothers and sisters. Consider this clear exhortation from Paul:

> Do not rebuke an older man harshly, but exhort him as if he were your father. Treat younger men as brothers, older women as mothers, and younger women as sisters, with absolute purity. (1 Timothy 5:1-2)

How various staff communities weave this rule into the fabric of staff relationships will vary. But healthy staff relationships will offer an honest blend of bridges and boundaries—bridges, so that coworkers of different genders can work together to enhance the ministry mission, and boundaries, so unhealthy relationships don't detract from the ministry mission.[15]

EVOLUTION OF STAFF RELATIONSHIPS

Another factor that shapes and sometimes impedes healthy staff relationships is tenure: How much turnover is there on the staff, and how do these transitions influence staff relationships? Mark Senter, professor of educational ministries at Trinity Evangelical Divinity School, discusses the normal evolution of staff relationships in terms of various stages. Let's examine three of these stages to assess the challenges a staff team might meet at various mileposts on their journey together.

STAGE 1: Getting Acquainted

When a youth worker takes a new position, a fog of euphoria generally covers the ministry landscape. The church or agency is pleased to be able to end its search successfully, and the youth worker is excited to have found a place to plug in for ministry. This honeymoon period is characterized by a sense of relief, discovery, and—most importantly—a sense of ignorance. At this point, staff members and constituents don't expect the newcomer to "know any better," so this forgiven ignorance should be used to the best advantage.

For example, this honeymoon period is a wonderful time for new staff to ask "stupid questions"—questions about jurisdiction, lines of responsibility, and expectations; questions that, if asked one year into the position, might give someone reason for offense. People are more gracious at this stage of the relationship—long-time staff members are themselves adjusting to a new team member and are more likely to flex. The key at this stage is to remember the old adage, "As the work begins, so will it go." We should balance our desires to push, probe, and test the boundaries with the reminder that first impressions often leave lasting impressions.

Dan was in a new position at a church in South Carolina when he sought to hire an intern whose denomination was different than the church's. It didn't seem like a big deal to Dan, and in some ways it probably wasn't. But it was a big deal to Dan's pastor. Dan wasn't allowed to hire the intern, and from that point on he never seemed to get back in step with the senior pastor. Dan left the position within a year.

STAGE 2: Getting Established

The "getting acquainted" stage usually ends with some sort of crisis. The willingness to overlook concerns simply because an employee is new has expired. This ushers the youth worker into a second stage in relationship to his or her colleagues—a stage in which the critical issue is trust or mistrust, credibility or lack of credibility.

If youth workers have earned the trust of their colleagues, it will generally be made manifest in some of the following ways:

- *Greater vulnerability*—staff members agree to admit that no one but Jesus walks on water.

- *Honest communication*—staff members feel free to express disagreement.

- *Job refinement*—there is some freedom to redefine the position now that you are in place and have seen up close the necessities of the situation.

- *Community*—there is support among the staff. Even in failure there is loving rebuke.

On the other hand, if the youth worker has *not* gained this kind of trust, it may be manifested in these ways:

- *Gradual isolation*—no one sits next to you at staff meetings.

- *Interpersonal conflict*—philosophical differences are exposed, and people begin to deal with one another on the basis of categories rather than on the basis of specific concerns.

- *Big hints*—the trustees remove your computer's hard drive and shut down your e-mail account.

If youth workers or staff members have not earned the trust of their fellow workers by stage two, they probably never will. The situation isn't likely to get better—and it will very possibly get worse.

STAGE 3: Gaining Momentum

By the time a youth worker has moved into stage three, the key issues professionally and relationally are growth versus stagnation. Having gained a certain amount of momentum thus far, will the youth worker be able to sustain it, or will he or she become stagnant? Growth at this stage is characterized by these elements:

- *Better time-management;*

- *Broader responsibility* given by the staff and/or supervisor;

- *Growing honesty and loving confrontation* among staff members; and

- *Systems being developed by the youth worker that enhance efficiency and expediency.*

Stagnation will be marked by some of the following:

- *Exhaustion*—physically, emotionally, and/or spiritually;
- *Feeling unchallenged by the job;*
- *New priorities*—usually something outside the church—that detract from job performance;
- *Financial worries;*
- *Withdrawal from staff relationships and an unwillingness to share honestly with others on staff.*

Senter's insights remind us staff relationships are organic and ever-changing. It's not like a group photograph that can be snapped while everyone is smiling. What is true of a staff in one moment in time will change over the course of its shared ministry. Maintaining staff cohesion is an ongoing effort that must be adjusted and adapted as time goes on.

SOME PRACTICAL SUGGESTIONS

Whether the issues are related to communication breakdown, gender differences, tenure dynamics, or any of the myriad other issues that impact staff relationships, the best rule of thumb is to be proactive. Just as faithful love isn't something you truly "fall into," so healthy staff relationships don't just bubble up out of the ground. Here are some simple, proactive steps to build healthy staff relationships:[16]

Each staff member should have a mandate as important as the mandates of every other member of the staff. In other words, staff members should feel and understand the vital significance of their own ministry roles to the whole mission of the church. For this to actually happen, the leadership of the congregation must set staff members free to do most what they do best. If youth ministry is what I do best, then I am freed and affirmed by my coworkers to do youth ministry, with just as much credibility as the person who is preaching, leading Bible studies, or directing a choir.

Each staff member must have equal access to the senior leadership person (usually the pastor). That access should be direct and reasonably immediate. One major cause of squabbles among staff members is the kind of professional jealousy we observe in the disciples jockeying to be closest to Jesus (see Mark 9:34, Luke 9:46, Luke 22:24). When the pastor seems more available to one staff member than to another, the neglected staff member may resent the extra attention, or suspect her contribution isn't really valued. To be sure, in very large churches with a high number of professional staff, it simply won't be possible for each staff member to have direct access to the senior leadership person, any more than it would be possible for every Microsoft employee to have access to CEO Steve Ballmer. The key is to have bridges of communication in place. All staff members need to have some means of connection, some reporting mechanism that validates their contributions, holds them accountable, and allows them to exercise real authority over their areas of responsibility.

Staff members must do what they have all promised to do—that is, act professionally. One of the major frustrations among coworkers in ministry is unpredictability: "Will she follow up on our conversation?" "Is he talking behind my back?" "Will their work be completed by the date assigned?" Nine times out of ten, a breach in staff relationships grows out of an instance in which someone acted unprofessionally.

Staff members should be allowed to develop their own constituencies. A lot of pastors feel threatened when they see other staff members closely aligning with power blocks in the congregation. But these support constituencies are vital. In the case of a youth pastor, these constituencies might include youth committees, youth groups, parents' support groups, or all of the above. Jealousy and insecurity leads to weak staff relationships. If staff members are encouraged to build support groups, those groups will give them the security they need to be vulnerable about mistakes, honest about concerns, and excited about other staff members' successes.

A RESOURCE FOR MINISTRY

The real reason for good, strong staff relationships is not a smoother operation. The real reason for good, strong staff relationships is that those of us in youth ministry need coworkers, and coworkers need us.

In his book, *Applying Modern Management Principles,*[17] Stanley Seashore provides empirical evidence that we're only handicapping ourselves when we limp along with non-cohesive staff relationships. Seashore's research draws these conclusions:

1. "Groups are superior to individuals in the solution of complex problems." The wider the range of knowledge needed to solve a problem, the more necessary it is to address the problem as a team. The writer of Proverbs put it this way: "Let the wise listen and add to their learning, and let the discerning get guidance." (1:5).

2. "It may take longer for a group to arrive at a solution to a problem, but it will typically be a better solution." Yes, it's harder to do

good group work; but good groups typically find better solutions than good individuals.

3. Groups working together are less likely to give up on a problem and abandon a solution than an individual working alone.

4. "Groups are able to generate a greater number of alternatives for solutions to their problems and are better able to see blind alleys than the individual who pursues the task alone."

In short, Seashore's research proves what the apostle Paul said two millennia ago:

> God has placed the parts in the body, every one of them, just as he wanted them to be. If they were all one part, where would the body be? As it is, there are many parts, but one body. The eye cannot say to the hand, "I don't need you!" And the head cannot say to the feet, "I don't need you!" (1 Corinthians 12:18-21)

Some of the greatest times in my life have been when I have stood shoulder to shoulder with brothers and sisters on the same staff, pooling gifts in an effort to glorify God. I will never forget the closeness I've felt in those times.

Likewise, I can still feel some of the pain of difficult encounters I've experienced with colleagues over the years. Those scars are as slow to fade as the memories of the good times. Even as I write these words, some of those conversations are as vivid as if they happened yesterday—and that hurts.

But most of all, I have learned through various staff relationships that God is good. He works through my coworkers to make me into the person he wants me to be. Looking back on some of those moments now, I understand: *I thought* I was discussing or arguing so I could build a better youth ministry. Now, from the perspective of time passed, I realize God's intention was to use those people in my life not to build a better youth ministry, but to build a better youth minister. When it all boils down, building a better youth minister is probably the best means and the best end of strong staff relationships. "Listen to advice and accept instruction, and in the end you will be wise" (Proverbs 19:20, NIV).

CHAPTER 8

The Essential Partnership: Working with Families

Hear, O Israel: The Lord our God, the Lord is one. Love the Lord your God with all your heart and with all your soul and with all your strength. These commandments that I give you today are to be on your hearts. Impress them on your children. Talk about them when you sit at home and when you walk along the road, when you lie down and when you get up.
(Deuteronomy 6:4-7)

It all began with a one-eared Mickey Mouse.

The year was 1989, and Stuart Cummings-Bond gave voice to the concern of a growing number of youth workers that many church youth programs, by default or by design, had become isolated from the remainder of the congregation.[1] Using a diagram that looked like a one-eared Mickey Mouse (Figure 8-1), Cummings-Bond observed that this segmentation was good neither for the youth group nor for the broader congregation. It was the perfect visual to depict a situation that was increasingly hard to ignore: The almost humorous picture of families coming to church in the same vehicle and then, upon arriving on church property, being shuffled off in different directions, segregated by age, so that in their respective Sunday school classes they could learn about the importance of being together!

Five years later, Mark DeVries observed that the church had become the place where teenagers "are most segregated from the world of adults."[2] Churches had unwittingly cultivated an environment where teenagers were being cut off from the very adult relationships that would sustain them through the turbulence of the adolescent years and by which they could learn about mature Christian faith. We were, in effect, nurturing in teenagers an appetite for a youth group from which they would soon graduate, while

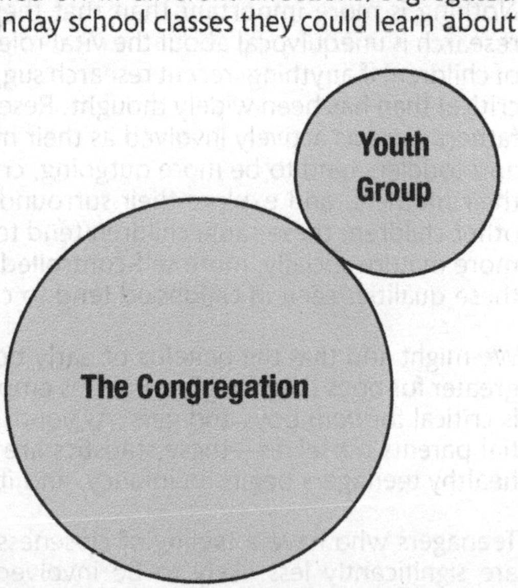

Figure 8-1: Cummings-Bonds One-Eared Mickey Mouse

weaning them from involvement in the broader church life that would sustain their spiritual growth as adults.

Except for the occasional Youth Sunday and the annual visit to sing Christmas carols for senior citizen shut-ins, teenagers were inadvertently amputated from the rest of the body of Christ. And the larger the church, the more dynamic the youth ministry, the more likely and stark was the separation. There were youth budgets, youth facilities, youth worship services, and youth ministry professionals who were assigned the role of nurturing the spiritual life of the teenagers in the congregation. The implicit message to parents was, "We are the professionals; we know teenagers; and we are the specialists who can help your kids find Jesus. Please do not try this at home." And parents, who often found it awkward and difficult to talk to their kids about spiritual matters, were all too willing to step back and let the experts take over.

Everyone was well-intentioned, of course, but the effect was not unlike when the overzealous rookie gardener pulled the plant out of its pot of soil so he could take it into the greenhouse and prune it. It was an approach that left teenagers with a very weak spiritual root system, dying on the vine and wilting under the pressure of post-high school temptations and pressures. Not a good result for churches and youth workers whose mandate is to "go and bear fruit—fruit that will last" (John 15:16).

THE FAMILY PLOT: A PLACE TO GROW HEALTHY TEENAGERS

When it comes to growing healthy teenagers, we can be certain of one thing: Nothing is more important than that they grow up in healthy families. The research is unequivocal about the vital role of both moms and dads in the lives of children. If anything, recent research suggests the role of fathers is even more critical than has been widely thought. Research has shown that children whose fathers were as actively involved as their mothers in parenting them as infants and toddlers tend to be more outgoing, cry less, are less overly dependent on their mothers, and explore their surroundings more eagerly. Compared with other children, these same children tend to be more at ease around strangers, more mature socially, more self-controlled, and more empathic. What's more, these qualities seen in childhood tend to carry over into the teenage years.[3]

We might add that the benefits of early bonding with the father appear to be greater for boys than for girls. But this emphasis on the role of involved fathers is critical for *both* boys and girls. As youth workers—and as parents or potential parents ourselves—these statistics are an important reminder that raising healthy teenagers begins in infancy, and it's not just the mother's task.

Teenagers who have a feeling of closeness and connection with their parents are significantly less likely to be involved in risky behaviors.[4] For example, boys who are deprived of a good relationship with their fathers in early childhood are more likely to manifest delinquency behaviors and engage in more overstated forms of masculinity, such as aggression, violence, defiance, and lawlessness.[5] While at one time the conventional wisdom might have been summarized by the notion that teenagers have to make a "break" from their parents if they are to become their own people, the vast majority of more recent research suggests precisely the contrary. Researcher John Bowlby explains it this way:

> Children tend unwittingly to identify with parents and therefore, to adopt, when they become parents, the same patterns of behavior towards children that they themselves have experienced during their own childhood. Patterns of interaction are transmitted, more or less faithfully, from one generation to another. Thus the inheritance of mental health and of mental ill health through the medium of family microculture is certainly no less important, than is their inheritance through the medium of genes.[6]

Should we think parental influence shapes only a child's emotional and relational health, there is ample evidence in both Scripture and research literature to remind us of the huge impact parents have in the spiritual lives of their teenagers. One of the most notable Scripture passages comes from Deuteronomy 6:4-7 in what is called the *shema* (Hebrew literally: *Hear*), a passage cited by Jesus when he spoke about the greatest commandments (Matthew 22:37-38; Mark 12:29-30; Luke 10:27):

> Hear, O Israel: The Lord our God, the Lord is one. Love the Lord your God with all your heart and with all your soul and with all your strength. These commandments that I give you today are to be on your hearts. *Impress them on your children. Talk about them when you sit at home and when you walk along the road, when you lie down and when you get up.* (emphasis mine)

And the evidence of adolescent research speaks just as clearly. Although Jesus never cited any of the findings of sociologist Chris Smith (at least to my knowledge), Smith speaks just as plainly about the importance of parents in the spiritual development of teenagers:

> Contrary to popular, misguided cultural stereotypes and frequent parental misconceptions, we believe the evidence clearly shows that the single most important social influence on the religious and spiritual lives of adolescents is their parents.[7]

This is a critical insight for folks in youth ministry because it reminds us again of the absolutely essential role of parents in the healthy development of a teenager. Youth ministry is not about helping teenagers cut the rope of attachment and become free climbers. At its best, youth ministry is about helping the parties at both ends of the rope maintain and strengthen their grips, and perhaps even trying to provide for them the proper equipment for the climb. But it surely is *not* about youth workers trying to offer teenagers an alternative rope, or an alternative route for the climb. Everyone understands there are families in which the relationships are unhealthy, and that some parents do not have secure enough footing themselves to offer their kids a safe line of support. But effective youth ministers will do whatever we can to facilitate a healthy connection between parents and teenagers, even when the climb looks steep, and climbers look weak. Ignoring the family relationships that have such profound impact on a teenager is like a farmer planting a crop without giving any thought to the soil out of which it grows.

A STRATEGIC ALLIANCE

The response of youth workers to this avalanche of research data has run the gamut from a heartfelt shrug that sighs, "Dude, we know parents are really important, but we're going to keep doing what we've been doing," all the way to sky-is-falling alarm that says it's *all* about families, and the whole concept of youth ministry is unbiblical because it "can't be found anywhere in the Bible."[8] Never mind that the Bible doesn't mention denominations or Vacation Bible School or church softball leagues, either. The real question is not whether youth ministry is *unbiblical.*[9] The real question to be asked here is ,*What is a biblical approach to youth ministry that protects and facilitates the pivotal role of families in the lives of teenagers?* And, I am convinced there are excellent resources that address that concern.[10]

In his classic book *Family-Based Youth Ministry,* Mark DeVries argues for a shift in the way we think about and execute youth ministry. The goal is not to "build a strong youth program" (i.e., get as many kids as possible involved in the ministry). Instead, the goal is a youth program that builds teenagers into people who will be mature Christians as adults, recognizing that nurturing strong families is a major element in that equation.[11] DeVries describes two key priorities for youth workers who intend to maintain a biblical emphasis on the role of family in Christian nurture:

- **Priority Number One: Equipping parents to do what God has called them to do and what they are uniquely suited to do—disciple their own children**. DeVries writes, "Parents need help in learning how to provide for the Christian nurture of their children. But youth workers must not merely do for the youth what their parents cannot or will not do for them. Instead, we must endeavor to equip those parents to communicate the faith to their teenagers themselves."[12]

- **Priority Number Two: Equip the extended family of the church.** "The 'my family first' attitude, especially among Christians, has, in fact, only served to sever nuclear families from the very structures that can give their children lasting values and clear identity. Without strong ties to specific extended families (for example, church, neighborhood, nation), nuclear families have

> become self-perpetuating breeding grounds for rootlessness and alienation...So the second priority of family-based youth ministry must be to provide a new 'first family' for our teenagers by allowing them to experience the extended family of the church (not to be confused with the extended family of teenagers in the church)."[13]

Two Points of Resistance

Sounds like a great idea, right? And it is, except for two groups of people who tend to be somewhat resistant to the concept: Youth workers and parents.

Youth workers. Historically, we have considered ourselves people who work with youth, not people who work with families. Why?

- *In part, because we are already busier than we should be.* It's hard to get excited about expanding the range of care. What we don't need is another whole realm of ministry and responsibility.

- *Family ministry intimidates us.* We know how to act around kids. But parents? They use a different "scoring" system, and working with adults doesn't exactly feel like our sweet spot—especially if we are closer in age to the teenagers than their parents.

- *In some ministry contexts, we might fear we're crossing into someone else's realm of responsibility.* Part of the unhealthy segmentation in some churches is that there are clear lines of division between "those who work with teenagers" and "those who work with adults." The youth minister who seeks to nurture teenagers *by* working with adults may meet resistance from the senior pastor or some other staff member who perceives family ministry to be more his or her role.

The reluctance of many youth workers to adopting a more family-based approach is summed up well in what author Steve Wright describes as "the three biggest mistakes" he made as a youth pastor:

1. I assumed parents didn't want to disciple their children;

2. I believed parents didn't have as much influence on their teens as I did;

3. I enamored students to myself and did not champion the influencers who would walk throughout life with the students.[14]

Parents. Often, the greatest resistance to a youth ministry that includes parents is the parents themselves. That seems odd. Why would we meet resistance from parents in trying to help them be who God calls them to be? There are several reasons:

- *Never trust anyone under 30.* Parents are reluctant to welcome the guidance and support of a youth minister because so many youth pastors are younger than the parents themselves. As one father put it, "What do you know? Both of your children are still under ten years old."

- *Parents fear we already have enough inside information to make them squirm.* Some parents are reluctant to get involved with us in family ministry because they don't want to air out any more dirty laundry on our line. I can distinctly remember a Tuesday morning sharing group when a teenager began sharing through her tears that she was worried about her parents' marriage, and that her dad had gotten "kind of violent" with her mom. I was stunned at her honesty in front of 12 peers around the table. But I'm sure I wasn't nearly as stunned as her parents would have been if they'd known what their daughter was saying in Covenant Group.

- *Parents have a different focus from youth workers.* Parents tend to look at the youth group through the eyes of their own teens. If the program is not working well for their kids, then it doesn't matter how helpful it is to other teenagers—it's a bad youth program. I vividly recall a conversation with a mother who wanted me to start a Bible study series on sex and dating within the next week. I told her we'd just completed a series on sex and dating four months earlier, but she persisted. When I asked her why, she blurted back, "Because Rachel has her first date Saturday night!"

- *Because they have a different perspective, parents evaluate our programs differently.* We get back from a mission trip on which three students got saved, one decided to be a career missionary, and five others decided they want to do short-term mission work, and we're ecstatic. The parents, on the other hand, are not impressed: "Sure, my kid will paint an orphanage down in Haiti, but I can't get him to clean his room." We might return from an awesome weekend retreat where God really worked, expecting we're about to be named youth minister of the year. Instead, the mother of the kid who got a sore throat calls Monday morning to complain that her son couldn't go to school. As far as that parent is concerned, it was a bad retreat.

We should expect then to meet some resistance as we begin to make this shift in ministry emphasis. That's why Mark DeVries suggests we take more of an "'undercover' or mustard-seed" approach.[15] He recommends that churches "begin to apply these principles slowly, adding one or two ideas [he suggests many in his book] each year. Typically, most churches will find that the more of these events they do, the more they will want to do and the easier they will become."

DeVries says his own rule of thumb as a youth pastor trying to build a family-based ministry was this: *If it works with youth, try it with youth and parents together.*[16] He continues:

> Just as in youth programming, some ideas worked beautifully; others were less successful. But, in general, family-based programming, used judiciously, is almost always more effective (and more fun) than having the adults and the youth apart.[17]

In most cases, the task of raising healthy, well-adjusted teenagers who are growing in Christ is just too big and too complex for either parents or youth workers to pull off alone. In-depth youth ministry demands that we transcend the imaginary boundaries between church and home. The most effective ministry occurs when youth workers and parents make a potent alliance.

Youth workers, after all, bring to the equation some significant skills. To begin with, we can talk to students. Our familiarity with youth culture gives us a different perspective on adolescent issues. We're not as apt to freak out if one of our kids gets her nose pierced. Plus, we know a side of the kids that their parents may never know. We see them with their friends, on their own. Over the years, teenagers have offered me the privilege of stepping into their worldsby talking with me about their doubts, concerns, worries, hopes, and fears. Sometimes they talk with me just because I'm available and willing to listen. Sometimes it's simply because I'm *not* their parent. But it is precisely *because* I am not their parent that my goal is to build those parent-teen bridges and nurture those key relationships that will be significant long after kids graduate from my youth group.

Parents bring to the equation an equally unique contribution. They know their children in the context of their daily lives, which we seldom see. The pictures of teenagers that their parents see may be shaded quite differently from the ones we view in youth group. Ironically, at times our perspective as youth ministers keeps us from ministering to teenagers in all the ways that are essential for their holistic development. If they're active in youth group and have signed up for the retreat, we generally feel as if their lives are well balanced. Parents can offer a broader perspective of their teenagers' growth—their educational progress in school, their ability to play constructive and cooperative roles in their families, their physical well-being.

One youth ministry buddy tells of a time when a mother barged into his Bible study because her son had promised to mow the lawn before he came to youth group. At first, my friend was really angry that this mother had intimidated her son in this way. He couldn't believe how insensitive she had been, reprimanding her son in front of the whole group. But the more he thought about it, the more it made sense. His final verdict: "More power to her. She's trying to teach her son responsibility and accountability. She did the right thing." It disrupted his Bible study (programming issue), but it hopefully taught the son about responsibility (maturity issue).

Plus, let's be honest: Parents love their children more than we do. Of course, there are the sad situations where parents are neglectful, self-absorbed, and even abusive. But by and large, no matter how committed we are to our youth, we youth workers will never make the investment in loving a teenager that his or her parents make. By the time kids arrive in our youth groups, their parents have already put in 13 or more years of nurture and care. And when we graduate a class or move on to other churches, our focus tends to turn to other kids. Not so with the parents. They are parents of those kids for life. It's easy for us youth workers to fall into an unholy arrogance that sees our care and concern for teenagers as deeper and more real than that of their parents. To paraphrase Job 38, "Where were we when diapers needed to be changed, when homework required extra help, when tuition needed to be paid, when they needed sick-care?" Let's not suppose ourselves the God-appointed guardian of every kid in the youth group. We don't really want to carry that load. And it isn't ours to bear.

STRATEGIES FOR TEAMWORK

Strengthening ties between parents and teens hasn't been our forte as youth workers. More often than not, the teamwork of the teenager, youth worker, and parents looks a bit like the Three Stooges trying to hang wallpaper. In our efforts at family ministry, the majority of us assume the role of *commentator*, giving scriptural teaching and describing problems from a safe distance. Other youth workers take on the role of *dictator*, threatening kids with Bible passages guaranteed to scare them into loving and communicating with their parents. (Proverbs 30:17 is a favorite verse with this group.) But the approach by which we can best serve our role as both disciple-makers and bridge-builders is the role of *facilitator*—one who opens lines of communication between teens and parents and does whatever possible to help them understand each other.

I've already mentioned some excellent books that offer in-depth strategies along those lines. What follows are four broad categories of planning that can help us better fulfill our role as facilitators so our youth ministries are more firmly rooted in family ministry.

Informing Parents

Keeping parents informed builds their trust in us and helps them better understand what we are doing. There are any number of ways to keep parents in the loop:

Parent briefings. Host quarterly (at least) meetings for just the parents of your youth. These meetings can include everything from announcing the schedule of upcoming events to getting parental feedback on youth activities, to simply explaining how a certain event or activity fits into the overall scheme of programming. One can even use an evening like this to take the parents through a simulated youth group meeting—complete with worship, skits, Bible study, and food! I've had parents who became much more supportive after attending a parent briefing and finding out why we were doing what we were doing. Don't be discouraged by poor attendance. Give this time to build. Remember, this is only one of a broad range of strategies.

Parent newsletter and Web site. Lots of youth workers nowadays communicate with their kids through texting and Facebook. The youth ministry Web site, which seemed so edgy and up-to-date a few years ago, is now almost routinely ignored by most teenagers. But it can still be a great tool for parents who are less fluent in social networking. The site could still be intended for the group, but you would add a link for parents where you'd post any of the following: The youth group calendar, a blog/column by the youth worker, book reviews, recaps of recent youth events, and links to articles and other Web sites informing parents about youth culture.[18]

Youth group hotline. It's simple to arrange a hotline number that parents (and students) can call to get up-to-date information about the youth group schedule. The hotline with a brief recorded answer can prevent the all-too-common scenario of little Johnny charging away from the dinner table with the explanation that he's just remembered "there's-a-youth-group-activity-tonight-and-mom-and-dad-I-need-to-have-twenty-dollars-or-Duffy-says-I'll-be-kicked-out-of-youth-group!!" Parents can just call the hotline and get the scoop well in advance.

In-home family visit. In the words of one youth counselor, "You don't really know a teenager until you've eaten with him, met his family, and seen the walls of his bedroom." One youth minister I know has a business card on which he has printed underneath his name this phrase: "Available most nights of the week for dinner."

Information about community resources. Prepare a laminated sheet that includes relevant phone numbers, not only for youth group contacts, but also for community agencies that might provide support in times of crises: Suicide hotlines, crisis pregnancy center, substance abuse counselors, pizza delivery, etc. Again, it might be helpful to list relevant Web sites as well.

Assisting Parents

Parenting teenagers today can be scary business. The average parent of an adolescent is worried—worried about the child's welfare, moral choices, friends, education, future, complexion, and the fungus growing on the walls of their teen's bedroom! It's usually while parenting adolescents that we learn what it means to pray unceasingly! Parents of adolescents understand that we go through labor twice with every child; it's just that this second time, the pains can last for about seven years. That's why we in youth ministry need to sensitively assist parents in their task of nurturing their teens. Here are some additional suggestions for doing that:

Seminars. In Merton Strommen's comprehensive study of parental concerns, *The Five Cries of Parents*, he asked 10,457 parents about topics they would have "much interest" in learning about. Most of the responses were predictable, but they are worth noting:

70%	Helping children develop healthy concepts of right and wrong;
66%	How to deal with the question of drug use;
62%	How to better communicate with their children;
60%	Helping children grow in their faith;
47%	How to exercise effective discipline;
44%	How to talk about sex;
42%	How to get support from other parents (see below).[19]

One church organizes a three-to-four-week course annually for both parents *and* teenagers. The topic changes each year, as students move from grade 7 through 12. Obviously, content and learning are an important part of these courses, but the major intent is to build bridges between parents and teens—to have them learning about and talking about these issues together. In other words, this is not simply a forum where parents and teens listen to a youth leader talk about these issues. The youth leader's goal is to present content in a way that allows *parents and teens to listen to each other*. The topic list is helpful:

7th grade:	Community building;
8th grade:	Drugs and alcohol;
9th grade:	Sexuality;
10th grade:	Communication;
11th grade:	Decision-making;
12th grade:	Preparing for college/adulthood.[20]

There would also be room, of course, for parent-only workshops. Hosting parent seminars about issues related to raising healthy teens can build bridges between the parents of teens in your group and may even be a means of outreach to the community at large. Invite a noted speaker to address a specific topic, or show one of the video seminars on the market.[21] Here's a sampling of additional topics that one might use:

"How to Pay for Your Child's Education"

"How to Keep Your Kids Free From Drugs"

"Bullying"

"Adolescent Suicide and Teenage Depression"

"Self-Injury: What Is It, and How Should a Parent Respond?"

"Family Traditions: The Gift of Memories"

"Eating Disorders and the Tyranny of Body Image"

"Social Networking: Is Facebook Taking up Too Much Face-Time in My Teenager's Life?"

"Lava Lamps: Making a House a Home"

Support groups. A group of youth workers were meeting at a Denver hotel to discuss parent-teen ministry. Following their enthusiastic interaction, a server on the hotel staff approached the youth worker who'd chaired the session. With tears in her eyes, the server said, "I couldn't help but overhear your discussions today. Please, when you do your seminars, tell people how lonely it can be to be the parent of a teenager." Her remark reminds us that organizing support groups is another important way we can assist parents. These occasional get-togethers or ongoing forums allow parents to discuss issues and questions, or to share some of the difficulties they face. The support groups can be for all parents or specialized to focus on a particular concern (substance abuse, teen pregnancy, runaways, single parenting). Perhaps there could even be a separate Facebook group for parents who want to participate.

Some parent support groups have found these kinds of gatherings help them develop common ground rules for curfew, in-house parties, and the like. If a group of parents agree they expect their teens to be in by 11:30 p.m., their solidarity can cut down on the dissension that begins with remarks like, "Well, Calenthia's mom lets her stay out later."

Opportunities for guided interaction. As often as possible, stage opportunities for teenagers to be in dialogue with their parents and other adults. Youth workers can serve as facilitators, leading students and parents in guided exercises. For example, it might be as simple as a Sunday school class in which teenagers interview parents—not about being parents, but about the pressures of being adults, husbands, wives, breadwinners. A forum like this can help students appreciate the world in which their parents function. What are my parents' concerns? What pressures do they face? And, of course, in the process, we are building bridges of communication.

Or, turn the interview around and allow some adults to interview teenagers about their lives: What's it really like at the high school? Why do they like that music? What do they expect from their parents? How can their parents best support them? Why do they wear their pants around their thighs? Although it's naive to expect total candor, parents can get a feel for teenagers' attitudes about music, styles, fads, and so forth. Teenagers are surprisingly willing to talk if they feel adults are interested.

Another communication exercise is to show both parents and teens a picture of an adult and an adolescent obviously having an argument, and then invite everyone to suggest what the argument is about. Allow the parents and the youth to gather in separate groups and come up with their scenarios independently, then bring them back together for dialogue. Ask questions about how the parent and teenager in the picture are feeling. How could they have avoided this argument?

Also, we can use role plays of teenagers facing their parents in various familiar situations—asking for the car, coming home after curfew, wanting money, or getting caught telling a lie. When doing these kinds of role plays, put parents in the roles of the teens and the teens in the roles of the parents. Then talk about the role play as a group.

Ask youth to write letters from their parents explaining why they (the parents) are running away from home. Ask parents to do the same—imagining they are in their kids' shoes, and writing a letter explaining why they've decided to run away. Allow both parties to read and discuss their letters. Encourage kids to reflect on what would it be like to be in their parents' roles. What would be good about it? What wouldn't be so good? Have parents ask themselves the same question: "What would it be like to be my teenage son or daughter?"

Lead adults through an exercise of remembering "the way we were," journeying with parents back into their teenage years to recall everything from which songs were popular, to which clothes were in fashion, to what the major areas of dispute were between them and their parents. One youth group has an annual *Back to the Future* night when parents bring in their old yearbooks and are asked to show and explain five pictures from them. These kinds of exercises facilitate parent–teen communication by giving kids and parents a chance to laugh together, listen to each other, and see each other as real people. There are a lot of teenagers who think their parents were born at age 40. Guided interaction can be a way of breaking through some of the stereotypes.

Family counseling. Despite all our efforts, there will be times when we need to intervene in difficult situations by guiding the whole family through a counseling session. In those situations, our role is not to act as amateur psychiatrists, but simply to be a third party who listens, interprets, keeps everybody honest, and (perhaps) referees. Although *there will be times when the most appropriate response is to refer the family to professional counseling*, sometimes families just need someone who can translate to make sure each party is hearing what the other is saying.

Big aunt/big uncle. There are times when kids growing up in single-parent households can benefit greatly from the presence of other caring adults. A teenage girl from a divorced family sometimes needs a "mom," even if it's not her real mom, or a boy might need a father figure for one-on-one basketball or a father-son retreat. The church can assist single parents by initiating a "big aunt/big uncle" program through which other adult church members are invited to "adopt" one of the youth group kids.

Parenting resource library. Begin collecting tapes, videos, and books relevant to the parents of adolescents. I've found that parents genuinely appreciate this kind of assistance, which allows them to receive help from us without having to actually tell us everything.

Encouraging Parents

Parenting teenagers can be discouraging. Many parents find that no one talks to them about their teenager unless the child has done something wrong. Youth workers can build strong friendships with parents simply by affirming and encouraging them regarding their kids.

Parent-appreciation events. Parent Sunday, thank-you dinners, mother-daughter or father-son events—there are lots of ways to affirm parents. One fun approach is to allow youth to host a dinner for their parents, preparing and serving the food, performing a skit or some kind of entertainment, and then letting several kids talk about what they appreciate about their parents.

Thank-you notes/e-mails/texts/phone calls. Parents always open a note from someone working with their teenager with a tinge of dread. What did she do wrong this time? Adults who work with the youth group should be encouraged to utilize the Character Trait ID strategy. The strategy begins when an adult catches one of the students in the act of doing something good. The adult identifies a character trait demonstrated in the student's behavior and then calls or writes the mom or dad to relate the incident. The youth worker describes the positive trait by saying, "It reminded me of something you would do," or, "If that were my son or daughter, that would make me very proud." For example, "When Jon ran over Mrs. Henderson in the church parking lot last Sunday, I noticed that he slowed down the car to allow her to get up. And I thought to myself, you know what? That's something his mother would do. Keep up the good work!"

Attending special events in the life of the student. Attending special events, concerts, recitals, sports games, and award ceremonies of the kids in our youth group offers encouragement not just to the teens but also to their parents. When we show up at the oboe recital or the Eagle Scout ceremony, parents realize there are a million other places we could be (and would probably rather be!) Our voluntary presence represents a special vote of encouragement.

Involving Parents

Youth ministry is a shared ministry. At its best, it incorporates the efforts of teenagers, their parents, and the youth workers. Sometimes we are shy about parents ministering with their own kids, but there are some significant strategies for involving parents in our youth ministries.

Care through prayer. Parents can meet weekly to pray for the youth ministry. Prayer garners support for the youth group from people who "don't know what to do" or "don't know how to help." People are not as quick to complain about a ministry they've been praying for consistently. Another added benefit: God answers prayer!

Organize a parents' council. One youth worker I know meets regularly with a team of parents who advise him about the junior high ministry. Sharing ownership of the ministry with the parents equips him to better handle parental complaints. He can always say, "Well, we discussed this matter with the Parents Council, and they felt it wouldn't be any problem." Plus, it can be a means for youth workers (especially younger ones) to gain the benefit of the parents' perspectives. For example, the gung ho, 23-year-old youth worker itching to make kids radical for Jesus might think an "Urban Plunge" solo overnight for junior-highers on the city streets seems like a great idea: "We'll challenge each kid to spend a night on the streets alone, to see what it's like to be really needy! It could be life-changing." Uh...yeah, but parents have a way of putting a different spin on these opportunities, and it might be just the sort of input that could avoid some major conflict.

Involve parents in youth meetings. One of our most memorable youth meetings was the night we brought three pairs of parents in for a discussion of dating. Utilizing a *Newlywed Game* format, we interviewed the moms and dads separately, and then brought the spouses back into the room to compare their answers to various questions. Parents were asked questions about their dating patterns: *Who was the first to say, "I love you?" Where was your first kiss? How did the actual marriage proposal happen?"* This helped students see their parents as real people who really did know what it was like to be in love and date. The students thought it was a riot. We had some great laughs, a few decent arguments, and only one divorce (just kidding).

There's no reason these kinds of activities couldn't happen on a regular basis. I'm not suggesting parents need to be invited to every youth group function.

But remember DeVries's dictum: "If it works with youth, try it with youth and parents together."[22]

Utilize parents in short-term service. When Walt Mueller of the Center for Parent and Youth Understanding was a youth pastor in suburban Philadelphia, he would periodically distribute parental involvement sheets that parents could use to volunteer their services to the group.

BREAKAWAY PARENTAL INVOLVEMENT SHEET

Your name:____

Phone Number:______________________________________

Please fill out and return to Walt Mueller by January 4.

Check any boxes that apply to you.

I WILL HELP WITH THE FOLLOWING EVENTS:

January 11: Family Potluck/Multimedia

- ☐ Set Up
- ☐ Kitchen Help

January 19: Third Day concert

- ☐ Drive Bus
- ☐ Drive Van
- ☐ Chaperone

January 23: Ski Trip

- ☐ Drive Bus
- ☐ Drive Van
- ☐ Chaperone

January 30: Family Fun Night at Lakeside

☐ Drive Bus

February 13: Women of Faith Gun Show

☐ Drive Bus

☐ Drive Van

☐ Chaperone

February 20: 76ers Game

☐ Drive Bus

☐ Drive Van

☐ Chaperone

March 6: Senior High Spaghetti Lock-In

☐ Drive Van

☐ Chaperone

☐ Cooking Help

MINISTRY IN THE CROSSFIRE

Our Lord described the role of the peacemaker as "blessed," but it has its ups and downs along the way. One pitfall for any youth worker who intervenes in a parent-teen conflict is the temptation to manipulate or side against one party to gain the approval and admiration of the other party. We also need to guard against becoming the blocker when a teenager wants to do an end-run around his or her parents.

We must also be aware that there are times when protecting confidences and remaining quiet about a teenager's problem steals from the parents their appointed role. We dare not take this liberty. To be sure, we have a sacred responsibility to maintain strictest confidence when students share with us their secrets, but certain kinds of information must be shared with parents, or we hinder their ability to carry out their God-ordained responsibilities.

Finally, we must resist the temptation to give up on a family. Some families may appear so dysfunctional that healing is impossible, but God can intervene. There are some parents who seem to want nothing to do with their children—whether it involves church, school, or any other area of a teen's life. But even then, God can work his purposes in young people. Just as surely as

Jesus healed people who were blind and lame, he can heal bruised and broken families.

The one-eared Mickey Mouse is dead. Wise youth workers recognize we have a significant and sacred role as a facilitator of family relationships—both the family that lives at a kid's house and the larger family that gathers in the house of worship. Whether that means involving, informing, assisting, or encouraging, we are called to be agents of reconciliation. Without question, this can be one of the more delicate tasks of youth ministry. But in the long run, we're not just building ministries; we're building teenagers into mature, healthy adult disciples of Jesus Christ. And that doesn't happen just through strong programs; it happens through strong families.

CHAPTER 9

Budgeting and Finance: Squeezing Blood from Turnips

"No one can serve two masters. Either you will hate the one and love the other, or you will be devoted to the one and despise the other. You cannot serve both God and Money."
(Matthew 6:24)

The first time I heard the evangelist Billy Graham in person it was at a pastors' seminar in North Carolina. I appreciated the chance to hear from this wise and fruitful servant in a pastor-to-(youth)-pastor context, and I took his words very much to heart as he spoke about the importance of personal integrity, maintaining the heart, the priority of family, and the temptations of life in ministry. But what stayed with me at the end of the day were these words: "The two main pitfalls of people in ministry are abuse of sex and abuse of money. Both have very real power, and both have the capacity to destroy people and ministries."

If anyone doubted his words that day (and I doubt many did), no one would do so today. Like wrecked cars on the side of a road, the burned out and gutted remains of too many ministries litter the church landscape because of a leader's poor choices in relation to sex or money. Listening to Billy Graham that day, we all understood he wasn't saying money is bad any more than he was saying sex is bad (can I get an "Amen"?). He was simply stating what folks in ministry have known all the way back at least as far as the apostle Paul: That sex and money have a very strong gravitational pull.

You may be a little disappointed (or relieved?) to hear that we are not going to address the sex issue in this book. But in a book on youth ministry administration, clearly we have to talk about money.

Whether he was writing a letter to the brethren in Thessalonica (1 Thessalonians 2:3-6, 9) or saying a final farewell to the church in Ephesus (Acts 20), the apostle Paul was quick to recall his financial dealings as proof of his love for Christ and of the sincerity of his calling. It's as if Paul recognized that his management of personal and ministry finances was a major way people would judge the integrity of his ministry. And 2,000 years later, church youth workers should understand we are under no less scrutiny in the way we steward ministry funds and personal finances. In the words of Titus 1:7, "Since an overseer manages God's household, he must be blameless—not overbearing, not quick-tempered, not given to drunkenness, not violent, not pursuing dishonest gain."

FUNDAMENTAL FACTS ABOUT FINANCES

Our handling of personal and ministry finances takes on even more importance in light of the following five basic facts:

Fact 1: Most youth ministers are not highly trained handlers of money. Our natural interests don't typically include budgeting and quarterly reports. If we're paid youth workers, we've probably discovered that a youth pastor's salary doesn't require that we spend much time working through investment portfolios. In one survey of both congregational and parachurch youth workers in which respondents were asked what they "really dislike" about their church or ministry organization, finances were a major source of stress, particularly among those who had to raise their own support.[1] We would rather focus on people than pennies. The training a youth pastor receives at the average Bible college or seminary is heavy on theology and light on financial management—which is unfortunate because of fact number two.

Fact 2: It's not unusual for youth ministers to deal with a heavy cash flow. An overseas mission trip can easily generate a budget of several thousand dollars. With a youth group of 50 teenagers, summer camp fees generate a cash flow of as much as $5,000. Web site design, food, software upgrades, food, printing, food, activity fees, food, transportation, or even an afternoon at the climbing gym or roller skating rink can be surprisingly costly. Anyone involved in the nuts and bolts of youth ministry knows that both nuts and bolts cost money. A lot of cash passes through our hands. (Sad to say, it usually passes through without stopping for a longer visit.) The frightening part is that we can hang ourselves decisively with as little as a few hundred dollars worth of rope.

Fact 3: Ironically, money management is one of the main criteria by which our congregations will judge our ministries. Typically, the members of the churches we serve won't know about the retreats, the growing turnout for Bible study, or the incredible ministry of one-on-one discipleship. But they will hear how the youth program overspent its funds or wants to increase its budget.

Fact 4: Authority equals the power to spend funds. A youth worker who is allowed to drive the van to the garage, find out what's wrong, and get an estimate for repairs, but who is not allowed to actually authorize repairs to the van without reporting to the C.E. board, doesn't really have authority for maintenance and upkeep of the van. The committee to whom that youth pastor reports is really responsible for van upkeep. The youth minister is only doing the committee's leg work. I don't mean to sound cynical or negative; it's simply a fact of life. If one doesn't have the authority to spend funds in carrying out a ministry (within a reasonable range of cost), then that person doesn't really have authority over that area of ministry.

I once worked for a church that, at my request, divided the annual youth budget by twelve and then gave us that amount on a monthly basis. We deposited the funds in a youth group account to spend at our discretion. It was great;

it gave us full responsibility. We could buy media gear, food, curriculum, or balloons without having to requisition three committees, get a presidential order, and cast lots. On the other hand, *full responsibility requires full accountability.* We had to be very careful to document how and why we spent every dollar, because we were well aware of the potential abuses in the system. There needs to be a balance between authority to spend and accountability for spending.

Fact 5: Youth ministry is an expensive proposition. Youth ministry probably costs more dollars-per-person-involved than any other ministry in the average local church. That's just part of the nature of the beast. When the five-year-olds finish a week of vacation Bible school, they are each given a little comb or key ring as a prize—total cost to the budget: three dollars. But at the high school graduation banquet, the gift of a comb or key ring just doesn't elicit the same excitement.

To some degree, the high cost of youth ministry is caused by the fact that teenagers have their own money and aren't dependent on the church for recreation and leisure activities. In a sense, the youth program is competing for the attention of students. Recognizing that most youth can access enough money to choose from many options outside of the church forces us to allocate more money for attractive, quality programming. And of course, this is complicated further by the fact that students don't expect to pay for church activities. Their unspoken assumption is that they are doing us a favor by being there. So youth ministry can be a costly enterprise.

PLANNING A BUDGET

When some of us hear about planning a budget, we feel a smirk coming on. It isn't hard to develop a plan for spending the zero dollars a year allocated to the youth ministry. Sometimes we feel like the Israelites under Pharaoh; we're being asked to make bricks without straw (Exodus 5:7). But whether the budget is large, small, or non-existent, all of us in youth ministry leadership have a responsibility to be faithful stewards of ministry funds. Certainly, one element of that responsibility is setting forth a fair and workable budget.

When we talk about establishing a budget, we're talking about financial planning that's done with enough care, foresight, and precision to enable faithful stewards of God's resources to effectively allocate the funds needed. Paul Borthwick suggests the best place to begin this process is by asking two questions:

1. What is the budget history of our church or organization?

2. What are we planning to do with our program over the long-term?[2]

Let's take some time to consider concerns in each of these areas.

Examining Budget History

Here are some key questions to keep in mind in looking back at past budgets for your church or group:

• *How does the church or organization calculate its budget year?* The budget year is sometimes referred to as a *fiscal year,* and there are typically two approaches used. One approach simply uses the calendar year—so the budget covers all income and spending from January 1 through December 31. The second, equally common, approach is for the organization to designate another 12-month period as its fiscal year. It could be July 1 through June 30, or September 1 through August 31. The fiscal pattern used depends on the unique ministry of that church or organization.

• *According to previous budgets, how much money has been allocated to the youth program over the last five years?* Has the figure held steady each year, or has there been an increase or decrease? What is the average percentage of increase or decrease in the budget over than span of time? If the figure has fluctuated, what were the criteria by which it was increased or decreased? The budget history will provide some *baseline* figures that will set the frame for the remainder of the budget picture. Without that baseline figure, preparing a budget is a shot in the dark. It's like wallpapering a room without laying a plumb line; we really have no sense of true up or down.

Katie had only been able to get her budget increased in one of the preceding four years, but the increase that year was almost 8 percent. By averaging that single 8 percent increase over the four-year period, she was able to go before the board in year five and justify an annual increase of 2 percent. If she'd had only the budget information from the previous year, she would not have been able to make her case. She needed a four- to five-year picture to see the pattern.

• *According to previous budgets, what is the budgeted money supposed to cover?* For example, at Lancaster Crossing Church, the youth budget never included expenses associated with the Sunday school program. Monies for purchasing Sunday school curricula had always come out of the Christian education budget. When the Christian education committee decided it didn't want responsibility for funding the youth Sunday school program, Lori had to request a sizable increase in the youth budget. But she wasn't actually proposing a larger budget; she was proposing that a line item that had previously been under the Christian education budget be moved to the youth ministry budget. Had she not made it clear to the finance committee that the youth budget had never before been used to fund youth Sunday school, she could not have justified such a disproportionate increase.

• *According to previous budgets, who controls the purse, and how does one gain access to budgeted funds?* I laugh about it now (sort of), but I can still remember playing tug-of-war with the church treasurer during my first full-time youth pastorate whenever I tried to access money budgeted to the youth ministry.

Making any purchase above my petty cash allotment of $50—whether it was ordering curricula or arranging for retreat deposits—was a tedious process, requiring several signed requisitions, committee approval, shameless pleading (which I was willing to do if necessary), and the promise of my firstborn child. I was reminded of the basic principle I'd learned playing Monopoly as a little boy: It is not always the banker who controls the flow of money; sometimes it's the one sitting closest to the bank! When evaluating an organization's budget process, find out who is sitting closest to the money.

Examining Long-Term Goals

The second consideration when budgeting involves what we are planning to do with our program over the long term. This is simply the process of taking a careful inventory of present *and future* need:

• *What are your dreams for the ministry, and what will it cost to accomplish these dreams?* How many retreats will there be? What other major projects should we be planning for?

• *Are there capital improvements that need to be factored in?* Capital improvements are any purchases that actually add to the ministry's assets (net value). For example, suppose we've decided to take advantage of the chance to buy some used backpacking gear, or redo the carpeting in the youth room, or replace the old data projector with one that has a working bulb, or put an upgraded Jacuzzi in the youth pastor's office. Unlike a purchase of curricula that's given out to teenagers, or food that's consumed at meetings, or monies paid out for the summer calendars given to every group member, these purchases add to the assets of the youth ministry. They are capital outlays or purchases.

• *What will it cost to subsidize students who can't afford to pay full price for some of the youth activities?*

• *What are the maintenance costs for equipment and facilities we already own?*

• *Does this budget plan for growth?*

• *Does this budget take into account price increases?*

• *Does this budget represent actual need?* For example, when volunteers pay their own way for an activity or retreat, it hides the actual cost of the event. Of course, it's generous and thoughtful for volunteers to subsidize their involvement in this way. But what about when those volunteers move on? Will the next volunteers be able to continue such largesse? If not, the added cost will look like a disproportionate budget increase when, in fact, someone is now simply seeing the cost for what it is. Even though it's done for all the right reasons, I'm convinced it's better for the ministry to discourage volunteers from subsidizing their costs. The same is true for the youth worker who spends her own money to buy supplies without seeking reimbursement. It's a wonderful gesture, but it camouflages the actual costs of the ministry.

Avoiding Budget Traps

Thinking about the budget history requires a backward look; thinking about future needs requires a forward look. Both are important. But be warned: There are some common mistakes that can distort our views.[3]

1. **The line-item trap:** In looking over a budget, remember that the money visible for the specific line item "youth ministry" may not represent the total funding available for youth ministry. There may be additional income under one or more line item categories. For example, there may be a line in the "missions" budget that shows money allocated to a youth missions trip, or funds listed under "staff" that are actually allocated for youth ministry interns.

2. **The higher-priority-means-more-money trap:** Be careful not to fall into the trap of assuming that giving more money to a ministry or program will raise its status or make it a higher priority. That assumption is based on a false premise—that money is the only measure of a ministry's status or value. In fact, every church has three budgets, and only one of them involves money. There is, to be sure, *the financial budget,* which defines how funds are dispersed, but there is also a *time budget* (How much time do members allocate to this ministry?) and a *pulpit recognition budget* (How often does the ministry get some sort of mention or shout-out from the pulpit?). Both time and recognition have value just as money does.

3. **The easy-compromise trap:** Both the missions committee and the youth ministry at St. David's Community Church wanted a 10 percent increase in their respective budgets. But the finance committee agreed there was only enough money to provide for about half the total increase the two programs had requested. Rather than trying to hammer out which budget line deserved which amount of money, both ministries were simply given a 5 percent increase. It was an expedient decision, and it prevented the finance committee making some harder choices, but it didn't clearly reflect the specific value of budget projections made by either ministry.

DISCIPLINE AND PRIORITIES

Unfortunately, for a lot of youth workers, "advance planning" means thinking four to ten weeks ahead. Good budget planning usually requires thinking about 15-18 months ahead. For example, if the budget for the next calendar year (Jan-Dec) is voted on in September, then the youth leadership team must decide in broad terms by August what it plans to accomplish through December of the following year. That's a 16-month lead time.

To make wise planning decisions about our ministries, we need accurate information gathered through careful research. "Winging it" is a good way to crash. Five years of budget totals give a picture broad enough to encompass the typical fluctuations of any youth ministry.

• *If our group continues to grow or decrease at its present rate, how many students are we apt to be working with?* Always begin your budgeting process with enrollment projections. If you plan for no growth, you'll probably achieve it.

• *How much has the group typically been able to count on through fundraising?*

• *How much has the group been spending per active student?* I know of one youth worker who was able to demonstrate to his church board that even though his budget was increasing, he was actually spending less money (good trick!). He thoroughly researched how much money was currently being spent per active student, and then divided his total proposed budget by the projected attendance increase based on the past history of his group. He showed that even with the budget increase, he would actually be spending less money per active student than in the previous year. His argument for the increase must have been convincing—the ministry got the funds he requested.

• *Have we prayed through budget priorities?* Prioritizing is the discipline of deciding which budget items are most important to the ongoing program. If the budget has to be cut back, which items will be erased first? If we can only take two retreats next year instead of four, which two will they be? If we must choose between sports gear and a mission-trip scholarship, which will we choose? Can we operate safely if we put off overhauling the van for another year? Prioritizing requires that we go back through the budget and tag certain items as more important than others. It's coming up with plans B, C, and D, in case we can't afford plan A.

When making purchases, make sure to exercise due diligence. Is this good quality equipment, and are you paying a fair price? For larger purchases it's usually wise to get at least three bids, so you can know (and prove) you paid the best price. Don't limit yourself to Christian-owned businesses; except in rare circumstances, getting the best price for the best service is the best stewardship. Speaking of stewardship, ask your church treasurer about a tax-exempt number. No need to render unto Caesar any more sales tax than necessary.

One method some churches use to build discipline and control into the budget is a system of *zero-based budgeting*. Perhaps, reading the word *zero*, you're thinking, "That sounds like our system!" But, in fact, zero-based budgeting is a very specific system in which the budgeting process begins with a zero in every projected expense line—no money is allocated to any program.[4] The church must then examine and approve every planned expenditure that goes in the budget. Church leaders are forced to evaluate every expense over against the church's total mission.

While this may sound like a tedious (nice word for *cheap*?) approach, it has some merit. First, it requires each ministry to do a thoughtful, annual reevaluation of its values, objectives, and strategies each year. Just using figures from the previous year, which were probably based on those of the year before that, which were based on the year before that, is not particularly good stewardship. Secondly, zero-based budgeting builds in direct accountability. If you say you can do the retreat with the $500 you proposed in your budget, you will be held accountable to "deliver" that retreat for $500. If, as the time draws closer, you decide it will require more money, the budget committee can say, "You have not because you asked not..." Finally, zero-based budgeting keeps everyone's eye on the ball: The youth worker is making sure she is wisely managing funds and planning ahead, and the supervising boards are attentive to needs because they are responsible for approving expenditures. Note that this does not negate *Fact 4* (above) and the relationship between authority and the power to spend funds. The question is this: Once the funds have been allocated, based on whatever budgeting method is used, does the youth worker have authority to spend that money?

INCOME SOURCES

Most of our discussion so far has been on the expense side of the ledger. But, obviously, good stewardship requires that we also think in terms of income. After we've come up with credible projections about financial needs and goals for our programs, we're ready to ask how we're going to come up with this money. In a traditional congregational ministry, we may have access to funds allocated through the overall budget, but that's seldom enough.

Money Magazine reported in the early eighties that a congregation generally needs to have at least two hundred members to sustain its ministry without the church having to look for a financial bargain either in facilities, programming, or pastor's salary. Based on inflation, we can assume that figure has increased. And there are a lot of churches out there with fewer than two hundred people.

So where does the money come from? There are several alternative sources of funding:

Ask the Youth to Pay. One obvious way to fund the youth program is to have the youth involved help fund it. They are, after all, the direct beneficiaries, and most of them have the money. A recent *New York Times* article reported that most national surveys peg the average monthly allowance of older teenagers at $100 or above.[5] That's a lot of cash, and most of these students are not buying groceries, paying utilities, purchasing insurance, or making housing payments. Most of the money is being used for discretionary spending. The advantages of having the youth support the program are readily apparent. First of all, paying for the program gives teenagers more ownership in it. They are apt to more responsibly care for equipment and property if they know that their money has been used to make purchases. Holding the youth responsible for paying their own way also helps them learn the value of work and the discipline of earning money. Heavily subsidizing the program through the church budget or another source may be underwriting teenagers' bad spending habits instead of helping them out. We've all watched the kid with the camp scholarship bound off with cash in hand to buy junk food every time the van stops, while the kid who paid his own way waits behind because he lacks the cash.

On the other hand, what about the kids who can't come up with the money for the ski retreat? Are they cut out of the ministry? And what does student-subsidized funding do to evangelistic ministry or a ministry of nurture? Common sense and experience tells us youth won't be willing to fund the program until they have a more mature commitment to Christ, and they won't develop a more mature commitment to Christ without the program. Which comes first? Typical teenagers are willing, perhaps, to pay for something they want. It may be more difficult to get them to pay for something they need.

Grants and Subsidies from Other Sources. It takes some experience to learn how to write the kind of grant proposals that will move foundations to support a youth program. But a number of enterprising youth workers can testify that the money is there. The process begins by knocking on doors. Start with major corporations or large businesses in your area. Business people sometimes feel they have more to gain by supporting a local project than an international charity. We needn't always ask for money, either. Sometimes a car dealer will donate a van or mark it down drastically. One church in Minneapolis was able to get several free computers from the Apple Corporation to use in its after-school tutoring program.

The main warning is that grant funding can be habit forming—and may even bring an unhealthy dependency. Ministries of all kinds have compromised their visions because they were too indebted to some sugar daddy who started using money as leverage to control their programming. Look carefully for strings attached to corporate gifts.

Low-cost and No-cost Activities. When we talk about budgeting in my classes at Eastern University, we inevitably find ourselves discussing this question: Does money equal value in ministry? In other words, if we spend more money, will we see more fruit?

There are justifiable reasons why youth ministry is more expensive than some other ministries in the church, but it's a fallacy that youth ministries need to be ultra-expensive. Sometimes budget increases are just excuses for thoughtless spending. The real cost-cutter is getting past the mindset that says money is always the answer. It's long since out of print, but Dennis and Marilyn Benson's *Hard Times Catalogue for Youth Ministry* was one of the first youth ministry books to make a persuasive case that creativity, ingenuity, and hard work can often provide what hundreds of budgeted dollars cannot.[6]

FUNDRAISING

The most common source of added funding is, of course, fundraisers. Just typing the word makes me think of car washes, gift-wrapping sales, and standing at the bake sale booth quietly wondering, "Is this really why I went to seminary?"

There are four basic types of fundraisers:

1. *Sell a product:* light bulbs, fruitcakes, gift-wrapping paper, medicinal marijuana;
2. *Sell a service:* Your kids can sell their services as yard-cleaners, snow shovelers, fence painters, house cleaners, or just about anything someone might want done.
3. *Sell "stock":* One youth worker and his group sold "stock" to raise funds for the youth missions program. Church members were invited to invest in the lives of student missionaries. Youth corresponded with their shareholders before, during, and after the mission trip. Following the trip, everyone was invited to a shareholder's dinner to enjoy pictures, videos, and testimonies of the project.
4. *Sell opportunity:* This includes auctions that offer gifts and unique opportunities (dirt-biking with the youth pastor, ringing the church bells, getting to play drums in worship band, the chance to wear the pastor's robe and vestments at Halloween), as well as the myriad of "-athons" which invite people to pledge on the basis of some activity kids are doing such as rocking (waste of time), walking (good exercise), running (too good an exercise!), picking up trash (neat idea), shaving (sexist), biking (best in areas where there are no hills), fasting (good discipline, but makes you hungry), or burping (not recommended).

We'll look at a few of my favorite fundraising ideas a little later in the chapter, but before we go any further, let me point out what should already be obvious: *Youth ministry and fundraising are not synonymous.* I still have occasional nightmares about beginning a new youth ministry position, and opening the office closet on the first day to find myself knee-deep in candy bars, light bulbs, and greeting cards. I told the board unequivocally that I felt the church's youth ministry was worth the congregation's support; if I'd wanted to get into retail work, I'd have applied for a job at K-Mart. Much to the relief of our youth (the sales force) and their parents (the consumer force), we got out of the retail business.

Yet the amount of time some youth workers must devote to raising money remains most disconcerting. I grew up in a large, wealthy church with a nonexistent youth budget. We held retreats so we could plan fundraisers, and we held fundraisers so we could afford the next retreat where we'd plan the next fundraiser! Certainly, in some cases, fundraising is a necessary evil. But I worry that many youth workers spend so much time trying to fund their ministries that they have very little time or energy left to perform those ministries. I routinely remind congregations that it makes no sense to hire an archer unless they can afford to pay for bows and arrows. Requiring youth workers to do an excessive amount of fundraising takes too much time and energy away from the youth worker—time that should be allocated toward making disciples and not making money.

But the fact remains: Many youth ministers need to engage their kids in some level of fundraising efforts. So here are some important questions to ask before we jump into any fundraising event:

• *Does your church or sponsoring organization have a policy on fundraising?* Some congregations don't allow it. Some congregations couldn't live without it.

• *What is your theology of money?* In other words, do you truly believe God will provide for the needs of his people—and, if you do believe that, does that have any bearing on *how* God provides for those needs? Suppose we want our kids to attend camp, but there just aren't funds in the regular church budget to make it happen. Are bake sales, rock-a-thons, car washes, and auctions part of God's plan for funding the youth ministry? Are they our back-up plan? Should we assume we don't really need what we think we need since God didn't provide for it? Or, are we trusting that God is meeting our needs, not through the gifts of his people, but through people who like cupcakes or have dirty cars? Of course, God can meet our needs any way he wishes. But it's a discussion worth having.

• *Do fundraising projects align with our mission as a church or organization, or do they lead us off-task? And how do these fundraising projects shape people's perceptions of who we are and what we believe?* Some churches don't want to do fundraisers because of the perception that the church is always asking for money. Putting the worst possible spin on it, it could be said that fundraisers announce to the community, *We don't care about our teenagers enough to fund their program, so we're hoping you'll help us do it by buying items you don't really need.* That may be way too cynical, and it certainly isn't what we intend to say, but that may be the message people hear.

• *Do we have any guidelines about who can use the church facilities?* Obviously, one way a church or youth ministry can supplement income is by renting out its facilities. If the youth program has a gym, game room, coffee bar, or some sort of special facility, renting this space might be a great way to make use of the building. On the other hand, you'll want a pretty clear policy about the terms of use. If one of your students wants to host a Sweet 16 party in the youth room, that could be a great outreach. On the other hand, if you get a call from the fraternity guys over at Phi Lusta Booza, you're going to have to think hard about making the place available. Who can use the church's name and facilities?

• *Who approves a fundraising activity?* Who grants permission for the youth group to have a car and pet wash, but, perhaps, draws the line at the medicinal marijuana sale?

• *How will the money be handled?* Make sure you've established a clear procedure that assures money accrued from the fundraiser goes to the proper place. Be prepared to file a brief-but-thorough follow-up report that gives public account (to any who want to see it) of how much money was taken in, what it cost to do the fundraiser, and how the collected funds were dispersed.

• *Are there legal issues?* Talk with a lawyer to assure you don't do anything that might jeopardize the church's tax-exempt status (or your status as a person with no police record). If you aren't clear how this could be a problem, Google *Jim Bakker* and *PTL Club*.

FAVORITE FUNDRAISING IDEAS

I have three simple criteria for any good fundraiser:

1. It needs to be quick (three weeks or less).

2. It needs to involve a maximum number of youth doing something useful or fun.

3. It needs to make lots of money!

The following are some ideas that, for the most part, live up to these standards:

Door-to-Door Car Wash. Rather than face the obstacle of getting people to bring their cars to your group for a wash, the Door-to-Door Car Wash sends car-wash teams into the neighborhood. Teens work their way down both sides of the street ringing doorbells and asking people if they would like their cars washed. The customers pay whatever they wish. Instead of washing 20 cars in the church parking lot over a five-hour period, a group that moves well can wash three times as many cars going door-to-door.

Free Car Wash. One of the all-time great fundraisers, the Free Car Wash involves a three-phase strategy.[7]

Phase One: Youth canvass the town to collect names, addresses, and pledges based on how many cars the group will wash on the day of the car wash. To help pledgers decide how much they are willing to pledge, give them a ballpark figure of how many cars the group might wash. If, for example, 20 students can each get 10 pledges of just a dime per washed car, the youth group will earn $20 every time they wash a car.

Phase Two: Host a *free* car wash for all comers. Ask local merchants to provide food for working students, jack up some tunes in the parking lot, and make it a party! Post a student in the street with a sign that says, "Free Car Wash." As cars enter the lot, a student requests the driver's name and address to verify the final total of cars washed and gives each driver a letter telling how the youth group will use the money received from pledges.

Phase Three: Go back and collect the money from those who pledged.

We had 85 students active in our youth ministry. We felt we could reasonably assume that at least 30 students would be able to collect 20 pledges of five cents each. That's $30 total per car washed. We knew from experience that we could use two hoses from two different buildings and, using "Y adapters," we could run two hoses from each source. That gave us four washing stations, each of which was staffed by six students. There were two students on each side of the car, plus one in front and one in back. There was one adult leader at each washing station for "quality control."

When we held our annual free car wash, cars were backed up in both directions on the street in front of our church. They would turn into our parking lot, get washed at one of the four stations, and pull on through the church lot, departing by the other entrance. We were able to wash about four cars every five minutes, which meant we were earning approximately $120 every five minutes. That's what I call a fundraiser! And that's why I dropped out of youth ministry to franchise the idea! (Not true.)

Scripture-athon. This "-athon" strategy solicits pledges on the basis of how many verses of Scripture can be memorized by kids in the youth group. The more Scripture the youth memorize, the more pledge money they collect. While I admit this may not be the best way to initiate interest in Scripture memorization, it seems a better use of time than having kids spend 12 hours in a rocking chair, rocking for pledges.

Shave-athon. The idea here is to invite everyone in the congregation to grow a beard (especially the women). Then hold an auction night in which people bid for the right to shave a certain person's beard. This may not provide a useful service (except in some cases!), but it would probably be a fun family-night activity.

BMX Competition. Several years ago, while serving as a youth minister at a church in San Juan Capistrano, California, Ridge Burns raised money by hosting a BMX biking competition in the church parking lot. Contestants paid to enter the competition in exchange for T-shirts, trophies, and the chance to compete for prizes. This event not only raised some money, but introduced the church to some students who might never otherwise come on the church property.

Home Building. Another ingenious fundraising strategy was developed by Young Life of Kansas City. They recruited ten adults from their local support committee to volunteer to build a house with a team from Habitat for Humanity. Then they asked each of those ten people to raise from acquaintances some donations for their work, all of which went to Young Life. The Young Life construction volunteers worked a combined total of 240 hours building homes for the homeless, raising $16,000 for the local budget of Young Life as a side benefit.

Bake Sale. For several years Young Life in Owatonna, Minnesota (a community of 20,000) joined a local radio station in co-sponsoring an annual cake auction. The strategy of the project was to sell cakes marketed in different ways. For example, 100 cakes were auctioned off to the highest bidder, and another 40 sold for a donation of $20 each. About one-third of the cakes have hidden inside them gift certificates donated by local merchants. That boosts the bidding significantly (and makes folks a little more cautious when they eat). The whole affair, well supported by the community, takes place on a Saturday in the lobby of a local bank. One year alone they raised $13,000.

THE FINAL PRODUCT: PREPARING THE BUDGET

Having taken into account both sides of the budget ledger—possible expenses and possible sources of income—we move to the final stage of the process. We're ready to draw up a readable, usable budget. The following sample models one possible layout and format of a youth-ministry budget.[8]

PROPOSED BUDGET: STUDENT MINISTRY

Wesley Baptist Church

INCOME:

A. Congregational Budget:	$4,100
B. Fund-Raising:	$3,300
C. Grants:	$500
D. Revenue Raised Through Youth Activities:	$750
Funds from Other Budget Sources:	
Sunday School Budget:	$500
TOTAL PROJECTED INCOME:	***$9,150***

EXPENSE:

A. CURRICULUM:

1. Cornerstone Bible Study:	
Junior High	$200
Senior High	$400
2. Covenant Group:	
Quiet Time Diary	$300
Study Materials	$250
3. Summer Trips:	
Study Materials	$200
4. Sunday School (7-12):	
Five classes	$435
Curriculum Total	***$1,785***

B. RETREATS:	
1. Travel:	
Sumatanga (Retreat)	$400
Winter	$400
Covenant Group	$150
Backpacking	$150
Summer Trip	$400
Fall Retreat	$400
Sub-total	*$1,900*
2. Honoraria:	
Sumatanga	$400
Winter	$400
Summer	$400
Fall	$400
Sub-total:	*$1600*
3. Scholarships	$500
4. Covenant Group Retreat Housing	$150
5. Ministry Team Expenses	$500
Retreat Total	***$4,650***

C. EQUIPMENT:	
1. Maintenance:	
Shelving, Curtains for youth room, displays	$100
Sports Gear	$200
Office Equipment	$400
2. Resource Materials	$150
3. Media Supplies, Software	$500
Equipment Total	***$1,350***

D. INSURANCE:

1. Automobile N/A Covered by general policy of the congregation

E. FOOD:

1. Covenant Group:

Weekly Mtgs	$350
Retreats (2)	$400
2. Sunday School: Drinks and Doughnuts	$400
3. Special: Halloween, Summer program, etc	$200
Food Total	***$1,350***
TOTAL EXPENSES (Excluding items noted below)	***$9,135***

Additional Items:

Youth Minister's Travel (comes out of Staff Budget)	$900
Continuing Education (comes out of Staff Budget)	$500
Summer Missions Trip (comes out of Mission Committee budget)	N/A

Note that this does not include these youth program-related items:

Postage expense

Printing costs

Telephone costs

The above information is respectfully submitted by David Williams, Minister with Youth.

____

Signature Date

Most of the budget is self-explanatory, but two ideas deserve more attention.

Budget Organization. This budget is broken down into five broad categories of expense: Curriculum, retreats, equipment, insurance, and food. At the end it lists a few additional ministry-related expenses that get folded into the overall church budget (such as continuing education, postage, etc.). These could vary, of course, depending on the ministry context. While it's possible to break down the budget in several different ways, what is most important is that it be broken down into components small enough to deal with. Asterisks are used to clarify in some way items not covered under the budget or items covered by another department's budget.

Appropriate Information. Budgets should provide enough information so that readers can clearly understand what the money pays for, but not so much information that people easily get sidetracked by details they might disagree with. For example, there's no need for a budget to specify which curriculum you're using, who the speakers are, or where the retreats will be. People have a right to take potshots at your budget, but why take pains to provide them with ammunition?

SOUND FINANCIAL POLICY

Once you have a working budget plan in place, there remain only a few final details necessary to hammer out a sound financial policy. These elements may already be codified somewhere in your church or organization's official documents, or they may need to be established. But, in any case, a wise youth worker will want clarity on these financial issues:[9]

• *What is the process for approving larger purchases?* Ideally, approval will not come from the same person who prepares the checks. Too frequently we hear news stories about some financial officer of a PTO or a Neighborhood Football Program who used organizational funds to fund personal expenses. The best way to protect against even the appearance of this kind of misuse is to have big-ticket purchases approved by someone other than the person who prepares the checks. Likewise, the person who prepares the checks should not be authorized to sign them.

• *Make sure there is a process whereby expenses can be reimbursed.* It should be as simple as possible, with prompt reimbursement and careful accountability (expense receipts should be made available to the treasurer).

• *Work with your Board to establish a scholarship fund for students who could not otherwise afford to participate in youth group activities.* Where will that money come from? By what criteria will people qualify for this help? How will the monies be dispersed?

• *Make certain there are clear policies regarding the reimbursement of travel expenses.* The IRS offers guidelines (read: commandments, not suggestions) about how much can be reimbursed for mileage, hotels, and food. That information is available online.

Again, the rule of thumb here is to keep everything exposed to daylight. Avoid even the appearance of evil.

THE JUDAS EXAMPLE

Money is a fact of life. We know Jesus and the disciples worked with some kind of treasury because we read that Judas kept the purse. We also know the last chapter in Judas' life was one of betrayal and tragedy. Whether it was the money that finally got to Judas, or some other sad confusion, we cannot be sure. We know only that his betrayal earned him thirty pieces of silver.

Any wise youth worker recognizes that the spirit of Judas is alive in all of us. No heart is incapable of betrayal, and no one is so spiritual as to be beyond financial temptation. The opportunity is there for the youth worker who betrays his Lord to pull down a few pieces of silver. It only takes a few instances of unwise or thoughtless financial mismanagement to tarnish a youth ministry and damage credibility. We should walk cautiously here, trusting God to provide for the needs of our ministries, and remembering the words of the apostle Paul:

> Now he who supplies seed to the sower and bread for food will also supply and increase your store of seed and will enlarge the harvest of your righteousness. You will be made rich in every way so that you can be generous on every occasion, and...your generosity will result in thanksgiving to God. (2 Corinthians 9:10-11)

CHAPTER 10

The Corps of Discovery I: Building a Team

The Lord said to Moses: "Bring me seventy of Israel's elders who are known to you as leaders and officials among the people. Have them come to the tent of meeting, that they may stand there with you. I will come down and speak with you there, and I will take some of the power of the Spirit that is on you and put it on them. They will share the burden of the people with you so that you will not have to carry it alone."
(Numbers 11:16-17)

"We are to ascend the Missouri River with a boat as far as it is navigable...This party consists of 25 picked Men of the armey (sic) & country and I am So happy as to be one of them pick'd (sic) Men... We are to Receive a great Reward for this expedition, when we Return..."[1]

These words, scrawled in the journal of Sergeant John Ordway on April 8, 1804, just ten days before Lewis and Clark's *Corps of Discovery* launched out for what surely would be the adventure of a lifetime, could also describe the thoughts and expectations of the thousands of church volunteers joined together in the adventure of ministry with teenagers. Counselors, coaches, tutors, mentors, friends, Bible teachers, worship leaders—this corps of youth ministry volunteers surely has some sense of the fear, exhilaration, and vivid hope that stirred Ordway that spring day two centuries ago. And like Ordway, they pursue the adventure with the very real anticipation of great reward.

There are few joys in youth ministry more real than partnering with like-minded people who share a vision for ministry. These marvelously diverse, unlikely crews of people working in churches and organizations all over the world are the heart and soul of youth work. As any experienced youth worker knows, such teams are all that stand between a successful venture and the perils of a solo voyage. But that's not to suggest that team ministry is easy. Doug Fields probably said it best: "Developing leaders is the best mix of blessing and burden that I know of in the church. It is a *blessing* to watch adults minister to students, and it is a *burden* to find the adults, train them, and motivate them."[2]

BURDEN AND BLESSING

Three weeks before I was scheduled to speak at a winter retreat for a youth group at Pearson Memorial Baptist Church, a suburban church outside a large Ohio city, I received a letter from the youth minister telling me about his group. As it happened, I found out much more than I wanted to know:[3]

> *When I came to Pearson, the youth group was about one hundred strong and had a group of twelve leaders. During a four-month interim between my arrival and my predecessor's leaving, the youth leaders formed a very close bond with one another and ran the program themselves—and they did it very well. They gave me the impression that they expected me to be responsible for the program and to take on much of the responsibility myself because they had jobs and families of their own. But when I did things my way—not theirs—we had constant conflict.*
>
> *These volunteer leaders were very dedicated Christians, but they were not supportive of the church as a whole. The youth group had become a sanctuary for disgruntled adults; they did their own thing in the youth group, and weren't real happy with the church, which, in fact, supported the youth group strongly. The senior pastor wasn't very happy with these leaders because of their lack of support for the church, so there was some open antagonism between him and our volunteer leaders.*
>
> *My first year and a half was one of conflict. The conflict became open and obvious in February when I had a program that several leaders opposed. Those leaders moved to organize a counter-meeting in one of their homes where we were already having a midweek group meeting sponsored by the church. We were able to resolve the conflict before the counter-meeting so that it never happened, but the stage was set for an exit.*
>
> *One of the volunteer leaders decided to leave the church, which meant that he would no longer be able to serve as a youth leader—this was my rule and the church's. When he insisted on continuing to be involved in our weeknight program as a leader, I asked him to stop. The Pastor-Parish Relations Committee backed me up on this. If he did not stop, we were going to cause the group to cease meeting.*
>
> *In August/September we had a mass resignation of ten leaders and college students in protest of our not allowing this person who'd left the church to continue serving as a youth leader. The whole group went to another church of our same denomination a mile from us and set up shop, involving that minister in their planning, beginning a Sunday night youth program, and setting plans for a fall retreat that would take place two weeks before ours. They actively recruited youth from our program, sometimes coming into our own church to do so. It has caused a great*

> *deal of heartache and stress in the church, with the youth, the youth group, and for me personally.*

Yikes! The above letter leaves little doubt about whether team ministry had been more "burden" or "blessing" in the recent experience of this beleaguered youth worker. He must have wondered if it wouldn't have been a lot easier to lead the youth program *without* any ministry team. After all, it's better to be alone on a solo hike than the guide for a mutinous, unhappy band of travelers. But, blessing or burden, the corps of discovery that sets out with us on the odyssey of ministry is not just a group of coworkers; these travelers are fellow members of the body of Christ. They bring to the journey gifts and skills that we and our ministries need. We risk the mission when we launch out on our own or demand too hastily that unpleasant fellow travelers, please, just get lost.

WHY TEAM MINISTRY?

Frustrations are a normal part of any team effort: Miscommunication, hurt feelings, botched plans, lack of dependability, lack of coordination, too many people shouting directions, and too few willing to walk the trail. These are all quite common. But there are also in team ministry deep satisfactions: The friendships melded through shared memories, the allegiance forged by standing together in ministry, the privilege of watching God use your combined efforts to do what none of you could have done alone, and the pleasure of being with other fun, resourceful Christians who are just crazy enough to want to work with teenagers.

My friend Mike Yaconelli put it like this:

> We have here a room full of rag-tag, foolish, unsophisticated, unfinished, work-in-progress, wandering, weak, disrespected ragamuffins who have been called to work with a group of rag-tag, foolish, unsophisticated, unfinished, work-in-progress wanderers called young people. Adults come up to us and say, "What's going on with this youth group? You've got all these scary people coming in here with tattoos and earrings and all kinds of strange clothes. They're loud; they're rowdy; they laugh a lot..." And you say, "Oh, yeah, well, that's our volunteer staff."[4]

What it amounts to is blessing indeed!

But the basic premises of volunteer youth ministry are anchored, not in good times or good friends, but in good theology. Preparing God's people for works of service is at the heart of the church's mandate (Ephesians 4:12).

THEOLOGICAL FOUNDATIONS

1. The model of Jesus: Server of the servants. One of the last and greatest lessons Jesus gave his disciples as he concluded his earthly ministry took place in an upper room as his disciples arrived for the evening meal (John 13:1-17). Stripped of his outer clothing, and with a towel wrapped around his waist, Jesus "poured water into a basin and began to wash his disciples' feet, drying them with the towel that was wrapped around him..." (13:5). The clear implication, both implicit and explicit (See John 13:12-17), is that leadership is about servanthood, and that *those of us in leadership are called to serve Christ's disciples.*

2. Gathered for God's purposes. Of course, foot-washing is very difficult work, and that's the burden of youth ministry leadership. Many a youth worker has burned herself out, hunched over, towel in hand, exhausting herself trying to meet the needs of an expanding group of *both* teenagers *and* adults. Little wonder volunteer ministry is so often neglected. Who needs more feet to wash?

But at the heart of this exhaustion is a misunderstanding of servant-leadership. It's true, service is sometimes exhausting, and, as Jesus' own example showed, it can be costly. But the key is to rethink theologically our resource and supply. Ministry with volunteer youth workers is not primarily about volunteers bringing refreshment to students, nor about youth pastors bringing refreshment to volunteers. It is about creating a space wherein people can find refreshment from Christ. It's about creating an upper room—holy ground where disciples can encounter Christ and be washed and refreshed *by him.*

In Numbers 11, we catch Moses in a moment of deep frustration. He is clearly tired of looking at dirty feet, and very nearly washed up. Moses is angry and frustrated, burned out and bushed, because, despite his best intentions, he does not have the resources to serve the people of God:

> [Moses] asked the Lord, "Why have you brought this trouble on your servant? What have I done to displease you that you put the burden of all these people on me? Did I conceive all these people? Did I give them birth? Why do you tell me to carry them in my arms, as a nurse carries an infant, to the land you promised on oath to their forefathers? Where can I get meat for all these people? They keep wailing to me, 'Give us meat to eat!' I cannot carry all these people by myself; the burden is too heavy for me. If this is how you are going to treat me, please go ahead and kill me—if I have found favor in your eyes—and do not let me face my own ruin." (Numbers 11:11-15)

Moses' complaint is real: Doggone it, he wants God to provide some volunteers to share *his* workload. "Do not let me face my own ruin." The Lord does provide others to share the load—but also reminds Moses whose work it is:

> The Lord said to Moses: "Bring me seventy of Israel's elders who are known to you as leaders and officials among the people. Have them come to the Tent of Meeting, that they may stand there with you. I will come down and speak with you there, and I will take of the Spirit that is on you and put the Spirit on them. They will help you carry the burden of the people so that you will not have to carry it alone." (Numbers 11:16-17, NIV)

There are two distinct promises in this passage. Kenda Dean has noted that youth pastors are apt to cling to the latter promise: "*They* will help *you* carry the burden..." (v. 17), and ignore the promise of the first part, "*I* will come down and speak with you there, and *I* will take of the Spirit that is on you and put the Spirit on them." Like Moses, we can easily forget it's not about *our* ministry; it's about God's ministry. "Numbers 11 calls us back to a form of ministry in which we gather people for God so that God can give them what we cannot: a share of God's spirit, the spirit that empowers ministry."[5]

3. *The priesthood of all believers.* Paul makes it quite clear that one central responsibility of those in ministry leadership is to equip the people of God to do the work of God, to equip the saints for the work of ministry. This shared labor is implicit in Paul's frequent use of the Greek preposition *syn* (meaning "with" or "together"), which he uses more than a dozen times in his letters, attaching it as a prefix to several verbs, actually creating compound words that are found nowhere else in the New Testament. Paul's clear intention is to communicate that ministry is a work we Christians must do *together*.[6] A youth leader who neglects this priority is like a football coach who takes the field by himself because he doesn't want to face the difficulties of recruiting and training a team. By definition, such a coach is no coach at all. Youth ministry is always *ministry with*...

4. *We are one body with many parts.* Paul's use of the "body" metaphor (1 Corinthians 12:14,17-20) clearly emphasizes the corporate nature of God's calling—that all parts of the body are essential to do what God calls us to do. No one is omni-gifted. The worship leader cannot sing to the gifted speaker, "I do not need you." The soft-spoken, insightful counselor cannot ask the jock, "Do you ever feel you're not needed, because, you know, you really aren't?" The contemplative leader cannot say to the wild and crazy game leader, "Just close your eyes and meditate for a moment on this: I do not need you (and I don't want to play your stupid games!)." We made this point earlier in the book, but it bears repeating: there's almost always an *and* in God's plans—whether we're talking about Moses *and* Aaron, Jesus *and* the disciples, or Bono *and* the Edge.

PRAGMATIC CONSIDERATIONS

But team ministry isn't just good theology. There are also some very good practical reasons to engage volunteers in our work with youth:

1. Continuity. Ecclesiastes 4:12 reminds us that "a cord of three strands is not quickly broken." A youth ministry that wisely incorporates volunteers in shared leadership is a youth ministry that's not hanging by the tenure of one or two leaders. It is a ministry that stays even when the youth minister moves on.

Volunteers Darrell and Erlene had been working with their church's senior high group for two years when the paid youth minister announced that he'd accepted a call to a new position. Because Darrell and Erlene had been equipped as part of a team ministry—trained to plan retreats, do Bible studies, and work closely with students—they ably sustained the work during the year-long search for a new youth pastor.

2. Diversity. Just as it's difficult to play a Mozart concerto on a piano with a single key, or write a romantic e-mail on a keyboard with only three letters, so it is difficult to give full expression to the Christian life through the lens of only one personality. One beauty of working with a diverse group of volunteers—young and old, athletic and musical, quiet and outgoing—is that it gives teenagers opportunities to see what Christian commitment looks like when it's shaded by different personalities. That opens up wider opportunities for rapport with a more varied group of youth, and helps break the power of negative Christian stereotypes.

3. Longevity. Hypothermia is a serious, and sometimes fatal, condition in which a person's core body temperature falls below 96 degrees. One of the oldest first response remedies to this condition is to lie down next to the hypothermic victim so the body heat of the rescuer can restore some of the heat of the victim.

Sadly, youth ministry sees far too many "hypothermic" youth workers who started out with a warm heart, but in working alone have simply lost their fire and passion for the journey. The best way to protect and prolong the ministry of youth workers is to recruit other youth workers who will "lie down beside them." (Please don't take this too literally.) Scripture reminds us:

> Two are better than one,
> because they have a good return for their labor:
> If they fall down, they can help each other up.
> But pity those who fall and have no one to help them up!
> Also, if two lie down together, they will keep warm.
> But how can one keep warm alone? (Ecclesiastes 4:9-11)

PEOPLE ARE THE PLAN

Several years ago, Ronald Wilson wrote an article for *Leadership* journal that ought to be required reading for any youth pastor working with volunteers.[7] Entitled "Letter From an Ex-Volunteer," this imaginary letter has an important message for us.

> *Dear Pastor Potter:*
>
> *You and some others are down in Finney Hall in the church basement stuffing 20,000 envelopes for the Madison County Deeper Life Campaign at the fairground. I guess I should be there. You asked for volunteers last Sunday, and I had my hand halfway up when you announced hymn number 263, "Work, for the Night is Coming."*
>
> *As you probably guessed, I'm feeling a little bad about that and about not getting to choir practice and dropping off the planning committee and canceling the literature distribution training session scheduled for our house last month.*
>
> *For one thing, pastor, I think I'm burned out—spent, pooped, empty. I've been hearing about it lately, and they say that if you're not careful, it can lead to dropout. I always used to say I didn't mind burning out for the Lord, but lately, I've been afraid I might go up in one big poof.*
>
> *...I haven't dropped out. Maybe I just need to hear you say it once more: "Wilson, it's the ninth inning, and we're two runs behind. We've got two outs and no one on and you're up. We're counting on you to hit. So go get 'em!"*
>
> *Your brother in the Lord,*
>
> *Ronald Wilson*

Change a few of the details, and that letter could have been written by almost any youth ministry volunteer. And it reminds us that good team ministry always begins with a good team mindset. It's a mindset that puts people at the heart of the mission, and a mission in the heart of people. Paul J. Loth articulates a list of seven "attitude competencies" that are essential for anyone who recruits ministry volunteers.[8]

1. Vision for potential volunteers to serve.

2. Belief that people are more important than positions and programs.

3. Willingness to work with volunteers to see them reach their full potential.

4. Love for the volunteers.

5. Belief in the importance of the youth ministry.

6. Desire to help volunteers develop.

7. A willingness to trust in the gifts of others.

The whole scope of effective volunteer youth ministry is shaped by a mindset that sees people at the heart of God's purpose. In the words of one wise youth worker: "Your ability to find volunteer leaders begins with how you view them."[9]

THE ENVIRONMENT OF RECRUITMENT

How can we cultivate the kind of ministry soil that grows strong, fruitful youth ministry volunteers? What are some of the values that might prepare that kind of healthy recruitment landscape?

Community (1 Corinthians 12:14-31)

Does our approach affirm the value of all people in the community while recognizing that not all people in the community are equally valuable to a particular ministry?

All Christians have been gifted by God's Spirit to serve him in the church. But they have not all been gifted to serve in the same ways, performing all the same tasks (See 1 Corinthians 12:4-6). Does that mean there are some God-loving, Jesus-serving, Spirit-filled people who probably shouldn't be doing ministry with teenagers? Yes. But it means more than that. It means that a wise youth worker will explore options for willing people to be involved beyond direct ministry with youth. In fact, one way we can be better stewards of those who are in direct youth ministry is by being stewards of those who are not in direct youth ministry. Doug Fields comments, "Many of us lose potential leaders because we limit our serving opportunities to two positions—All or Nothing. Everyone in your church is a potential youth worker if you provide serving opportunities that are more simplified and less threatening than working directly with students."[10]

Statistically the vast majority of volunteers give only a few hours a week, and only 14 percent have been estimated to volunteer five or more hours a week.[11] What we want to say to members of the community is, "Just because you can't do everything, that doesn't mean you can't do anything." Not only does this incorporate broader-based support and community involvement for the youth ministry, it lightens the load for those leaders who are both inclined and gifted for direct ministry with teenagers, and sets them apart to do what they have been called and gifted to do.

In his ministry at Saddleback Church, Doug Fields divided volunteer involvement into four types of positions (Figure 10-1).[12] The deeper the level of involvement, the more difficult it becomes to fill the position. But by utilizing the will and the gifts of those in the upper levels of involvement, it is possible to protect and better utilize the gifts of those more deeply and directly involved.[13]

Sensitivity

Does our approach take into account the concerns of volunteers and potential volunteers?

There are at least four reasons that many people are reluctant to do volunteer ministry with youth.[14] Youth workers run head-on into these all the time. The degree to which we are sensitive in addressing these concerns will greatly affect volunteer involvement in our ministries.

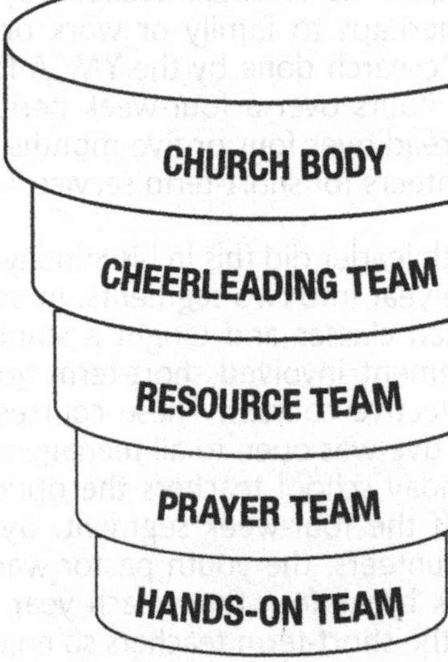

Figure 10-1 Fields's breakdown of volunteer involvement

Concern 1: "I don't know enough about the Bible to work with the kids." One fear often voiced by volunteer leaders is that they simply lack the biblical knowledge that they need. They are afraid students will ask questions they can't answer, or that they'll answer a kid's question wrongly, and that kid will start a cult when he grows up!

Remedy: Bible knowledge is important, and yes, it's a wonderful asset in a volunteer leader. But leaders also need to be assured that their lack of knowledge will be supplemented by user-friendly curriculum and ongoing in-service training. They also need to understand that students are rarely attracted to someone based solely on their theological expertise. Teenagers don't respond to Christ by listening for knowledge from the leader's head, but by experiencing care and friendship from the leader's heart. (See 1 Corinthians 2:1-5.)

Concern 2: "Um...how long am I signing up for?" People have an intuitive fear (often verified by experience) that any volunteer commitment in ministry is a lifetime enlistment—that any ministry volunteer who attempts to retire prior to death and decomposition will be considered a flagrant slacker and seriously AWOL.

Remedy: While an open-ended commitment might seem to offer the greatest freedom, in fact, such an arrangement is beneficial neither for the volunteer nor for the ministry. Any leadership position description should define a set length of tenure, followed by review, after which the leadership responsibilities can be reaffirmed, downgraded, or ended.[15] There are good, sound reasons why both parties might wish to end or downgrade the commitment in time.

For example, the volunteer leader may have had a change in circumstances—related perhaps to family or work or both. People don't want to be "tied down." Research done by the YMCA found that people were more willing to work 50 hours over a four-week period than to work that same number of hours spread over four or five months.[16] That means we need to find ways to use volunteers for short-term service.[17]

One youth leader did this in his Sunday school program by dividing each quarter of the year into two segments. In one segment, students were divided into age-graded classes and taught a standard curriculum. Then, a second four-week segment involved short-term volunteers who were recruited to teach special elective courses. These courses were based on student interest, and each elective was open to all teenagers, regardless of age. That gave the long-term Sunday school teachers the option of attending the elective course or taking off the four-week segment. By using the short-term commitment of some volunteers, the youth pastor was able to offer his long-term workers a four-week break four times each year. And the unexpected benefit was that some of the short-term teachers so enjoyed their experience that they offered to make a more long-term commitment.

A predetermined length of service for volunteers protects a youth ministry against rapid turnover on the one hand, and *no prospect of turnover* on the other. Sometimes the latter problem causes the greater pain. The only thing harder than getting good leaders on the team is gracefully getting bad ones off the team. A pre-service agreement on tenure can make that process a bit easier.

What if we do need to ask someone to step down from a volunteer leadership role? I like the approach very carefully laid out by Mark Senter in his book, *Recruiting Volunteers in the Church*:[18]

Preparation:

(1) *Prayer.* Focus prayerfully on the best interests of the ministry and the person.

(2) *Documentation.* Document the issues that are raising concern.

(3) *No Surprises.* Some type of ongoing volunteer performance review (formal or informal) will keep the leader from being caught off guard. For guidance on bringing a complaint before the church, see Matt. 18:15-17.

Timing:

(1) *Don't rush.*

(2) *Don't renew.* If possible, rather than dismiss a volunteer, it is always better simply not to renew the relationship. But, as Senter points out, "Absence of renewal does not mean absence of communication."

(3) *Don't delay.* Where moral or theological problems have arisen, don't let procrastination and wishful thinking overrule leadership responsibility.

Procedure:

(1) *Private appointment.* Obviously, the dismissal should not be public. There should be one other third party available as a witness and mediator (if needed), but any more than that can feel like an ambush.

(2) *Self-evaluation.* The supervisor should first ask the volunteer for an appraisal of the situation. Sometimes the volunteer will acknowledge a problem without the supervisor having to say too much.

(3) *Confront if necessary.* (Cf. Galatians 6:1)

(4) *Affirm positive qualities.*

(5) *Allow resignation.* After the problems have been defined, ask the volunteer what he/she thinks might be the best course of action for the ministry.

(6) *Redirect talents.* If possible, try to help the volunteer leader get plugged in elsewhere.

(7) *Follow-up.* Even in the midst of a difficult situation, the goal is redemption of the individual and the relationship.

Concern 3: "I understand there's a need for ministry with teenagers, but is it...er...uh...safe?" Many adults are intimidated by youth ministry because they assume all teenagers are barbarians, incorrigible, just a step above lower primates, and that going into a room or meeting alone with them is to risk being taken hostage.

Remedy: Again, as with the previous concern—let's be honest—these assumptions are occasionally verified by experience! But experience also paints quite another picture, and that picture, colored by the privilege of sharing life and Jesus with an adolescent, far outshines the more troubling image.

Often this concern can be addressed by a pre-service period of observation. For example, a youth worker in San Antonio invites prospective leaders to tag along for a weekend retreat as guests of the youth ministry, or to sit in for a few weeks of youth group, so that they can see firsthand what goes on. Looking from the outside in, before they are fully inside, gives them a more realistic picture of both the challenges and the joys of ministry with students.

Concern 4: "But my wife and I are really involved in our own Sunday school class." Twenty years ago most adults were only too happy to pass up the adult Sunday school program, bailing on curricula they perceived to be outdated and irrelevant. Now, an adult volunteer who misses Sunday school may be passing up anything from a creative class on Christian financial management to a video by one of Christendom's greatest teachers. And, as more and more congregations move to Sunday school-based fellowship groups, some adults fear the heavy involvement necessary for youth ministry may cut them off from the broader life of the community. A growing number of adults are unwilling to forego the nurture and care of their own Sunday school classes to work with teenagers on Sunday mornings.

Remedy: First of all, this is less a problem in parachurch ministries like Young Life, where a larger proportion of the volunteer force is made up of college students or twentysomethings. They're less likely to feel the close connection to a local congregation, anyway. For them, the Young Life leadership team may represent their best source of nurture and fellowship. Plus, most parachurch programming takes place at times that don't conflict with traditional Sunday morning programming. So, for parachurch ministries, this isn't usually a big concern.

For parish-based youth ministries, it is important to provide adult leaders opportunities for personal growth and fellowship. This may come through the sort of staggered teaching schedule described earlier in this chapter or, at the very least, by making available videotapes of special Sunday school courses or podcasts of sermons so leaders can take them home and enjoy them on their own time.

It is also vital that volunteer leaders perceive the others on the team as friends, not just as coworkers. People are far more likely to remain committed to relationships than they are to a job. One writer, in commenting on the uncanny loyalty British soldiers show to their regiments, observed that there is a strong emphasis on regimental unity and continuity. "Men may enlist to serve their country, but they will fight hardest to protect their friends."[19]

Some of the best experiences I've had with volunteer teams have happened when we were out together as friends (with no students) for a day of white-water rafting. Those afternoons paddling the Big South Fork of the Cumberland River melded our volunteer team into a fellowship of friends who laughed together, helped one another, sweated together, faced death together (!), and reminisced together.

It's hard to leave teams like that. It's like leaving friends and family. Whether it's a potluck dinner or a yearly backpacking trip, volunteers need to experience team-building, praying together, dreaming, and bonding that shows them they are important, even when no adolescents are around.

Integrity (1 Corinthians 4:2)

Does this approach find the "right" people for the ministry and screen out the "wrong" people?

Are there *right* people and *wrong* people for youth ministry leadership? Based on considerations that are biblical, legal, and practical, the answer is clearly *Yes*. And, whatever else might be said about the *wrong* people (and we will say a bit more later in this chapter), the *right* people should share these three essential traits:

A love for Christ. The most basic law of reproductive biology is "like begets like." Humans give birth to baby humans; not baby aardvarks. The implications in the spiritual realm are obvious. If we hope to *reproduce* maturing disciples of Jesus, the process must begin with maturing disciples of Jesus Christ—not people who are perfect, but people who are in pursuit (See Philippians 3:12-17). Paul encourages the Corinthians to imitate him as he seeks to imitate Christ (1 Corinthians 11:1). The writer of Hebrews echoes the same idea: "Remember your leaders, who spoke the word of God to you. Consider the outcome of their way of life and imitate their faith" (Hebrews 13:7). The number one criterion for selecting prospects for a role on the youth ministry team should be the fruit of their relationship with Jesus.

A love for students. At the heart of any effective youth ministry is a love for teenagers. In referring to his own ministry, Paul wrote (2 Corinthians 6:4-6), "...As servants of God we commend ourselves in every way: in great endurance; in troubles, hardships and distresses; in beatings, imprisonments and riots; in hard work, sleepless nights and hunger; in purity, understanding, patience and kindness; in the Holy Spirit *and in sincere love* [emphasis added]." It should be said that a love for teenagers is quite different from a love for the front of the room, or a need for teenagers—both of which are all too common in youth ministry. Richard Foster offers some guidelines for discerning the difference between service rightly rendered and service wrongly rendered.[20]

True Service	***Pseudo-Service***
Doesn't distinguish between large and small tasks.	Enjoys the spectacular.
Is willing to serve behind the scenes. Not afraid to be out front, but neither seeking the limelight.	Likes the spotlight. Motivated by the attention and admiration of others.
Finds contentment in the service. Leaves the results in God's hands.	Very results-oriented. Scorekeeper mind-set. Measures performance by comparison with others.
Servant of all.	Picks and chooses who will be served, and how they will be served.
Consistent in service. Motivation not based on mood swings or short-term passions.	Motivations shaped by the moods and affections of the moment.
Service is fruit of the Spirit.	Service is work of the flesh.

A Love of the Church. The third essential is a love of the church. The story at the beginning of this chapter reminds us that the youth ministry can often become a gathering place for a congregation's disgruntled adults. When that happens, these adults will likely transfer their own dissatisfaction with the church to the youth. And when disenchanted adults wean teenagers from a local church, they seldom help those teens find nurture in another congregation. That's not healthy for the student, and it's not responsible Christian leadership. This is not a plea for phoniness or unthinking approval. It is a reminder that, while no congregation is perfect, the church is Christ's body, and one of the greatest predictors of a teenager's long-term commitment to the faith is his or her assimilation in a local church.[21] Volunteers who can't or won't nurture that commitment should not be working in youth ministry.

Having identified these three essentials for the "right" kind of youth ministry volunteer leader, it is worth asking if there are issues or conditions that might suggest that someone is the "wrong" kind of volunteer leader. It feels uncomfortable to talk about *right* people and *wrong* people, but biblical teaching, legal mandates, and common sense dictate that extreme care be given in placing people in a role of ministry leadership. Inclusiveness is wonderful, but nobody wants the fox to guard the hen house.

Here's a pretty good list of "red flags" to watch out for:

- A brand new Christian or a person new to your church
- A history of short-term commitments
- A critical spirit
- Going through major life crisis or transition (for example, death of a family member, divorce or separation, major career change)
- High expectation for staff to be best friends or for ministry to provide personal experiences
- Hidden agendas—desires and expectations that are counter to the ministry's values and goals
- Not committed to a lifestyle above reproach
- Unsupportive spouse[22]

This isn't about being judgmental; it *is* about exercising good judgment. As Marlene Wilson points out, this kind of vigilance is important because a lot is at stake:[23]

The welfare of the youth is at stake. This is not just a question of a leader's integrity; it's also a question of the teenagers' safety. The ministry is, first and foremost, for the youth. Therefore, care must be taken to provide for them a place where they will be protected from spiritual, physical, or emotional injury.[24]

Richard Hammar, editor of the *Church Law and Tax Report*, cites research indicating that "70 percent of churches are doing absolutely nothing to screen volunteer youth workers."[25] Hammar goes on to say:

> ...Trust, but verify. Church leaders tend to view the church differently than other institutions in society. It's an institution predicated on trust. It's a sanctuary. It bothers people to have to go through metal detectors or have their fingerprints taken in a church setting...But the courts in this country have ruled that what is needed is very minimal. We're talking about an application process that includes reference checks...
>
> In my church, we perform criminal record checks on paid employees and male volunteers with minors. More churches are performing these checks, which are being used more often by nonreligious charities. At some point, a court may say they are necessary in screening youth workers.[26]

The ministry's reputation is at stake. The apostle Paul wrote, "We put no stumbling block in anyone's path, so that our ministry will not be discredited"

(2 Corinthians 6:3). He understood that in ministry, trust and credibility are paramount (See 1 Thessalonians 2:10). For that reason, carelessness in recruiting volunteer leaders can bring grave harm to a ministry and, even worse, to the name of Christ.

The morale of other team members is at stake. The self-perception of other volunteer leaders can be adversely affected by careless recruiting. All the pep talks about the importance of excellence in ministry ring hollow when it is clear to everyone that the qualifications for service are minimal.[27] If you communicate that "Any idiot can do this," don't be surprised when you wind up with a team full of idiots.

The welfare of the misplaced volunteer is at stake. Pushing a volunteer into a position for which he or she is not spiritually, emotionally, or temperamentally equipped is like trying to build a tree house in a small tree. It's bad for the tree house, yes, but it also crushes the tree—a tree that in time, with proper nurture and care, might have provided a sturdy and capable support. Although a youth ministry's first concern must be the youth, there must also be concern for the potential leader as well.

THE TWO BIGGEST ISSUES

That still leaves us facing the two biggest concerns in building a strong leadership team: *How do I find good volunteers?* and *How do I keep them?* We'll address those issues in the next chapter.

CHAPTER 11

The Corps of Discovery II: Finding and Keeping Good Volunteer Leaders

When morning came, he called his disciples to him and chose twelve of them.
(Luke 6:13)

In the previous chapter, we inventoried several values that can help us to build the sort of environment we need to build a strong corps of youth ministry volunteers:

> ***Community:*** *Does this approach affirm the value of all people in the community while recognizing that not all people in the community are equally valuable to a particular ministry?*
>
> ***Sensitivity:*** *Does this recruitment approach take into account the concerns of the recruited?*
>
> ***Integrity:*** *Does this approach find the "right" people for the ministry and screen out the "wrong" people?*

There are two additional key values that point us to questions at the heart of building any sound team ministry: ***Opportunity*** *(How do I find these people?)* and ***Longevity*** *(How do I keep them?)*.

Opportunity

Does this approach provide the widest possible pool of good candidates?

Whether the context is parachurch ministry or congregational ministry, there will always be a pool of potential volunteers. Hersey and Blanchard observe that this pool is made up of four types of people at various stages of *readiness.*[1] If we define readiness in terms of two variables, *ability* and *availability,*[2] there are those who are: (1) willing and able; (2) unwilling and able; (3) willing and unable; and (4) unwilling and unable (Figure 11-1).

One implication of Hersey and Blanchard's insights is that the search for volunteers must be broad enough to include possible volunteers who are at a much lower state of readiness. Too many recruitment efforts are limited only to those in Quadrant 1. The other clear implication is that differing means of

	Willing	
Quadrant I Able	**Status**	Willing/Able Prospective Volunteer
	Needs: Encourage	Talk to them about the opportunity, and invite them to commit.
	Expose	Give them a chance to view the ministry to check out where they feel they might best contribute.
	Educate	Provide pre-service training.
	Explore	Specific areas of interest
Quadrant II Unable	**Status**	Willing/Unable Possible Volunteer
	Needs: Encourage	Everyone is gifted for something. Probe for the areas of inadequacy, and explore the areas of ability. Are there youth ministry stereotypes that are preventing them from seeing themselves in a leadership role?
	Expose	Give them a chance to see the ministry up close.
	Educate	Give them training in the areas they feel (and, in fact, may be) inadequate.
	Explore	Are there other places they could serve that might better suit their gifts? Could the barriers to their involvement be addressed effectively though training and experience?

Fig. 11-1 Potential Volunteers

recruitment are needed to reach those at differing levels of readiness. Both observations are important, and they affirm the value of building a youth ministry leadership team from the widest possible pool of good candidates.

Many potential leaders exclude themselves (or are excluded by short-sighted youth workers) from the realm of the willing and able (Quadrant 1) simply because they are *perceived* as unable. And often this is solely because they appear to fall short of inaccurate youth ministry stereotypes: "...young, funny,

Unwilling		
Quadrant III Able	**Status**	Unwilling/Able Post-Volunteer
	Needs: Encourage	Encourage them to support the ministry in some other way that fits them better (prayer, short-term projects, etc.).
	Expose	Let them know of ways they could be involved on a smaller scale.
	Educate	(It's pretty tough to train people for a job they are unwilling to take.)
	Explore	Possible reasons for disenchantment (past issues, present concerns, etc.)
Quadrant IV Unable	**Status**	Unwilling/Unable Pre-Volunteer
	Needs: Encourage	Address concerns cited in the previous chapter: Concern 1: Inadequate knowledge. Concern 2: Fear that the job will never end. Concern 3: Fearing teenagers. Concern 4: Isolation from the fellowship and nurture of the larger congregation.
	Expose	Through congregational announcements, bulletin inserts, and reports in the services, keep promoting the youth ministry across the congregation. That arouses interest.
	Educate	Make certain people know what the youth ministry is and what it isn't.
	Explore	Perhaps explore some other places where they might be willing and able to serve the Lord.

Fig. 11-1 Potential Volunteers

athletic, good in front of crowds, strong teacher, has Bible knowledge, outgoing personality, charisma, understands youth culture, owns a van..."[3] There are too many wonderful characters who have done amazing work in youth ministry to think these stereotypes are valid.

There is 60-plus-year-old Grady who's been working as a volunteer with his Louisiana youth group for well over a decade. With his warmth and easy laugh, Grady has touched the lives of hundreds of Baton Rouge teenagers.

And Mary, also well into her sixties, whose genuine love for special needs kids has made a remarkable contribution to the Capernaum ministry of Young Life. Those kids don't see in Mary a young, edgy, guitar-playing youth ministry chick. What they see is someone who loves them, and that is more than enough to make her a vivid signpost pointing teenagers to God.

For Will, it was his love of art—not a flashy personality or extreme athletic prowess—that became a connecting point with teenagers in Colorado Springs. And, through that love of art, Will has gained access to the high school and the lives of countless teenagers who might never have known Christ if not for his unique ministry.

God uses all kinds of people to reach teenagers.

In fact, as Joseph Galbo discovered in his research on "Adolescents' Perceptions of Significant Adults,"[4] when asked to identify the significant adults in their lives, excluding their own parents, the adults selected were usually over 24 years of age and, in one study, at least 9 percent were over 66 years old.[5] That fact, in and of itself, dispels one chief myth that makes adults reluctant to work with teenagers—that they are too old to do youth ministry. Galbo cites another study of the relationships between adults and various gang and non-gang youth in which the youth were asked to provide no more than four names of adults other than family members with whom they regularly interacted. "The ages of these adults ranged from 35-47. No young adults were mentioned."[6] Teenagers typically named as significant adults those who were of the same gender, with 83 percent of the males in one study choosing other males, and 52 percent of the females choosing other females. Again, this has real implications for any ministry team.

Also noteworthy are the qualities teenagers look for in those they describe as "significant adults." The literature indicates that understanding and openness to communication were, by far, the most important qualities mentioned.[7] Other important qualities that came up were intelligence, strong personality, generosity, honesty, and premature hair-loss (just kidding). Absent were qualities like "buff," "young," "hip," "wild and crazy," and "massive facial hair." All of this underlines the importance of developing a leadership environment broad enough to embrace people of all ages, personality types, backgrounds, and body types, with a wide variety of skills, interests, and strengths.

Longevity

Does our ministry keep the right people in the right places?

One of the most important and most basic tasks of Christian leadership is equipping folks for ministry—discerning, developing, and deploying the gifts of God's people. In the context of youth ministry volunteer leadership, that means helping the right people find the right places in which they can best grow and utilize their gifts. Research on volunteer involvement typically defines longevity in terms of three variables: Tenure ("I want to keep doing this"), commitment ("I'm willing to invest significant time into this ministry"), and satisfaction ("I really enjoy doing this").[8] Anything we can do to nurture these three variables is going to build longevity into our volunteer team.

Les Christie, in his book *Unsung Heroes*, estimates the annual turnover rate among volunteer youth leaders is about 30 percent.[9] Mathematically, that adds up to an almost complete turnover every three years. With all the effort that goes into recruiting qualified youth workers, that kind of turnover rate represents a huge waste of time and talent. We want to be sensitive to tangible ways that we can increase the tenure of our volunteers and motivate them to stay engaged in the work.

In their studies in motivation and organizational behavior, Litwin and Stringer cite nine factors that can help us build longevity into our ministry's *organizational climate*.[10]

- **Relationships.** What are the relational dynamics of the ministry team? Is there clear definition in terms of job definition? Does everyone know his or her role? Is the relational environment one of trust or distrust? Is there a sense that all members of the team are vital and valued?

- **Rewards.** Is the ministry intentional about affirming and expressing thanks to volunteer leaders?

- **Warmth/Support.** Is time together focused entirely on program items, or is there space for nurture and fellowship? Are meetings characterized by laughing, crying, praying, arguing, or voting?

- **Conflict.** Is conflict allowed—and is it done in a positive, productive way?

- **Physical setting.** Is the meeting space similar in style to a formal "living room," or does it have the feel of an informal "family room"?

- **Identity.** Do team members feel they can be real—accepted and valued as they are? Do they collectively feel a sense of team identity?

- **Standards.** Is the team identity clear enough and secure enough that standards of behavior and commitment can be established and taken seriously?

- **Creativity/Risk.** Is there room to experiment? How often are the phrases, "We always….," "We never…," or "It won't work…" used in team meetings?
- **Congregational Expectations.** Are the specified rules and roles reasonable? Are volunteers laboring under needless "administrivia" or unhealthy time expectations?

TEAM MINISTRY: FROM CALL TO CULTIVATION

Okay, so we have these basic values—Community, Sensitivity, Integrity, Opportunity, and Longevity— that affect your ministry's environment. How do we begin to build a team in the context of that environment?

Essentially, it boils down to four basic initiatives:

- Call them,
- Court them,
- Coach them,
- Cover them.

CALL THEM

Calling the right people for the right positions is perhaps the area of youth ministry that causes the most frustration and headache. How do we find the people we want? How do we decide what kind of people we want to find? How do we avoid finding people we don't want?

Four Basic Approaches

There are four approaches commonly used in recruiting youth leaders. All of them have some merit,[11] but each must be measured carefully by the values articulated above.

1. The public appeal method. Typically, this approach means the pastor or youth pastor stands in front of the congregation on Sunday morning and publicly pleads and bleeds until some poor, unknowing soul is driven by guilt to respond. Usually it sounds something like this: "Maybe you folks don't care if our youth are getting pregnant or using drugs, but if you do, we have a wonderful opportunity for you downstairs with our junior high Sunday school program."

While this is the most common means of volunteer recruitment, it has some obvious flaws. Notably, it is the precise opposite of the approach Jesus took. There is no evidence indicating that Jesus ever went into Jericho and announced, "If anyone is willing to be a fisher of men, please sign up over near the well or see me after the service." Nor is there any record of Jesus putting an ad in the synagogue bulletin asking for "volunteers to help perform miracles and cast out demons."

Another concern is that this approach seems to say, "We need *you* to help *us* serve God," instead of, "We want to invite you to discover God by serving teenagers." The first is a plea to share a burden; the other is an invitation to share Christ—to be, in Kenda Dean's words, a "Godbearer."

The main advantage of the public appeal approach is that it casts the widest possible net—the need is expressed to the broadest range of people. As Jane Eisinger, associate editor of *Association Management* explains, "Sometimes it's the simplest step that gets the job done. Tell your members you need them. If asked, 63 percent of people will volunteer compared with 25 percent who volunteer without being asked."[12] On the other hand, the wider the appeal, the greater the likelihood for getting undesirable recruits. And, trust me, it's much more difficult to get rid of volunteers you don't want than to find good volunteers you do want.

2. Youth recruiting leaders. Imagine how the following invitation would melt some of the initial resistance of a potential volunteer youth worker: "You know, we asked the kids whom they would like to have working with them in their youth group, and sure enough, with one voice they began chanting your name." Granted, youth are occasionally attracted to certain adults for reasons other than those that might actually make someone a strong leader. ("We love Bill! He buys our beer for us so we don't have to use our fake ID's!") But we can presume any adult recommended by the youth possesses basic interpersonal skills and has shown at least some ability to relate to teenagers. That's a major hurdle.

3. Volunteers recruiting volunteers. Investors are much more likely to put their money in a stock when they know the broker making the sale has already invested in that same stock. Current volunteers can be much more believable than youth pastors when recruiting new volunteers. Active volunteers can pass on a realistic idea of the challenges and rewards of answering the call of youth work. Plus, they can answer with credibility the misgivings prospective volunteers might have about balancing ministry with parenting or working full time or concerns about not having adequate training.

4. The one-to-one call. Jesus assembled his team by praying thoroughly, seeking the people he wanted, and calling them individually by name. One strength of such an approach is that it allows us to meet and get to know each person who's considering joining the ministry team. And, just as important, it affords them the opportunity to meet and get to know us as well. In *The Volunteers,* David Sills reports this:

> The role relationship most frequently employed in recruiting is that of friendship: 58 percent of all volunteers who were recruited into the Foundation [March of Dimes] were asked by a friend. This is perfectly in accord with the conclusions reached in several studies of how people are influenced—what to buy, what to think about publications, what entertainment to seek, whom to vote for—all have been shown to be decisions in which personal influence plays a very large part.[13]

The table below (Figure 11-2) offers an evaluation of each of the four approaches in light of the values articulated in this and the preceding chapter.

Means of Leadership Recruitment	***Community***	***Sensitivity***	***Integrity***	***Opportunity***	***Longevity***
Public Appeal	+	0	- -	+ +	0
Youth Recruiting Leaders	+	+ +	-	+	0
Volunteer Leaders Recruiting Volunteers	+ +	+ +	+ -	+	+ +
Personal Contact	-	+ +	+	- -	+ +
Scale: [++] positive, [+] potentially positive, [0] neutral, [-] potentially negative, [- -] negative					

Figure 11-2 Comparison of Four Basic Approaches to Recruiting Youth Ministry Volunteer Leaders

COURT THEM

The average volunteer youth worker receives very little affirmation and encouragement for his or her labors. Oh, to be sure, there will be the pulpit announcement: "Henry and Sadie have told the C.E. board that they are willing to start working with our youth group. We praise the Lord for their availability and openness to this vital work." And that will be followed by a congregational euphoria that lasts all of about ten seconds. But then almost immediately there is the collective, inaudible sigh as pastor and people think to themselves, "Thank goodness. Now we don't have to think about the youth ministry any more until these two quit."

And quit they will, if we aren't able to create intentional ways to help them know they are appreciated and valued. In "How to Light a Fire Under People Without Burning Them Up," Ed Dayton and Ted Engstrom identified several ways a youth ministry can foster a positive, affirming environment for volunteers.[14]

1. Keep good lines of communication. Youth workers are busy people. They can appear to be aloof and hard to contact. Some youth ministry professionals have incorporated basic report sheets so volunteers are not haunted by the fear of the phantom youth worker who never seems to be in the office or never makes himself available for consultation or coaching. It could be something as simple as asking volunteers to fill out a form like the one below so that they are reassured they are not going to be left in the lurch by some superhero youth pastor who only drops in dramatically in a moment of crisis (Figure 11-3). Notice that the form puts the onus of responsibility for contact on the youth pastor. It's a way of promising accountability and availability.

YOUTH MINISTRY REPORT SHEET

Please submit to Shelly after each ministry activity. Thanks.

Class/study group: ____________________

Leader's name: ____________________

Topic of study: ____________________

Total attendance: Regulars: ______ Visitors: ______

Comments: ____________________

Materials you need: ____________________

Shelly, please get in touch with me this week. Yes ______

(Figure 11-3)

Gary Newton presents research that 75 percent of all the church volunteers he surveyed cited *a specific supportive gesture* as the factor that influenced them to maintain involvement in their ministry roles.[15] We don't want to underestimate the power of those tangible gestures that say, "You are not on your own; we are doing this together."

2. Practice accountability. Follow up on requests and delegated tasks. If a volunteer is given an assignment, follow up to see that the assignment is completed. That affirms to volunteers that their efforts are important.

3. Give volunteers a chance to succeed. A wise leader creates for volunteers working conditions that say, "We take your ministry seriously." That means well-lit rooms, clean blackboards with functional chalk, markers that actually mark, and projectors that really do project.

4. Be generous with affirmation. Use notes, texts, phone calls, public recognition, and comments on their Facebook walls. Recognize effort as well as results. And be specific. Rather than saying, "You did a good job Sunday night," say, "The game where you had the kids chew Silly Putty was really ingenious. What a creative idea! I've never seen the kids that quiet. How long did it take the EMT to get Jimmy breathing again?"

5. Express gratitude and offer recognition. Special T-shirts or hats for the leaders, appreciation dinners, notes, phone calls, free babysitting from youth group students—all these are ways of saying "Thanks for doing what you do." Good youth ministry leadership courts volunteers, makes them feel appreciated, makes them feel wanted, lets them know that theirs is an important ministry.

In Ronald Wilson's imaginary "Letter From an Ex-Volunteer," he underlines this point.

> *Take Eddie Turner with his five kids, three of them teenagers. He's into everything. Practically eats and sleeps at the church. Now what if someone said to him, "'Hey, Eddie, two kids in the youth group accepted the Lord this week. All that driving around you've done to take the kids to Camp Ocheewahbee and the roller rink and everyplace really helped. You had a part in it." Not that Eddie needs anyone to say thanks, you understand. But the way he's going, he's going to need a little encouragement.*[16]

Don't underestimate the power of symbolic rewards. In their research on volunteer performance, Cnaan and Cascio[17] tested a variety of symbolic rewards to see if they had any influence on the three key longevity variables: Tenure, commitment, and satisfaction. Some of the variables examined were these:

- Thank you letters
- Certificates of appreciation
- Prizes

- Organized trips
- Parties
- Free meals
- In-house lectures
- Conference participation
- Newsletter publicity
- Luncheons
- Annual dinner
- Media publicity
- Volunteer of the month/year award
- Service pin
- Free parking
- Free medical service

Of these 16 items, only two (in-house conferences and media publicity) showed no correlation with any of the performance variables. Awards significantly associated with tenure were thank you letters, certificates of appreciation, and luncheons. Savvy youth workers will be intentional in affirmation and take every opportunity to "consider how [they] may spur [their volunteers] on toward love and good deeds" (Hebrews 10:24).

Job Design: Fitting Jobs to People Instead of Fitting People to Jobs

Consider the following case study. Cheryl has been working with the eighth-grade Sunday school class at your church for four years. She's recently said she is thinking about "taking some time off." Although you agree that she may just need a little break, you're concerned there may be other issues, and that she may end up leaving the team permanently. After all, she did make a point of saying, "I'm just not finding the job fits me the way I feel it used to."

Assuming the problem is with the position rather than some external problem (such as struggles with her marriage or job), how do you respond? Is there a way to keep this valuable veteran on your youth ministry team? You have several options:

- ***Let her have the break, and take the risk that she might not come back.*** Maybe all she needs is a little break to recharge her batteries—and then she'll be back. But a person like Cheryl is going to get plugged in somewhere, and it's a shame to lose someone with her skills, relationships, and experience. There must be a way to keep her involved.

- ***Bribe her to stay.*** Forget it. There isn't enough money in the youth budget to bribe anybody!

- ***Promise she'll never, ever have to do lock-ins again.*** No way. That's a lie, and besides, you need experienced people like Cheryl at the lock-ins so you can leave the church at 10 p.m. and go home to get some sleep.

- ***Give her a one-year sabbatical from youth ministry.*** This is a good idea, but a year is a long time. People get interested in other areas of ministry, and we lose them.

- ***Tell her scary stories about teenagers' problems, the need for willing volunteers, and the judgment of God.*** If Cheryl has been through four years of lock-ins, nothing is going to scare her!

- ***Redesign the job we're asking Cheryl to do.*** Rather than working so hard to change Cheryl's mind, change the design of the ministry to better use Cheryl's gifts and help her feel satisfied and challenged in her ministry. People are more important than positions. We recruit people. We don't recruit positions. The key is to make sure good volunteers find ministry roles that are personally satisfying and make good use of their unique gifts.

There are three specific strategies of job design by which we can tailor a position to fit the volunteer instead of changing volunteers so they fit the position: Job enlargement, job enrichment, and job simplification.

Job enlargement. One way to court Cheryl's commitment may be to enlarge her ministry, increasing the breadth of her responsibilities. Perhaps she isn't asking to step away from the ministry as much as she is asking to step away from her current role in the ministry. Maybe the ministry "doesn't fit her as well" not because she's weary, but because she's bored. Giving her more of a challenge could be one possible way of keeping her engaged.

For example, we might offer a new assignment as a "troubleshooter"—a teacher who rotates among the various youth Sunday school classes. After four years with the eighth graders, she knows most of the high-school students and has gained some valuable insights through her experience. So she's well-suited to this increased responsibility.

Another way to affirm Cheryl's ability and make use of her experience is to ask her to present teacher-training workshops for the other volunteers. Or maybe she would feel more challenged teaching a larger, combined junior-high Sunday school class, working with a team of volunteer helpers. She might feel motivated by leading a small discipleship group one afternoon a week in addition to her Sunday school responsibilities, or she might even prefer one-on-one discipling of two or three teenagers in her class.

Caution: When using job enlargement, assign jobs that really need to be done. Three meaningless tasks are probably not going to add up to one meaningful task.

Job enrichment. It may be that the better way to court Cheryl's commitment is not by changing the breadth of her ministry, but by changing the depth of her ministry. Most tasks have three main components: Planning (before), doing (during), and evaluation (after). Thus far, Cheryl's input in the youth program has been at the *doing* level. She has faithfully taught her class every week for four years. But someone else has decided what material she should use, where the class will meet, when it will meet, and whether or not it will include both guys and girls. Job enrichment is a strategy of redesigning Cheryl's ministry so she becomes more involved in planning and evaluation, keeping her fresh, fulfilled, and on the growing edge.

The kind of job enrichment we offer depends on the volunteer's unique gifts. Sheila had been playing guitar for the worship team; now she is asked to lead the team. Jim had been the bus driver for all youth outings; now the church asks him to head a committee overseeing the service and maintenance of the bus, and the possible purchase of a new bus. Charles and Marie had been leading a weekly Bible study group; now the council on ministry asks them to head up a youth committee. All of these are examples of job enrichment.

Job simplification. Of course, Cheryl may not be looking for broader or deeper responsibilities at all. Perhaps she's groaning under the burden of her many responsibilities as mom, wife, and part-time employee at the local bookstore. Like many of our volunteers, she's looking for less to do, not more. Thus, the third strategy of job redesign is simplification—taking a difficult task and breaking it down into more manageable responsibilities.

Cheryl's current responsibilities in an average week as Sunday school teacher include the following:

- Preparing her own curriculum
- Calling or visiting at least two of her students
- Sending a text to any students who were absent
- Picking up doughnuts before Sunday school
- Teaching her class during Sunday school

- Making announcements in worship pertaining to the overall youth program
- Securing all necessary media supplies for her lessons
- Making sure the classroom is cleaned up before she leaves
- Attending the monthly C.E. board meeting

To simplify her job we eliminate, delegate, or design a plan for sharing some of her tasks. In a team-teaching role, Cheryl could cut her load almost in half just by sharing some of the ongoing tasks of teaching, visitation, and curriculum preparation. Perhaps we could recruit one person who would tend to the media needs of all the youth teachers, freeing Cheryl of her weekly rummage through the media closet in search of an extension cord. Cheryl could delegate to students the responsibility of buying doughnuts and cleaning up the classroom. Maybe all the teachers could be represented at the C.E. board meeting by the youth minister or chair of the youth committee, or by a different teacher each month on a rotating basis.

What so often burns out the average volunteer is not jobs that are too challenging, but those that are too trivial. Are we asking volunteers to fill out detailed reports no one ever reads or heeds? Do we require that they attend extra meetings that neither train nor inspire them, just so we can say we've had our departmental meeting this week? These duties can exasperate good leaders.

COACH THEM

Luke reports that Jesus appointed 72 people to serve as his advance team in co-ministry. They were sent out "two by two ahead of him to every town and place where he was about to go" (Luke 10:1). But what is especially intriguing about Jesus' method with these folks is not that he sent them out; it's that he called them back. In Luke 10:17-20, we see Jesus with the 72, sharing and celebrating what has happened in their travels. It's like the locker room at halftime, and the coach has brought the team together to discuss strategy and give critical instruction.

The Master's model highlights the need for instruction and counsel if volunteer leaders are going to be equipped to complete their mission. Numerous studies have shown a positive correlation between good training and volunteer retention.[18] The great fear of most volunteers is that they'll be thrust into a small dungeon-dim classroom with a room full of adolescents and given absolutely no training on how to survive (sort of like latter-day gladiators). Unfortunately, this happens more than anyone wants to admit.

Volunteers can travel only so far on God-given talents. Even the best workers need to have their abilities honed and sharpened. We need leaders who send us out to do ministry, but then call us back, so we can discuss what worked and why, what bombed and why. People need to be trained gradually, at a pace that neither insults nor threatens them.

One of the most common paradigms for pacing a successful training process is by using what some refer to as the Four Phases of Ease:

- ***"I do it—you watch."*** The volunteer simply observes the job being done. Allow new volunteers to attend youth group or club for a few months before asking them to lead anything. Help them get used to the theatre before they are expected to take part in the play.

- ***"Let's do it together."*** At this point, the volunteer still isn't pedaling her own bike, but she is riding tandem. She's getting a feel for how this new role handles and turns, and what it takes to keep everything in balance. In practical terms, a leader might suggest to the volunteer something like this: "Look, next week's Bible study has four sections to it. You've watched me do Bible study now for about four months. You know most of the kids. Why don't we share responsibility for next week's Bible study? I'll do the opening and closing, and you do the two middle portions of the study."

- ***"You do it—I'll watch."*** In this critical phase of the training process, volunteers take steps independent of the supervisor's help, but the supervisor is still walking beside them in case they fall. This is what happens when students in college youth ministry programs serve as interns in various ministries, and then in class meetings the following week, evaluate what happened and, in some cases, what didn't happen. It's learning by doing.

- ***"You do it—I'll go train someone else."*** At this stage the volunteers have developed a level of competence that allows them to exercise their own ministries within the context of the youth group. No one has to constantly tell them what to do or how to do it. They have developed some instincts for what will and won't work in youth ministry. They still need to be updated on new resources and strategies, and they need ongoing feedback, evaluation, and encouragement. But they are now beginning to transition into fuller responsibility.

Effective training of youth volunteers requires training both before they start the work (pre-service training) and after the work has begun (in-service training). Although training procedures vary, certain basic training applies to any youth program. The following are sample topics that might be covered at the pre-service and in-service levels (Figure 11-4):

POSSIBLE VOLUNTEER TRAINING CURRICULUM
PRE-SERVICE:
Intro to Youth Group • A look at youth culture • Understanding our philosophy of youth ministry • Understanding how the youth program works (why we do what we do and why we've chosen to use certain programs)
Procedural Issues • What is my role within the team? • Who are the people I'm working with? • Where do I get teaching materials, resources, etc.? • How am I reimbursed for ministry expenses? • What happens in a medical emergency? • What happens in case of fire? • What is our procedure in case of discipline issues, fighting, etc.?
Youth Ministry 101 • Student-centered learning • Teaching the Bible in a way that puts students in the heart of the investigation instead of using a teacher-centered lecture approach • How to discipline in a youth group • How to get close to kids (contact work)
IN-SERVICE: • How to use questions effectively • Counseling kids who are hurting • Discipling students/One-on-one ministry • Stretching muscles of creativity

(Fig. 11-4)

We all tend to enjoy most what we feel we do best. If we want our volunteers to enjoy their work, we need to counsel them on how to do youth ministry well. Our biblical mandate as leaders is to "prepare God's people for works of service, so that the body of Christ may be built up" (Ephesians 4:12, NIV).

COVER THEM

By the time a youth worker has made the investment of recruiting, affirming, and training volunteers, stewardship suggests the investment should be protected. That's why the ongoing priority will be to cover the volunteers, protect them for long-term involvement—protect them from themselves, from the parents, and, paradoxically, even from the students.

Themselves. It is not the people who find youth ministry tedious and unpleasant who burn themselves out. It's the people who so enjoy their work with kids that other parts of their lives get out of balance. And that's sad, because the people youth ministry needs most are the very people most likely to burn out. Youth ministry is legendary for its abysmal record of retention. We go through leaders so fast that the kids they work with can scarcely learn their names, let alone build with them any kind of in-depth relationships. Volunteer ministry will need to be envisioned and explained in ways that protect the leaders.

For example, design a team approach that allows volunteers to have occasional days off. I have often told "Mom and Pop" volunteer youth leaders that they should take off one Sunday night in every eight just to have a Sunday evening with no ministry responsibilities.

"But what if there is no one else?"

Then don't have youth group that night. Better to have "no one else" for one out of every eight weeks than "no one else" for eight out of eight weeks. A volunteer who misses one meeting every eight weeks for three years is far more valuable than a volunteer who meticulously attends every meeting for eight months and then quits altogether due to exhaustion.

Parents. Nothing discourages volunteers as much as discovering how unappreciated they are by the parents of students with whom they're working. Except for those volunteers who are also parents, I don't believe volunteer team members should attend parents' briefings. When I have permitted volunteers to attend, I have occasionally been embarrassed for the parents and resentful of the way volunteers were treated. Honest criticism can always be passed along to volunteers through gentler, more sensitive channels. I ask parents to come to me first; then, if there is a legitimate concern, I translate that to the volunteer staff.

Students. Ironically, the more effective we are with students, the more apt we are to be smothered by them.

Bill was a volunteer leader who naturally drew students to himself. He was always spending time with kids. If he wasn't leading a Bible study with kids, he was preparing to lead a Bible study for kids. He was one of those dream volunteers who was always ready. Over the course of time, however, it became evident he was spending time with the youth group kids at the expense of time with his family. It was beginning to affect his marriage. Finally, at his wife's request, I took him to lunch and told him he would have to step down from the ministry team for at least a month or so to spend more time at home; that he needed to regain some balance in his life. It was a difficult conversation and a painful step to take, but it made more sense to release Bill in the short term so we could protect him and retain him over the long haul.

Although spending time with the students earns volunteers the right to be heard, so does a balanced and healthy life. We must make sure volunteers aren't neglecting family time, personal time, or other responsibilities at work or in school. If we care about our volunteers, we owe them that.

EACH DEPENDENT ON THE OTHERS

Trying to do youth ministry without a team, or with a team that is not fully utilized, is a common recipe for ministry exhaustion. But it's also an approach that loses the privilege of community, fun, shared adventure, fellowship, and the great pleasure that comes when God's people dwell in unity (See Psalm 133:1). It's not just an issue of burning out; it's an issue of missing out!

The four men who took to the roof to get their friend to the feet of Jesus (Mark 2:1-12) demonstrated a classic example of team ministry. They accomplished together what none of them alone would have been able to do. And by laboring together, risking together, hoping together, and caring together, they were able to bring a broken man into the healing presence of Christ. That is team ministry.

In describing the resolve of Meriwether Lewis and his determination to maintain the bond of his Corps of Discovery as they opened the American West, Stephen Ambrose uses words that, with some minor changes, could be used of a team of youth ministry volunteers venturing out into the frontiers of outreach and discipleship:

> The men of the expedition were linked together by uncommon experiences and by the certain knowledge that they were making history, the realization that they were in the middle of what would without question be the most exciting and important time of their lives, and the obvious fact that they were in all this together, that every man—and the Indian woman—was dependent on all the others, and they on him or her.
>
> Together, under the leadership of the captains, they had become a family. They could recognize one another at night by a cough, or a gesture; they knew one another's skills, and weaknesses, and habits, and background: Who liked salt, who preferred liver; who shot true, got the cooking fires going quickest; where they came from, what their parents were like, what dreams they had. Lewis would have hated to break them apart. He decided to hold them together. They would triumph, or die, as one.[19]

SECTION FOUR

MAINTENANCE

CHAPTER 12

Evaluating Your Ministry

The wisdom of the prudent is to give thought to their ways, but the folly of fools is deception.
(Proverbs 14:8)

Steve had just graduated from college with a degree in youth ministry. He began his first full-time position with high hopes. It was just the sort of position for which he'd been preparing for four years, and it seemed like a great fit. As one of his former professors, I was excited for him, and excited about what God was going to do through his ministry. I can still vividly remember exactly where I was when I got the phone call from Steve telling me he'd been fired. I can even remember the first words he said when I answered the phone: "I've been a full-time youth pastor for three months, thirteen days, and ten hours—and this morning, about twenty minutes ago, I got fired."

Tim was a youth pastor in a fairly large congregation. He knew the economy was turning the screws on the church budget, but it wasn't until he received a memo about the skate-park ministry that he realized how bad it was. He was told in that memo of the board's decision that the church could no longer justify the expense of this unique outreach ministry. It was not that they thought it was a bad idea. In fact, they loved the idea. But something had to be cut, and, in the grand scheme of things, the outreach efforts at the skate park seemed like a lower priority than some other items on the table.

Thea had taken her youth group to the same conference for three straight years. Everyone looked forward to that week. But then she heard about a different summer conference that would include all the normal program components—band, speaker, media, etc.—but with the added element of a mission service project in which every kid would participate. She knew it wouldn't be a popular decision, but she made her choice. This summer, it would be a new kind of camp experience for her kids.

In one form or another, each of these situations involves youth workers and their churches making serious choices that center around questions of evaluation. What are we doing—and how well are we doing it? What are we doing wrong? What could we do better? Are we seeing the results we want? Are we doing anything that really makes a difference? How do we set our priorities? Are those priorities reflected in our practical ministry decisions? These are important questions.

How do we evaluate a youth ministry program? By the size of the group? The size of the budget? The size of the youth worker's paycheck? What are some practical ways of sizing up the strengths and weaknesses of a youth ministry?

STOP, LOOK, AND LISTEN

"If you have completely lost your bearings, try to get to a high vista and look around."

—Joshua Piven and David Borgenicht,
The Worst-Case Scenario Survival Handbook[1]

Like most other males of the species *homo sapiens*, I would rather drive aimlessly, hoping to find my way, than pull over and actually look at a map that shows me the way. Don't get me wrong; maps are great. When I'm on the right road headed in the right direction, they can be very affirming. But maps are also ruthlessly honest. If I'm on the wrong road and moving in the wrong direction, there is little room for self-deception. The only reasonable response is course correction. And that may take me on a route I hadn't wanted to travel, or perhaps a route where the scenery is less pleasant. But if I really have a destination in mind, and I really and truly want to get there, I have little choice but to stop my car, look at the map, and listen to what it tells me to do. That, in a nutshell, is evaluation.

For a wise youth worker seeking to be a good steward of opportunities and resources, evaluation is an essential discipline. So why do we resist it?

Evaluation Can Make Us Uncomfortable. The way I eat is no different from most children. I like hot dogs, hamburgers, fast food, and special delicacies like Spam, cream of mushroom soup, and rice casserole. What I don't like is pizza, dressing on my salad, and any dish I've never tasted. When the subject of my diet is discussed, as it often is, I'm inevitably asked this question: "Duffy, you sure have a different kind of diet. Do you ever have any trouble with your cholesterol count?"

My answer: "No."

"What about your triglyceride level? Are you having any trouble with a high count there?"

Again, I answer: "No."

Astonished, these people glance down at my plate of Hamburger Helper and look back with disbelief. "Man, that's incredible. How do you do it?"

That's when I tell them my secret: "I never get it checked. It's wonderful. I've never had a high reading in my life."

To be completely truthful, I recently had my cholesterol checked (and yes, it was fine, thank you). But I think I avoided that check-up for the same reason heavy people don't weigh themselves and people who haven't brushed aren't eager to go to the dentist. None of us is thrilled to find out where we are missing the mark. To some of us, a performance review feels a bit too much like a firing squad. Evaluations can be intimidating.

Whether we're talking about cholesterol levels or youth ministry, ignorance may be bliss, but it is also very risky. Serious youth ministers cannot afford to gloss over evaluations. "Whoever heeds correction shows prudence" (Proverbs 15:5). Evaluation is not always a pleasant exercise, but it is an important one.

Evaluation Seems a Little Unfaithful. One of the quasi-spiritual myths that haunts the church is the idea that *God's blessing means God's sanction.* In other words, we too easily assume that, if our ministry is growing and flourishing, then we must be doing everything right. But flourishing youth ministries are no indication that God sanctions either our methods or our attitudes. In fact, when we think back about the ministries of guys like Moses, Elijah, Jeremiah, Jesus, and Paul, we begin to recognize that our ministries may sometimes experience serious struggle precisely *because* we are doing God's will. God's blessing in our ministries says more about his abounding grace than about whether we have chosen right or wrong courses in ministry. We can't excuse ourselves from evaluation just because God is blessing our work.

Evaluation Feels Unnecessary. This resistance to evaluation can play out in two ways: As arrogance or as ignorance. (1) *Arrogance: We're already doing things the best way they can be done.* With that arrogant assumption, we put off evaluation, smugly assured that no one knows how to do the job better than we do. We've peaked. There is no way to improve on what we're doing. The corporate claim of Hewlett-Packard is, "We never stop asking, 'What if?'" Unfortunately, many of us in youth ministry never stop asking, "Why should we?" (2) *Ignorance: What do we know? We're doing what the experts say.* We like to be assured that the experts know best. We love the safety of doing what *they* say. That gets us off the hook. That places upon the experts the responsibility for our ministries. We don't have to risk experiments and tough thinking because we do only what the experts say to do. But the fact that a method has been published in a youth ministry book somewhere doesn't mean it's the best one; it just means it's the best one known to that author. Experts are only experts because they've made almost every mistake once, and *they took time to evaluate why it didn't work.*

Evaluation Seems Sort of Unspiritual. Any real evaluation of a youth program has to include an assessment of the ministry team. But many of us feel reluctant to render judgment about the performance, or even the spiritual maturity, of current or potential teammates. I mean, come on, didn't Jesus say, "Do not judge, or you too will be judged"? Obviously, we expect some kind of scrutiny in a secular job, but is it appropriate in a community of brothers and sisters? Do we really have the right to evaluate another person's work or suitability for spiritual leadership?

The answer is, no, it is not our right to judge others; but, yes, it is our responsibility to judge others (See Matthew 7:15-20; 1 Corinthians 5:1-13). This is not a role earned because we're better and more spiritual than others; it's a role required because whether we be volunteer or paid, we're called to be good stewards of God's household, and that means faithful, thoughtful use of people, time, and money (See 1 Corinthians 4:1; 1 Peter 4:10).

Evaluation Is Scary. I once made the mistake of looking for a pen under the cushions on our sofa. What I discovered was a nightmare of leftover cookies, popcorn, used Kleenex, and a smashed doughnut. And I was faced with the unhappy prospect of having to clean up the mess (except for the doughnut, which was a little dry, but otherwise not too bad). I've since made it my policy to never lift up the cushions on our sofa.

We neglect evaluation because we are afraid of what we'll find. And we're afraid of the mess involved in trying to clean it up. It's easier not to ask too many questions.

Effective Evaluation Can Be Difficult. Ultimately, a lot of us resist evaluation simply because we lack the know-how. We hear students remark, "That was awesome," or, "That was boring"; we hear parents worry, "You're doing too much"; we hear deacons and board members complain, "You're doing too little"; we hear some nice old lady comment, "The young people's group is a blessing." But how do we assess all this stuff?

The writer of Proverbs counsels us to "give thought to (our) steps" (14:15). For thoughtful youth ministers, that means we should be doing the kind of evaluation that affirms specifically what we're doing right and demonstrates specifically what we're doing wrong. Let's look at how this works.

STAGE 1: CLARIFY THE VISION

It is impossible to evaluate our ministry marksmanship if we don't have a clear sense of the target. We begin the process of evaluation by determining goals. Whether we develop a vision statement or hammer out a philosophy of ministry, whether we are reaffirming old goals or establishing new ones, it is absolutely critical that we begin the evaluation process with this stage. It's impossible to tell how close we are to the mark if no one is willing to define it. Proverbs 14:15 reminds us that a simple person will believe anything, but the prudent give thought to where they are going.[2]

STAGE 2: EXAMINATION

José is a conscientious youth worker. He loves the Lord, and he loves teenagers. But he's troubled by recent facts and statistics that rattle around in youth ministry cyberspace:

- A majority of youth group seniors drop out of church after graduating.
- A long-term study of youth group graduates shows that 40-50 percent of students struggle with their faith beyond high school.
- One pastor calls youth ministry a "50-year failed experiment"[3]

But how does José get his arms around his own youth ministry so he can do serious evaluation? I'm convinced that a thorough inventory must explore four different elements of a youth ministry: *Program, Protocol, Personnel, and Personal.*

I. PROGRAM Evaluation: Three Vital Signs

The evaluation process is essentially about asking basic questions: What are we doing right (our strengths)? What are we doing wrong (our weaknesses)? What can we do better (improvements)? In measuring our programs against these questions, there are three vital signs we must examine:

- Finances,
- Attendance, and
- Goal achievement.

Finances. Although it's probably the least reliable barometer of ministry effectiveness, a simple cost analysis can offer a youth worker valuable information about his or her ministry. I'm not talking about some lengthy accounting process that requires banking experience. Cost analysis simply involves looking at each element of the youth program to see what it actually costs. This allows the youth worker to compare the cost of a specific program to its value for the youth group.

My most vivid experience in cost analysis was when we evaluated our youth program's involvement in a church basketball league. After accounting for all expenses entailed in our participation (league membership fees, gym rental fees, uniform expenses, insurance, transportation costs), I divided the total cost of the program by the number of guys on the team. With only eight or nine regulars, the cost came to over five dollars per student per game. That may not sound like much at first, but we began discussing as a ministry team if we really wanted to spend five dollars per kid per week to get guys to play basketball. It seemed a bit ridiculous.

As we measured the expense of the basketball league against other elements of the youth program where the money might have been used, we considered three options: a) require members of the basketball team to pay all costs associated with the league; b) require kids involved to assume some of the costs and, in addition, to complete certain "homework" assignments that might contribute to their personal spiritual growth; or c) cancel the program. We knew students wouldn't cough up five bucks a game; and after trying option b for one season, we found team members did not support that alternative either. That left us only option c. We simply couldn't justify the money and time the basketball team was costing us.

The same basic method can make other information available to us. If we want to find out how much our ministry spends per teenager per year, we would simply divide the total program budget by the number of active youth. If the total youth ministry budget is $4,500 and there are 85 youth active in the program, we can see that, on the basis of the youth ministry budget alone, it's costing the church approximately $52 dollars per year—or one dollar per week for each student in the youth program. Now, obviously, this does not take into account the salary of any paid youth ministry staff. But the point is not to gloat over inexpensive ministry; the point is to try to find some ways of gaining financial data about the ministry.

It's important to remember that finances are the *least* reliable criterion of evaluation. Some activities will be consistently self-sustaining in terms of finances, while others will consistently lose money. But let's remember that our goal is to make a prophet, not a profit. I'll fund a Bible study over a beer blast any time, although the latter might predictably draw a bigger crowd. A youth ministry shall not live by "bread" alone.

Attendance. One eternal truth of youth ministry is that kids vote with their feet. If they don't like a program, they won't come to it. To that extent, attendance is a good criterion for evaluating a youth program. But as an indicator of faithfulness, attendance is only slightly more reliable than finances. Evaluating on the basis of attendance generally measures wants, not needs.

The Penner Park Church was one of those congregations in which numbers were used to evaluate almost everything: *How many members did we gain? Do we have as many in Sunday school as we did last year?* The youth workers at Penner Park were so preoccupied with numerical growth that they began to forget why they were there. Programs that might have helped students grow spiritually were replaced by programs that offered fewer opportunities for growth, but drew larger crowds.

A drop-in center in which any Christian witness was somewhere between low-key and nonexistent replaced the weekly Bible study. Christian music was dropped for music the youth said they liked better. Predictably, attendance increased. The drop-in center began to draw about a hundred kids weekly. And everyone was so exhilarated by the increased attendance that folks forgot to ask this question: Is a drop-in center that draws a hundred students a better ministry than a Bible study that draws twenty students?

When churches become more interested in building numbers than in building disciples, they forget the fundamental principle that *as commitment increases, attendance decreases*. When our programming calls for a greater level of spiritual commitment from kids, we shouldn't be surprised that fewer kids are willing to make that kind of commitment. That means that if we evaluate a program strictly on the basis of numbers, we'll have a program that's high on crowds and low on discipleship. On the other side of the coin, we're kidding ourselves if we offer only "quality programs" that don't actually draw students. It's not how many healthy meals we cook; it's how many hungry mouths we feed. It's impossible to do youth ministry without youth, and to that extent, *numbers do matter*. Those numbers represent people, and people are who Jesus died for. Numbers count, so we have to count numbers. But we can't put so much weight on numbers that we forget the core mission of making disciples.

Goal achievement. Every year, each of the ten senior staff members of Lima Bible Church presents to the elders a list of goals for the upcoming year. Then periodically throughout the year, the executive pastor and the staff reflect on how well they are meeting these goals. This process of evaluation uses goal achievement as its major criterion.

Perhaps some of us read about this church and say, "Who needs to evaluate? They must be doing something right! We don't have as many kids in our youth group as they have on their senior staff!" But that, of course, is precisely the point. The more a youth ministry grows in attendance, the more important it is that it not be driven by numerical growth, but by asking, "Are we accomplishing anything? Are we moving in the direction of our vision?"

Larry Richards recommends evaluating a youth ministry by a model that defines goals in three key areas of the youth-ministry program: Bible, Life, and Body.[4] Using Richards' approach, we evaluate group needs and design program goals based on three key questions:

- Bible: Are our students growing in their basic knowledge of biblical teaching?
- Life: Are our students weaving that biblical truth into the fabric of their everyday lives?
- Body: Are our students living out kingdom relationships—are they being the body of Christ?

Designing specific objectives based on these questions allows leaders to evaluate how effectively their youth programs are moving the group in the desired direction.

Another goal achievement assessment is based on a concept conceived by Dennis Miller.[5] It imagines the overall youth program as being shaped like a funnel (Figure 12-1)—wide enough at the top to bring students in, but intentional enough at the bottom to accomplish our objectives. Using that funnel design, the program is evaluated on the basis of students' movement through various levels of Christian growth:

- *Come Level*—an initial contact with the program;
- *Grow Level*—a willingness to attend programs where spiritual growth is involved;
- *Disciple Level*—a desire to take the initiative for their own spiritual growth;
- *Develop Level*—a willingness to assume responsibility for the spiritual growth of other youth (at this level we *develop* their gifts and abilities to do ministry);
- *Multiplier Level*—an ability to assume some responsibility for their own personal ministries.[6]

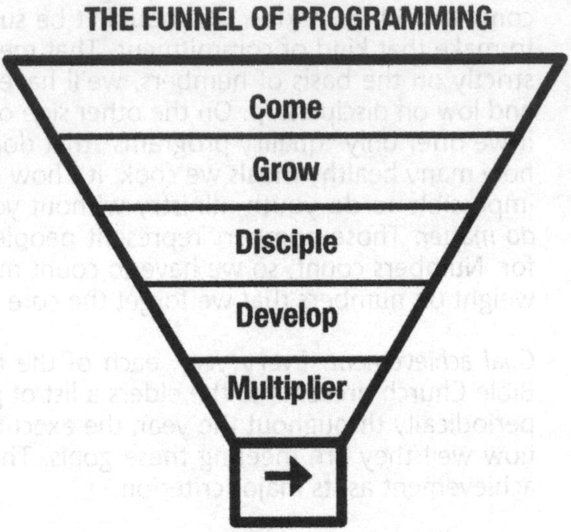

Figure 12-1

We could evaluate our programs by asking two questions in relationship to this funnel of commitment: Which of our activities minister to students at the various levels of commitment? Which students do we have at the various levels of commitment?

Some youth pastors have designed informal survey tools to get feedback about the program from volunteer staff on a weekly basis. The key to such a process is making it convenient for volunteers. We don't want to saddle team members with a lengthy form they will have to fill out (and we will feel obligated to read) on a weekly basis. But a short form that gathers input from team members could be a valuable way to stay current, particularly in a larger ministry.

You could use a similar process to collect feedback less frequently. The form that follows is quite a bit longer than anything I would suggest for a weekly evaluation. It was designed as a means of inviting quarterly input.

QUARTERLY LEADER EVALUATION
FIRST CHURCH

NAME:____

DATE:________________

Program Evaluation: Sunday

1. Please give your overall evaluation of our Sunday night Breakaway meetings.

2. Any suggestions concerning the program or the overall ministry?

Bible Study: Wednesday

Middle School

Sr. High

1. Please give your overall evaluation of the Wednesday night Bible study.

2. Any ideas of suggested topics of study?

Contact Ministry (time spent with youth outside of regular programs)

1. Who are some of the kids you've been investing in over the last quarter?

2. In what contexts (small group, contact work apart from program, Onward Bound)?

Any other thoughts, concerns, threats, input?

While there are a number of different models that can be used, evaluating programs based on goal achievement boils down to one basic strategy: It begins with defining our goals, and then identifying specific objectives that will help us meet our goals or specific outcomes that will indicate that we are meeting our goals. These objectives or outcomes must have three important qualities: 1) They need to be *measurable:* We need to know whether we're meeting them or not. Example: "We plan to start two small discipleship groups for high-school-age youth by October 1." 2) They need to be *reachable:* It does no good to set goals we cannot possibly reach. Bad example: "We will have U2 play in our Sunday morning worship on Mother's Day, with the pastor singing lead and his wife playing tambourine." 3) The objectives must be *ownable:* Each objective must be embraced by enough of our leadership and youth that it can be accomplished without destroying the youth group. Example: "We plan to do one mission outreach project every other month, and take one major mission trip this July."

Having formulated specific objectives, we can then assess how effective specific elements of the program are meeting those goals and objectives. Rather than just spending time and money on programs because "we've always done this" or because they are well attended or because nobody has a better idea, we ask ourselves the following kinds of questions before and after each specific activity:[7]

- Which of our goals does this program or activity help us attain?
- Does this activity fit into our program and ministry objectives?
- Do we understand what this program or activity is about? What if it were wildly successful? What would it look like? What would it accomplish for us?
- Do the kids own this program or activity? (How can we increase the buy-in among our students?)
- How much time, effort, and cost is required to do this program or activity?
- Do we really have the right talent to lead this program or activity?
- Does it fit the unique ministry context of our group (group size, group personality, commitment level of students)?
- Does the current physical setup (room arrangement, etc.) maximize the effectiveness of the program?
- Is there some sort of training we could offer to our leadership team that would make this program or activity more effective?
- What risks are involved in this program or activity?

- Assume Murphy's Law for a moment (Anything that *can* go wrong *will* go wrong). What could go wrong with this activity? What are the consequences or costs if that happens?

Part of our sacred responsibility in youth ministry is careful evaluation to make sure we are faithful trustees of both opportunities and resources. It begins with the program, but it extends to three additional key areas as well.

II. PROTOCOL Evaluation: Do Everything Decently and in Order

When the apostle Paul exhorted the Corinthian church do all things "decently and in order" (1 Corinthians 14:40, KJV), he was talking about their corporate worship. But earlier in that passage, he makes this comment: "God is not a God of disorder..." (1 Corinthians 14:33), observing that God is the one who makes order out of chaos. Because an effective youth ministry will reflect that same value in the way it functions, it is important, probably on an annual basis, to do an evaluation of the ministry protocols.

Now, if, when you read the word *protocol*, your mind immediately went to Jack Bauer, CTU, and the TV show *24*, I have two comments: First of all, you watch too much television, and secondly, Chloe for President. But what we're talking about here is a little more mundane than a real-time terrorist plot. When we talk about evaluating *protocols* we're really talking about "the efficiency and effectiveness of policies and procedures."[8] Admittedly, this stuff is easy to ignore, partly because it is so mundane, and partly because it focuses more on process than product. Most of us are in youth ministry to cultivate "fruit that will last"; we're not as keen to worry about keeping count of the plants, maintaining the greenhouse, and having a plan in place if the sprinkler system goes haywire.

Here are some practical questions to help you think about your youth ministry protocols:

Maintenance Protocols

- Who is responsible for maintaining youth ministry-owned equipment (data projector, computer, software, XBox, hot tub, etc.)?

- What are the protocols for making surface changes (painting, carpeting, furniture) to spaces used by the youth ministry?

- Do we have a means of keeping accurate attendance records?

- What is our procedure for handling monies paid into the ministry for youth activities? Are there accountability safeguards built into that process? (For more on this, see chapter 9.)

- What is our protocol for following up on first-time visitors or students who make first-time commitments to Christ?

Emergency Protocols

- Do we have an evacuation plan in place if our facility catches fire during a youth meeting—something more elaborate, say, than "Grab the laptop, head for the exit, pray that kids will get out okay"? And do our leaders know that plan?
- Do we have a procedure in place in case of serious injury during a youth activity? And do our leaders know that procedure?
- What are the guidelines by which we decide to cancel a youth ministry activity (for reasons weather-related or otherwise)?

Discipline Protocols

- What is our protocol for dealing with violence at a youth activity (bullying, fighting, etc.)?
- What is our procedure for dealing with acute discipline problems? (On what terms might we decide a student be disallowed to come to youth group?)

For most of these issues, it won't be necessary to change protocols on a regular basis. But there are good reasons for reconsidering these questions annually, including group changes (attendance, age, size), facility changes, and protocol inadequacies (Our procedure doesn't really address our needs).

III. PERSONNEL Evaluation: Exegeting Your Ministry

Youth ministry veteran Dean Borgman likes to say that one of the first steps in doing ministry is "exegeting your community." Basically, that means taking a good look at the people to whom you are ministering, taking time to understand the soil into which you plan to sow the seed of God's Word. In this phase of evaluation, we turn our attention away from the youth program itself (See Phase 1) and refocus attention on the youth *in* the program. We consider, at least, these three questions: *What are the needs of our youth? How do they perceive our program? Are our youth growing spiritually?*

What Are the Needs of Our Youth?

I will never forget my week at a Bible conference in Florida one winter. I thoroughly enjoyed the in-depth teaching and preaching. I learned a lot. But I observed something about the culture of the average midwinter Bible conference in Florida. The week I attended, 95 percent of the people in the audience were over the age of 70. That's why I was so amused when one of the preachers devoted the bulk of one of his messages to the issue "Why premarital sex is unbiblical." I whispered to my wife that a more appropriate title might have been "Why premarital sex is impossible!"

We in the church have a bad habit of scratching where nobody itches. As youth workers we can easily fall into this same trap, doing youth ministry based more on seasons, habits, expectations, or the latest youth ministry fads than the needs of the youth around us. But how do we assess those needs?

There are several different kinds of tools:

Paper Surveys. Before doing a four-week series on sex and dating, I surveyed my high-school students to get some idea of their values and opinions. The survey was unscientific, but we hadn't actually planned to submit it to *Scientific American*. We asked the youth to give us honest, anonymous responses to a few basic questions like these:

1. I want to marry someone who is a virgin.

Strongly Agree   Moderately Agree   Neither Agree nor Disagree   Moderately Disagree   Strongly Disagree

2. It's okay to be involved with someone sexually if (check the one that *best* represents your opinion):

☐ you really love them

☐ you like them a lot

☐ they will let you

☐ you have been dating for at least three months

☐ you can remember their name

☐ Other

3. At least three of my friends are currently dating someone seriously. (True or False.)

4. Define what you consider to be "serious dating."

I chose these four questions because they represent four different formats. Question 1 uses what is called a five-point Likert response scale. It's helpful in giving youth a shorthand way to express their attitudes. Question 2 offers youth an opportunity to complete a sentence. It was actually shaped with the specific intent of tying it into a specific point in one of the studies. Question 3 is formatted with a True/False response. Essentially, it was designed to set the stage for the open-ended Question 4.

Now, obviously, a survey like this is only as good as the questions used. So care should be taken to make the questions simple, clear, and unambiguous. Try to craft your questions so that they address only one idea.[9] You'll probably want to add some basic questions that will provide demographic background (age, gender, frequency of attendance) as well. One caution when you use a survey like this: Unless you have a very large youth group, your survey sample is too small to draw any grandiose conclusions. If one of your four students is involved with his girlfriend, the survey will show that 25 percent of your students are sexually active (and if the girlfriend is in the youth group, the figure shoots up to 50 percent!). So try to resist the temptation to generalize too much.

Online Surveys. These require a little more know-how in terms of the technology. But the benefit is that they can offer maximum anonymity, and can be designed so respondents are not allowed to skip a question. If you use an instrument like this, make sure all your students have access to a computer so no one is left out.

Facebook survey. Less formal, and unscientific. But, depending on your purposes, it could still be an easy-to-use, helpful tool.

How Do the Youth Perceive Our Ministry?

The youth ministry is for the youth—so why wouldn't we want to know their attitudes about our ministry?

I once served in a youth ministry that had two different kinds of small groups—some were coed and others were gender-specific. I made the mistake of suggesting to one high school girl that we combine the two. It seemed like a good idea to me. I thought the kids would be relieved by the cutback in scheduling. In response she gave me a look that fluctuated between outrage and confusion—as if I had proposed filling the baptistry with jellybeans. One easy way to find out what the youth in your group think is to ask them. This is best done informally, in the course of normal conversation. Youth are remarkably responsive when they believe we sincerely want their opinions. We may not always hear what we like, but we may hear something we need to hear.

As with our inventory of the needs of our youth, we could get feedback on their attitudes about the youth ministry by using some sort of paper or online survey. The following is a sample from an inventory originally appearing in *Group* magazine.[10] It asks teenagers to offer their input on the youth program using the imagery of weather. Frankly, I'm not sure I like the questions so much. But I appreciate the idea of surveying students' attitudes by using creative categories of response.

Check the box that fits your opinion.

Our youth-ministry programming...

	Sunny	Partly Sunny	Partly Cloudy	Cloudy	Stormy
...Involves young people in the planning process.	☐	☐	☐	☐	☐
...Uses surveys, needs assessments, and conversation to discover kids' needs.	☐	☐	☐	☐	☐
...Meets young peoples' needs and is relevant to their lives.	☐	☐	☐	☐	☐
...Publicizes well in advance so kids know what's coming.	☐	☐	☐	☐	☐
...Communicates to the whole congregation what young people are doing.	☐	☐	☐	☐	☐
...Sets clear, specific goals and objectives.	☐	☐	☐	☐	☐

Are the Youth Growing Spiritually?

One question we'll want to be asking is whether we are seeing the fruit of the Spirit—love, joy, peace, patience, kindness, goodness, faithfulness, gentleness, and self-control (Gal. 5:22-23)—in the lives of our students. Jesus said the best way to learn something about a tree is to observe its fruit (Matt. 7:15-20). Of course, any attempt to make an appraisal of a student's heart is going to be limited. But acknowledging those limitations, we could use the following exercise to *observe the fruit*:

> *Step 1:* Each member of the leadership team (students or adults) lists all nine fruit Paul mentions in Galatians 5. Each leader then adds two to three other fruit of the Spirit implied in other portions of Scripture. (Ephesians 4:29, for example, implies the fruit of encour-

agement—an ability to build others up. Philippians 2:5-7 implies the fruit of humility—a willingness to put others before oneself.)

Step 2: Each leader writes out one practical way each fruit might be manifest in a group of teenagers. (For example: Self-control—youth exhibiting this fruit are willing to be quiet when others are speaking or sharing with the group.)

Step 3: Combine the various lists of fruit and their manifestations, and allow youth and/or leaders to grade the group on how well they exhibit the various fruit described (perhaps using a scale of zero to ten, with ten meaning "very evident," and zero meaning "nonexistent").

Or you could use a questionnaire tool. Several years ago I developed a test teenagers could use to help evaluate their own spiritual growth. It's based on the idea of going to the doctor for a physical. The full text of this survey appears elsewhere.[11] But a sampling of some of the questions offers an idea about how it would work.

A SPIRITUAL "CHECKUP"

I. Pulse: Are you a Christian?

Describe your relationship with Jesus Christ.

On a scale of 1 to 10 (1 = potential axe murderer, 10 = the next Mother Teresa), how would you rate your relationship with Christ? Why?

II. Red Blood Cells (carry the oxygen that prevents anemia or sluggishness)

A. Devotional life:

1. Do you spend any time during the week reading the Bible or praying on your own? Describe these times and about how often you do this.
2. How would you like to see these times get better? And what do you think is keeping these devotions/quiet times from being all they could be?

B. Relationships that keep the arteries open:

1. In what ways do you feel you and God have friendship together?
2. Do you have a church fellowship where you try to regularly take part in Sunday worship? Describe.

III. White Blood Cells (disease fighters for inner spiritual cleansing and renewing)

A. How does your faith in Christ affect your ability to be accepting, loving, and forgiving?

B. How do you deal with feelings of guilt?

IV. Brain Scan: Check out your mind

A. What are three of the biggest doubts or questions you seem to struggle with?

B. What are you doing to deal with those doubts and questions? What could you be doing?

C. How would you describe your understanding of the Bible? Pick one of the following phrases that best sums up your ability to find helpful answers in the Bible:

1. Bible? What's a Bible?
2. I can't ever find anything I need when I need it.
3. I'm okay with the New Testament, but the Old Testament is like an old "B" movie with blurry subtitles.
4. I think I'm beginning to get more out of the Bible when other people teach or speak from it.
5. I'm a regular Bible whiz kid: Next stop is memorization of Leviticus.

D. How well do you feel you understand the basics of the gospel? Try to write a simple answer to the following questions:

1. What is sin?
2. What are the effects of sin?
3. Who is Jesus?
4. How does he deal with our sin?
5. Why does God offer us the gift of life with him?
6. How do you receive that gift?
7. Who is the Holy Spirit and how does he fit in all of this?
8. If you were a contestant on a TV game show and the host asked you to explain the following terms, which could you *not* explain? Circle them:

SANCTIFICATION	JUSTIFICATION	GRACE	FAITH
CONFESSION	REPENTANCE	FRUIT OF THE SPIRIT	

E. How would describe your ability to fight off temptation? Choose the phrase below that best describes your approach.

1. Hot dog! This looks like fun!
2. Honk if you love Jesus!
3. Get the heck out of Dodge.
4. Pray.
5. Get with some people who are stronger than me.
6. Other.

IV. PERSONAL Evaluation: "Search me, O God, and know my heart..."

The fourth and final area of focus for a thorough evaluation of the youth program is the assessment of ourselves. This is the most critical area of examination and, unfortunately, also the most neglected. It is far too easy to just "keep on keepin' on" week after week—stoking the fires of the program, neglecting the flame that kindles our hearts—until, finally, something snaps. We stand up to shine and the light has gone out.

I remember when I first read the book *Dance, Children, Dance.*[12] It was one of those books I saved for vacation, waiting to read it until I had time to fully "dialogue" with the author. By the time I had finished the first chapter, I was so captivated by the story that I finished the book in two days. *Dance, Children, Dance* is the autobiography of Jim Rayburn, the founder of Young Life, a man who is both a legend and a pioneer in the field of youth ministry. His life story captured wonderfully the drama, the joy, and the high adventure of ministry with teenagers.

But, just as clearly, it gave a portrait of the grave danger stalking even the most gifted youth minister: The danger of an unbalanced life. His story of damaged health, a less-than-healthy marriage, and a family of people who both loved and resented their ever-absent father hit close to home. That book inspired my wife and me to take time for some stout, honest, personal evaluation.

There are no easy tricks for self-examination. It requires the following:

Time. Reflection takes time. Promise yourself at least one day every six weeks.

Accountability. Follow-through is more likely to happen if we know someone is going to follow up on us.

Openness. David's prayer in Psalm 19 takes us right to the difficulty in this task. "Who can discern their own errors? Forgive my hidden faults" (19:12). Like rats in the basement, our sins usually hide in the dark places of our self-deceit. In a rare moment of self-discovery we may glimpse what those around us have seen—missed opportunities for conversation and refreshment, a diminished sense of joy and contentment in our work, shortness of temper, various and sundry other balls that get dropped along the way. But rather than admit the rats are there, we blame the droppings on other factors. For this sort of self-examination we need to pray for openness to the Spirit's enlightenment.

Contemplation. Contemplation is intentional listening to God. It is cultivating quiet spaces in our lives, not so that we can shut down, but so that we can shut up long enough to hear the voice of God. As Gordon MacDonald reminds us, the contemplative person "has learned that there are some things best heard in silence...The contemplative [person] has sensitive spiritual fingertips like the proverbial safecracker who can feel the slightest movement of the tumblers behind the dial on the vault."[13]

Spiritual Direction. It may be helpful to ask someone to meet with you on a regular basis with the sole intent of asking that person to help you listen for what God is doing in your life. I have seen firsthand the impact of this kind of ministry through my wife, Maggie, a spiritual director who meets several times a week with college students, pastors, working moms, and an assortment of other earnest folks who simply want someone to help them carve out a space, a time, and a context for hearing God in their lives.[14]

A Bible. This living and active Word that judges the thoughts of the heart (Hebrews 4:12) keeps us from wandering into self-persecution or navel-gazing.

What Am I Looking For?

The work of self-evaluation takes place at several different levels.

Interpersonal support. Am I cultivating a group of people who hold me accountable and build me up in faith? How do I relate to these people? Am I open to their input?

Leadership behavior. Am I the sort of leader who has to control everything? Am I a shepherd who pastors the youth, encouraging them in their baby steps of growth, or am I a sheriff who pesters them, always nagging kids about what they aren't doing? How do I function within the leadership team? Am I developing and deploying the gifts of others? How do I handle decision-making?

Family life. Do I ask my spouse to honestly evaluate my ministry to my family? In what ways do I celebrate my family? Am I making my family as special and fun an experience as I make my youth group? Am I as willing to have my plans interrupted by a family member as I am by one of the youth group kids? Am I taking a consistent day off with my family? How are we as a family protecting our unique community so that we maintain our special identity and intimacy?

Spiritual vitality. Is my heart still warm for Christ? Do I take time to maintain a personal devotional life that is completely separate from my preparation time for youth group? Am I trying anything that really forces me to have genuine trust in God to help me succeed? Am I reading books that deepen and enrich my understanding of the faith?

Personal growth and enrichment. What am I doing to feed my mind? Am I seeking out books, articles, or podcasts that take me deeper than next week's message and beyond the latest youth ministry hot topic? Am I exposing myself to sources of input that stretch me to think about theology, culture, and the world outside the youth ministry biosphere?

STAGE 3: STAYING ON TRACK

Evaluation is an ongoing process. In that sense, there's no such thing as a *final* stage. But, there is an inherent pattern to the process. First, we pause to reconsider and reaffirm our ministry vision (stage 1), and then we perform a thorough inventory that assesses the program, protocol, personnel, and personal aspects of our ministry (stage 2). But what gives the pattern shape and consistency is the third stage of the process: A commitment to staying on track.

When I first moved to Massachusetts from North Carolina, I was amused at the six-foot poles with flags attached that lined the roads near the seminary I attended. I couldn't imagine the purpose of those markers—until about two months into winter. I discovered that these markers were to guide the plows as the snow got deeper and deeper. No matter how many times the road was plowed, new snowfalls meant new confusion about where the road was and where the road was not. I can only assume that a few lawns were inadvertently snowplowed before someone realized the need for these markers.

In the same way, a youth ministry that is thoroughly evaluated can stay on course through future blizzards of busyness and activity only if consistent markers are put in place to keep that ministry on the right track. Having plowed through the evaluation process, here are some markers that will keep us on course:

Regular Meetings. Meet consistently with volunteers, student leaders, parents, and others who share the vision. Encourage and challenge one another to keep true to your common vision of discipling teenagers.

Frequent reevaluation. Frequent reevaluations with small adjustments are not nearly as difficult as once-a-year (or less frequent) evaluations that may reveal numerous problems that can be healed only through major corrections and radical surgery.

Cold-blooded programming decisions. If a program doesn't help your ministry reach the prescribed goals, cut it. Be wed to the message, not to the method. If Plan A seems to be ineffective, then it should be scrapped—cut off—neat and clean. When we experiment with new ways of solving problems, our attitude should be "Yes, and..." rather than "Yes, but..."

Good records. A clear picture of the youth ministry's past gives a much clearer picture of its future.

Long-range planning. Long-range planning allows us to get a better idea of where a program is taking us. The long-range picture provides perspective that allows us to see where the program is presently and where it is going. It is easier to chart a westerly course by following the sunset than by rechecking the compass at every turn in the road.

In *The Genesee Diary* Henri Nouwen gives an account of life within a monastery community. He tells the story of a day when, while baking raisin bread as part of his community responsibility, he made an interesting observation.

> For four and a half hours I worked with Brother Theodore and Brother Benedict at the raisin washer. Theodore washed, Benedict collected the raisins, and I folded empty boxes. Suddenly Theodore stopped the machine and knocked with his fist against his head. Not knowing sign language, I said, "What's the matter?" "A stone went through," he said. I asked him, "How do you know?" He said, "I heard it." I asked, "How could you hear it between the noise of the machine and the raisins cascading through it?" "I just hear it," he said, and added, "We have to find that stone. If a lady gets it in her bread, she can break her tooth on it and we can be sued!" Pointing to the large bathtub-like container full of washed raisins, he said, "We have to push those through again until we find that stone."
>
> I couldn't believe it. Benedict hadn't been able to detect the stone while the raisins came out, but Theodore was so sure that objection was senseless. Millions of raisins went through again, and just when I had given up ever finding that stone—it seemed like looking for a needle in a haystack—something clicked. "There it is," Theodore said. "It jumped against the metal wall of the washer." Benedict looked carefully and moved his hands through the last ounce of raisins. There it was! A small purple-blue stone, just as large as a raisin. Theodore took it and gave it to me with a big smile.
>
> In some strange way this event meant a lot to me...We were looking for a stone among millions of raisins. I was impressed, not only by Theodore's alertness, but even more by his determination to find it and take no risks. He really is a careful diagnostician. This little stone could have harmed someone—a lady or a monastery.[15]

Effective youth ministry means becoming careful diagnosticians. We are doing a work for Christ, and the impact of our ministry is felt directly in the lives of students. We simply cannot afford to be sloppy in our work. Frequent, ongoing evaluation is a part of our calling, part of caring. And caring is what youth ministry is about.

CHAPTER 13

When the Tie Binds: Dealing with Conflict

They had such a sharp disagreement
that they parted company.
(Acts 15:39)

Joe, the salaried youth minister at First Church, has been faithfully employed by the congregation for three years. His wife, Jane, has been a willing co-minister with Joe, volunteering significant time with the youth and consistently serving the Lord, the church, and her husband. This spring, however, Joe is facing a problem that's becoming a major obstacle in his ministry. And Jane is not a happy camper.

For the past three years, the youth group has done an annual missions project. It's the part of the youth program that's most personally satisfying to Joe, and most strategically effective in his work with the kids. The funds for the mission project have always been under the jurisdiction of the missions committee, chaired by the outreach pastor, Napoleon Pickabone. This year, the missions committee wants Joe and the youth group to participate in a denominational missions project in South Dakota. Joe feels the project will not be nearly as valuable for his group as what they've done in the past three years. In fact, he's not even sure the project is valid.

Joe wants to see the funding system changed so the youth mission project funds are directly under his supervision. He feels the present system effectively puts this important part of the youth program under the control of Napoleon Pickabone and his committee. Aside from this particular missions trip, Joe feels there is a principle at stake here.

The pastor of First Church is the Reverend Genghis Warren. He's told Joe to back off. He feels the issue is not worth getting Napoleon and his committee up in arms. That committee's role in raising money for mission outreach is critical, and if a problem erupts with them, it will be a serious problem indeed (read: "It will hurt giving"). Joe is disappointed that Pastor Warren is siding with the missions committee and Napoleon instead of trusting in his leadership. Joe sees the whole issue as being one of trust.

As emotions and tensions accelerate around this issue, Joe's wife doesn't like what she sees happening to her husband. Two months after the issue emerged, with no resolution in sight, Jane suggested that maybe it's time to move on to another ministry. Jane's pain makes Joe even angrier...

THE "C" WORD

Most of us in the church don't like to talk about conflict. As children we were told: *If you can't say something nice, don't say anything at all.* We were taught that nice people don't argue, and that "niceness" is the cardinal virtue.

Yet the implicit message of Scripture is that there are times when conflict is appropriate and godly behavior. In fact, it's quite clear, if we have something against a brother or sister, or if we feel another Christian has something against us, the *last* thing we should do is sit on it and stew (Matthew 5:23-24; Ephesians 4:25-27).

As a demonstration that believers are not immune to conflict, Acts 15:36-40 gives us a rather surprising glimpse into a clash between Paul and Barnabas, two titans of early church life.

> Some time later Paul said to Barnabas, "Let us go back and visit the believers in all the towns where we preached the word of the Lord and see how they are doing." Barnabas wanted to take John, also called Mark, with them, but Paul did not think it wise to take him, because he had deserted them in Pamphylia and had not continued with them in the work. They had such a sharp disagreement that they parted company. Barnabas took Mark and sailed for Cyprus, but Paul chose Silas and left, commended by the believers to the grace of the Lord.

Notice those words: *They had such a sharp disagreement.* They jut out of the passage like a jagged shard on a smooth surface. This is Paul (the church's first and greatest missionary) and Barnabas (the "son of encouragement"), for heaven's sake. We prefer to think these heroes of the early church would never be involved in any kind of conflict—certainly not a conflict that they couldn't just pray through, talk out, and resolve. This is like Billy Graham taking a swing at Mr. Rogers!

It gives us an opportunity to make two preliminary observations about conflict:

1. Conflict is normal, even among godly people. This intriguing narrative of the troubled relationship between Paul and Barnabas confirms that godly people who are walking in the Spirit, sensitive to God's Word, and burdened for ministry are quite capable of coming into conflict with one another. There's just no way to dismiss their "sharp disagreement" as an insignificant squabble.

These two men, having faced unbelievable ministry challenges together, now, in the face of disagreement, are so divided that they decide to split up.

2. Conflict isn't necessarily bad or immoral. We also note that Luke's account in the Book of Acts gives no hint that the early church was particularly embarrassed by this conflict—which is pretty surprising in light of how much Paul's letters emphasize the importance of unity among believers. It appears the church accepted certain kinds of conflict as valid, normal, and a fact of community life. Indeed, we are told that Paul and Barnabas went off in their separate directions, "commended by the believers to the grace of the Lord."

MYTHS ABOUT CONFLICT

To say youth workers are not immune to conflict is an understatement along the same lines as "Well, General Custer, looks like we might not make it back to the fort in time for movie night." In a survey for *Group* magazine, youth workers cited a wide range of conflict causes: "The senior minister's abuse of power, families with money or influence seeking to control the church, gossip and rumors, the youth minister's lack of clout, power plays over the church budget, negative people on church boards, adult expectations overruling the youth group's need, committee red tape, and money-making ministries getting priority."[1] And we could add to that list theological disagreement, conflict over worship styles, disenchantment with the organizational climate of the ministry (staff relational styles, understanding of what it means to be *professional*, supervision style), generational differences, and more. Unfortunately, not much has changed since Paul wrote these words two thousand years ago: "I hear that when you come together as a church, there are divisions among you, and to some extent I believe it" (1 Corinthians 11:18). If we do youth ministry for very long—perhaps a day or two—we will have to deal with conflict.

If conflict has been part of the church since the first covered-dish dinner, why do we fear it so much? A number of misconceptions breed our fear of conflict.

Myth 1: Only dysfunctional and ineffective ministries experience conflict. The word *conflict* comes from the Latin word *fligere*, which means literally *to strike together.*[2] In practical terms, conflict occurs when "two or more people (or parties) perceive that what each one wants is incompatible with the other."[3] The writer of Proverbs uses the metaphor of *iron sharpening iron* (Proverbs 27:17), which reminds us that if the sparks don't fly occasionally, then one of your striking pieces isn't made of the stuff you think it is. To imagine a staff or ministry where conflict never happens is to imagine a staff or ministry where most of the people lack passion, initiative, creativity, or all of the above.

Myth 2: Conflict must always be avoided or suppressed. We often act as if the only appropriate response to conflict is to reduce, stifle, or eliminate it. But as former senior pastor Earl Palmer observes:

> It can be a good experience for a staff to have even a painful confrontation. Our staff has had that happen several times, and in each case it's been for the good of each of us. We never would choose confrontation gleefully. No one likes confrontation because it means admitting that we've failed each other somehow. But we ministers are in a prophetic tradition. We shouldn't run away from that positive heritage of confrontation, yet it has to be done with skill and love."[4]

Forest fires can be terribly destructive, but the National Forest Service often ignites controlled burns, clearing out deadwood that impedes new growth and protecting biodiversity in the habitat. Conflict is not always to be feared, but it is always to be wisely and honestly managed.

Myth 3: Conflicts are the result of clashing personalities. Personalities do not conflict. Behaviors do. Two people, one of them wild and crazy, the other serious and thoughtful, can work together for years without having any trouble—until their *behaviors* conflict.

It's true that people with certain personalities tend to exhibit certain kinds of behaviors, and that those behaviors may rub people of different personalities the wrong way. But it is the behaviors—and not the personalities—that cause the conflict. Ron Susek, in his book *Firestorm: Preventing and Overcoming Church Conflicts*, offers three possible responses to potential conflict:[5]

- Acceptance (I *choose* to want you, and I will learn to tolerate our differences even though they sometimes cause me frustration.)
- Adjustment (I *choose* to change for you, so that our differences can complement, or, at least, not detract from each other.)
- Appreciation (I *choose* to understand you, and I recognize that your personality and your gifts bring to the table some strengths that I do not have.)

Making a clear distinction between personalities and behaviors is a crucial component of dealing with conflict. Every potential conflict makes several choices available. Conflict doesn't have to happen just because there are two or more people with contrasting personalities. If it were so, a staff member could approach his supervisor and say, "Y'know, Pastor Joe, I've been having some struggles lately with Jill. I know she's a great Worship Pastor, but would you be willing to ask her to change her personality?"

GETTING CLEAR ABOUT CONFLICT

One of the first steps in resolving any conflict is making sure we understand what we're fighting about! This process of conflict definition is primary. We can't be peacemakers if we don't know who the combatants are, where the battle is taking place, and what the fighting is about. One way to think through this information is by understanding what Ron Susek calls the Four Levels of Conflict.[6]

LEVEL ONE: Facts or Data. A Level-One conflict occurs when parties simply have different information. This is the easiest kind of conflict to resolve.

I used to do a weekly radio show in Philadelphia with my good friend and teaching colleague at Eastern University, Tony Campolo. Our show was called *Let's Talk It Over*, although we jokingly referred to it as Let's Over-Talk It. Anyone who listened to our show realized Tony and I had different political leanings. Tony comes from a more liberal political perspective, while I come from a more Christian perspective (just kidding). But every now and then we would quarrel over something that was not a matter of differing viewpoints or interpretations—but a matter of fact. Tony would suggest, for instance, that unemployment rose under a certain president, and I would insist it decreased. This kind of conflict was easily resolved by going back to data from the Bureau of Labor Statistics and uncovering the actual facts (which neither of us was willing to do!).

Within the realm of youth ministry, a Level-One conflict might involve a dispute over which topics the students want to study, how much the youth budget has increased over the last five years, or whether or not the last four summer retreats have all been in mountain locations. To resolve a Level-One conflict, we simply postpone further discussion until we have the accurate information on hand.

LEVEL TWO: Processes or Methods. Joy, the youth worker, and Mark, the Christian education director, both know there's been a decrease in attendance since the church began using new curriculum. The facts about attendance are not in dispute, and they both feel the downturn is connected to the curriculum change. But they disagree on how to turn the trend around. Mark says to scrap the new curriculum. Joy says the problem is not the material itself but the teacher-training process. She believes they need to do a better job training the teachers who will use the new curriculum.

Generally, the key to resolution of a Level-Two conflict is compromise. Since the issue is more a question of "How do we get there?" than "Where should we go?" compromise is usually a realistic option. Joy and Mark agree that Sunday school attendance has decreased, and that this negative trend needs to be reversed. How they do so is negotiable. For example, Joy might suggest offering better teacher training during the next four months; if attendance does not improve, then they would drop the curriculum.

LEVEL THREE: Goals or Purpose. At this level, the parties in conflict cannot agree on a proper goal for their mission. Perhaps Mark feels attendance is not even an appropriate criterion for evaluation: "We should be focused on discipling a few students and training them to reach their friends for Christ. Let's not get hung up on how many kids show up!" Joy says, "Our kids aren't going to reach out to their friends until they're more spiritually mature, and they won't mature if we can't get them to come to nurturing activities like Sunday school. So we have to be concerned about attendance!"

Negotiations at this level take patience and skill. Many youth ministers retreat from this kind of conflict because they simply are not of the temperament to work through the hard issues and uncomfortable dialogues that often accompany resolution of a Level-Three conflict. Clearly, one key to resolution at this level is having a strong mission statement the group can use as a guide for staying on course (see chapter 5).

LEVEL FOUR: Values. The deepest and most serious conflicts relate to values—the parties disagree about basic meanings. Both Joy and Mark feel burdened to "reach the students for Christ," but John and Marilyn, a married couple on the volunteer team, feel that what gets called "reaching students for Christ" is nothing less than brainwashing. They are uncomfortable with what they describe as "fundamentalist, fire-and-brimstone evangelism." Dialogue at this level becomes tremendously difficult because the parties are using the same words with different meanings.

Frankly, resolution of a conflict that's rooted in different core values is almost impossible. The only thing more ludicrous than asking someone to change his or her personality is asking people to change their core values and convictions.

Overlapping Levels

Defining the level of conflict can help us choose appropriate, positive routes to resolution. Unfortunately, most of the time, conflicts aren't neat. As we explore and excavate conflicts, we may discover that a disagreement between coworkers that seems to be at one level is really a smoke screen for the real conflict at another level. The following case study illustrates how one situation may include several different overlapping levels of conflict:

> A designated gift had been given to benefit the church's mission program. At its next regular meeting, the church staff began to brainstorm about how the funds might be used. Some staff members felt the issue should be decided by the staff. One felt the finance committee, representing the entire congregation, should decide. Still another felt the congregation should ultimately be allowed to vote. The pastor felt the money should be used for their local radio ministry as a home-mission project. The youth pastor felt the money should be used for a mission trip to Haiti. The children's minister

felt the money would best be used to start a childcare outreach in the community. Another staff member felt the matter should not even be discussed in a staff meeting. He felt the church was wrong to accept a designated gift in the first place. He feels it gives a single individual too much control over the finances of the congregation.

As you reflect on this case study, identify at least one example of each of the four levels of conflict.

Level One:____________________________________

Level Two:____________________________________

Level Three:__________________________________

Level Four:___________________________________

Causes of Conflict

The first and best way to deal with negative conflicts that are draining and disruptive is to recognize the circumstances that give rise to such conflict. If you don't want to breed rats in you house, you'd better deal carefully and completely with the garbage. The question for youth workers is, *What kinds of garbage cause disruptive conflicts in a youth program?*

Fuzzy Lines of Responsibility. In our opening case study, Joe felt that, as youth pastor, all aspects of the youth ministry were his responsibility—particularly the annual youth missions project, which Joe identified as one of the most significant aspects of his work. On the other hand, Napoleon and his committee were acting on a mandate the church had given them—to allocate funds for missions projects. The problem here is that, to some extent, both Joe and Napoleon were right. The conflict surfaced not because one person or one group was power hungry, but because there was no clarity about who was responsible for the decision regarding a youth missions trip. Ambiguous jurisdiction is one of the quickest ways to brew unproductive conflict.

It was Benjamin Franklin who said, "Love your neighbor, yet don't pull down your hedge." Almost two centuries later, Robert Frost gave us the more familiar proverb, "Good fences make good neighbors." It may feel uncomfortable to confront an interviewing committee or church board with specific questions about lines of responsibility and authority, but direct and straightforward inquiry is the most loving and thoughtful way we can circumvent some of these problems.

Conflict of Interest. Conflict may grow out of competition for scarce resources—financial, human, or physical (such as available rooms or vehicles). For example: The youth committee wants to buy a new van. The worship committee wants a new sound system for the sanctuary. Both groups know the pie is only so big. If the youth committee gets a bigger slice of the pie, the worship committee feels it is being starved.

Communication Barriers. One of the most basic facts about communication is that it is meaning exchange, not word exchange. It's like the old cartoon from Gary Larson's "The Far Side" which offers two pictures of the same incident. In frame number one, entitled "What we say to dogs," a guy is yelling at his dog, "Okay, Ginger, I've had it! You stay out of the garbage! Understand, Ginger? Stay out of the garbage or else!" In the second frame, entitled "What they hear," we see the same bemused little pooch staring up at her master as he yells, "Blah, blah, Ginger, blah, blah, blah, blah, blah, Ginger, blah, blah, blah..."[7]

Of course, we need to have our facts right—but the right facts communicated in the wrong way can sound a whole lot like wrong ideas. Joe made some assumptions about the funding from the missions committee. The missions committee made some assumptions about their authority over monies designated for youth missions projects. Since neither group had carefully articulated their assumptions, a conflict erupted. Building in strong lines of communication for honest and frequent dialogue among team members, staff members, youth, and parents is an essential for avoiding needless conflict in any youth ministry.

Body Odor in the Body of Christ. Have you ever argued with a stranger who's in an elevator with you? Probably not. Why? Because even if your riding companion is whistling off-key or smoking a cigar or exhibiting some annoying habit with his nose, you simply won't be spending enough time with him to make it worth attempting honest dialogue about the areas of offense. On the other hand, co-ministers, staff members, or members of a youth ministry team spend a lot of time together and will face a host of decisions they cannot avoid. They simply will be occupying the same space at the same time for too long a time to avoid all conflict.

Need for Agreement. The more important it is that a group reach total agreement on an issue, the less likely it is that the group will be able to avoid conflict. If it's a question of how to grill hot dogs, people are open to lots of different opinions. My wife likes to use tongs, my buddy uses a fork, and, being a true man, I just use my hands. Our differences breed little conflict because a grilled hot dog is a grilled hot dog. The stakes are just not that high. We agree to disagree. On the other hand, if my wife thinks we should have another child, and I am happy to stop with two, there is more likely to be serious conflict. We can't resolve this issue by saying, "Let's just agree to disagree."

If Joe and the missions committee were trying to decide between a Saturday clean-up project and a weekend overnight at a homeless shelter, the issue might not provoke as much emotion. They could do either one—or maybe even do both. But when it comes to the annual missions trip, and what Joe perceives to be the more basic fundamental principle of trust and authority—it's much more difficult for him to simply agree to disagree.

Generational Differences. Some older people in the congregation feel uncomfortable when the worship incorporates some new and creative element they aren't used to. The pastor can't understand why the younger members of the staff keep asking for time to meet together when, in fact, the staff meets for two hours every Monday to conduct congregational business. The church treasurer—a wonderful, faithful gentleman in his late seventies—can't comprehend "Why we need all this computer stuff for the young people when we used to just have a Bible study in the church basement." Parents can't understand why the youth director shows up for Sunday school in jeans, shaved head, and sporting an earring. After all, she's the mom of one of the kids! (Just wanted to see if you're paying attention.)

We run into these generational differences all the time. And, again, they often stem from the fact that these situations have different meanings for different individuals. The youth worker who wears jeans to church wants to make sure teenagers know they're welcome regardless of their dress or appearance. He may not realize that what's intended as a gesture of warm welcome to one group of people is seen as a gesture of disrespect by another group of people. Sometimes conflict is born solely from these differences in generational perception.

Theological Disagreement. The youth worker doesn't emphasize water baptism as much as the pastor feels she should. The pastor feels the youth group is too charismatic, and worries that "things are going to get out of hand." The youth minister, on the other hand, feels the pastor's preaching lacks an adequate emphasis on the missional nature of the church. The board thinks the youth ministry should put more emphasis on the theological distinctives of the denomination. One group of parents thinks the youth pastor's use of secular music and movie clips communicates a worldly message to the young people.

Missed-communication. Miscommunication is when two or more parties misunderstand each other (see "Communication Barriers" above). Missed-communication is when the communication between the parties just never happened. The parents are angry they weren't informed that the youth group is beginning a fairly in-depth study in sex education. The youth worker forgot to tell the pastor of his plans to use the sanctuary for an all-nighter.

One of the first lessons to learn in youth worker diplomacy is that neither parents nor pastors like surprises. Certainly, there are times when it is "easier to get forgiveness than permission." But don't be shocked when the decision to bypass requesting permission makes it harder to get forgiveness.

Diversity in Perspective. One member of the youth staff feels we need to spend more time emphasizing personal holiness. Another feels our students are weak in the area of service. Another feels that the kids get enough serious stuff at school: "Let's show them they can be Christians and still have fun."

Majoring in Minors. Insisting that:

- the youth minister be at every meeting;
- the youth pastor always wear a tie or a dress (or both);
- any youth ministry intern must be from the congregation's denominational background;
- the Sunday school should always use the denomination's official curriculum;
- the youth retreat always end on Saturday so students can be back for Sunday morning worship.

The more lines that are drawn, the more likely it is that someone will step across one.

Environment. Sometimes conflict is born out of the organizational climate. Is it too rigid? Too formal? Too traditional? Too restrictive? Too lax? Too directive? Not directive enough?

Lack of Relationships. Comments, criticisms, and incidents that might warrant only a blip on the radar between parties with a history of friendship and trust can become seismic issues between parties who lack that same relational history. A volunteer might feel angry and hurt by the youth pastor's semi-negative feedback about the volunteer's teaching technique. The breakdown may come, not so much because the criticism was unmerited or too harsh, but simply because the two people had no relational capital to draw from.

Reflection Exercise

Go back and reread the case study that opens this chapter about the mission project funds at First Church. Rank the characters in order of who is most at fault in the conflict (1=least at fault):

________ Joe, the youth minister

________ Jane, Joe's wife and a ministry volunteer

________ Napoleon Pickabone, outreach pastor and chair of the missions committee

________ Missions committee

________ Genghis Warren, pastor

Now, here's a key question: What kinds of issues do you believe brought the saga of Joe and the mission trip to such a grim threshold? Or, to put it another way, which of the factors we've reviewed in the previous paragraphs might have set the stage for this drama of conflict?

In the list below, check the factors that you think are present in the conflict, and then rank (1-5, with 1 being the key factor) what you consider to be the top five factors that caused this conflict.

☐ ____ Fuzzy Lines of Responsibility.

☐ ____ Conflict of Interest.

☐ ____ Communication Barriers.

☐ ____ Body Odor in the Body of Christ.

☐ ____ Need for Agreement.

☐ ____ Generational Differences.

☐ ____ Theological Disagreement.

☐ ____ Missed-communication.

☐ ____ Diversity in Perspective.

☐ ____ Majoring in Minors.

☐ ____ Environment.

☐ ____ Lack of Relationships.

ANATOMY OF A CONFLICT

As we've seen, the sources for conflict are many and varied. Take one or more of the circumstances we've just listed, toss them in a cauldron with a dash of miscommunication or missed-communication, and you'll soon have some genuine conflict brewing. Sometimes it takes just one incident or remark to bring the whole thing to a boil. When that happens, the basic formula is fairly simple. It can be understood in terms of the diagram on the next page (Figure 13-1).[8]

The conflict starts with a *frustration*. In our case study, the frustration centers around the disputed funds for the youth mission trip.

Then, that frustration gives birth to a *conceptualization* about what lies behind the frustration. *Why is this happening?* And, of course, everyone involved in the conflict perceives the situation a little differently. If we take a moment to think through the perceptions of the various characters in our case study, we begin to see how conflict heats up so quickly.

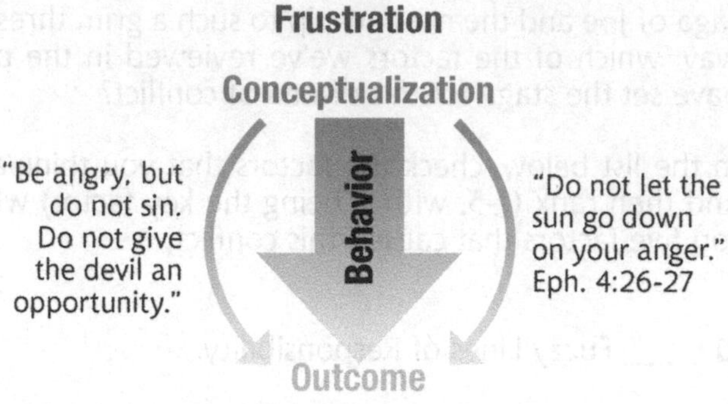
Frustration
Conceptualization
"Be angry, but do not sin. Do not give the devil an opportunity."
Behavior
"Do not let the sun go down on your anger." Eph. 4:26-27
Outcome

Figure 13-1: Anatomy of a Conflict

- JOE: For Joe, the youth pastor, this is about trust. Joe feels Napoleon and his committee don't trust him to do what is right for the students. And, even more painful, Pastor Warren doesn't seem to trust or respect him enough to step in and protect Joe's authority over the youth ministry.

- JANE: For Jane, this is about respect. Clearly, these people are not giving her husband the respect he deserves.

- NAPOLEON: Napoleon feels Joe's complaints are a power play. Napoleon and his committee are in charge of missions. It's a responsibility they have taken seriously, and they've valued their involvement and support for the youth ministry through the South Dakota mission project. *Why is this a big deal for Joe all of a sudden?* Is he trying to re-draw the boundary lines of responsibility? Napoleon and his committee refuse to become a rubber-stamp dispenser of mission funds. They will continue to do their work conscientiously and strategically. If Joe doesn't like it, he can get his funding from another source.

- GENGHIS: At this point, he feels the whole affair is primarily an annoyance. From his office, it looks like Joe is whining, and that Jane is behind his discontent. He wonders if she just wants to leave, and perhaps feels that this is an opportunity for her to drive a wedge between Joe and his colleagues on the church staff.

It's like the old story about the six blind men and the elephant.[9] One man touches the beast's tusk and thinks the elephant is like a spear. Another touches the elephant's tail and thinks the elephant is like a rope. Another, upon touching the ear, says that the elephant is like a big fan. Still another, who touched the animal's massive belly, proclaimed that the elephant was like a great wall.

A fifth, embracing the massive leg, thought the elephant was more like a giant pillar. And the sixth man, holding on to the elephant's trunk, said that all of them were wrong because the elephant was more like a great pipe. Often when we're in conflict, each person has his hands on the same situation, but each one feels something different. This is where communication, trust, and cool heads are so important, because, as the diagram indicates, people begin to act on the basis of their perceptions.

The *behavior* of the various individuals may confirm the perceptions of other conflicting parties, or it may help redefine the perceptions of other conflicting parties. Let's look at how each of these dynamics might happen:

> *Confirm:* Joe feels he's not been trusted by the mission committee, and feels disrespected by the pastor. Ultimately, he feels his ministry is not being valued by others at the church. So Joe puts out some feelers to other ministries, wondering if, perhaps, it's time for him to move on. Even though a move was not Joe's initial intention (nor was it Jane's), if Genghis gets wind of this search, that could confirm his perception of the whole affair.

> *Redefine:* On the other hand, suppose Genghis, demonstrating leadership that we've not seen before now, goes to Joe and asks if he and Jane are feeling restless. And, in the course of that conversation, Genghis assures Joe that, notwithstanding the current skirmish, he *is* a much valued member of the team. On the basis of that conversation, Joe begins to wonder if there is more to this conflict than his being disrespected. And, on the basis of his conversation with Joe, Genghis begins to see he was wrong in assuming Joe wants to leave.

Joe and Genghis recalibrate their perceptions of each other, they may behave differently toward each other, and may even develop different conceptions of the funding issue itself. Recognizing this, we can see from the diagram the importance of following the biblical injunctions to be proactive in dealing with conflict (Ephesians 4:26-27; See also Matthew 5:22-25).

It is not wrong for people to get angry, any more than it is wrong for six blind people to form six different perceptions of the same elephant. We are limited human beings, and our perceptions are not always accurate. What is wrong is to let those false perceptions fester into something that infects the body of Christ. That's why Paul offers his sharp command, "'In your anger, do not sin': Don't let the sun go down on your anger..."

DEFINING, DEFUSING, AND DIFFUSION

If conflict often stems from differing perceptions of the same situation, one of the best ways to defuse conflict is to re-define the situation. The best way to facilitate this re-defining process is to give those touching the elephant an accurate sense of the bigger picture. We can't help that our biases and prejudices impact how we see, but we can pool our various perceptions with the hope of getting a better view of the whole. This is akin to what Larry McSwain and William Treadwell refer to as diffusion.[10] Here are some basic strategies of diffusion:

1. Be sure everyone in the group knows the facts of the situation. Again, all of us are blinded to some degree. None of us can claim what Leonard Sweet calls immaculate perception. So the first step is to make sure everyone is working with the same set of facts. We all know how quickly misinformation travels through a ministry community. It's key to get out ahead of the gossip and untruth so those involved at least start with accurate information. "Don't give the devil an opportunity..."

Having said that, let's add this word of caution: This doesn't mean involving a whole new segment of people who are not involved in the conflict. That will provide just enough hot air to fan the spark into a firestorm and inflame the situation needlessly. It would be like announcing over the loudspeaker at a large sports event, "Your attention, please: A few people have shared their concerns that the large dome roof above your heads is about to cave in. If you've heard anything about this, or even if you haven't, we just want you to know, it's not true." This is not about cover-ups and denials; it's about discretion. We don't need a whole lot more blind people touching the elephant. We need those who are touching the elephant to get a better sense of the big picture.

2. Try to uncover the history of the conflict. If you've ever watched a tussle break out in a football game, you know that most such incidents have a history. Maybe it was a hard block on the previous play, or a harsh word spoken to the press in the previous week. It doesn't usually begin with the offense the ref saw. It probably began earlier, with some offense the ref never knew about.

Most conflicts are perceived in terms of relative simplicity: He said and she said. In fact, to fully pull the weeds of conflict out of the ground, we have to recognize there are usually deeper roots beneath the surface. What sort of history might have led Joe to believe the South Dakota trip would not provide the kind of mission experience he wanted for the group? Are there other backstories between Joe and Napoleon, or Jane and Joe, or Jane and some member of the missions committee, that might be at the root of the conflict we now see above the surface?

3. Get the right people involved—no more, no less. Looking through binoculars to get the very best view of the landscape requires focus. Sometimes the lens needs to be adjusted in (you're too far out); sometimes the lens needs to be adjusted out (you're too close). The clearest focus is somewhere between these two viewpoints. In solving conflict, we often face the same kinds of difficulties in gaining an accurate focus on the problem.

Too far out: We don't want too many people involved in the definition/resolution process because that can only lead to distortions. Six blind men touching an elephant have six different opinions about what they see. But the situation isn't improved by bringing in someone who has never seen or touched an elephant—someone who, were it not for a meeting called to discuss the matter, would not even be aware there was such an animal. There's no need to involve a lot of people who have no vested interest in the problem. That only spreads the conflict and makes the conflict look bigger than perhaps it should.

Too close: On the other hand, sometimes expanding the view beyond just what can be seen by the immediate parties can provide a better context for conflict definition and resolution. The six blind men might be helped greatly by a seventh blind man who is able to touch two or three parts of the elephant at the same time. That would offer a way to correct their personal perspectives.

It would be easy for Joe, Napoleon, and the others in our case study to see this conflict as primarily a personal one. But, in fact, this isn't a personal conflict between Joe and Napoleon, it's a conflict about funding a mission trip for the teenagers. Joe's opinion about the trip may be shared by the entire youth committee. But if Joe is the only one given an opportunity to represent that position in a meeting, the chances of positive engagement are lessened, because it too easily decays into something personal. It might be worthwhile to invite members of the youth committee to advocate for their position rather than having Joe stand alone. Or, instead of framing this conflict as a duel between Joe and Napoleon, perhaps the dialogue could take place between members of the youth committee and members of the missions committee.

Conflict resolution begins when we have the problem in clear focus, and clarity of focus is what we gain by having the right number of people involved in the process—no more than we need, and no fewer than we need.

4. Delay action until there has been time to manage the conflict. This is tricky. There's a fine line between letting the sun go down on your anger, and acting so quickly that you just start shooting from the hip before you really know what the target is. These first five steps of diffusion are, in part, designed to slow down the process of conflict so cooler heads can prevail and information can be gathered.

These steps of diffusion usher the parties into what McSwain and Treadwell describe as the problem-solving analysis process.[11] In this stage, the parties can begin to

- Consider all the gathered facts, feelings, and opinions about the point in contention;
- List possible options for resolution, considering carefully the pros and cons of each option;
- Prioritize the options on the basis of pros and cons;

- Depersonalize the options so the decision centers on an issue, and not on a personality. (Again, that's probably one factor that's made our case study a little sticky—it's been framed as *Joe vs Napoleon*.)
- Try to develop a consensus for the option that best resolves the problem. Remember (chapter 6) that different kinds of solutions might be better suited to different kinds of problems.

CONFLICT RESOLUTION IN THE REAL WORLD

Of course, conflicts don't always fit the nice schemes and prescribed questions. We find ourselves dealing with two groups who don't even *want* to resolve their conflict. Or we discover the issue at stake has been discussed, and we weren't even invited to the meeting. Or we find ourselves confronted by an issue that's so hot it threatens to divide the youth group down the middle, and we can see no route to resolution. Every situation dictates its own approach. Yet even when there aren't any obvious solutions, the following are some general principles we can abide by in conflicted situations:

- *The "win-win" principle.* Look for a solution that makes both parties winners. It isn't always necessary for one party to lose for the other party to win.
- *The principle of involvement.* Any time we can involve the disputing parties in the process of finding a solution, we are moving in the right direction. It is much easier for people to follow through on solutions they have initiated. When the youth of a certain congregation complained that Sunday school was dry, boring, irrelevant, obtrusive, and a waste of time, the youth minister formed a team of students to survey the youth group and propose a Sunday morning program that would meet the needs of the youth as well as the goals of the youth ministry. Almost immediately, the complaints dropped off. We youth workers tend to always accept complaints as *our* problem. We zoom back to our programming kitchen to cook up some new idea we hope kids and parents will like. And when they complain, "No, this time it's overcooked," we rush back to try some other concoction. The better approach may be to show the parties the ingredients we're working with and allow them to come up with their own recipe.
- *The "nip-it-quick" principle.* The sooner we deal with conflict, the more effective we will be. Our tendency is to hope it isn't happening, pray it will stop happening, and turn our heads the other way while it's happening. But Scripture and experience urge us to action: "Get rid of all bitterness, rage and anger, brawling and slander, along with every form of malice" (Ephesians 4:31). A sapling can be pulled from the ground with just one hand. But a

full-grown oak tree cannot be pulled up with even a hundred pairs of hands.

- *The principle of positive assumptions.* Conflicts are much easier to resolve when each party agrees to assume the best about the other. If the youth worker enters the process convinced the board doesn't really care about the youth program, he generally comes away with the same conviction. Negative assumptions trap us into being reactors instead of initiators.

- *The principle of the here and now.* The trustees complain that the church van has returned from the last two youth retreats dirty enough to warrant health inspection. Rather than dealing with the issue under dispute, the youth minister responds, "Well, nobody made any big speech about the elementary Sunday school Christmas party that left the place looking like "King Kong Meets Santa's Workshop." In conflict, our best progress occurs when the parties focus on the problem at hand. Historical baggage unrelated to the current issue under dispute hinders resolution. Save other issues for a separate discussion.

- *The principle of first agreement.* Always begin conflict resolution by having parties focus on their areas of agreement. We usually "get down to business" by saying "here's the problem." We should begin at the other end of the equation—by asking, "What do we agree on?" This establishes common ground that allows us room to maneuver for a resolution.

- *The dangerous-opportunity principle.* I am told that the Chinese symbol that represents the word *crisis* is a character that combines the symbols for the words *danger* and *opportunity.* Seeing conflict as a "dangerous opportunity"—a chance to find new alternatives, stimulate new thinking, open new dialogue—we're more likely to approach the process with optimism, making resolution more probable.

BLESSED ARE THE PEACEMAKERS?

I once heard Gordon MacDonald tell of a time when he and his family were stopped on the highway by traffic backed up in both directions waiting to get under an overpass. When he stepped out of the car to see what the holdup was, Gordon discovered a bewildered skunk, standing in the middle of the highway, struggling to get a Nestle's Quik container off its head. MacDonald was intrigued by the notion that all these people wanted to help this skunk get out of his predicament, and any of them had the ability to do so. Yet nobody made a move because nobody wanted to risk the smell that might happen if they were to get involved.

That's the predicament we often face in dealing with conflicts in a youth program. Sometimes being a peacemaker doesn't seem like much of a blessing. Even less of a blessing is being a wave-maker—the kind of person who realizes that sometimes conflict is necessary, regardless of how unpleasant it might be.

When the apostle Paul describes our ministry as disciples, he calls us to be agents of reconciliation. We must take this mandate seriously—whether that means seeking reconciliation with another staff person, with a member of our youth ministry team, or even with one of the youth. Seeking reconciliation doesn't mean we will always be ducking back into some turtle shell of martyrdom or accommodation. Nor does it mean we should always charge into conflicts like *Teenage Mutant Ninja Turtles*. What it does mean is that as youth workers we must be prepared for the hard work of conflict. As the apostle Paul reminds us: "Do not repay anyone evil for evil. Be careful to do what is right in the eyes of everyone. If it is possible, as far as it depends on you, live at peace with everyone" (Romans 12:17-18).

CHAPTER 14

Comings and Goings I: Finding a Position that Fits Your Passion

"For I know the plans I have for you," declares the Lord, "plans to prosper you and not to harm you, plans to give you hope and a future. Then you will call on me and come and pray to me, and I will listen to you. You will seek me and find me when you seek me with all your heart."
(Jeremiah 29:11-13)

Google the words *Venus flytrap* and you can learn that these feisty, hungry plants need three things to thrive as what one Internet source describes as a "healthy, happy little...trap": Pure water (not tap water), lots of light (a minimum of four hours of direct sunlight daily), and, apparently, very poor soil (fertilize these guys and it will likely burn the roots, leaving you with a plant that's unhealthy and unhappy—if it's still living at all). Without implying that there are any similarities between your vocational aspirations and the survival needs of small carnivorous plants, let me begin this chapter by posing two simple questions about what *you* need to thrive in ministry:

1. *In what kind of ministry environment do you think you would most flourish? What sort of place would provide you with the best possible environment for ministry and personal growth?*

The second question is the flip side of the first:

2. *What kind of ministry environment do you think you would find most difficult?*

Or, to put it another way, think about this: What kind of characteristics are you looking for in a youth ministry position?

- Are there any non-negotiable factors?

- Do you have any strong preferences with regard to ministry context (urban, suburban, rural, lap of luxury, cross-cultural, local church, parachurch)?

- Would geography factor into your decision?

- Do you wish to be near family, or in a particular region of the country? (In other words, are you convinced God loves you too much to lead you to a place with a climate inhospitable to palm trees?)
- Are there special considerations you must make for your family (such as spouse's employment or needs of children or extended family)?
- Where do finances come into play?
- Do you have long-term debts or financial obligations that might limit your range of choices?
- Are you hoping for some sort of overseas mission assignment?
- If you were to serve in a local church, how important to you is worship style, preaching style, ministry style?
- What unique talents or gifts factor into your decision? (Are you looking for an opportunity to use your gifts in drama, music, dance, sports, or media technology?)
- To what extent do your theological convictions play into your thought process?
- Are there practical ministry issues that are important (freedom to choose curriculum, strong emphasis on missions and service, a strong team of adult volunteers already in place, etc.)?
- What would your responsibilities be in your ideal ministry position?

To help you dig a little deeper, let's do a little *ministry dream inventory.* Using the table below, make a list of the factors that are important to you as you think and pray about a potential youth ministry position. You can use the questions from the previous paragraph to stir your imagination, but feel free to list other criteria important to you. Whether you are already involved in ministry and considering a move or making your first venture into full-time youthwork, which factors do you consider important in making the decision about where you will invest your heart, your gifts, and your life? List those factors in Column 1.

Column 1: Factors for Consideration	***Column 2***

Column 1: Factors for Consideration	**Column 2**

Now, reread your list in Column 1, and think about priorities. Suppose you're not able to find an open position that completely matches your personal dream job. You find jobs with some very attractive features, but those same places have other features you're not so excited about. On which of the preferences in Column 1 are you willing to make some compromises? As you read back through the list this time, assign in Column 2 a numerical value to that preference—the higher the point value, the more important the factor. Let's say you have 100 points total to spend—what relative weight would you give to the various preferences?

Sample:

Column 1: Factors for Consideration	***Column 2: Points***
Factor *A: Theological Compatibility*	35
Factor *B: Near Extended Family*	5
Factor *C: Congregational Worship Style*	30
Factor *D: Spouse Can Find Job*	5
Factor *E: Youth Ministry Philosophy*	15

Factor F: *Work With a Large Staff Team*	10

Now, having considered what kind of ministry position would be the best match for you, there's one more question I'd like you to consider—a very important one. This one is mission-critical:

How will God guide you to such a place?

THE MYSTERY OF GOD'S WILL: WALKING BY FAITH, NOT BY SIGHT

When my youth ministry students at Eastern University were working through this exercise, one of them protested that it didn't feel right to him. He said that, somehow, coming up with a menu of preferences didn't seem like an approach that did justice to the mystery and wonder of God's guidance. I responded by asking if he'd ever thought about whether he wanted to get married and, if so, had he thought about the type of girl he'd like to marry. He said, "Yes," he had, in fact, "given that a lot of thought." That led me to wonder aloud why it was okay to dream about how God might guide us in one area of life, but inappropriate to dream about how he might lead us in another area.

Thinking about the kind of ministry in which we'd most like to serve is not about placing an order from the divine take-out menu and waiting for God to deliver. It's about surveying the contours of the ministry landscape to gain some sense of where you could dig in and do ministry for maximum harvest. It's about recognizing that God guides us through his Spirit, through his Word, through the wise counsel of friends and mentors, and *through the divine alchemy of circumstances and personality.*

There are lots of great books on understanding and discerning the will of God.[1] I don't intend to treat that subject here in any detail. Obviously, being obedient to God and serving him with delight is at the core of our calling as Christians. Yet it's equally obvious that how God works his will in our lives is an immense and amazing mystery. In my experience too many youth workers have a great deal of trouble navigating the road that leads from their desire to serve God to the actual ministry address that fits their passions and gifts.

One of the biggest misconceptions about the will of God is the belief that God would never call us to do something that gives us great pleasure. There is an attitude: "God couldn't be leading me to do this because I like it too much!" Not only does such a notion betray the goodness of God, it also betrays his wisdom. Certainly there are times when God calls us to sacrifice, times when we must do in obedience what we do not want to do. But why wouldn't God create us with a desire to do what he calls us to do? In a sense, that is what makes Christian vocation such a place of freedom. Frederick Buechner described it this way, "The place God calls you to is the place where your deep gladness and the world's deep hunger meet."[2]

What we shall consider in the remainder of this chapter, in practical terms, is how to find that place.

"SHOW ME THE MINISTRY!"

In the movie *Jerry McGuire*, sports agent Jerry McGuire is having an intense phone conversation with one of his clients, Arizona Cardinals wide receiver Rod Tidwell, who's upset that his contract doesn't allow him to receive wider amounts of cash. As the conversation heats up, Tidwell reaches his flash point and yells into the phone a line that has become a movie classic: "Show me the money!"

In looking at a youth ministry position and discerning the will of God, "Show me the money!" is just about the worst place to begin the conversation. Taking a youth ministry job for the money is like going to work on a farm because they give you a good price on eggs. In seeking out a position that fits your passion, the best place to start is by examining the ministry itself.

THE CHURCH OR ORGANIZATION

If the ministry isn't compatible with your convictions and priorities, then it's not a good fit for you—regardless of where the job is or how much you'll be paid to do it. The kinds of questions you ask about the ministry will be as varied as the responses to the survey at the opening of this chapter. But certainly some of the essential questions would revolve around ministry compatibility.[3] Here are a few steps you'll want to take:

Ask to see the mission or purpose statement of the church or agency. Most churches and organizations have a mission statement—and the youth program of a larger organization may even have its own mission statement. These documents are important to examine. You could use the information discussed in chapter 5 (Visioneering) as a way of sifting through and reflecting on these documents. If no such documents exist (or if people begin to look at you funny when you mention *vision*), that should be considered a bright red flag.

Quite often, when evaluating a new ministry situation, a discerning youth worker will realize the ministry has a very clear and succinct *articulated* philosophy, but the philosophy by which the group actually operates (its *operant* philosophy) is quite different. It all looks good on paper, but the words never become flesh—the philosophy never becomes program. We need to be alert for these kinds of disconnections—and if we see them, they will be important talking points.

Learning how to evaluate the operant philosophy in a ministry situation is important because the way an organization operates often says more about its philosophy of youth ministry than does any vision statement. Figure 14-1 describes the various elements of the four most common youth ministry philosophies:

Four Common Operant Ministry Philosophies[4]		
PHILOSOPHY	***Pragmatist [Focus on ideas and strategies]***	***Realist [Focus on being culturally relevant without be being biblically relative]***
Essential Youth Ministry Issue:	Does it meet the needs or wants of our students?	Can we do this, while remaining faithful to our biblical mandates, and attentive to our ministry context?
What is the apparent criteria for starting a new program?	Numbers: students would probably attend if we do this.	Sure, we can get students there, but will it meet our goals? Or, yes, it will meet our goals, but we won't get any students to show up.
What are the apparent goals for ministry?	To see the program grow (in numbers, budget, popularity, etc.)	To see people grow from where they are to where God calls them to be.
What is the apparent criteria for evaluating the program?	Is the program growing?	Are we seeing fruit?
What is the apparent criteria for ending a program?	A better way is found that attracts more people.	It no longer seems to meet needs.
Underlying assumption:	Our job is to reach people—the more the better.	It does little good to reach people if we cannot help them know God's embrace. On the other hand, it won't do any good to talk to people about God's love if they are unwilling to listen.
Inherent strength of this approach:	While there is wide and justified criticism for a ministry that focuses only on numbers, there is the obvious fact that numbers represent individual human beings. And human beings are whom Jesus died to redeem. To dismiss the focus on numbers as shallow and irrelevant overlooks the obvious fact that a youth ministry without any youth is not very effective youth ministry.	This approach is sometimes maligned as being too purpose-driven, too based on the notion that "the end justifies the means." This is not entirely fair. The emphasis in this philosophy is not "the end justifies the means" so much as it is that every method and program (means) must be measured by its contribution toward the final goal (end).

(Figure 14-1)

Four Common Operant Ministry Philosophies[4]		
PHILOSOPHY	***Idealist [Focus on faithfulness to ideals]***	***Traditionalist [Focus on connection to denomination or movement]***
Essential Youth Ministry Issue:	Is it right? Is this what God calls us in his Word to do?	Is this in keeping with our tradition? How does this line up with others in our denomination or organization?
What is the apparent criteria for starting a new program?	Scripture calls us to this, so we'll do it, and whatever happens is what happens.	This is a part of our tradition to which we have not been faithful so we need to begin doing it; Other congregations (areas, districts, dioceses, etc.) are doing this and we have been requested to join them by organizational or denominational headquarters.
What are the apparent goals for ministry?	Faithfulness to God as he has made himself known in the Scripture.	To help people be faithful to our mission, tradition, etc.
What is the apparent criteria for evaluating the program?	Are we being faithful to the truth?	Are we maintaining union with those in our denomination or organization?
What is the apparent criteria for ending a program?	That's one of the problems of this approach. Once everyone agrees this is what God wants us to do, people are unlikely to be open to change. (Changes in hymnody, worship style, Sunday school scheduling, mid-week prayer service, missions conference, etc.)	Ministries end only when there is a change at the broader level—which is very seldom. That's why large institutions tend to develop their own momentum.
Underlying assumption:	God's word does not return void (Isaiah 55:11). It is his work and he will bless it (1 Thessalonians 5:24).	There is strength and balance in unity.
Inherent strength of this approach:	Some would criticize this approach as being too inflexible and unrealistic, and, of course, it could be. But one person's "inflexibility" is another's "conviction." At least with firm ideals a ministry is prevented from being too market-driven, or so culturally relevant that it ceases to be biblically faithful.	The word *tradition* has gotten a bad rap in a culture that is marked by immediacy and the arrogance of the now. But, in fact, tradition can be an important corrective that allows the iron of one generation to sharpen the iron of another generation. (cf. Proverbs 27:17).

(Figure 14-1)

Ask if the church or agency has ever done any kind of self-study, or if they've had a consultant prepare any kind of report on the ministry or agency in the last five years. A ministry engaging in some kind of self- or outside-examination is more common than it used to be, and the findings of any such study would certainly be information worth having.

If you're considering work in a church, try to get a sense of how both the congregation and the pastor understand the pastor's role. Is the pastor primarily teacher, shepherd, program manager, equipper, generalist, specialist? This will be important in terms of the pastor's role, but may also have some bearing on how the congregation views other pastoral staff.

Review the doctrinal statements of the church or agency. Again, if it's a church, you'll want to read these documents—but the best way to get a sense of the doctrinal positions of a congregation is to listen to the preaching. If the church is being seriously considered, try to listen to four or five sermons by the senior pastor. That may tell you more about the doctrinal stance of the congregation than a document that some members of the congregation may never have read.

Seek out the history of the church or organization. You don't need to know that the congregation you're considering was founded by the Smith family back in 300 B.C. as a place they could store their collection of ancient handbells. But it would be helpful to know if the congregation was a church-plant, for example, and from which congregation was it planted. That kind of information about a congregation's DNA might tell you something. Was the congregation born of a split? How long has the agency or organization been working in this community? Is there a parent organization?

Find out about the demographics of the youth ministry, the congregation or agency, and the community. Understanding something about not only the youth you'll work with but also the surrounding community's economic factors, ethnic mix, religious preferences, and employment picture can give you an idea about the soil into which you hope to sow the seed of the Word.

Take note of the attendance patterns of both the youth ministry and (in the case of a congregation) the worship services and Sunday school.

Budget history. It's very important to look closely at the youth ministry budget, as well as the budget of the larger church or agency. Use material from chapter 9 (*Budgeting and Finance: Squeezing Blood from Turnips*) to think through some of the critical issues (What does the budget cover? How is funding determined? Are there additional funds under different budget lines?) Consider whether the church or organization has a lot of debt, and how much of the budget goes to pay off that debt. Too many youth workers have found their hands tied (or their jobs cut) by budgets stretched to pay off building programs and unpaid debts.

Do a thorough survey of the facilities. Is the space adequate for the programming planned? Are there any plans for building?

THE POSITION ITSELF

If we're comfortable with the church or organization, then we can begin to think about the specific job they're asking us to do. Again, note that the first question is, *Would I want to work at a place like this?* If that's a yes, then it's worth asking the next one: *What sort of work would I do? How would I use my gifts in this place?*

You'll want to ask for a *clear, written job description.* If one is not available, ask that one be drawn up. I once interviewed with a congregation that asked me to draw up my own job description! I did, they hired me (I was a perfect fit for the job!), and I thoroughly enjoyed my work there. Hopefully, the church or organization will have already hammered out the details before they begin their search, but it doesn't always happen like that.

What would be your specific responsibilities? Would this be more of an oversight role, an equipping role, a hands-on role? What sort of freedom would you have in this position? (Would you make curricular choices or decisions about retreats and mission programming?)

How does the process of change happen in the ministry? What we're really looking for here are sacred cows, to gain a sense of which ones will need to be fed and which ones might someday need to be butchered.

To whom are you responsible? Do you answer to the senior pastor or organization director? To a committee? To the board?

Find out about staff history. What is the average tenure of the current staff? How do they relate to one another? How often do they meet? Is the staff operating on a Fellowship Model or a Functional Model (see chapter 7)? How do they handle differences of opinion between staff members? You'll definitely want to interview some staff members to get a sense of who your coworkers will be. Again, be listening in those conversations for information about the operant philosophy of the ministry, church, or organization.

Inventory the demographics of the youth group.[5] Try to get hard evidence about real live teenagers. When it comes to the number of people involved (and some other kinds of data), congregations and ministry agencies are notorious for stretching the truth, or for being what is known as *evang-elastic*. When they say, "We have about 75 kids on the rolls," remember that the most literal translation of that statement may be, "We've managed to accumulate a mailing list of 75 kids, and we've actually seen about ten of them here at the church."

Try to get a feel for some of the "hot topics" in the ministry. Whether it's outreach issues, the way kids dress, music styles, or retreats that keep the kids away on Sunday mornings, every ministry has issues it struggles with. If it seems like there aren't any tough issues to deal with, you probably haven't looked hard enough. Try to meet not only with the ministry's supporters, but also with its critics.

Listen and watch for informal and hidden networks within the congregation. These networks don't show up on any organizational charts, but navigating those networks will be an important key to effective ministry.

Will you have any role in public services of worship? Will you have opportunities to preach? (Do you want opportunities to preach?) Will there be other ways you can serve the congregation at large?

And then, finally, here are some additional questions you might ask to get a better sense of the ministry and the role you might play:[6] What is it about my gifts that you think might fit the needs of this ministry? What has been the most significant event in the life of this ministry since you've been a member? What has been the most upsetting event? What do you see as the main areas of concern for the youth involved?

If there isn't a sense of confirmation from God regarding these first two areas of concern—your compatibility with the overall ministry and with the needs of the specific position—then there isn't any reason to move to the final area of concern. But if it still feels like a fit, then we consider the compensation for the position.

Compensation

A compensation package is a support built on three legs: Salary, benefits, and housing allowance. Let's take some time to look at each of these individually

Salary

When considering the appropriate pay for a job in youth work, there are some larger questions that need to be considered:

To which secular profession should youth work be compared in determining a fair salary? One of the more widely accepted and reasonable ways of pegging the compensation of a youth worker is by looking at the compensation of secondary school teachers in the local school district. First of all, this takes into consideration differences in regional cost of living. Secondly, most school systems base compensation on a combination of educational background and years of experience. So, again, that provides a framework for a church or ministry organization to calculate a fair wage. The pay of a youth worker with a master's degree and ten years of full-time experience should be similar to that of a secondary school teacher in the district with a similar educational background and similar length of experience. The weight given to factors like education, experience, and whether the candidate is ordained or not will vary—but most ministry organizations take these elements into consideration.

What is the salary range of other people on the ministry staff and, even more important, what was the basis for determining those salaries? The goal here, of course, is fair compensation, not fare competition. You don't need to know the compensation of each individual staff person. But to determine a fair wage, it's helpful to understand how salaries are structured within the ministry. For example, there are lots of youth workers who serve in ministry at a lower wage in ministry than they might command otherwise, yet they understand that similar sacrifices are being shared across the board by others in the ministry. It's not as if the budget is being balanced on the backs of one or two low-wage workers while the other staff members are relatively well-paid. This kind of information provides a context for understanding the compensation package.

What are the average salaries of those with comparable jobs within the denomination or ministry organization at large? In many cases, the best source of this information is the denominational or organizational headquarters. Another excellent source for this data is the Web site churchlawtoday.com. This organization issues a very thorough compensation survey biannually so boards and executive pastors have the data necessary to make this kind of assessment.[7]

If it's a church position, is compensation based on the membership, the size of the Sunday morning congregation, the size of the youth group, the range of responsibilities, or something else altogether?

What is the process by which compensation is increased? This is especially important because one might be willing to take a position for less compensation if one could see that there is a clear path to increased compensation. The four basic criteria by which salary adjustments are made are these:

1. Education: Pay increases when someone gets an additional educational credential or some new professional certification;
2. Experience: As experience increases, generally, compensation increases;
3. Responsibilities: Increased responsibilities earn increased compensation;
4. Merit: Strong performance is rewarded with increased pay.

It's reasonable to ask if any of these factors merit an adjustment in compensation, and what the review process is to make these judgments.

Of course, a paycheck is only one of the three legs that support a compensation package. We've addressed some of the models organizations can use to assess a fair cash salary. But what about the other two legs of the support structure: Benefits and housing? First, let's talk about benefits.

Benefits

When it comes to the various benefits a church or organization might include in a staff position, the possibilities are extensive, and make a huge difference in the overall value of a compensation package. Here are some of the questions you'll want to ask:

What non-salary contributions does the church or organization make on behalf of the employee? Is there medical insurance? Workers and unemployment compensation insurance? Liability, disability, and/or life insurance? A dental plan? Retirement or pension plans? Social Security contributions? These are the kinds of issues we tend to think of first with regard to the benefits included in many compensation packages. But there are many other possibilities to be considered:

Is there a travel allowance? Youth workers have to be fairly mobile. In fact, I know more than a few youth workers who think of the car as their primary "office." Is there a mechanism whereby car expenses can be reimbursed? How does that system work?

Is there a communication allowance? An increasing amount of contact ministry is now done online through Facebook, cell phones, and PDAs (personal digital assistants). There is every justification to ask churches and agencies to provide an off-salary allowance for these expenses, as well.

Is there an allowance for conferences or continuing education? Some ministries pay for conference registration fees, but not travel costs, presumably so their staff will think long and hard about trying to find educational opportunities close to home. Others provide for travel costs, but not registration. Some offer both. I have met many youth workers who attend conferences by paying the event costs out of their own pockets. That's fine, as long as everyone understands that going in. But it's probably a conversation worth having before signing day.

Will the church provide an allowance for other professional expenses (books, subscriptions, professional dues)?

Are there other forms of non-cash compensation or payments-in-kind that should be factored into the package? For example, some churches offer free tuition at a Christian school or daycare center to the children of their employees. Or, if the position is on staff at a camp, the family may be allowed to eat meals and use facilities on the property. Sometimes churches have recreational facilities that rival the local YMCA, and free use of those can be a welcome part of the youth pastor's compensation.

How many days off are employees given each week? Generally, churches allow 1.5 to 2 days a week. Listen carefully to this part of the discussion for any disconnect between the stated policy and the reality. Are staff encouraged to take seriously a Sabbath rhythm, or there is an implicit message that *real* servants stay on the job 24-7?

What is the vacation policy?

Does the church have a policy of providing sabbaticals or study leave? Some churches and Christian organizations allow senior staffers and professional workers to take a week a year for study leave, and, in some cases, after a set period of time (usually six to seven years) an extended sabbatical study leave of one to three months.

Will the church license you to preach? What about ordination? There are tax advantages to ordination. While that's no reason to be ordained, it does have some impact on the compensation package. It would be wise to talk about this issue. Will the congregation help you seek ordination? Does it intend for you to seek ordination?

Housing

Although policies vary from denomination to denomination, and even from church to church, and also depend to some degree on ordination status, most churches provide a housing allowance for pastoral staff as part of the compensation package. Others expect the staff member to live in ministry-owned housing, often referred to as a *parsonage*. If a parsonage is provided as part of the compensation package, one important question to ask is whether this provision is optional. Do staffers have the choice of receiving a housing allowance instead? This is important to consider, because there are both advantages and disadvantages to living in ministry-owned housing.

Let's consider first the advantages of ministry-owned housing:

Why a youth pastor might prefer ministry-owned housing:

- First of all, it may very well be that your income won't allow you to own a home. Making a down payment and paying a monthly mortgage may require too much of your income. And, in that case, a ministry-owned home may be your best bet for good, economical housing;
- You don't have to deal with any of the hassles of home ownership. Somebody else cares for the old, burned-out hot water heater;

- The congregation is your landlord, and presumably, they would be more attentive than if you were simply renting the property from a stranger;
- Housing near the church or agency may be unaffordable. A ministry-owned property may provide the youth pastor with more house for less money, in a convenient location;
- No maintenance concerns, no utilities to pay, no homeowners insurance;
- When it's time to move on, you don't have to worry about selling a house.

Why a church or agency might prefer ministry-owned housing:

- Tradition: "This is where one of our pastors has always lived!"
- It allows a church to make profitable use of a property that might be tough to sell (read: *white elephant*);
- Owning the house allows the congregation to gain equity—a way of building net worth;
- It's a simple way for a church to meet the housing needs of a pastoral staff member;
- Some church and agency executives believe it to be less expensive than providing a cash housing allowance. (This may be a fallacy, but it's a widely held assumption.)[8]

Now, what about the other side of the coin? How might both the youth worker and the ministry organization benefit from a housing allowance that enables the employee to find his or her own housing?

Why a youth pastor might prefer a housing allowance:

- There are also some very real tax advantages for ordained people who own their own homes. Talk to an accountant in your congregation or someone who can give you good information about this matter;[9]
- An allowance gives you a choice about where to live;
- If you buy a house, the monthly mortgage payment is like forced savings because you gain some equity in the value of your home;
- Having a home that must be sold if you relocate forces you to think harder about moving. It develops deeper community roots;

- In the event of job loss, long-term disability, or death, the pastor (or his or her family) will not necessarily need to relocate immediately. This is not the happiest question to consider (you'll notice that I tried to be gentle and placed it lower on the list), but what happens to families in these situations if they're living in ministry-owned housing? How long can the church or agency provide housing to a youth worker or family if the youth worker is no longer employed?
- In a roundabout way, a housing allowance helps a youth pastor plan for retirement. After all, if you are moving from parsonage to parsonage throughout your working life, what happens when you are no longer able to work? This has been a problem for some pastors in denominations where parsonage use is the tradition;
- Owning or renting a home in the neighborhood allows the clergy family to feel more like a part of the community;

Why a church or agency might prefer a housing allowance:

- It keeps the church out of the real-estate business. They don't have to worry about maintaining an additional property;
- It avoids the possibility of a *white elephant* property;
- It gets the youth pastor and his or her family out into the community;
- It avoids the limitations that a parsonage might place on who can take the job. It would be a shame to lose a good candidate because the parsonage is too small to accommodate a large family;
- It simplifies church budgets;
- It eliminates the congregation having to choose and decorate a home for someone they don't know;
- It makes much less awkward the questions surrounding housing in the event of job loss, disability, or death.

Ultimately, my personal opinion is that a housing allowance that's large enough to allow a youth worker to buy a home is almost always a better deal for the youth worker than living in a ministry-owned property. When the youth pastor lives in ministry-owned housing, it is basically a transaction between the ministry and the youth worker that says, "You work for us, and we will provide you housing." But when the youth worker moves on, the ministry keeps the house and the youth worker walks away with nothing. In essence, it's as if the ministry paid the youth worker a certain amount, and the youth worker turned around and used his or her paycheck to buy *the church* a house. It's very generous, but most youth workers probably can't afford that. They need to put their incomes toward homes for themselves—so that when they decide to move on, they can gain some benefit from the money they've earned. But, as we've discussed, if you can't afford to buy a home, then there are some real and tangible advantages to a parsonage.

Before we leave this topic, let me say that in the real world of ministry, there is a wide variation in compensation packages. *Don't expect that every church will be able to fund all the items listed above.* It is fair to ask, but probably unreasonable to expect. But, again, this is ministry—and ministry is service. Jesus had the audacity to compare it to washing feet (John 13). In reality, you are much more likely to pick up a towel than pick up a large conference allowance or pension contribution. On the other hand, the joy and excitement of seeing God move among a group of people—and of somehow being allowed to play a part in that movement—is a privilege beyond price.

IF YOU GET THE JOB: YOUR FIRST FOUR WEEKS IN YOUTH MINISTRY

My recent graduates tell me there's nothing more exciting—and more intimidating—than stepping into an office and sitting down behind a desk your first day in a new youth ministry position. After you put all your office equipment in place (both the iPod *and* the laptop), you begin to look around the room at the blank walls. That's when it hits you: *These people expect me to do youth ministry!*

And, of course, by God's grace and power, that is just what you will do.

But it can still be daunting to call the first signal and put the ball in play. What follows are some simple suggestions for what you should do in your first four weeks of youth ministry at a new position. Whether you're a veteran who has been on the field for years, or a rookie seeing your first live action, here are some ideas for how to get started.

1. TALK with everyone close to the youth ministry: Kids, volunteers, senior pastor or administrator, outgoing youth minister, parents, elders, etc. And then, talk to people who are *not* close to the ministry, such as staff in other parts of the organization or kids who haven't shown up. These conversations may be your best source of information about whether you are on offense or defense, and which plays to call first!

2. MEET with parents *en masse* as soon as possible to share your vision, hear their concerns, and make sure they know the youth ministry is a ministry you share with them.

3. DRAW INPUT from as many sources as possible to gather information about any adjustments that might be immediately necessary. Make sure you allow for a broad scope of input. Sometimes the people most eager to talk are the ones who are disgruntled. They want to make sure *you* get off on the right foot by getting full advantage of *their* opinion. Their opinions are important, but remember, theirs may not be the majority opinion.

4. SURVEY the current youth population to determine

(a) potential leaders

(b) possible areas of need (see chapter 12, *Evaluating Your Ministry*)

(c) state of the ministry (see chapter 12, *Evaluating Your Ministry*)

5. Get a clear understanding of the way ***FINANCES*** work in the church. Talk to the treasurer of the church or organization. This is your best chance to make this person an ally instead of an adversary.

6. INTRODUCE yourself to the students at the first meeting. Don't try to make that first meeting so "normal" that you don't acknowledge that there's been a huge change here. Sports metaphors aside, this is not the same as sending in a new quarterback. This is more like transplanting a body part.

7. LEARN about your geographical area: Service opportunities, recreational opportunities, school calendar, community calendar, retreat centers, Christian bookstores, printing/shipping stores, etc.

8. RE-CATALOGUE current files so you can benefit from them. You will recognize that some of it can be thrown away immediately. It may also be just as wise, if you're not sure, to hold on to some of it until you have time to recognize whether it should be thrown away. A document that doesn't look important in the first four weeks may look very important when you're five months into the work.

9. CONTACT local schools. Your goal is to introduce yourself and see if there's any way you can serve them. Solicit their ideas about community needs.

10. PLAN your first six months. You can always make changes later, but there's something about seeing a plan on paper that provides a sense of momentum.

11. Develop a ***NETWORK*** of youth ministry contacts. If a local network already exists, find it and join it!

12. Do an ***INSURANCE EVALUATION.*** Has your name been added to the church or organization's policies? Find out about coverage. For example, that iPod and laptop—if they are lost or stolen from your new office, are they covered under the church's policy?

13. REVIEW POLICIES for both volunteer and paid staff.

14. KNOW who your resources are. As soon as possible, seek out names and contact information for the following:

- Christian counselor
- Suicide hotline
- Drug Counseling
- Christian Crisis Pregnancy Center
- Local Police/Fire
- Local Chick-fil-a

Of course, as important as a strong start is a strong finish. In the next chapter, we'll think about how a good departure can underline what God has done—and a bad departure can undermine it.

CHAPTER 15

Comings and Goings II: The Grace-Full Exit

They all wept as they embraced him and kissed him.
What grieved them most was his statement that
they would never see his face again.
(Acts 20:37-38)

Two veteran youth workers are being interviewed in one of my upper-level youth ministry classes at Eastern University. The topic of the day is "When to Leave a Ministry." Paul is the first to share his story.

A Departure Bred by Divergent Visions

> After nine years of what I have considered to be effective youth work, I'm leaving my position at Church of the Holy Comforter—an Episcopal church—to accept a youth ministry position with a growing and progressive Episcopal church in the Southwest. One reason I'm leaving is because while I attempted to follow the steps in my most recent five-year plan for reaching kids for Christ, the hierarchy of the church started throwing up roadblocks.
>
> Now that's not necessarily a reason to leave. If my vision is not in tune with the vision of the church, I could bend my goals to fit what the church is doing. However, when it begins to affect the ministry—the relationships I have with students—then I need to sit up and say, "Hey, what's going on here?"
>
> What happened was that we were experiencing tremendous growth in all three areas for which I had responsibility: Junior high, senior high, and college. I needed help. So for the last five years I have submitted in my budget a proposal for a full-time, salaried youth ministry assistant. Every year they put it off. "Maybe next year," they said. But then, over the last two years my administrative work load skyrocketed, making it tough for me to get out from behind my desk. Obviously, that began to affect my relationships with kids.
>
> This year I had a student who had accepted Christ through our program and later graduated from Syracuse come back to me and say, "I want to be involved in ministry." So I brought him on as a part-time assistant, and the church, in a sense, told us they would bring him on full time by the end of the year.

> Not only did they not hire him full time, but in the last two years my operating budget has decreased by 60 percent. At the same time, the vestry—the board—says that our number-one priority is our youth. So I went twice before the board to ask: If youth ministry is our highest priority, why are we walking backward after we've built it up for so long? And why are we jerking this one kid around who wants to come back and get involved in ministry? I've felt a tremendous amount of anger in the past two years—anger that affected my wife and my child, and my relationships with my students.
>
> Also by this point, I had been receiving offers for youth-ministry positions with different churches. Until last Christmas I would just toss them in the wastebasket, because I really was committed to Holy Comforter and to the kids there and to the Episcopal Church. But over Christmas, while my wife and I were praying, she said to me, "You know, Paul, maybe you should listen to some of the offers from these other places. If you just keep throwing them out, you may be limiting how the Holy Spirit wants to lead us."
>
> So I said, "Okay, I'll do that." That week I received a second offer from this one church out west, and I said, "I'll go down and take a look." I went down there and it was real exciting work. But at first I didn't trust my judgment. When you've poured yourself into a ministry for so long only to see your plans go haywire, another offer from another church is very seductive. Am I leaving because I'm angry? Am I leaving because of pain? Or am I leaving because this is truly God's call for me to leave Holy Comforter? When I finally decided to leave, I felt it boiled down to a difference of vision between myself and my board.

After Paul answered a few questions from students, there was a second story. This one, from Dan, focused on what he considered an integrity issue, and how conflict over the issue led him to resign his position in the church.

The "Wrong Kids" Start Coming, the Youth Pastor Decides to Go

> I've been serving the same United Methodist congregation for about five years—so I'm not a short-term, fly-about youth worker whose idea of commitment is a one-year stint. I've faced tough situations and difficult decisions without losing my optimism about being a youth minister. I'm still committed to teenagers and excited about God's call. But I guess it came down to a few significant cues that told me, "It's time to leave."
>
> The first was that both our senior pastor and associate pastor left the church. The new leadership ushered in a new vision and a new concept of our congregation that I didn't feel was as conducive to my approach to youth ministry.

Another problem was that our church was going through a very difficult time with finances. My budget was decreased significantly. The church leadership decided they would cut both my salary and the music minister's salary in half; but there was no change in our responsibilities. They still wanted us to be there full time. So...uh...we decided this also might be a sign it was time to look around a bit!

Another issue that arose—and this was probably the major issue, believe it or not—was an issue of integrity. In my ministry I've always made it my habit to put a welcome mat in front of my office door. It's a way of saying all kids are welcome into the church and into the youth group. We often reminded our students that their friends were always welcome—not just their "good" friends who were Christians and carried their Bible to school, but all their friends.

The problem occurred when the kids started bringing friends who were not the kind of kids some parents wanted hanging around our youth group. We're talking about kids who wore earrings and chains in unusual places. I felt these kids needed Christ as much as anyone else, and this was precisely the place where they should be. But that opinion was not shared by a small, powerful minority of parents.

One night, just as one of these parents was dropping her son off at youth group, she saw another student getting out of the car accompanied by this kid with long black hair with blonde streaks, who was wearing earrings and chains. And that was the spark that lit the firestorm. She went to the board and said, "This cannot be; it's a bad influence on our kids."

Well, when both she and the board came back to me with this concern, I said, "There are a lot of things we can compromise on: Whether we serve hamburgers or hot dogs, whether we meet at 6:00 or 7:00, and all those kinds of things. But there are some issues on which I will not compromise, and one of those is whether I will say to a kid, 'Because you're dressed like this, or because you look like that, you're not welcome in our youth group.' That is a non-negotiable."

Well, they backed down a little bit for a short while, but that really set the wheels in motion. They began to watch, and they saw me going on campus, and bringing in kids who were "undesirable." And over time my support just eroded. It didn't happen overnight. But my wife saw it too—probably a good thing because we really operate as a team. Finally, it came down to the point where we both felt God was leading us out of the church. That's when we decided to move on.

THE REVOLVING-DOOR SYNDROME

For years, one favorite stereotype of youth workers has been that they are fickle, undependable, slippery, and hard to hold on to. And, as if it's not enough to be described with such endearing, snake-like features, that description is often ratified by someone citing this statistic: *The average tenure of professional youth workers in any one position is between twelve and eighteen months!*

The good news is that, like so many urban myths, this statistic is untrue. Like the rumors that Coca-Cola is an effective contraceptive, that pouring Coca-Cola on a piece of raw pork will cause worms to crawl out of it, and that drinking Coca-Cola combined with aspirin will get you high,[1] there is absolutely no evidence that youth workers are more mobile than other church professionals. Jonathan Grenz's 2002 study of 154 current and former youth ministers published in the *Journal of Youth Ministry* shows that while there certainly is movement, the average length of time that youth ministers stay in one position is 4.7 years.[2] Other research demonstrates an average tenure ranging from 3.7 years to 4.8 years.[3]

The Benefits of Staying

These numbers are important, because longer tenures almost always breed deeper ministry.

There's no study that can prove in any absolute way that there's a correlation between long tenure and more effective youth ministry, but the anecdotal evidence generally points in that direction. Consider the benefits of a long tenure in one ministry location.

First of all, as students become convinced you are in for the long-term, they will be more willing to trust you, which is one of the absolute keys to more effective ministry.

Secondly, remaining long-term on one plot of ministry ground allows you to see fruit that is visible only after several growing seasons. There are few joys in ministry more vivid than the joy of seeing the kids who were part of your youth group return to the youth group years later as adult volunteers.

Third, credibility with parents will increase. As youth workers invest in families over time, they gain a shared history with families—a shared history that knits deeper and more vulnerable relationships.

A fourth benefit is that with longer tenures among ministry staff, volunteer leaders are exposed to a more consistent philosophy and strategy of ministry. It gradually becomes part of the ministry DNA.

And, finally, over time, the long-term youth worker gains professional credibility with the congregation at large. He or she comes to be viewed, in effect, as the church's expert on adolescents and as the youth ministry trainer-in-residence.[4]

ISSUES THAT MOVE US

So, having banished the myth that youth workers are genetically predisposed to job-hopping, and having taken stock of the benefits of staying put, it's reasonable to pose this question: What are some of the factors that work *against* long-term youth ministry? Let's consider some of them.

The Marathon Factor. Doing ministry—any kind of ministry—is like running a marathon. At the beginning of the race, as we prepare for the starter's gun to sound, people are there to witness our ordination or installation and there's a lot of enthusiasm. The crowd is there, nodding their approval, showing their support. From the starting line, it's hard to see the hills on the horizon that will test our mettle soon enough. But those hills do come, and the cheers of the starting line start to fade in the distance.

Youth ministry is hard work. And people—good people who love Jesus—begin to feel they do not have the stamina for such a race. Grenz's survey of people who once served as youth ministers but no longer serve in that role indicates they stayed in youth ministry for about 7.8 years on average.[5]

Not surprisingly, this marathon fatigue is true even among senior pastors. One study of United Methodist clergy showed that 41 percent of ministers dropped out of parish ministry within ten years of their ordination, and 58 percent had dropped out within 20 years.[6] A 1998 survey of 5,000 ordained clergy from 15 denominations found that by age 50, 33 percent had left local church ministry.[7]

If this is true for senior pastors, we can imagine it might be even more true for youth workers. People get into youth ministry thinking it will be all fun and games—only to discover that even the fun and games aren't all fun and games! When we get into *anything* full-time, we discover that *starting* is much easier than *continuing*, and that elements of the job that were fascinating at first become mundane with familiarity. What someone thought would be a sprint, or maybe even a cruise or a coast, turns out to be a grueling and difficult journey—exhilarating at times, yes, and every now and then downright inspiring; but, still hard. Certainly, no one is suggesting this is unique to youth ministry (though youth ministry does seem to be one of those occupations that looks easier from a distance).

Getaways to Get a Raise. In the late 1960s and early 1970s, when inflation was punishing the U.S. economy, the government felt it needed to do something to fix the problem (usually a bad sign). Facing rising prices and decreased buying power, President Nixon instituted what became known as a "voluntary wage and price freeze." The plan was that industry would voluntarily agree to freeze prices and wages at current levels so production costs could be maintained at the current rates. And then—at least this was the hope—with production costs frozen in place, pricing could be maintained at a stable level, thereby stopping or slowing the rise of inflation.

Now, this may shock you—but the government plan didn't work out exactly as they'd hoped. There were several unintended consequences.

About a year into the plan, *The Wall Street Journal* began running stories about the problem of executive mobility. People in top positions were moving from job to job with discouraging frequency. What was happening, it turns out, was that with the wage freeze, the only way people could get raises was by changing jobs. If they stayed in their present positions, their salaries were frozen. If they moved to new jobs, they could negotiate for higher wages. In short, executives were being penalized for being faithful and were being rewarded for being fickle.

Frankly, the same dynamic works in today's youth ministry climate. While the rest of the country has moved beyond the wage and price freeze of the 1970s, many churches still seek to hold costs down by freezing salaries. Although many churches increase salaries to keep pace with inflation—a cost-of-living increase—fewer churches give their youth ministers, or any other staff members, an actual increase in spendable income. In short, that means that when financial burdens increase (due to a growing family or some kind of financial emergency), youth workers have to tighten their belts—or find new positions. A youth worker has to decide, "Do I stick it out here and let my family's income shrink, or do I move to the church down the street that's offering a few thousand dollars a year more?" We end up rewarding those who move and penalizing those who stay.

In one survey of Canadian youth workers, respondents repeatedly cited money as the greatest frustration that challenges them. Thirty-nine percent of those who left youth ministry either disagreed or strongly disagreed with the statement, "My salary is competitive with other youth leaders I know." Of that same group (former youth workers now working in other fields), more than three of four either agreed or strongly agreed with the statement, "The financial compensation I receive now is greater than when I was in youth ministry."[8] Similar data is reflected in other youth worker surveys.[9]

Because of the low professional regard most people have for youth ministry, youth workers are especially vulnerable to price-freezing strategies. The average hiring committee views youth workers as desperate for a position, perhaps doing youth ministry because they are unable to do some other kind of more "legitimate" ministry. So churches often pay incoming youth ministers enough to get them, but not enough to keep them.

Seller's Market. In the offices of the youth ministry department at Eastern University is a notebook of job openings we have posted for the benefit of our graduates. I'm always fascinated that we consistently have many more positions to fill than graduates to fill them.

Most youth ministers with any kind of track record get occasional offers from other churches and organizations. The solicitation from another church or ministry is always flattering, and the promise of a salary increase along with a fresh start and a clean slate can be fairly seductive. Familiarity breeds contempt, or at least a lack of appreciation. When constituents in your current position don't seem to value you as much as potential constituents in a new position, it's attractive. It's a short trip from wooed to wowed, and in a climate where there are more youth ministry positions than youth ministers, it's little wonder that many youth workers wander off looking for new relationships.

Empty Bag Syndrome. Too many youth workers approach ministry on the basis of new ideas, rather than on the basis of vision. As long as they're able to pull off activities that are bigger and better or do programs that are wilder and zanier, they maintain ministry momentum. But when the idea count runs low, their ministries become anemic. One reason youth ministers leave is that all the fresh ideas have grown stale and the new programs have become old. Now that their bag of tricks is empty, these youth workers move on looking for new audiences in the next stage of ministry.

Discouragement. Even worse than running out of ideas is running out of hope. When youth workers begin to believe they're farming bad soil—or that they lack the equipment to farm it well—that's when some of them decide to kick the dust off their feet and move on to other fields. Kageler's 2006 survey of just under 400 youth workers showed this to be a particularly sensitive issue for youth workers who have resigned from their positions. When asked why they left their most recent ministry, three of the top five reasons cited were related to discouragement:[10]

Felt isolated or lonely	43 percent
Spiritual dryness, unfed soul	39 percent
Criticism	35 percent

This is consistent with extensive research by Strommen, Jones, and Rahn involving almost 2500 youth workers that indicated six common concerns on the minds of youth workers, four of which reflect a deep discouragement.[11]

- Feelings of personal inadequacy
- A growing loss of confidence
- Feeling unqualified for the job
- Burnout

Loss of Necessary Support. It's tough to stay long-term in a ministry position if you don't feel supported by your supervisor, your staff colleagues, or the people to whom you minister. The loss of support might stem from poor diplomacy (*we don't like you*), imprudent decisions (*we don't trust you*), perceived incapability (*we don't think you can do the job*), or just good old church politics (*you weren't there when we voted*). Of senior pastors who leave the ministry, this appears to be the number one reason: Conflict with parishioners, with other staff members, or with denominational officials.[12]

Such loss of support is often closely related to a growing distrust of the youth worker. In *Before You Move: A Guide to Making Transitions in Ministry*, John Cionca cites a number of common "trust-busters" that can fracture credibility and put cracks in a pastor's support base. His comments are related primarily to the dismissal of senior pastors, but several are relevant to those of us in youth ministry:[13]

- Being defensive when given correction or negative feedback;
- Poor decisions (lack of discernment);
- Lack of dependability, not following through on commitments or responsibilities;
- Inability to handle conflict;
- Distraction by some sort of extra-curricular ministry/business/ occupation;
- Preaching *you* rather than *we* (i.e., communicating truth without communicating love—see 1 Thessalonians 2:8);
- Making major program changes without consultation of those involved;
- Inappropriate moral behavior;
- Dishonesty in interactions—saying different things to different people;
- Lack of preparation (programming by the seat of the pants);
- Missing significant events in the life of the ministry (not being there when families need us—funerals, times of crisis, etc.).

Nobody wants to be a quitter, and there are clearly times when one must stand strong, even in the face of opposition. Anyone can lead when everyone is willing and eager to follow. The best leaders are able to find ways to keep the ministry moving even in the tough times.

Yet one ceases to be a leader when *no one* (or not many) is willing to follow. And that's when it may be better to seriously consider a strategic retreat. Why waste your emotional resources, time, gifts, and the sanity of those who love you by fighting a war you cannot win?

And are there unwinnable wars? Absolutely.

WARS YOU CAN'T WIN

One former pastor with extensive experience as a consultant in interpersonal and church relations suggests not only that there are unwinnable wars in the ministry setting, but also that those unwinnable wars have some fairly distinct characteristics.[14] He offers some questions worth considering if you ever find yourself lacking support to the point where you feel you may need to leave your ministry:

1. *Is there a history of factionalism in the church or organization?* Some churches and agencies have a track record of chewing up and spitting out people in ministry. Sometimes you can pick up on this before you go in; other times you don't realize it until you are between their jaws. As we mentioned in the last chapter, Jesus declared peacemakers blessed—and maybe God has called you to bring reconciliation to a very difficult situation. But not very many people survive a shark attack by using reason. The best course is usually to swim away.

2. *Have overtures of peace and reconciliation been rejected?* Remember that Paul writes, "If it is possible, as far as it depends on you, live at peace with everyone" (Romans 12:18). The key word there is *if.* Sometimes it just isn't possible, and there is no support—despite every effort to build a bridge or make peace with the complaining party. That may mean it's time to move on.

3. *Are you (and your family) and the staff willing to pay the price to win the support you need to be effective in your ministry?* Some wars are winnable, but only at great price. If the collateral damage of confrontation destroys the ministry you're trying to lead, or if it destroys your personal or family life, perhaps it's better to leave the battle un-fought, at least for now.

4. *Is there enough current support to continue the fight to gain the support you need?* It's not enough that there is *some* support for your ministry. Most capable youth workers will always have someone who is willing to stand with them and say, "Stay and fight; we need you." But unless you think of the Alamo as a shrewd battle strategy, you'll want to think twice about whether it's worth dragging a few supporters down with you in a battle you can't win, even *with* their support.

5. *Are those withholding support open to compromise, or do they want your head?* If it's the latter, it's fair to say that you may find it difficult to settle on terms you'll find suitable.

6. *Do you know for sure why you're fighting?* Before you scrap and claw to gain the support you need to stay in your current position, ask yourself why this war is important. Are there substantive issues at stake? Is the life of the church or the ministry at stake? Is your integrity or future ministry at stake? Or is this just about winning because none of us likes to lose?

MAYBE A MOVE IS A MOVEMENT OF GOD

There are many reasons why someone in youth ministry might feel inclined to move to a new position, and some of those reasons are totally legitimate. Tenure is a good thing, but moving isn't always a bad thing. In fact, often, it's not just a good thing—it is very much a God-thing!

The following are some questions we can ask ourselves as we move through this process:

1. *Have I been here long enough to reach my most effective years?* According to the Institute for American Church Growth, the average tenure for pastors in the country's largest churches is 21 years. While there is clearly a correlation between long tenure and large churches, no one is certain which causes which. Are pastors of large churches apt to stick around longer because those churches can pay better and offer broader ministry opportunities? Or are we to infer that one key reason some churches grow is because their pastors have stayed long-term?

Surveys of Lutheran, Presbyterian, and United Methodist churches have all shown that long pastorates are more effective in attracting and holding members. And many pastors believe the most fruitful years of ministry with a particular congregation come after six or seven years of tenure. I once heard a pastor put it this way: "In the first two years of a pastorate, either you leave, or the people who think you can do nothing right leave, or you change, or they change, or you both change. By the seventh year, you start to really get productive."

2. *Do I have a dream for this ministry?* Can you remember what it's like to be excited about your work, to dream about what God is going to do with your group? One of the sad hazards of staying in one place too long is that we begin to do the work only with our heads, but not with our hearts. Imagine a ski patrolman who has been working the slopes for so long that he's forgotten the joy of gliding across a snowy landscape, or a restaurant critic who used to come to the table for taste and delight, but now comes only to write an article about food; or the professional golfer who got into the sport because she loved the game, but has long since forgotten what it was like to think of

golf as a game. It is the difference between doing a job with passion and doing a job for pay.

Henri Nouwen spoke of "that dead-end street...where all the words (are) already spoken, all events (have) already taken place, and all the people (have) already been met."[15] When we find ourselves on that street, when we've lost the ability to dream for a ministry, it may be a good sign that it's time to move on. Of course, we don't need every day to be a thrill-packed adventure of "Harry Potter and the Lost Middle-Schoolers" or "The Lion, the Witch, and the Youth Pastor"—but beware of a professional stagnation that comes from a lack of vision and a lack of challenge.

3. *Do my spiritual gifts match the present needs of this ministry?* In speaking to a group of youth ministry students, one former youth pastor explained that he left his position at one church after three years because he felt the ministry had grown to the point that it needed someone who was a better administrator. He felt his gifts and call were more in the area of one-on-one discipleship. Rather than try to fit himself into a changing role, he resigned from his paid position and found another job to support his family. He continued to minister within the group as a volunteer, and the funding freed up when he resigned was used to hire his replacement.

Stories like this are rare, but these circumstances are not so rare. Ministries change and needs change. A program that once needed someone with a strong gift for outreach may develop into a program that needs someone with more of a discipleship ministry. Such shifts don't always necessitate leaving a staff position. If we've built a genuine team ministry, it will be possible for us and our teams to stretch and flex with the changing needs of a ministry. Nonetheless, there are times when we may sense that, even if we don't personally feel we need a change, we may feel the youth program does.

4. *Is my philosophy of ministry compatible with my church?* Over 30 percent of the youth workers in Kageler's study who were fired listed disputes over "philosophy of ministry"—making it the most frequently cited reason for their firings.[16] It boils down to the simple question raised through the prophet Amos: "Do two walk together unless they have agreed to do so?" (Amos 3:3). This is the kind of issue Dan was dealing with in the second of the two stories that open this chapter: Could he continue to serve as youth minister of a church in which the leadership and some parents were trying to restrict the kind of students with whom he could actually minister? For Dan, that was a non-negotiable. He decided to move on.

5. *Are people still willing to follow me?* Titles don't mean much in youth ministry. We may have been hired as a "youth leader"—but if the youth aren't willing to follow, then it's time to reassess whether we can really be their leaders. We're all familiar with the image of the solitary Old Testament prophet, standing alone and prodding an unwilling Israel to follow. That's a valid ministry, no doubt. On the other hand, it takes a certain amount of parental, youth, and

board support to make any progress in ministry. When we've lost that support, it sometimes makes more sense to move on.

Ben was a youth pastor at a large church in North Carolina that underwent two or three years of painful upheaval which finally led to the senior pastor's dismissal. Although the turbulence had little to do with Ben's work with youth, the support framework he needed to do effective ministry in the church had been deeply eroded. After several conversations with him, my recommendation was to move on. We've only one life to live for Christ. Time is too short to waste it fighting to be a leader of people who don't want to follow.

HOLD IT...DON'T TOUCH THAT RESUME

On the other hand, not every situation that gives a youth worker itchy feet is a sound reason for leaving a ministry position. Here are a few circumstances which, while they may make us uncomfortable, are not necessarily solid grounds for walking out on a ministry.

Plateaus. *The youth program has no appreciable growth numerically and seems to lack momentum.* Youth groups normally go through ebbs and flows in attendance, sometimes solely due to demographic changes in the youth population.[17] Even school districts experience these fluctuations in enrollment—and that's with compulsory attendance. Leaving a youth ministry just because it's reached some kind of numerical plateau may simply be a reflection of our own need to feel we run the "fastest growing" youth group in the area. God doesn't call us to have groups that are always increasing enrollment. God calls us to be faithful to Christ and entrust the results to him.

Problem people. *A student, parent, parishioner, or board member is making us miserable.* My former pastor, David Seamands, used to playfully refer to these troublesome people as "assistants to the Holy Spirit"—people who are there to convict us just in case the Holy Spirit misses something. The problem with running from these people, of course, is that they are omnipresent. Run from these people and you will never stop running.

Financial dissatisfaction. *We have an offer for a higher paying youth ministry position.* As we've noted already, inadequate finances are a recurring concern. But if every youth worker moved whenever they learned of a better salary elsewhere, there would be almost perpetual motion, because it's almost always possible to find another position that pays $1,000 to $3,000 more than your current salary. Finances are important. It takes money to support a family; and it's tough for us to do our best in youth ministry when we're worried about paying the bills. On the other hand, youth ministers who are lured by a hook dangling a slightly higher salary are going to be darting from job to job like guppies in a fish tank.

Clearly, finances are a concern. But given the high costs of relocation, closing costs, and down payments, moving frequently isn't smart, even on financial terms. And there are other intangible costs to be considered. What about uprooting the family? What about children having to change schools? What about having to acclimate to a new community? What about having to start back at square one in building ministry credibility? What about the will of God? Chasing a dollar to a new position is usually a poor way to discern God's leading.

Hurt feelings. *We feel underappreciated, under-affirmed, under-supported, or just plain hurt.* If someone hurts our feelings, it's understandable that we will be angry. What is not understandable is how our departure from the ministry will make things right. Our departure will hurt the students we're working with. It will hurt our families by putting them through the trauma and trials of a move. It will hurt those in our congregations who support us. And none of this additional hurt will make our pain any less.

And, of course, after you've played this trump card, you can't play it again. By leaving a ministry, you effectively disenfranchise yourself from the process of change. Departure because of some hurt or offense usually brings additional pain and rarely offers satisfaction. We will not find a ministry without pain. Probably that's what Jesus was getting at when he said, "I am sending you out like lambs among wolves" (Luke 10:3).

WHEN IS A MOVE APPROPRIATE?

Despite all we've said in this chapter about the value of longevity, some things are more important than a long tenure. In my estimation the following four scenarios might justify a move:

1. When staying with the present church violates your integrity.

Bill was working in a large United Methodist Church in the Southeast. Like many other members of the congregation, he became aware that the church's choir director was having a not-so-discreet affair with one of the choir members. It gnawed at him to watch his unfaithful colleague take a leading role in worship week after week. He even told me of a Sunday when he'd watched this choir director serve Communion to the husband of the woman with whom he was having the affair!

By the time Bill spoke with me, the situation was eating him up inside. He felt he'd become an accessory to the charade taking place in the choir on Sunday mornings. When he'd confronted the choir director, he'd been strictly rebuffed, with the choir director saying it was none of his business. When he went to the pastor about his concern, he was told there wasn't enough evidence to take any action. Why start a disciplinary process that could ruin two good families? In essence, Bill was warned not to make waves.

My recommendation was straightforward and direct: "You've done all you can to confront and remedy the situation. If the church tolerates the situation, you must leave for the sake of your own conscience." At some point, trying to make peace with a deceit like that can do damage to your soul. That's when it's time to get out.

2. When family needs would be ignored by staying.

We're not talking here only about financial concerns. There are times when our ministries may place unfair expectations on family members, prevent us from spending adequate time with our families, or inhibit us responding to the special health requirements of a family member. In these and other family situations, we may find it necessary to leave. Our first responsibility is to the ministry God gives us with our families. Any job responsibility that effectively prevents us from carrying out that ministry gives us grounds to resign from our posts.

3. When your relationship with the congregation has deteriorated beyond reasonable hope of reconciliation.

Whether it's due to bad decisions, interpersonal conflict, or other factors, sometimes a pastor's relationship with a congregation is beyond repair. When this occurs, a move might be justified. See "Wars You Can't Win" above.

4. When it is clearly the will of God that we move to a specific new ministry.

This kind of call grows out of mostly positive circumstances—an instance of being *led to* a position rather than being *driven from* a position. Sometimes the Spirit of God leads us to new work. Our decision may seem beyond the understanding of the people in the ministries we leave behind, and may not even make sense from our own human standpoint. But if God says move, we'd better move (see the book of *Jonah*).

The longer we live under the hand of God, the more we begin to trust that God wants us to know his will more than we want to know it. We don't have to fret and worry that God may be trying to lead us in a new direction, but we are missing his point. If God wants us to move, he has ways of getting us to pay attention! My personal conviction is that God is not so concerned that we specifically work in this or that location; God's major concern is that we have faith in him (John 6:28-29). God can use both positive and negative situations to nurture that faith—in fact, sometimes he can better use the negative situations to build our trust in him.

The LEAVE Principle

In my thirty-plus years of youth ministry, my family and I have chosen to go through the uncertainty and dislocation of moving to a new ministry three or four times. On one of those occasions, I sought counsel from a friend who referred me to what he called the LEAVE principle. My friend suggested that there are five good reasons for making a ministry transition—reasons that echo much of what we've said in this chapter:

> ***L***ack of personal growth
>
> ***E***xpenses exceed income (not enough income to support my family)
>
> ***A*** breakdown in relationships (among staff, students, parents)
>
> ***V***ision has ceased
>
> ***E***vidence that God is leading elsewhere

IF YOU DECIDE TO GO: LEAVING WELL

Since we speak to teenagers week after week, most of us in youth ministry have come to appreciate the power of a good closing line. We understand that those last few sentences of a message will stick in the listeners' memories after we cease to speak. So we choose our final words carefully, staying away from lines like:

> "And if you don't like it, that's tough."
>
> "Since I see you're leaving, I guess I'll wrap up."
>
> "And in the words of Forrest Gump, that's all I have to say about that."
>
> "Is it just me—or was that an amazing message?"
>
> And, my favorite,
>
> "But, hey, what do I know?"

In the same way, when we leave a ministry position—for whatever reason—we do well to think carefully about our exit lines. How we leave a ministry can make a statement that underlines all the good God has done in a ministry, and it can undercut all the good God has done in a ministry. Here are some basic principles to remember as you write your exit lines.[18] Whether it be in your resignation letter, or your everyday conversation, or the inevitable round of good-bye events, let these thoughts guide your interactions in the final days of a ministry:

Focus on the positive. Your ministry tenure may be filled with great memories, or it may be that the memories are mostly bad. But there is almost nothing to gain by slamming the door on the way out. One denominational executive observed, "During almost twenty-two years on a presbytery staff and as a Presbyterian executive, I spent countless hours repairing the damage of destructive good-byes to both congregations and pastors."[19] It is never appropriate to write a "Take this job and shove it" letter as you leave a position. The ministry will exist after you exit, and you will exist after you exit the ministry. What is best for the cause of Christ is that both parties move ahead with a positive direction.

Communicate the difficulties of making the choice to leave. By the time you leave, the decision may feel like a "no-brainer." But any thoughtful exit decision is a tough one, and communicating the difficulties of that struggle to those who are left behind is a way of communicating respect and appreciation.

Express gratitude. A good resignation letter recognizes that folks have honored you with their trust and allowed you the tremendous privilege of pastoral care. Be clear in expressing your thanks for that.

Affirm the good. In a good situation, there is much to celebrate—and that should not be overlooked. But even in a bad situation, we can celebrate the goodness of God. In spite of all the grief and heartbreak Joseph suffered at the hands of his brothers, he had the grace and wisdom to understand that God could redeem those difficult experiences for his purposes (Genesis 50:20).

Offer hope. Whether the departure is on good terms or bad terms, it's easy for those in the congregation or ministry you've left behind to feel a sense of despair. They have to go through a search process, endure a period of transition, and struggle through a trial of uncertain leadership. They need to hear you clearly affirm (in your resignation letter and elsewhere) that *God is not finished here* and that the future is as bright as God's promises.

Explain your decision. It isn't enough to say, *"God is leading me elsewhere."* Everyone wants to know *why*, especially the students and their parents. It simply isn't fair to walk away from a ministry without offering some word of explanation. And if you don't establish the narrative about why you are leaving, others will—and that can lead to accusations, rumors, and speculation. Obviously, your reasons for departing need to be stated discreetly—not as camouflaged complaints or sanctified boasting. But articulating three or four factors that have shaped your decision will help people come to terms with your departure.

Be clear about your departure date. An exit period that lingers long-term is like a slow bleed. Be specific about the timing and the process of your departure.

When the decision to leave has been finally made, the message you want to leave behind is a message that affirms the goodness and wisdom of God. It should be part healing salve, part benediction, part explanation, part testimony, and part statement of faith. You're leaving; God isn't. His purposes are best served by bearing witness to both of those statements as clearly and as positively as possible.

CHAPTER 16

Growing Old without Growing Stale: Staying Fresh in Long-Term Youth Ministry

Even when I am old and gray, do not forsake me, my God,
till I declare your power to the next generation,
your mighty acts to all who are to come.
(Psalm 71:18)

It might feel a little weird reading a chapter about "growing old" in youth ministry. After all, we work with teenagers. And working with teenagers is all about being young and cool, right? For those of you who are just starting out, it feels like turning to the last chapter of the book when we've just barely gotten through the Table of Contents. And for those of us who've been at this for a while, it feels a little incriminating, like picking up a book entitled *So, You Struggle with Lust?*

As of this date, I'm 58 and counting (read: breathing). For 36 of those years I've been involved in some form of full-time work in youth ministry. It has been an amazing adventure, every step of the way. But as the journey continues, now well into a fourth decade, I've seen that there are clearly both benefits and challenges that come with the long walk.

Some years ago, Chuck Swindoll preached a sermon on aging gracefully, and he began his message with the following series of statements. Each of them begins, *You know you're getting old when...*

> *...your back goes out more often than you do.*
>
> *...you see an attractive person of the opposite sex and your pacemaker opens the garage door.*
>
> *...the little old lady or little old man you help across the street is married to you.*
>
> *...you sit in a rocking chair and you can't get it going.*
>
> *...you look forward to a dull evening at home.*
>
> *...your knees buckle but your belt won't.*
>
> *...the gleam in your eye is a refection off your bifocals.*

...finding your hair takes longer than combing it.

...you sink your teeth into a steak and they stay there.

Okay, thankfully, I'm not at the point where all of these apply to me yet, but Swindoll's list is suggestive of some common ways we think about aging in youth ministry. *You know you're getting older in youth ministry when...*

...you decide that, from now on, all lock-ins will end at 8:30 p.m.—with your interns in charge.

...your Woodstock illustrations don't work anymore.

...you find yourself doing more contact work with the kids' parents than the kids themselves.

...you need to take your microwave to camp to fix your own stewed prunes.

...a student has to explain that text is something you do, not something you read.

...you stop taking off your shirt at pool parties (men only).

...you look out at the senior high group and recognize two of the kids as your own daughters.

...you stop with the kids at McDonald's and you pull out your AARP discount card;

...your idea of an "all-nighter" is sleeping through to the morning without getting up to use the bathroom.

In ministry, as in life, there are two possibilities: We can grow older or we can die young. For right now, I prefer the first option. But growing older in youth ministry without growing stale requires grace and understanding. In this final chapter of the book, we'll consider some of the pluses and minuses of long-term youth ministry.

SO YOU'RE GETTING OLDER

Over the last decade, the median age of youth workers has slowly crept higher and higher. One study prepared by *Group* magazine in the early 1990s showed the median age of North American youth workers to be 33 years (remember: A *median* age of 33 means half of all youth workers are younger than 33, *and half of all youth workers are older*). More recent surveys reflect the same phenomenon. A 2005 study of youth workers in Australia's Uniting Church found that "the average age of youth workers in some synods has increased dramatically and the length of time serving in ministry and in specific placements has also increased....*A significant number of Specified Youth Workers are around 40 to 50 years of age" [emphasis added]*. A newsletter of the Evangelical Free Church of America reports the average age of youth workers in that denomination as 37 years old.

In an excellent 2009 study of 810 Canadian youth workers, 32 percent were between the ages of 31 to 40 (the largest group); 15 percent were age 41-50; 4 percent were age 51-55, 1 percent age 56-60; and 2 percent were more than 60 years old.[1] That's one of every five Canadian youth workers in the sample who are age 41 or older. In their broad study of youth work in the United Kingdom,[2] Alison Gelder and Phillip Escott found that two of every three youth workers were under the age of 40 (compared to one in eight senior ministers). Yet they still found a remarkably high number of youth workers—three out of every ten—between the ages of 40 and 59.[3] It's become quite common to meet people in their forties or even fifties who are still doing youth work.

This maturing of the youth worker population has some profound implications for those of us in youth ministry. In fact, one could probably make a very strong case that most of the changes in the youth ministry landscape over the last two decades have happened *not because teenagers have changed, but because those of us who work with teenagers have changed.*

Think about it. Aging changes the way we think about almost every facet of youth work. Consider these areas:

Family ministry. Was it mere coincidence that youth workers began to discover the importance of family ministry back in the early 1990s? Was it a flash of divine insight? Or was it because the first generation of long-term youth workers began to see their own children showing up for youth group?

I remember the first time my own daughters were part of the audience when I did my usual "sex talk" for a group of kids. My wife commented later, "You weren't as funny as you usually are." And I said, "You bet I wasn't; those were our girls out there. This isn't funny!"

Back when the first group of trailblazing youth ministers were all 25-35 years old, teenagers were just these people who showed up at youth group. We loved them and cared for them. But a funny thing happened as we got a little older. *Suddenly, those teenagers were our kids.* That changed the way we thought about youth ministry and family. All of a sudden we were talking about the importance of working with parents, ministering to whole families, and being supportive of what was happening at home. Why? Well, it probably had to do with the fact that these were *our* kids and those were *our homes*!

Safety issues. Three decades ago, nobody ever talked about safety issues in youth ministry. We were all young, naïve, and game for anything. I remember a massive food fight breaking out at a Youth Specialties convention years ago.

Now, three decades later, we sound like parents: "You know, it's dangerous to cram thirty marshmallows into your mouth..." and "Let's make sure that we don't put students in situations where there is the danger of abuse..." We used to approach safety issues as if we were pals; now we approach them as if we were parents.

The Focus of Ministry. Growing older even affects the way we see youth ministry itself. Goals shift from short-term to long-term, from survival to impact. A newsletter article from one North American denomination put it well:

> The long-term effectiveness of these ministers cannot be overstated. They have shed the "bag of tricks" stage of their youth, the "program to death" stage of their adolescent years, and are now focused on equipping others for ministry. Most of them have been equipping throughout their tenure. But now equipping takes on an urgent tone because they know their time is short, and they realize that those so equipped will be their legacy.

Eventually, we all come to a point where we realize we won't last forever. At that point, we begin to ask: "What am I building here that will last longer than me?"

"AM I TOO OLD?" OR "AM I STILL CALLED?"

There's no disputing the fact that as we age in youth ministry, some things that once came easily to us become more difficult. But the reverse is also true: Some elements of youth ministry actually become easier with age. What it really boils down to is this: In terms of effectiveness with teenagers, age is not the central issue. Indeed, the central question in youth ministry is not, "Am I *too old* to do youth work?" but, "Am I *still called* to do youth work?" In an effort to offer a framework for thinking through that question, let's consider some of the benefits that can come from staying in youth ministry for the long haul.

Increased Credibility. Older youth workers are generally taken more seriously by other people in the congregation and leadership structures. When we start out in ministry as twenty-something "wonder-kids," congregations appreciate us the way one might appreciate a St. Bernard puppy. We're seen as young, cute, and playful—but certainly not the ones you call out for the serious rescue. Aging works to change that.

Clearer Vision. Aging gives us a better grasp of our own youth ministry philosophy. When you're young and starting out in ministry, your thinking is often a bit like this: "*Something* must be done. This *is* something. Therefore, it *must* be done."

We spend a lot of time in our early years trying to prove ourselves, not just to others, but also *to ourselves*. It's like the first *Rocky* film, when Rocky is running through the streets of Philadelphia with trumpets blaring, pushing himself to win the big fight (and make several additional mediocre movies). When asked why he did it, he says, "So, I can prove I'm not a bum!" As we grow older in ministry—if we're in a place of spiritual and emotional health—we don't feel we have as much to prove. We come to understand what we can do, and just as importantly, we come to terms with what we cannot do. Age forces us to rethink and clarify our vision. We don't have the energy to do everything, so we learn to focus less on activity and more on productivity.

The Joy of the Harvest. Aging in youth ministry allows us to experience more fully the joy of the harvest. Any seed-sower will tell you that harvest is all about seasons, and seasons are about time. One of the greatest personal privileges I've experienced in my own ministry is getting to see the fruit of seeds sown over many seasons of youth work. Recently, I was approached after speaking at a youth retreat by three smiling teenage girls who announced, "Our Dad told us to tell you 'hello.' He says you know him."

When I asked, "Who's your dad?" they gave me the name of a guy who'd been in my own youth ministry almost 25 years ago. It was a wonderful gift. To see these young teenage girls, and to see their dad's faith reflected in their own growing faith, I was stunned that God would give me the opportunity to see my ministry come full circle. When I related the story later to a friend, he said, "Does that make you feel old?" I said, "No. It makes me feel *grateful!*"

Better Perspective. For the sailor on his maiden voyage, every swell seems to rock the boat, every storm looks like a killer hurricane, every crew complaint feels like a potential mutiny. But when you've been on the open water of ministry for a while, you gain a sense of perspective. Failures don't loom as large. Negative comments don't sting quite as long. Emergencies don't seem quite as catastrophic. Not only do you begin to gain confidence that you can weather the storms, you also gain a deeper appreciation for the mystery and adventure of the voyage.

Of course, any old salt would probably tell us that familiarity has its disadvantages as well. If we're not careful, we start to become numb to the wonder around us. Like the aging seafarer who no longer notices the splendor of the sunset, or the captain who knows the waters so well that he becomes careless in keeping to the course, experienced youth workers must guard against the cynicism and arrogance that can comes with many years of ministry. When you start to think you've seen it all, expectancy fades into complacency.

Less Stress. When I arrived at the church a few minutes before midnight, every window was flooded with light, and every lighted window showed a room full of kids. The place was jam-packed—every nook and cranny of the building was throbbing with excited teenagers. When I finally found the youth worker, he was clearly in shock.

He'd wanted to do an outreach event, but he didn't really expect his event to reach out *this* much! He was like a fisherman who'd cast out hoping for bass and ended up hooking a shark. Now that he had the fish on the line, what was he supposed to do? Jason's wide eyes met mine with a sense of panic—and it was all I could do to keep from laughing. I grabbed him by the shoulders and said, "You know what, Jas, God is in the midst of this thing, and it's wild, and it's wall-to-wall pandemonium. But the Lord's going to bring us through it, and the sun's going to rise tomorrow, and you're going to make it."

That is the blessing of experience—knowing that the ministry doesn't rise or fall with this one event, that my gifts are not defined by this one study, that the measure of my call is not calculated by this one weekend—whether it was good *or* bad. That takes away a lot of the stress.

Professional Respect. If you've been in youth ministry more than 20 minutes, you've probably come to understand that this is not a work generally held in high esteem—inside or outside the church. I can't count the number of times I've shared a flight with some high-powered business traveler, eager to network, who asks expectantly, "And what kind of work are you in?" When I say, "I'm in youth ministry," his smile fades and his eyes glaze over. It's as if I've said, "Oh, yes, my job is to follow the elephants in the parade."

In the church environment, at least, there are some small and positive changes in the climate. The number of youth workers who are staying longer in youth ministry has helped to redefine our profession. People are beginning to understand that youth ministry is not just a stepping-stone to the big leagues—something one does until one is qualified to do almost anything else. In North America, at least, this increasing respect is reflected in better compensation for full-time youth workers (especially those with ten or more years of experience) and broader recognition of youth ministry as a legitimate field of academic study.

In that sense youth ministry is like a marathon race. The start of the race is cluttered with so many competitors that no particular runner attracts much attention. But for those who stay in the race and go the distance, there is a growing consensus of respect.

Youth Ministry Keeps Us Young. We don't survive very long in youth ministry without being open, flexible, and growing as a person. Those are good traits to cultivate because they keep us "young" in some of the principal ways that most adults show their age: Loss of playfulness, stuck in the past, little or no appetite for adventure, dulled sense of discovery, and jaded attitudes towards the promises of God. When I'm around certain non-youth ministry folks who are my chronological peers, I'm often struck by how they seem so...um, old. You just don't sense the fire, the hunger, the openness, the creativity.

Please understand: There are parts of adolescence that are better left behind—The obsession with being edgy, the pathological fear of being uncool, the suspicion of anything older than this moment, the misconception that freedom is doing whatever one wishes. Our ability to grow beyond these things as we age is a genuine plus for authentic ministry. But one of the hazards of growing old is the possibility of growing stale. Working closely with teenagers can help us grow up and keep growing.

TRANSITIONS AND CHANGES

As someone who has officiated quite a few weddings, I've often thought to myself that the most important part of the wedding vows is the promise, "I [groom] take thee [bride] from this day forward, to have and to hold, *for better or for worse...*" For those who take vows seriously, it's a sober reminder that—even if you never get a divorce—the person you marry today will not be the person to whom you're married 10, 15, or 20 years from now. People change; they grow older, they develop different preferences and strengths, they function differently over time. Lo and behold, she marries *Mr. Right*, only to discover ten years down the road that he is *Mr. Wrong*—and she becomes *Miss Left*.

In the same way, youth workers who are committed to long-term youth ministry should understand that the person who begins the journey will not be the same person who maintains it. Your approach to ministry priorities, volunteer relationships, and operational approaches will change and evolve over time. And, contrary to popular belief, the trajectory isn't just one long-sloping nosedive that begins with strength and crashes and burns with ineffectiveness. Sure, some of our strengths as young youth workers diminish a bit as we age. But some of the weaknesses we have as young youth workers can also diminish as we age. Healthy long-term youth ministry is a matter of understanding these changes, and then trusting God to give us the grace and insight to make realistic and honest adjustments in our evolving circumstances.

What follows is a description of the various stages that youth workers tend to experience over the course of a long-term career in youth ministry, and an examination of how the adjustments that accompany these stages might play out with regard to a number of issues. The observations here are largely anecdotal and, to some extent, autobiographical. But they describe some of the milestones and potholes on the road of long-term youth ministry. Let's look first at the stages themselves:[4]

> ***Stage One (S1):*** In this first stage, we're just starting out. Perhaps our first taste of youth ministry is as a volunteer or intern who works with a group while completing college studies, or simply as an older teen who is no longer in high school but remembers what a strong ministry or caring Christian adult can mean for a teenager, and we want to provide that kind of support for others.

Stage Two (S2): This second stage emerges in the mid-twenties, post-college years. Perhaps now we've completed some seminary work as well, gaining some sort of graduate preparation for ministry.

Stage Three (S3): With stage three we're clearly getting our ministry footing. Now, in our late twenties to mid-thirties, we've landed a full-time ministry position and are beginning to develop some sense of competence.

Stage Four (S4): Somewhere between late thirties and mid-forties, we reach stage Four in which we're firmly established in our role as a professional youth worker. That's not to say there aren't struggles and questions. But for those who have survived to this point in youth ministry, clearly there is some sense of confidence and know-how.

Stage Five (S5): Late forties and beyond, into the fifties and sixties.

Stage Six (S6): Death. (Just kidding.)

As we move through these stages, there are a range of issues and relationships affected by the aging process. What are they, and what kind of strengths and risks characterize these stages?

Issue 1: Relationships With Students

S1: When we start out in youth ministry (often as a late teen or college student), youth tend to view us as an older peer. "Basically, she looks like us; therefore, she is one of us." In terms of dress, musical tastes, everyday linguistic idioms, comfort level with digital technologies, and even marital status (in most cases), our life situations are very similar to those with whom we're doing ministry. This is indigenous mission work—like reaching out to like. But there's a subtle distinction to make here. Despite how *we* might see ourselves, they do not see us *as* a peer, they see us *like* a peer.[5]

Strengths: We can move among teenagers incognito; we look like them. Plus, we have the time, freedom, and energy to be more spontaneous. If it's 10 p.m. or even midnight, and a kid suggests going to a movie, we say, "Sure"—whereas in later years if they say, "Let's go to the midnight movie," we're more inclined to respond, "Okay, sure, I guess I can just sleep in the car."

Dangers: The danger at this stage is that we try to use our youthfulness as our greatest asset. In other words, we try to connect with teenagers by acting like a teenager—and that's almost always unhealthy. First of all, if you're not in high school, it's not very authentic to act like you are. Second, when adults *act* like teenagers, that very often degenerates into just plain acting immature, and that's the last thing teenagers need to see modeled in their leaders. Finally, unless we succeed where Ponce de Leon failed and find the Fountain of Youth, with each passing year we remain in ministry, we'll become less effective because of the way we've defined ourselves to kids.

S2: As we get a bit older, perhaps now a graduate of college or even seminary, our relationships with students become more that of a significant other—not necessarily a peer, but, somehow, not necessarily an adult either.

S3: Now, into our late twenties or early thirties, youth begin to view us perhaps as more of a benign adult—kind of like a friendly uncle or aunt. We're definitely seen as an adult, but we're trusted enough by the teenagers in our spheres of ministry to be invited where many adults are not. This is a rare privilege, a hard-earned trust that allows kids to feel safe around us in ways that they don't feel safe when they're around other adults.

S4: As we get older still (late thirties or forties), the teenagers we work with see us more as a father- or mother-figure, particularly if we have children who are approaching their own teenage years. Being at peace with this particular transition is a huge factor in the equation of growing old without getting stale. I can still recall my horror when a bunch of my students and I were riding in the church van and Melissa, without catching herself, started to say something to me: "Dad...er...I mean, Duffy..." The kids all laughed, but I almost drove into a tree. It was the first time I realized what the kids had known for years: *I was not one of them*; I was an adult, an older person, and they recognized that. But it was also a moment of great relief, because I realized they were okay with that. The question for me then was; *Am I okay with it?*

Danger: If we see ourselves as the eternal teenager, Rev. Peter Pan, this stage can become very uncomfortable (for all involved).

Strength: If, on the other hand, we see ourselves as adults who care about teenagers, and who value our role in ministering to families, we can begin to see this transition as the onset of a newly strategic ministry moment—because it's not until we get to this stage that parents really begin to see us as someone who understands *them*. Some of the most in-depth ministry happens when the teenagers no longer see you as a peer, but the parents do.

Danger: A second lurking danger at this point is the temptation to become "SuperParent"—to see ourselves as surrogate parents who can offer kids a second opinion when their own parents don't understand them. As we affirmed earlier in chapter 8, ours is the role of a bridge-builder. What makes us effective at this stage of ministry is our increased ability to bring *both ends* of the bridge together.

Strength: A significant advantage of this stage, especially if we have teenagers of our own, is that we're able to see the youth with whom we work through different eyes. The perspective we bring as a non-parent adult, who thinks like a parent, is a wonderful gift for ministry, and it's a strength that most of us lack in our early years of youth work.

S5: As we move into our fifties and sixties, some of us are still quite comfortable with and capable of doing front-line direct ministry with teenagers. That's great, and we've already seen that there's no reason older age necessarily precludes effectiveness with teenagers.

But, there are others, still committed to youth ministry, who, for various reasons, find that their roles have changed. They do less on-the-field ministry, and more coaching from the sidelines. Or, their involvement may primarily be the role of advocates—supporting the troops from a distance so they can maintain effectiveness in the trenches. Others take on a supervisory role, like a principal at school—although, for a lot of us, that's not exactly a warm, fuzzy image. They care about teenagers, but their responsibilities are more removed from direct adult-to-student interaction.

In my opinion, this is one of the trickiest transitions in long-term youth ministry. Direct interaction with kids is partially what drew us into youth ministry. It strikes right at the heart of our call, and our sense of self-definition. Being a youth worker who doesn't work directly with youth is like being named *Abraham* (lit: "father of a nation," Genesis 17:5), and not having any children. And, we sense, also, that if we get too distant from the kids, we'll lose our edge. The challenge is maintaining that balance. It's a willingness to be a coach, who still has contact with the game, but feels that it's more strategic for younger players to take the field.

Issue 2: Ministry Objectives

S1: When we start out in youth ministry as a young person, we tend to be in activity mode. Our landscape of experience is so small that it's hard to even think of long-term goals. Long-term goals are things like *getting home safely* and *completing the lock-in without burning the building down*. In those early days of ministry, we're sometimes so intent on just completing the task that we can forget to ask why we're doing the task. It's like the first run down a hill on skis: So much effort is being spent on not crashing that there isn't time to enjoy the snowy landscape of the wider mountain-top vista.

Also, much of ministry at this age is shaped by a simple philosophy: *How can I get the kids to like me?* Partly as a factor of age, that's still a fundamental lens through which late teens and early twenty-somethings see all of life. Plus, intuitively, we tend to think of our ability to relate as a natural strength.

Danger: The danger on both points is confusing *survival* with *fruitful*. We're not called primarily to get kids to like the ministry or the minister; our call is to grow mature saints who can serve the kingdom of God.

S2: After graduation, be it from college or seminary, there's a bit of a shift in ministry emphasis. Especially if someone has been engaged in theological study, the ministry emphasis becomes more about teaching. After all, why waste all of this incredible knowledge gained in the classroom? Fresh from an environment in which big philosophical questions and theological issues have been the daily diet, it's only natural that we would want to make use of those big books we were required to read.

Strengths: The strengths of this shift are obvious. The training we've had should enable us to build more substance and depth into our teaching.

Danger: The danger is that we become so absorbed with these issues that we teach more out of our own spiritual journey than to our students' spiritual journey. The debate between *consubstantiation* and *transubstantiation* is interesting and important, but let's not plumb its depths before our youth have been introduced to the atonement. Nor should we spend so much time teaching students doctrinal gems that we neglect to talk about the lifestyle issues they face every day as thirteen- or seventeen-year-olds. Finally, there's a danger of becoming condescending and cynical towards those who are not asking the same kind of deep, thoughtful questions we're asking (see 1 Corinthians 8:1).

S3: As we move into the third stage of the ministry journey, there is often still another shift. By this time, we've developed some teaching skills, we've addressed some pet theological topics, and we've learned to hold a crowd with our message or put together an effective Bible study. But as we move into a second decade of ministry, that's no longer enough. We yearn to see life-change, and the desire to make kids good listeners becomes eclipsed by the desire to help them become disciples of Christ who are being changed into his likeness. To use the language of Jesus, we want to see fruit, "fruit that will last" (John 15:16).

S4: As we adapt to the more parental role of stage four, our ministry emphasis continues to evolve in the direction of developing disciples.

Strength: Viewing teenagers from this parental/adult perspective, our teaching becomes more practical, more real life, more *what does this look like at home with your family?* That's a good thing.

Danger: The danger is that the parental vibe can come with a nagging vibe. Right? In that role, we're trying to keep everybody safe. ("Hey, guys, don't ski on those black diamond slopes; the last thing you need is to break a leg two weeks before report cards.") And sometimes, the parental role even slides into what almost feels like disgust: We've just gotten tired of teenagers acting like teenagers. *Why can't they be (fill in the blank): quieter, cleaner, more serious, more interested in listening to sermons?*

One of the real tragedies of long-term youth ministry is that people sometimes get to this point and remain in youth work primarily because it's what they know. They aren't sure they can do anything else. If you find yourself in that situation, for the health of all involved, this is a great time to trust God to lead you elsewhere. These feelings don't mean you're immoral or sinful. In fact, those feelings about teenagers are probably shared to some extent by about 90 percent of the adult population. (Other people feel the same way about young children or senior adults.) But those attitudes are an indication that you probably won't be a very effective youth worker. It's hard to do effective youth ministry when you look across the room at the students and start thinking, *This could have been a great meeting if the kids hadn't come!*

S5: By the time you reach stage 5, your approach to ministry is very much centered around multiplying yourself and training others to do the work of ministry. You realize both your time and energy are limited, so you focus more on giving away the ministry.

Strength: By this time, you may very well have students from your ministry who have planted youth ministries of their own, so your role as a mentor becomes very significant (and satisfying). You get to see the fruit of your ministry.

Danger: Part of giving ministry away is...well, giving ministry away. And that's hard sometimes, when we begin to see the new leadership making choices we would not have made—not necessarily bad choices, just different ones. There is in most of us, I think, a natural and unhealthy tendency to want to clone ourselves—to raise up disciples who think like us and serve like us and lead like us. It's almost like we've forgotten that the goal is not to equip people to follow us; it's to equip people to follow Christ. I've had to remind myself that God called me to reproduce myself spiritually, not replicate myself spiritually. The goal is Christ-likeness, not me-likeness, and sometimes that will lead students into ministries that look very different from my own.

We also have to be careful in this stage to recognize that amid the bright lights of new leadership it's easy for the shadow of jealousy to fall on those of us in the old leadership. Rather than celebrating the fruit, we commiserate that we are under-appreciated and out to pasture. It takes a special grace to say with John the Baptist, "He must increase, but I must decrease" (John 3:30).

Issue 3: Approach To Staff And Volunteers

S1: In our earliest days as youth workers, we typically approach volunteers as if they were there to help us do *our* ministry. At this point in our life, adults still kind of freak us out. We're not super comfortable dealing with them as peers, and certainly not as people under our tutelage. Maybe we're even a little threatened by some of the folks on staff or in our congregations who've been working with teenagers longer than we have. Plus, we're not really sure we know enough about how to do youth ministry to train others, and, at one level, we might be afraid that our efforts to offer training will only confirm that we're making it up as we go along. Better just to do everything ourselves and hope they don't see us sweat.

S2: As we move into stage 2 we begin to see volunteer staff as valued co-workers. Since we're most interested in teaching anyway (see stage 2 of "Ministry Objectives" above), we're more willing to make use of staff. We see these people as allies: "You guys plan the event. I'll be in there studying. Call me when it's time to come out and say something profound."

S3: By stage 3 we can begin to see the benefit and privilege of nurturing these volunteers. We tend to see them more as disciples who need to be equipped rather than merely as equipment for us to use while we disciple the students.

One factor that probably plays into this transition is that, as people get into their late twenties and early thirties, they often begin having children. That means that many of the volunteers who are our peers are now stepping back so they can concentrate on raising a young family. That puts us in the position of being among a new group of younger stage 1 and stage 2 youth workers.

S4 and S5: This training role becomes even more galvanized as we move into our forties and beyond. We're secure enough in our own role and competence that we can see the volunteer staff as a valued team. And just as our relationships with students become a bit more distant, our relationships with team members become more immediate and more direct. They are the eyes, arms, and ears through which we love the students.

Strengths: Perhaps this is the first time we can truly and unreservedly celebrate when one of our team members is gifted in an area that we are not. If we're willing to work to this point in ministry, it is almost always a place of great joy.

Issue 4: Evolution Of Role In Church

S1: When we start in youth ministry, especially if we're working in a congregational setting, we tend to be seen as this cute, off-the-wall Pied Piper type of figure—appreciated more for novelty than wisdom. Everyone in the congregation is willing to be our parents. Folks are more forgiving when we make mistakes.

S2: By the time we graduate from seminary or college, with our theology finely honed and doctrinal positions neatly worked out, we'll appoint ourselves as the conscience of the congregation—sort of a prophet in residence.

Strengths: Fresh ideas and fresh voices can help people think in fresh ways.

Dangers: Sometimes highly educated people who lack life experience (and faith experience) communicate fresh ideas in a way that just sounds fresh and arrogant. That's a good way to make enemies.

Very likely, when we are in stage 2, the congregation sees us as *preparing for something else*. In other words, from their perspective, we aren't doing youth work because we're called to do it. We're doing youth work because we're trying to figure out what we're called to do. In that sense, we're probably seen as transient and not to be counted on for long-term tenure.

S3: If we stay in youth ministry into our thirties, we start to gain professional credibility. We are, perhaps, taken more seriously as a pastor. Having paid our dues and proven ourselves trustworthy, it's also possible we've added responsibilities that include occasional preaching. Rightly or wrongly, that usually adds to our professional stature. Barriers begin to come down, and we are seen more and more as a peer by the adults in the congregation. That opens up new relational and ministry opportunities that can extend our ministry into the broader community.

S4 and S5: The credibility and extended influence increases as we move into our late thirties and beyond—particularly among parents of teenagers, who are, in many cases, our own peers.

Strengths: This added credibility provides a much better platform for the kind of bridge-building family ministry we talked about in chapter 8. People in the congregation begin to see us as advocates, not just for teenagers, but for teenagers *and* families.

Dangers: These added responsibilities can make it increasingly difficult to maintain our focus on youth ministry. If the congregation does not value youth ministry, there may be the added subtle pressure for us to *graduate* into an associate pastor or other pastoral role.

Issue 5: Professional Development

S1: In stage 1, professional development usually isn't even on the radar. We don't so much choose youth ministry as it chooses us: We're in our youth and we want to do ministry, so we do youth ministry.

Strengths: There is something about that initial passion and excitement that is vital. We want always to cultivate that sense of urgency and adventure in ministry.

Weaknesses: That youthful exuberance won't be enough to sustain us long-term. Some young people get into youth work because they don't want to leave youth group, or maybe because the youth group was the last place they actually felt affirmed and accepted. Those positive feelings aren't durable enough to carry us very far in the rough and tumble of ministry. There has to be a call anchored in the conviction that we are doing what God has called us to do.

S2: In the years after college or seminary, we begin to think more about our long-term calling. We begin to test our gifts. That's one reason people in youth ministry have the reputation of being transient. A lot of young youth workers are trying to figure out what we should (could?) be doing.

S3: Moving into a second decade as youth workers, we have gained more confidence about who we are and what we're are called to do. It's at this point we become more focused on professional issues like organization, staff relationships, and ministry systems and protocols.

S4: To be a youth worker in his or her late thirties and forties is to face some pretty serious questions. We've possibly seen peers in other fields advance into prestigious roles and good-paying jobs, and we wonder if we're settling for a smaller, less significant sphere of influence.

Strengths: This provides a healthy motivation to think about how we can maximize our impact for the kingdom. Do we invest ourselves more deeply (start a more intentional mentoring or intern program, invest in some younger local youth workers, or offer to teach a training series for volunteers from several area youth ministries)? Or, do we invest wider (maybe do some writing, speak on a broader level, or assume some role in denominational, district, or network leadership)?

Dangers: We have in youth ministry unintentionally cultivated the notion that those who aren't writing books and doing seminars all over the country aren't doing significant ministry. Beyond the obvious flaws in this premise, this mindset can also distract good youth workers from impacting deep (locally) because they feel they need to impact wide (nationally). The heart and soul of youth ministry will always be the person who sows the seed, works the soil, and nurtures the fruit among a group of kids they love week in and week out. These other ministries have value, but let's not assume they are more valuable because they are often more prominent.

S5: My experience is that the majority of those who stay in youth ministry through stage 5 tend to specialize. They find a particular area of expertise and contentment within youth ministry and focus intentionally on that area. My Dad used to say, "Find someone who will pay you to do what you love, and you'll never have to work a day in your life." That's the secret of many lifelong youth workers.

In this stage, many youth workers seek to develop a more intentional youth ministry intern program. A congregation or ministry board recognizes the youth worker's unique skills and gifts, but recognizes those gifts and skills are in an aging body that can't do everything it used to do. So, they say, "Fine, we want you to lead the team, but we'll hire some young horses as interns to help pull the wagon." This seems to be an increasingly popular way for youth ministries to retain and celebrate the experience of aging youth workers.

Ultimately, the question of whether or not we move through these stages of long-term ministry will largely be based on how we respond to the following questions.

STICKING IT OUT OR STUCK IN IT

***(A Personal Inventory for Assessing Your Long-Term Call to Youth Ministry)*[6]**

MOTIVATION: Why am I remaining in youth work? Is it because I still take delight in the work? Do I find it stimulating? Do I still feel a genuine burden for teenagers? Some people like youth ministry more than they like teenagers, maybe even more than they like Jesus.

TRAINING: How much is enough? Can I remain in a place of mental prosperity if I remain in youth ministry? One of the dangers of long-term youth ministry is that we know enough to teach, but not enough to thrive. Can I stay in a job I know well and maintain the discipline of being a life-long learner?

PROFESSIONALISM*: *Am I comfortable with being a professional youth worker? Can I live with the lack of affirmation and minimal recognition that often accompanies a long-term call to youth ministry? And can I absorb that (usually unintended) disrespect without growing bitter or resentful?

CHANGING ROLES: Am I willing to transition from kids seeing me as their "peer" to seeing me as their "pastor"? And am I able to balance both roles? One particularly vivid example of this tension is what happens when your own children become part of the ministry. Being able to maintain balance, separation, and authenticity in the various roles we play out is critical for our own long-term health and the health of those around us.

DELEGATION: Am I willing to give the ministry away? For some, this is the make or break question of long-term youth ministry. Do I always have to "minister to..." or can I develop the habits of "ministering through..."? Those who love a sport know they will have a longer career as a coach than they will as a player. The goals are exactly the same, but some never seem to feel as comfortable on the sidelines as they were on the field.

ECONOMICS: Am I in a place where there is adequate financial support for me to continue youth ministry and still fulfill my responsibilities for the financial welfare of my family?

FAMILY: What is the impact of my continuing youth ministry on my family? How does it affect my spouse? My children? Maybe it's temperament or maybe it's ministry circumstances, but some families are just more comfortable with the special demands and opportunities that come along with youth ministry. If my family isn't one of those families, that may be a clear indication of God's direction.

CONFESSIONS OF A "LIFER"

Even though I am well into stage 5 myself, I don't honestly know if I will do youth ministry for my whole life. If God should make it possible, that would be awesome. But I didn't invite "youth ministry" into my heart on that weekend retreat back in 1969. I invited Jesus into my heart. That means that my first allegiance is to Christ, not to my peers and dear friends in youth ministry.

In the early days of youth ministry—when youth ministry was the ugly duckling of clergy life—we used to encourage one another to do God's will, *"...even if it's youth ministry."* Now, there is so much emphasis on being a "lifer" in youth ministry, we may need to begin encouraging one another to do God's will, *"...even if it's not youth ministry."*

There are advantages to the life of the long-term youth worker, and disadvantages as well.

But I firmly believe the key issue will never be just a matter of age. For most of us, the question we must continue to revisit is not, "Am I too old?" but, "Am I still called?"

EPILOGUE

Whatever you do, work at it with all your heart, as working for the Lord, not for human masters, since you know that you will receive an inheritance from the Lord as a reward. It is the Lord Christ you are serving.
(Colossians 3:23-24)

As I close out the final pages of this book, it's intriguing for me to think about what your feelings might be after wading through these nuts and bolts issues. It's hard to be inspired by topics like budgeting, conflict, decision-making, and team building. As we said at the very beginning of the book, most of us don't get into youth ministry because we're eager to deal with those kinds of issues.

By this point, you might feel a little overwhelmed. Whether you're volunteer or paid, full-time, part-time or intern, it seems like a lot to consider. But if that's what you're feeling, let the weight of those concerns bring your faith into balance. Until we're working somewhere beyond our own abilities, we're not really trusting in Christ's abilities.

When that group of guys lowered their friend through the rooftop that day in Mark 2:1-12, no one knew how it was all going to turn out. There must have been some unsettled people up on that roof: *Will this work? Can we pull this off? Will we really get to witness the Lord at work? Are we absolutely sure this is the right house?*

As you think back through the challenges confronted in a book like this, you may be asking some of the same questions. If so, let me remind you of another passage of Scripture we cited earlier in this book. Jesus spoke these words in one of his final discipleship training sessions prior to his arrest and crucifixion.

> *"The man with the two talents also came. 'Master,' he said, 'you entrusted me with two talents; see, I have gained two more.' His master replied, 'Well done, good and faithful servant! You have been faithful with a few things; I will put you in charge of many things. Come and share in your master's happiness!'"* (Matthew 25:22-23, NIV)

There is perhaps no quality more important in the nuts and bolts of youth ministry than plain old diligence. Like the servants in Jesus' parable, each of whom was given a different number of gold coins (called "talents" in the text), we have all been uniquely gifted and called to be faithful in investing what God has given us to maximize our impact for him. We all know youth workers who seem to have an infinite number of talents, but Scripture and experience bear testimony to the fact that the number of talents is not nearly as important as our willingness to make diligent use of all we've been given.

In youth work, this requires that we overcome two major obstacles:

Obstacle 1: Laziness. When the Master of Jesus' parable confronted the unfaithful slave in Matthew 25 (see verse 26), it wasn't because he had only one talent, or because he lacked any particular ability. The Master condemned him as a "wicked, *lazy* slave." We looked earlier in this book at the risks of slothfulness—a life lived unintentionally, without purpose. What we see clearly in this passage is one of the principal symptoms of slothfulness—laziness. It's not just unintentional living; it's leaving some life un-lived. Perhaps the unfaithful servant was not as gifted as the other servants, but clearly Jesus' rebuke was because he had not made use of the talent he did have.

Youth ministry is a field in which one can be either incredibly energetic and creative or woefully laid back and sloppy, and for the most part, very few people will notice the difference. It's remarkable how few youth workers ever enjoy serious, constructive accountability. Nobody seems to know (or care?) what we're doing until something "drastic" happens (a bus breaks down, the kitchen is left messy, a hymnbook is marred in the sanctuary, or someone made a call to the "Nasty Talk" 900-line on the church phone).

If a youth worker doesn't have enough diligence to be a self-starter, it's quite possible there will be no start at all. We're not talking here about either legalism or clock-watching; just earnest, responsible effort. For a professional youth worker this might mean something as simple as keeping regular office hours. To be sure, our work with teenagers will mandate a schedule that stretches beyond "9 to 5." On the other hand, church secretaries, other staff, and parents are often frustrated by our aloofness and unpredictability. I called a youth worker recently only to be told by his secretary, "We have no idea where he is; we never do. You might try Pizza Hut." It took an hour for my ear to thaw out.

For the volunteer, this diligent approach to ministry will be manifest in a desire to take the ministry seriously—to approach it with as much creativity and excellence as we might if it were our full-time position. Actually, from a biblical standpoint, ministry *is* our full-time calling, whether we are paid for it or not. We simply can't afford to get in the habit of thinking, "Well, we could probably do more, but it'll be okay for teenagers..."

At the same time, diligence is not the same as feverish activity. As one writer put it, "The Father bids us to do His business, not to fill our schedules with busy-ness." I have met lots of youth workers who are whirling dervishes of activity—even to the point of neglecting their families and their own personal walks with God—but they seldom get anything of significance done. The key is not activity, but productivity. In his excellent book *The Normal Christian Worker*, Watchman Nee puts it this way:

> It is not feverish activity of people whose restless dispositions keep them ever on the go that will meet the need, but the alertness of a diligent servant who has cultivated the upward gaze and can always see the Father's work that is waiting for his cooperation...[Jesus] did not just come to make contacts with men; He came to seek them out and to save them...Some Christian workers seem almost devoid of any sense of responsibility; they do not realize the vastness of the field; they do not feel the urge to reach the uttermost ends of the earth with the Gospel; they just do their little bit and hope for the best.[1]

Obstacle 2: Intimidation. The other obstacle to diligence in youth ministry is intimidation, the feeling that we simply aren't cool enough, talented enough, or young enough to impact a student's life for Christ. In the words of the unfaithful servant (Matthew 25:25, NIV), "I was afraid and went out and hid your talent in the ground."

One of the remarkable aspects of this parable is that every servant was given at least one talent. And Jesus didn't belittle in any way the servant who had only one talent while the other servants were better endowed. The issue was never how much the servants had; the issue was whether they were wisely investing whatever they'd been given.

I believe there are very few people who simply are unable to do youth ministry. The tasks of youth work are diverse enough, and the kinds of students are so widely varied, that I am convinced most people can be effective with students if they're plugged into the right roles with the right amount of support. Furthermore, youth ministry allows people to use lots of wonderful gifts that aren't as readily recognized elsewhere—whether it's the ability to hang out and get close to teenagers, the ability to tell stories, the ability to put biblical ideas into remarkable media images, the ability to use a Frisbee to build a relationship with a cynical teenage guy, or the ability to speak loudly by sitting quietly in a coffee shop with a hurting teenage girl. In youth ministry there's a place for almost every talent.

On the other hand, I have seen many volunteer and professional youth workers through the years who either dropped out or burned out because they were constantly comparing their talents and abilities with the talents and abilities of other youth workers—never focusing on what they *could* do for the Master, but focusing rather on what they could *not* do. The diligent servant will accept the fact that God has uniquely and adequately gifted each of us for the ministry to which he has called us. What great encouragement to remember that this is God's work, and that he is able to accomplish it through people like us (1 Thessalonians 5:14, 24)! Our response is faithful obedience and joyful investment.

When that happens, by God's power, we can break through rooftops, help teenagers come to the feet of Jesus, and watch God do amazing and crazy things in our midst. And that *is* why most of us got into youth ministry! What a privilege! To God be the glory!

APPENDIX A

How to Find a Youth Pastor[1]

It was the fourth such phone call that week:

"Hi, Duffy, this is Pastor Herman Nutick, and I'm calling from First Church out here in Pleasantville to see if you might be able to help us find a new youth pastor. We've had a little bad luck with our last four youth pastors. They've all come and gone in a very short period of time. But I've tried to explain to our board that we're just having a bad month.

"We need somebody who is seminary-trained, married, and mature; a seasoned veteran with about ten years' experience who's about 23 years old. We have a pretty good situation: 150 kids on the roll, including three girls and one guy who attend regularly—or two guys, if you count the kid's probation officer. And I think our compensation package is pretty good. After all, if you're a good steward, $23,000 can go a long way!

"Whaddya think? Can you help us find someone before the car wash and rake-a-thon this Saturday? We really need your help."

ANOTHER CHURCH, ANOTHER SEARCH

Every other week I hear reports of job searches that take too long only to hire youth pastors who leave too soon. Committees get discouraged, opportunities are lost, enthusiasm is wasted, money is spent, and the youth pastor position goes unfilled. Why does this have to be so difficult?!

As a person who wants very much to place effective youth workers in places where effective youth ministry can grow and bloom, I sometimes feel like I'm in an *eHarmony* commercial for search committees. I really want to help them find a match, but I want to make sure the process doesn't lead to a really messy split at some point down the road. Finding the right youth worker—or the right place to do youth work—is a dance of faith, courtship, marketing, discouragement, hope, due diligence, and the sovereignty of God.

What follows is not so much a complete overview as some initial thoughts for an ongoing conversation. This appendix certainly does not provide everything a church or agency *should* know about hiring a youth worker. But it's offered here as a primer—a short inventory of what a church or agency *must* know about hiring a youth worker.

Let's begin with some of the myths that have contributed to the woefully bad track records that many congregations have when it comes to finding (and hiring and keeping) a youth worker.

MYTH 1: These people are desperate and need a job.

One won't be involved in a youth pastor search process for very long before it becomes clear this is a "seller's market." I know of numerous churches whose youth pastor searches have lasted for more than 18 months, including one that was offering a compensation package of over $50,000 plus a $25,000 interest-free relocation loan. After more than 35 phone calls to prospective youth workers around the country, the church found only four who were "willing to consider" the position. (A lot of senior pastors have just read that sentence and are beginning to feel a special burden and call to youth ministry!)[2]

Search committees need to recognize that searching for a youth pastor is a bit more involved than shaking the youth pastor tree and then picking up whoever fell to the ground. If you're looking for someone right out of college, yes, there are a lot of potential candidates available—some of them quite capable. But don't expect to hire a person with zero years of full-time experience and have that person perform like someone who has 10 years of full-time experience. Fruit takes time to ripen, and so do good youth workers—just like good workers in most every field.

If you *do* want the person with 10-plus years of experience, those folks are much more difficult to find. As we saw in chapter 16, youth ministry is like the Boston Marathon: A lot of people start out, but not nearly as many run the race long-term. So if you are looking for experience, you need to assume you'll be competing with several other churches and that your potential candidate has many options.

MYTH 2: High turnover is a fact of life when hiring youth workers.

Actually, the truth of the matter is that high turnover is a fact of life when we pay people sub-standard wages, give them little hope for any increase in pay, offer them almost no room to grow professionally, and treat them like second-class citizens on the church staff. The conventional wisdom that youth workers are migrant workers who should never be expected to work the same field more than 18 months straight is a comfortable cop-out for a congregation that doesn't want to ask hard questions about why it has trouble keeping youth pastors.

If you think good youth workers are fickle and easy to move, try to hire one. People stay where they feel fruitful and fulfilled.

MYTH 3: Youth group + job opening = irresistible opportunity.

As a faculty member in the youth ministry program at Eastern University, I am still appalled at how many churches apprise us of their job opening by sending a little five-line postcard announcement that conveys all the vision and excitement of a doorknob. Wise search committees realize everybody wants to be wooed. Good youth workers want to be wooed by a church that seems to have vision and passion.

How can we possibly expect to capture the imagination and allegiance of a talented, gifted, in-demand youth worker with this notice: "Job Opening: Youth Worker, First Church, Salary commensurate with experience"? We're asking youth workers to consider giving us their gifts and time and energy, relocating their families, and leaving ministries in which they already feel quite comfortable, and the job notice reads like a dog food coupon! Passion is attractive to passionate people. If we want to attract a youth worker who will start a fire in the youth program, we need to communicate that there's already some kindling in the woodpile.

MYTH 4: Any idiot can do the job.

To use a variation of an old proverb: *If you search for no one in particular, that is exactly who you will find.* One of the biggest mistakes congregations and agencies make in filling a youth ministry position is underestimating what it takes to do the job well. The mindset seems to be: "Well, he's willing to do it, he plays guitar, and his blood count seems normal—let's hire him."

There are two things worse than going through a youth pastor search: One is finding the wrong person, and the second is having to go through the search a second time to find the right person. A wise search committee will give some serious thought to these questions:

- ✓ What makes a good youth worker?
- ✓ What is the task we are asking a youth worker to do?
- ✓ What is there about our situation that will attract the kind of person we want?

SEARCHING WELL

Most of us have heard those haunting words from the prophet Ezekiel: "I looked for someone among them who would build up the wall and stand before me in the gap on behalf of the land so I would not have to destroy it, but I found no one" (22:30). If you've ever served on a youth pastor search committee, it probably wouldn't take much imagination for you to hear the prophet's lament in slightly different terms: "I looked for someone among them who would go to the mall and stand in The Gap..."

Having considered some of the myths that confuse and subvert congregations as they search for a youth pastor, let's look now at some of the steps churches can take to make their youth pastor searches more fruitful.

Step 1. Decide what you want someone to do before you search for someone to do it.

The single biggest mistake churches and organizations make in searching for a youth worker is failing to stop and consider *exactly* what they want that youth worker to do, and then communicating that clearly and honestly to potential candidates.

In his survey of youth workers who have resigned, been fired, or been summarily executed (most of those folks were unable to respond to the survey), Len Kageler offers a sampling of unfortunate but familiar stories, in which the failure to take this first point seriously is the central narrative. One youth pastor explained, "My senior pastor was very corporate. Our philosophies of how the church should run were very different. There were no angry words or arguments, it was just very apparent we were going different directions. My emphasis was more on discipleship, and his was more on getting bodies in the door."[3] Another reflected, "My senior pastor had no philosophy of ministry. He never thought about it. He felt threatened when I tried to say we should have one."[4]

A congregation that's not prepared to answer, "What?" is not prepared to ask, "Who?" This "what" discussion will involve two essential tasks:[5]

✓ *Task 1: Articulating a vision statement for the agency's or congregation's youth ministry.*[6]

One way to approach this first task is to:

1. *Enjoin the search committee to brainstorm this question:* Suppose we hire a new youth pastor, and this person has now been in our employ for twelve months. And let's suppose it's been an amazing 12 months. This new member of our staff family has more than fulfilled our dreams for the youth program. *What have we seen in those 12 months that justifies such a positive report?* You might make a list with adjectives describing this ministry.

2. Then, *prayerfully consider the list*: Are these biblical goals? Are they realistic? Are they contradictory? (Can we simultaneously become

more intimate as a group and grow our group into the size of a small country?)

3. Then, *edit the list down to a clear, biblical vision.*[7] This is a step too often neglected, and it's absolutely critical. We don't just jump into the cab and ask the driver to take us *somewhere* (and see how many young people we can cram into the cab with us). We look for a cab driver who understands *where we want to go*, and has the ability to get us (and our young fellow travelers) to that place.

✓ Task 2: Hammer out a written job description that specifies these expectations, as well as specific goals, lines of authority, and basic principles of understanding about what the youth worker is being hired to do.[8]

It's not enough to hire the cab driver. You'll want to make sure you are very clear in your instructions to the driver about where you want him or her to take you. Are there important stops along the way? Are there expectations about when you will arrive at this destination? Are there expectations about what will happen in the cab during the journey? Who is the dispatcher holding the driver responsible for staying on course? How often does the driver need to report his position to the dispatcher? How will the driver's progress on the journey be determined? The position description needs to be very clear on these kinds of matters.

Step 2. Develop a profile of the person the congregation is seeking.

A congregation that wants to develop long-term spiritual growth may decide that spiritual depth is far more important to them than youthfulness, athletic ability, or a zany personality. A congregation that sees its youth ministry as a bridge-building enterprise that emphasizes whole-family ministry may decide an older youth worker would be better able to relate to parents than a twenty-something late adolescent. A congregation that takes theology seriously will want to know if the candidate has spent more time reading the Bible than he or she has spent studying the latest youth ministry book, *Devotionals You Can Do With Water Balloons.*

Does it matter if the candidate is from the same denominational background? Must the candidate be ordained? What kind of spiritual gifts should this candidate possess? Are we willing to pay the price of attracting someone with a youth ministry track record? Or, are we willing to nurture a younger person and support her as she learns the ropes of youth work? What kinds of lifestyle issues are important to us? How important is it to us that the candidate subscribe to certain stances on issues like rock music, smoking, drinking, dancing, etc.?

Step 3. Know where to look.

A lot of congregations begin their search by contacting denominational seminaries or colleges and asking for a list of candidates. But since the amount of youth ministry training offered by many of these schools falls somewhere between zero and none, this will probably prove less than satisfactory. A better approach would be to go to schools and organizations that actually value youth ministry training.

Contact one of the many Christian colleges that prepares students with a BA in Youth Ministry.[9] Or write to the placement office of some of the seminaries that do offer extensive youth ministry training at the graduate level.[10] Go to the Web site for Youth Specialties, one of the largest and most respected youth ministry resource outlets in the country (www.youthspecialties.com). Youth Specialties keeps a running file of job openings that are made available to youth workers upon request, and are frequently updated on the Internet.

Step 4. Pay attention to the process of courtship.

I always tell my students, "When a congregation is trying to hire you, they will put on their very best face. If they treat you with little respect and only moderate consideration before you come, how will they treat you six months from now when they take you for granted?"

All of us like to be wooed. An experienced youth worker with a strong track record gets wooed almost once a month. To really get the attention of one so well qualified, a congregation will have to expend some effort. Here are some suggestions:

1. *Put together a recruitment packet that sets forth the congregation's or organization's mission, vision, and core values.* The packet might also include some information about the congregation's recent history and its dreams for the future.

2. *Include information about your community and the surrounding area.* This is not a snow job. No one is suggesting that your church or agency has to transform Des Moines into *the Paris of the Plains*. We are called to go where the Lord leads us. But, like potential candidates in any search, youth ministry candidates will likely consider the setting for the ministry—schools, recreational opportunities, socioeconomic factors, etc.

3. *Bring the candidate (and his or her spouse) for a relaxed exploratory visit.* Let your potential employee get a taste of what God is doing in the church.

4. *Recruit both the parents and youth of your congregation to communicate with the candidate by phone and mail about why they feel this*

might be a good fit. I remember one church trying to recruit me for a youth pastor position, and they had both parents and teenagers call to tell me about the group and about why they felt it could be an exciting place to do youth ministry. It made an impression.

5. *Don't forget that, in most cases, you're not just recruiting a person but recruiting a family.* Give some thought as to how spouses and children might be made more comfortable with the thought of relocation to a new church.

SAMPLE INTERVIEW QUESTIONS:[11]

1. Talk to us about why you feel called, at least for this next season of your life, to do youth ministry.

2. How do you understand the role of family in youth ministry? How would that vision be reflected in your programming?

3. As you think about making *disciples*, what words would you use to describe what *teenage discipleship* looks like? What, in your mind, are some of the essential traits of a *teenage disciple*?

4. Use five words or phrases to describe what you think of when you think of *effective youth ministry.*

5. Tell us about your experience in terms of relational ministry. What kind of experience have you had with building a bridge to area school campuses? Tell us how you would approach the opportunity to get on our local campuses.

6. If you were to give us five questions that you'd like us to use in evaluating your ministry one year from now, what would those questions be?

7. Tell us about your experience in recruiting, training, and motivating youth ministry volunteers.

8. Talk to us about how you understand a youth ministry's relationship to the life of the broader congregation. How has that vision been worked out in your previous youth ministry position(s)?

9. What five words or phrases would you use to describe what you think of when you think of effective staff relationships?

10. Tell us about the last student you led to Christ.

11. Suppose we were a group of teenagers who've been coming to youth group for a while, and now, tonight, after your Bible study, we ask this question: *What does it mean to become a Christian?* How would you respond?

12. If youth ministry is about bearing fruit, what could we as a congregation or agency do to provide for you the very best conditions for the harvest?

13. What three memories of your ministry thus far bring you the greatest satisfaction? Be as specific as possible. If the candidate is currently serving in a youth ministry position: What is the greatest source of satisfaction in your current position?

14. What three elements of ministry have thus far been the most frustrating for you? Be as specific as possible. If the candidate is currently serving in a youth ministry position: What is the greatest source of frustration in your current position?

15. What unique strengths do you think you bring to youth ministry? How might we cultivate those?

16. What weaknesses do you think impair your ability to do ministry? How could we help you address those?

17. Tell us about the rhythms of your normal week. How much time is given to Internet, to study, to personal devotions, to family, to exercise? Is there a day off? What time of day are you at your best?

18. How does your family feel about this move?

19. What is it about this position that interests you enough to talk with us? What is it about your current situation that makes you willing to talk with us?

20. Tell us about some of the books you are reading or have read over the last six months. Which of those books was your favorite, and why?

21. On a scale of 1 to 10, how would you rate your abilities in each of the following five areas?[12] Very important: Why would you give yourself that score?

Basic Knowledge of Scripture:

1--10

Basic Knowledge of Central Christian Doctrines:

1--10

Interpersonal (People) Skills:

1--10

Ability to Work with Parents, Staff, and Adults Older Than Yourself:

1---10

Communication (Speaking/Teaching) Skills:

1---10

AN OPEN LETTER FROM A YOUTH PASTOR TO A SEARCH COMMITTEE

As anybody on eHarmony knows (as someone who's been married for 37 years, I'm not myself a frequent visitor to the site), it isn't enough to simply advertise availability. It's all about moving through the various stages of communication from interest, to initial contact, to getting to know one another, to courtship, to engagement, to marriage (and eHarmony, I guess). In many ways it's not unlike the process of finding a good youth pastor.

The following was originally written as a blog by a youth worker who wrote it as an open letter to a search committee. It gives us a glimpse into what that process looks like from inside the mind of a youthworker:[13]

> *Dear Search Team or Committee,*
>
> *I have applied to your open youth minister position and would like to pass on some information from my perspective of the search. Before I begin by giving you some advice to improve your communication with those of us who have applied for your position; allow me to share these thoughts. First off, thank you for being a part of the group who will determine the next minister to the students. I understand you have a big decision ahead of you and it should not be taken lightly. I appreciate all the extra time, effort, and energy you have put into the process (not to mention all of the meetings). One last thing you should know about me—I am praying for you as much as you are praying for me. I pray God gives you wisdom, strength, and the ability to discern the right choice.*
>
> *As a search team moving along in the search process, I would suggest you keep these few things in mind (in no particular order). You will notice that throughout this list I will use the word "appreciate" often; because none of these ideas are requirements for you, they are just things I would appreciate.*
>
> *1. Use Technology. You do not have to waste a stamp. Since we are living in an age of technology, with email and text messaging being more prevalent than snail mail, you do not have to send me a letter. You can*

send me an email letting me know you are not pursuing me any longer. This is especially true if all of our communication has been done via email.

2. Communicate, communicate, communicate. At the beginning of the process, I understand it might take months for you to make any sort of decision. I do not expect a weekly email letting me know what number I am on your list of potential youth workers, but I would appreciate notification when the process moves forward. As we move farther down the process, I would appreciate knowing what is going on. As the list of potential youth ministers is narrowed, and I'm still on it, I would expect to be informed on the progress. Even if the search team has not met for a month, I would appreciate knowing.

If I end up being the "chosen" youth minister, I am learning a lot about the way the leadership in the church works. If there is a pattern of poor communication during the search process, I will be more likely to decline your offer to be youth minister. Why would I willingly walk into a situation where communication is not a strength for the leadership? On the other hand, when a search team communicates well during the search process, I will willingly join that team.

3. Honesty is a must! For me, this is a huge issue. In fact, this might be the biggest issue I consider. And as much as you are deciding if I am the right person for this position, I am deciding if you are the right congregation for me. I do not want to work with a group of people who are not completely honest. When it comes to the search process, do not lie to me. If you are interviewing two other people, tell me. If you are worried that I will not work well with the senior minister, let me know. The worst thing you can do is make me feel I am the person for the job while I am visiting, when you know I am not.

There is no reason to drag me along, just to keep me as a "back-up" if the real #1 choice doesn't work out. If you want to pursue one candidate at a time, then be honest and let me know that at the beginning of the process. I will not be offended if you want to be specific and strategic in your search, even if it means I am not going through the first round of the interview process. I would rather know from the beginning what the search team's intentions are, than to believe a lie about where I stand. Being honest is one of those qualities Christians are supposed to possess, so it needs to be a quality the search team possesses as well.

4. Silence conveys a message. I have found that when a youth ministry search team is silent for an extended period of time, it usually is not a good sign. Silence from your team conveys one main thing—I am no longer being considered for the position. I understand this is not always the case, but it is the conclusion I will come to when I do not hear anything from a search team for an extended period of time. Silence also conveys the message that your team is not willing to honestly tell me what you think about my ability to minister to the students in your congregation.

As I am patiently waiting to hear back from your committee, I would appreciate an occasional (at the least) update. Even if the search team is hesitant to have a difficult discussion with one of the candidates, that is no reason to avoid communication. Some conversations will be difficult, but you should have known that when you signed up to be on the team—even in the church, the hiring process is difficult. You need to know that I am not going to talk or think negatively about you if you phone and tell me I am not the right person for the position. I will respect your team and appreciate the manner in which you handled the situation.

If you are silent after I have already interviewed, I believe one of two things is happening: You are calling another candidate back and you are hoping if that candidate says "no" then I'll still be willing to come for another interview. Or you do not know how to tell me that I am not the right candidate and hope I'll find another position before you have to tell me.

5. Respect my time. This comment goes along with the silence one—as you are going through your process remember that the candidates are waiting to hear back from you. Just because you only want to meet once a month does not make it appropriate to only contact the applicants every other time you meet. Do not drag out the process for any candidate longer than necessary—as soon as you know a candidate is not going to be the right person for the ministry the best thing you can do is let him or her know.

We, the candidates, are not just waiting to hear back about a job. We are waiting to hear back about the city we will live in, the church our family will attend, and the people we will become friends with. Taking on a new youth ministry position entails all of our life and family. So, as you are considering your decision, please keep this in mind as you keep us abreast of the situation. And please try to meet as a group more than once a month.

Thank you for reading this letter. I hope it helps you have a better understanding of what the youth minister candidates are feeling and thinking during this search process. I pray God gives you wisdom and discernment in your search and you find the right minister for the students.

Sincerely,

A youth minister candidate.

NEEDLES IN A HAYSTACK: SOME STICKING POINTS

Anyone who's ever tried to recruit a youth pastor understands firsthand what it means to look for needles in a haystack. And like the proverbial search through the haystack, finding sharp ones can be a painful process. Let's conclude then with some fundamental presuppositions that will keep your search process from getting stuck.

1. The youth program is first and foremost a ministry for youth. It is not a place to heal broken adults, provide service opportunities for needy people, or offer therapy to hurting church members. This is not a search for flawless Christians who can lead our youth from a posture of perfection, but it is a search for healthy, growing Christians who can model holistic Christian spirituality. To accept any less is as foolish as hiring a blind man to be a security guard so he won't feel self-conscious about his lack of vision. It might be nice, but it isn't wise.

2. There are clearly some factors that disqualify a person from ministry leadership. This is not some legalistic line drawn in the sand. It is simply to say that if the surgeon has a disease he may well infect the patient. As caretakers of the patient, we must not cast out the surgeon, but neither should we put him in a place where his wounds will be exposed in ways that will endanger others. Each congregation will have to draw these guidelines for themselves.

You may think this point is just common sense—and you're right. But, in almost three decades of ministry I am still amazed at how uncommon "common sense" can be. People find this uncomfortable to talk about, but the apostle Paul did not (1 Timothy 3:1-13, Titus 1:6-16).

3. Pray hard. Consider these two passages:

> "Then he said to his disciples, 'The harvest is plentiful but the workers are few. Ask the Lord of the harvest, therefore, to send out workers into his harvest field.'" (Matthew 9:37-38)
>
> "One of those days Jesus went out to a mountainside to pray, and spent the night praying to God. When morning came, he called his disciples to him..." (Luke 6:12-13)

If you're on a search committee, be encouraged to know that Jesus faced a challenge similar to your own: He was looking for people who could be trusted with shared life and ministry. Granted, being God, he had some advantages we don't bring to the process! But, like us, he understood that these are serious decisions, and that serious decisions must be bathed in prayer.

4. As hard as it is to find the right person, it is much easier to find the right person than to get rid of the wrong person. Dismissal of any staff member can be an embarrassing, awkward, and even divisive process. And, with the relational ties that often accompany youth ministry, the dismissal of a youth pastor can be an especially painful process. The best way to handle this snake is to see it coming and walk around it! Even though finding the right person is difficult, it is nowhere near as difficult as having the wrong person on your staff.

APPENDIX B

A Pastor's Perspective: How to Get Hired as a Youth Pastor

Some time ago I received in my office at Eastern University the following letter from a local pastor. The letter was sent to a number of Christian colleges and seminaries in our area, so I knew it wasn't aimed at our students in particular. But I also knew our students would very much benefit from hearing his perspective—and from his suggestions about preparing a resume and interviewing for a job. I think his letter and the material that accompanies it offer a vital complement to what was written in this book about "Finding a Position that Fits Your Passion" (chapter 14). There have been a few edits—for the sake of brevity. But, essentially, what we have here are the words and thoughts of a local pastor as he wrote them.

Dear Prospective Youth Pastors:

What follows are pages of practical wisdom you will need while seeking a youth ministry position. I've put them together out of frustration because of the things I'm seeing and hearing from people seeking to be considered by our church. I hope you will read through these materials so you can avoid these obvious mistakes and even find ways to improve your resume and interviewing skills.

In the application and interview process, your life will be under a microscope. It should be, because you are applying for an awesome, powerful, life-changing position. You are not building a youth group; you are equipping eternal souls. The person or persons doing the hiring know that, and you must communicate that you know and believe the position of youth pastor is an awesome and high calling.

A word of advice about churches. You may want a full-blown contemporary worship experience, all of the equipment and facility resources you've been learning about, and a large starting salary. Get real. Most churches are not there. You must accept a church for what it is and where it is, just like they must accept you on the same basis. We trust that basis is rooted in the Savior and loaded down with the fruit of the Spirit.

Consider how your words are received when you tell a church you can only worship God in a contemporary music format. You are telling them how little you think about God. Consider your statement—it's on the same level as a man saying he can only love his wife when she is wearing blue jeans. What nonsense! Ministry is not about your preferences, it is about serving God and the people of God. Until you can get that reconciled in your life, perhaps you need to do something else.

I want you to remember that methods are only that. The heart of the matter is people—God's people. A church simply wants a youth pastor to love them and their kids. Nothing else matters. You can have the purest doctrine, the greatest speaking ability, the craziest programming, and the most creative worship experiences, but it doesn't mean a thing if you don't love the kids you work with. "If I speak in human or angelic tongues of men and of angels, but do not have love, I am only a resounding gong or a clanging cymbal" (1 Corinthians 13:1).

As a pastor with 27 years of experience, I'm willing to listen to a youth pastor fresh out of college. But I always remember that this person has very little life experience, and has walked with the Savior for a relatively short time. I love enthusiasm and passionate faith. It is also important for me to listen to the voices of mature faith and long experience of walking with the Savior. Ministry is always a balance of enthusiasm and wisdom.

Sincerely, Rev. Wylie W. Johnson

Pastor, The Springfield Baptist Church, Springfield, PA

HOW TO WRITE A RESUME

1. Write and send your resume with prayer! This is a business of the Holy Spirit; ask for God's help and power.

2. Professionals always keep a resume. You never know when you might need it. Update your resume periodically for accuracy and relevance.

3. First impressions matter. Spend a lot of time making your resume right. First impressions count far more than you might imagine. Read your resume 100 times and fix it 100 times.

4. Make it appropriate. Don't send the same resume for different jobs. Tailor it to fit the job.

5. Use business format. This means one or two pages, printed in black & white on standard paper. Resumes will need to be copied for committee members, and churches are not interested in or impressed by color copies. Use a standard word-processing program like Word or Word Perfect. A good place to start is with the resume template on your word processor. Additionally:

   a. Use Times New Roman. No variation in font, and a limited use of bold and italics.

b. NO colors, artistic license, etc.

c. NO graphics, arrows, or cutesy-pie stuff.

d. NO fancy and non-standard paper, envelopes, embossing, ragged edges, etc.

6. Don't change contact information after you've sent your resume. You will miss any opportunities for response because you are unreachable.

7. Tell churches what they want to know. Your honesty and willingness to be transparent goes a long way.

a. BLUF (Bottom Line Up Front). Tell them what you are looking for—write a real purpose statement that communicates your desire to follow Jesus in ministry.

b. Be sure to include everything they ask for!!!

c. Are you born again / seeker / fundamentalist / liberal / evangelical / charismatic?

d. Provide brief information about your family (if you have one). Are you married, single, divorced, remarried, any children, other dependents? An interviewing committee may not ask specifically about these questions, but they will certainly want to know. And clearly, your family (again, if there is one) is an important part of who you are and what you bring to a community.

e. Relevant Skills?

f. Denominational commitments / rejection of denominations / new wave?

g. Ordained / Licensed / seeking ordination?

h. Include a photo—but keep the file size small if you're emailing materials (under 250K). Lots of people are on dial-up, even if you aren't.

8. Previous work experience. Tell it straight and unvarnished. Don't assume we know what that means—give some indication of what you really did. The committee isn't interested that you made change at McDonalds, but they are interested if you were a shift manager. Tell them if you taught, led someone to Christ, took leadership or responsibility, or planned and led ministries.

9. Education. Specifying the particular classes you've taken doesn't matter unless you haven't completed a degree (and then it probably doesn't matter, either). Don't list your high school.

10. Don't be a poser. Fluff and smoke are easy to spot and make you look stupid—or worse.

11. Considerations and abilities. What do you bring to the position that others don't? Managerial experience? Computer skills? Language? Music ability? Other skills?

12. Proofreading. Get someone knowledgeable to read, advise, and correct your resume for spelling, professional presentation, and wisdom. Check and recheck it for accuracy.

UNDERSTANDING A SEARCH COMMITTEE

1. A search committee is comprised of working adults with lives of their own, who are reading 10 to 50 resumes each week. How much time do you think they will spend reading yours? Not much. Get to the point.

   a. About 5-10 percent will become A-list candidates

   b. About 30 percent of candidates will be immediately rejected.

   c. 60–65 percent of applications will become reserves to be reconsidered if the A-listers don't work out. The chances of a B-lister getting selected is pretty high.

2. A search committee is looking for three things:

   a. Something that catches their attention and makes them interested in you.

   b. Do you have everything they've asked for (education, experience, etc.)—or something that will go one better? If not—rejection!

   c. Is there something else in your resume that causes them to reject you?

3. Understand your audience. Church committees are composed of lay people, most of whom probably don't do a lot of hiring and don't really understand your field. You must make it understandable for them. You must answer these questions:

   a. Why should we trust our children to you? "I have a solid track record."

   b. Do you have the maturity to do this ministry? "Check my references."

c. Just what do you do? How do you do it? Why do you do it?

d. Are we going to have to search again in 6 months? A year? 18 months? Communicate stability and commitment.

4. K.I.S.S. (Keep It Simple, Stupid) Use language that everyone will understand. Include something that humanizes you. A short word about your faith, and short philosophy of ministry.

5. Attitude. Candidates who communicate a superior, know-it-all attitude get rejected quickly. Consider how your words will be received by people who are older than you, who have children, and who have a lot of responsibility in life. Humility is still a Christian virtue. Don't confuse your own haughtiness for enthusiasm or competence.

6. Ministry is more like a marriage than a job. It has to be a love match. And you must demonstrate that you will love that church and really want them to love you.

7. Work Ethic. Ministry is not a 9-to-5 job, nor is it a 40-hour week. The church wants to know that you will put your entire effort into their shared ministry. Ministry means lots of nights and weekends. Ministry also means personal sacrifice. Churches want to know that you will see things that need to be done, and you'll do them. They are interested in hiring a shepherd—with a work ethic!

8. Be careful about bragging; it can get you rejected quickly. Accurately list your accomplishments, but don't brag, especially about nonessential things. Let others, preferably your references, tell about how wonderful you are.

STRATEGY FOR ONLINE POSTING OF YOUR RESUME

1. Post only what is most important. When it comes to online resumes, less is more. Include enough to give prospective employers a sense of who you are, but don't include everything. Save the more detailed info for your resume submission.

2. Post your resume in as many places as you can afford. Some sites are free, or free for the first month or two. Take advantage of the Internet's wide reach.

3. What is most important to post online?

a. Ministry history for the past five years. Indicate if there is more, and make them interested to hear more!

b. Work history for the past five years—indicate if there is more.

c. Post-high school education. Skip the high school diploma unless that's all there is. Don't list numerous courses taken—again, save it for the resume.

d. Denominational preference.

e. Are you married, single, etc.?

f. Photo—churches may repeatedly browse resumes over time, and your photo will help them remember you.

g. Contact information.

4. Be aware of how your words open or close doors. Say only what you want to be heard, and speak the language of churches.

5. Understand the system. Remember, the longer your posting is online, the further it is down the list. If you regularly go online and update your posting, it will move back to the top of the list. Don't get buried behind 200 other job candidates.

6. When you receive a contact, respond immediately and send your resume. Do not ask the church to go online to see your resume; send it yourself.

7. When you send your resume, send it in the format in which you want it seen. It annoys me to have to rescale someone's resume so it'll fit on two pages, but I will sometimes do that—and all the formatting you've given so much attention to is instantly gone. Get down to business by sending your resume in two power-packed pages.

8. Finally, check your postings on Facebook, YouTube, and any Web sites including blogs. If your posts include anything detrimental, embarrassing, or compromising (including coarse language), delete them immediately! Employers all over the map now do a Web search seeking information about anyone they might hire. If you have put up something stupid, take it down immediately.

AVOID THESE RESUME DISASTERS!

1. Focus on Self: Your first response to a church is "How much is the salary, and how much vacation comes with it?" That communicates that you don't have a work ethic and that this isn't a ministry, it's just a job.

2. Insert Politics: "I could never work at a church that worships [insert politician you dislike]!" Even church members who share your politics may find such statements to be immature. Stay focused on the task, and don't let stupid remarks take you out of the running.

3. Mysterious Statements: "My goal is to stay six years." Then what? What does this mean? Better to say, "I intend to commit to a minimum of six years at my next church."

4. Inattention. Spelling mistakes. ("I realey du hve a callege edcation.")

5. Inadequate Identification. Sending a resume with no name, address, phone, or email. Your contact information should be at the top of every page.

6. Outdated Contact Information. Don't send your resume out and then change your contact information (telephone, address, email) so those interested in following up cannot find you.

7. Format. Too many pages (six, eight, ten, twelve pages) = Too much to process!

8. Bizarre. 10mb of graphics, video, photos, moving objects, colors, fonts, circuses, and fluff. Most churches ask for a resume with cover letter. They are not impressed with your computer ability—they want a peek at your faith and heart.

9. Unrequested Inclusions. Sending letters of reference, multiple photos, testing results, spiritual gifts inventory, ordination certificates, graduation diplomas, philosophy of ministry, etc. If the church is interested they will ask for more. Send additional information only when asked for it.

10. Insensitive or Stupid? Applying for a pastoral position with the email address: beermeister@xyz.com. Even if alcohol isn't an issue at that church, your emphasis upon beer demonstrates immaturity. (By the way, in a secular business they would see it the same way!)

11. Attitude. Your attitude reveals a whole lot about the servant's heart that you do or do not have. Remember, you're seeking the job and want a fair consideration. You must be teachable, a team worker, and submissive to authority. Humility is still a Christian virtue.

12. Show Stoppers. "I am not presently in ministry because of a moral failure." OUCH!!! This requires a whole lot of explanations—especially regarding what positive steps you've accomplished to make sure it never happens again. But know that trust is very hard to build after a moral failure.

13. Argumentative. Churches aren't looking for candidates who come in to convince them their theology is wrong. Nor are they interested in the *American Idol* response to rejection: "You don't really know what you are talking about!" Such responses make two things obvious: 1) you don't really understand what it is they want, and 2) you don't know how you come across. Learn from rejection, be gracious, and do your homework. Don't apply for something where you do not meet the basic requirements.

14. Compliance. If you are asked for a resume, send a resume. Don't say: "You can find my resume at xxx@web.site" Don't get upset about a committee not doing it your way. There really are a lot of people applying for these jobs and you will disqualify yourself very quickly. There is no reason why they should begin the relationship by making exceptions for you.

15. Detail. Send everything they ask for. If you send less, you should expect rejection.

16. Sloth. Respond to questions quickly. Answer requests in a timely manner. Meet deadlines.

17. Hidden Agenda. We've received numerous resumes where the applicant is plainly unsuited but is seeking to immigrate to the U.S., or hoping to find someone to fund a move to the East coast.

18. Bragging. "I am the most dynamic Youth Worker you will ever meet!" That remains to be proven, but you have shown yourself to be a braggart. Describe yourself with some reality and humility.

INTERVIEWING STRATEGY

You are no longer a student, but a ministry professional. You must act, look, and talk like a professional. Churches are impressed by maturity, politeness, spiritual earnestness, and preparation.

1. Dress Appropriately. Don't come looking like a slacker, a beach-babe, or someone who slept in his/her clothes. Get a haircut, wear makeup, look the part of a professional. You can always dress down, but it is impossible to dress up after you've arrived.

2. Be Prepared. Know something about the church, their theology, their pastor, their ministries, the position you are applying for, their community. Read their whole Web site, call someone who knows the church, read the denominational directory—do your homework.

3. Rehearse. Have someone ask you questions a committee is likely to ask. Do it more than once. Discuss your answers and how they come across. Have concise, honest, straightforward answers to basic questions. If you don't want to answer a question, have a tactful response ready.

4. Develop. Have your own list of important questions you will definitely ask, some you would like to ask, and others you'll ask if it seems appropriate. Rehearse these questions. And be sure to really listen to the answers!

5. Be Early. If you aren't early, you are late. No exceptions to this rule. No excuses.

6. Be Organized. Take notes if appropriate. Bring photos, recordings, and written work (such as lesson plans) that the committee can look at after you have departed. Leave a lingering impression.

7. Listen First, Listen Second, Then Remember to Listen. Listen with your ears, your heart, your head, and your soul. Work at understanding the real issues and the real intentions.

8. Be Humble. Just because a church doesn't have high-speed Internet, video projection, and a gymnasium doesn't mean you cannot minister there. Remember the priority is people, the priority is people, and in case you forget, the priority is people.

9. Don't Criticize. Churches know their faults. They don't need you to tell them. Observe and make your own decisions about the position after the interview. (See #14.) Remember, churches talk to one another, and we can never quite know how people are connected—you may find an interview at another church torpedoed because of what you did at this church.

10. Be Honest. Your life will be under a microscope. It should be, because you are applying for an awesome, powerful, life-changing position. You are not building a youth group; you are equipping eternal souls. Let the committee ask probing and uncomfortable questions—and be honest.

11. Be Winsome. Figure out who needs to be won over. Listen to people's questions and answer them directly and honestly. Skip the smoke and mirrors. Let them know you think their concerns are important. Remember, one key vote can win the others, but one negative vote can end your candidacy.

12. Have Integrity. Don't accept travel expenses to interview with a church you have no intention of serving. Don't schedule another interview on a day you're expected to spend with church members. Account for your reimbursable expenses with receipts, and submit them in a timely manner.

13. Assess. When you get home, take some notes. Ask yourself: 1) What did I do right? 2) What did I mess up? 3) What could I have improved? 4) How can I pray for these people? Learn from your assessment so that your next interview better reflects the dedicated professional you really want to present to churches.

14. Follow Up with a Thank You. Your professionalism follows you. If you don't get this position, they may pass your name on to another church, or you may find yourself coming back to the same place at a later date. Build relationships; don't burn bridges (See #15).

15. Always Leave the Door Open. The committee may eventually come back to you, even after passing over your candidacy at first, and you might change your mind as well. Tell them you would be open to a second look if the committee changes its mind. Keep your options open.

Questions a Search Committee Is Likely To Ask

1. Tell us about your relationship to Jesus Christ, and your devotional/spiritual routines.

2. Why do you want to minister here? What do you think you can do to make this ministry better? What do you see about this position or church that attracts you?

3. Why are you leaving your present position? Why aren't you currently in a position?

4. Are you currently interviewing for another position? When are you available to begin ministry? What do you need to move into this community?

5. What is your relationship to authority? How do you respond to criticism and correction? Do you learn from mentoring and coaching, or are you resistant to another's help?

6. Do you agree with the doctrine and teachings of our church?

7. What are your salary expectations? Do you have a second ministry or business?

8. Do you have a criminal record? Will you submit to a criminal record check?

9. Are you in debt? How much? Have you ever gone bankrupt? Will you submit to a credit check?

10. If you are single, how do you live out your faith in your dating and relationships to the opposite sex?

11. If you are married, do you have a good, stable, solid marriage? Would others describe your relationship that way?

12. Have you been married before? Have you ever co-habited with another person?

13. What is your philosophy of youth ministry?

14. What are your views on pre-marital sex, homosexuality, abortion, alcohol consumption, recreational drug use, popular music, co-habiting, cutting, etc.?

15. What are your personal goals in life? Family? Education? Professional?

16. What limitations do you have personally or in ministry?

17. Tell us how you work with young children, parents, girls, boys, and volunteers.

18. Do you have experience in preaching and teaching?

19. Would you describe yourself as organized? Relational? Able to multitask?

20. What other gifts and abilities do you have that we should know about?[1]

APPENDIX C

Nuts & Bolts Web Sites

Researched by Thea Lamberson

The Internet has become an amazing tool for ministry. Yes, it can be a distraction, and yes, the cool sites we find today may be gone a week later. But what follows is a partial list of Web sites especially relevant to some of the issues covered in this book. *Please understand that this is not meant as an exhaustive list of all helpful youth ministry web sites!*

The following sites were chosen specifically because they offer help in addressing some of the nuts and bolts issues of youth ministry. Some of them are very well known already. Others are not well known at all. We've already referenced a number of very helpful Web sites throughout the text of the book, so we won't repeat those here. But hopefully you'll discover one or two sites you didn't know about. Be sure to check out not only these sites themselves, but explore the links as well. There are some wonderful free tools available online to help you better do youth ministry administration.

General

Nya.org.uk has national news affecting youth work and teenagers. Although it specializes in issues in the United Kingdom, there are many helpful resources for youth workers in the U.S. as well. Searchable, archived, and featuring plenty of links to other interesting sites.

Wynet.org is the Wycliffe Center's site. Another UK-based organization, its purpose is to equip youth for mission. It includes games, program outlines, and fundraising ideas.

Yom.org is the site for Youth on Mission here in the U.S. This site has information about what short-term mission should be (according to YOM), but doesn't include many resources that can be used outside of their organization. The primary purpose of the site is to help users plan a trip with YOM.

Personal Management

Treepad.com organizes personal information and serves as a database, word processor, and even a photo album. A free trial version is available or a complete, upgraded version can be purchased and downloaded. It's a bit hard to use, especially if you already have a system of organization you're comfortable with. But it could be helpful if you don't yet have an organization system you feel good about.

Netvibes.com lets you create your own newsfeed with customized information all in one place. You can even customize the aesthetic aspect of the Web site. You can access your e-mail, Facebook, favorite Web sites, and search engines all on one site in addition to being able to download "widgets" to suit your interests. Great time saver because you don't have to click around to a bunch of a sites because it's all right there. You can find up-to-date information at a glance and choose what you want to look at in more depth.

Sendible.com helps you access all of your social networks and send out reminders and notes to people. You can save time by creating reminders and notes all at once in advance which will be sent out to people according to a schedule that can be customized. It's also helpful to have all the social networking sites connected and keeps everyone informed. Definitely useful for people who like to plan ahead.

Sched.org allows you to create, edit, and send out schedules for major events and conferences. It also allows you to coordinate and delegate responsibilities to people on the trip. A great organizational tool for large trips where details can often be overlooked, it keeps all the leaders and students informed. However, you have to pay for a yearly subscription to get most of the more useful features and it's pretty pricey.

Bing.com is a search engine that allows you to take a peek into a site without actually having to go there. For example, any video results play when you hover your mouse over them. Good search engine, but some of the previews of the sites do not display the most relevant information about the site.

Spezify.com is another search engine that displays results in an idea map layout with large thumbnail pictures, article excerpts, videos, music, and links to other sites. You can even specify if you want to see only text, only pictures, etc. The layout of the results can be time-consuming to sort through, but visually appealing. When the "display text" option is used, there is a tendency for a lot of Twitter updates to show up in the results, which are unhelpful.

Visioneering

Mindmeister.com is a site that makes it simple to create visual mind maps. With a paid subscription, you can create mind maps in real time with other users, which allows for productive brainstorming sessions that keep everyone up to date with new additions. This feature could be super helpful for large planning/brainstorming sessions if people have busy schedules.

Family Ministry

CPYU.org, the site for the Center for Parent/Youth Understanding, is, without question, one of the best resources for helping parents and youth workers understand the world of teenagers. Filled with fresh content and helpful insight, CPYU.org is the home site for Walt Mueller, one of the leading voices in understanding youth culture. Also has some excellent links.

Parenteen.com is a Web site developed by Chap Clark and his Parenteen team. Has a good section of "Tips for Parents" that could be a good resource for youth workers to use in serving parents of teenagers.

Fulleryouthinstitute.org provides thoughtful, up-to-date articles on how youth workers can do holistic ministry with teenagers. Offers summations of recent research in adolescent development and adolescent spirituality to help youth workers develop practices rooted in solid theological and developmental principles.

Evaluation

Ymarchitects.com is the site of Youth Ministry Architects, considered one of North America's leading providers of youth ministry consulting. YMA partners with churches and youth ministers, working alongside key stakeholders—including senior pastors, youth ministers, parents, and students—to customize strategic plans for building successful and sustainable youth ministries. This web site is the home base for Mark DeVries, author of *Sustainable Youth Ministry* (IVP, 2008). Lots of great resources, sample forms, informative articles, and links for parents, volunteers, and youth workers.

Percept.com and the parallel site ***ministryarea.com*** offer an excellent way for youth ministries to gain up-to-date demographic information about the communities in which they work. The information—including data about religious and/or denominational affiliations, unchurched households, family demographics, and socioeconomic factors—can be broken down in any number of helpful ways. The biggest downside is that the information is not cheap, although it certainly is affordable for most congregations. Don't go to this Web site looking for lots of free information. But, the information it offers, if you can pay for it, is quite good.

Team Ministry

Xywrite.it allows people who are not in the same room to create documents together. People can share documents, track different versions, and export them in different formats. It can be helpful when planning events, brainstorming, or just sharing information. Allows documents to be updated online, which makes it easy for everyone to see the progress being made and other people's contributions without having to send out a slew of emails.

Onedrum.com lets users share and edit documents using your choice of applications (such as Word) and always have the latest version. Available features enable changes to be tracked and synchronized; those changes can be merged together into one document that is backed up and accessible online. Easy to use and a great way to track changes made among the group. Currently, there is only a beta version available but the full version will be ready for release in a couple months (or so it says on the Web site). There will also be a premium version that will be a subscription.

Diarised.com is a tool that helps choose the best meeting times for people. The administrator sends out details about the event and possible meeting times and days, all the invitees choose which times work best for them, then diarised sends a summary of which days and times would work the best. A great way to coordinate calendars without sending a million emails! There is no sign-up required and the site can be used immediately.

Just Plain Cool

Posterazor.sourceforge.net lets you turn any picture into a poster. Choose an image, and this program helps break it up into separate pieces of paper that can be printed and assembled to form a poster. Easy to use and could be a great resource for advertising and creating something that is larger than just one sheet of paper.

Animoto.com. Upload your pictures, videos, and music, add narration or text, and this Web site makes the video for you! The videos can be uploaded to social networking sites or downloaded to share with others. No two videos created by the Web site are the same. The site offers a free version that can create thirty-second videos or the premium version with full-length videos for a subscription fee. Could be really helpful when advertising for an event because the movies made are similar to a movie trailer.

Smilebox.com lets you create slideshows, e-cards, scrapbooking pages, and postcards using your own photos or free designs on the Web site. With a paid subscription, creations can be printed or burned to a DVD. This site could be really helpful in creating unique announcements. With the free version, everything is digital and online. It may not be the most effective way to send information since most people are unlikely to click on links to e-cards in their email.

Anyvite.com allows users to send out personalized invitations and RSVP via the Web. After the event, they can upload photos and comments. A page that was originally an invitation has now become a way to remember the event. A great way to inform people about what's going on in a fun and creative way. The feature of being able to add photos and comments before, during, and after the event seems like it'd be a great way to get people involved.

Tumblr.com is a blogging site that can be used to keep people informed. Material can be posted to any social networking site or simply shared by distributing the link. Text, photos, music, quotes, slideshows, and more can all be incorporated into this very creative and aesthetically pleasing blogging site. It's easy to use and update and can accommodate a lot of different uses.

Aviary.com is a photo and video editing site that was created by a team of graphic designers who wanted to make image editing accessible to everyone. This Web site is a great idea, but does take a while to use. There are a variety of tutorials available on the site as well as feedback from other users, but it's not a site that can be easily used immediately.

ENDNOTES

Chapter 1

1. Henri Nouwen, *The Wounded Healer* (New York: Image Books, 1979), 42.

2. Ben Patterson, "Is Ministry a Career?" *The Leadership Handbook of Management and Administration,* ed. James D. Berkley (Grand Rapids, MI: Baker Books with Christianity Today, Inc., 2000), 20-21.

3. Frederick Buechner, *Wishful Thinking: A Theological ABC* (New York: Harper and Row, 1973), 95.

4. Os Guinness, *The Call* (Nashville: Word, 1998), 4.

5. Gordon MacDonald, *Ordering Your Private World* (Nashville: Oliver-Nelson, 1984), 32-42; 55-62.

Chapter 2

1. Denise VanEck, *Leadership 101* (El Cajon, CA: Youth Specialties, 2005), 19-20.

2. See also 1 Samuel 16:7 NASB, "Do not look at his appearance or at the height of his stature, because I have rejected him [speaking of Eliab]; for God sees not as a man sees, for man looks at the outward appearance, but God looks at the heart."

3. VanEck, 19.

4. To underline the importance of skill, note also Exodus 36:1-7. Moses chose Bezalel and Oholiab to help build the Tabernacle because they had the skills needed to do the job. See also Ezra 3:8-9. Ezra selected Zerubbabel, Joshua, Kadmiel, and other Levites to supervise and oversee the rebuilding of the Temple because they were craftsmen with the necessary skills. See also Daniel 1:17-20.

5. J. Russell Hale, *Who Are the Unchurched? An Exploratory Study* (Washington, D.C.: Glenmary Research Center, 1977), cited in Harvie M. Conn, *Evangelism: Doing Justice and Preaching Grace* (Grand Rapids, Zondervan, 1982), 20.

6. Dietrich Bonhoeffer, *Life Together,* trans. John W. Doberstein (New York: Harper and Bros, 1954), 97-99.

Chapter 3

1. Eugene Peterson, *Working the Angles* (Grand Rapids: Eerdmans, 1987), 7.

2. Peterson, 7.

3. John Kotter, *A Force for Change: How Leadership Differs from Management* (New York: Free Press, 1990), see especially pp. 4-18.

4. Bernard Bass characterizes *transactional* leaders as those who work within the situation and *transformational* leaders as those who redefine the situation to make sure work is profitable (Bernard Bass, *Leadership and Performance Beyond Expectations* (New York: The Free Press, 1985), ch. 1-2. For a theological and practical look at this style of leadership, see Leighton Ford, *Transformational Leadership* (Downers Grove, IL: InterVarsity Press, 1991).

5. Thomas Peters and Robert Waterman, *In Search of Excellence* (New York: Warner Books, 1982).

6. Oswald Chambers, *Workmen of God* (London: Marshall, Morgan, and Scott, 1937), 86.

7. Peters and Waterman, 202.

8. Peters and Waterman, 202.

9. Peters and Waterman, 235.

10. http://www.ijm.org/getinvolved/youth

11. From Youth Specialties, CORE 2008 one-day seminar notes.

12. http://www.hoopsofhope.org/index.cfm

13. Ken Walker, "The Kiva Effect," *Christianity Today*, December 2009, 17.

14. Peters and Waterman, 280.

15. Thomas J. Watson, cited in Peters and Waterman, 280.

16. Bernard Swain, *Liberating Leadership* (San Francisco: Harper and Row, 1986), 30-31. Swain wants to make sure we do not contrast this kind of *style* with *substance*, as with the familiar criticism, "more style than substance." In this understanding of *style*, style *is* the substance of leadership.

Chapter 4

1. I searched for the first few lines and there were 239,000 hits on Google.

2. Godfrey M. Lebhar, *The Use of Time*, 3rd edition (Chain Store Publishing Corp, 1958). Lebhar also wrote the definitive history of chain stores, *Chain Stores in America, 1859-1959* (Chain Store Pub. Corp; Centennial edition, 1959). A *must* read!

3. Robert Banks, *The Tyranny of Time* (Downer's Grove, IL: InterVarsity Press, 1983), 27-35.

4. In Colossians 4:5, for example, Paul's counsel is neither that we see as many "outsiders" as possible, nor that we limit our contact with "outsiders." His counsel is that we "act wisely toward outsiders, making the most of every opportunity."

5. Fred Smith, *Learning to Lead* (Nashville: W Publishing Group, 1986), from the online edition of the book, http://www.ctlibrary.com/lebooks/theleadershiplibrary/learningtolead/ldlib05-6.html.

6. For a full and excellent study of this phenomenon, see Eugene Peterson and Marva Dawn, *The Unnecessary Pastor* (Grand Rapids, MI: Eerdmans, 2000).

7. Eugene Peterson, *The Contemplative Pastor*, (Carol Stream, IL: Christianity Today, Inc., 1989), 45.

8. Claude Levi-Strauss, *The Jealous Potter*, trans. Benedicte Chorier, (Chicago: University of Chicago Press, 1988), 90.

9. John Ortberg, "Confessions of a Lazy Pastor," in Richard Exley, Mark Galli, and John Ortberg, *Dangers, Toils and Snares* (Sisters, OR: Multnomah, 1994), 52-53. I am indebted to Ortberg's article for much of this material on slothfulness.

10. Buechner, 89-90.

11. Cited in Smith, *Learning to Lead*, from the on-line edition of the book, http://www.ctlibrary.com/lebooks/theleadershiplibrary/learningtolead/ldlib05-6.html.

12. Doug Fields, *What Matters Most: When NO is better than YES* (Grand Rapids, MI: Zondervan, 2006), 23ff.

13. Marlene Wilson, *Survival Skills for Managers* (Boulder, CO: Volunteer Management Associates, 1981), 249

14. Wilson, 261

15. William Bryk, "The Collyer Brothers," *New York Sun* (April 13, 2005), http://www.nysun.com/on-the-town/collyer-brothers/12165/.

16. I recommend *Youth Ministry Management Tools* (Youth Specialties/Zondervan, 2001), by Ginny Olson, Diane Elliot and Mike Work as an excellent resource to help you do this. See especially pp. 43-58.

17. Alec MacKenzie, *The Time Trap: Managing Your Way Out*. Cited in Wilson, *Survival Skills for Managers*, 249.

18. Carl von Clausewitz, *On War, Book 2*, (IAP) Ch 2, paragraph 24.

19. Schwartz and Mackenzie, "Time Management Strategies for Women," cited in Marlene Wilson, *Survival Skills for Managers* (Volunteer Management Associates, 1981), 232.

20. Patrick Lencioni, *Death by Meeting* (San Francisco: Jossey-Bass, 2004), 224.

21. Eugene Peterson, *Working the Angles* (Grand Rapids, MI: William B. Eerdmans, 1989), 46.

Chapter 5

1. I've written some of these books myself (although maybe not the excellent ones). I recommend *Purpose-Driven Youth Ministry* (Zondervan) by Doug Fields, *Contemplative Youth Ministry* (Zondervan) by Mark Yaconelli, and *The God-Bearing Life* (Abingdon) by Kenda Creasy Dean.

2. For the most thorough statement of my own youth ministry philosophy, see *This Way to Youth Ministry* (Zondervan), chapter 12.

3. Norman DeJong, *Education in the Truth* (Nutley, NJ: Presbyterians and Reformed, 1974), 61-63. DeJong was addressing the issue of educational philosophy, but his philosophical ladder is quite helpful in shaping a philosophy of ministry as well.

4. Josh McDowell, *Evidence That Demands a Verdict* (Nashville: Thomas Nelson, 1999).

5. Richard Dawkins, *The God Delusion* (Great Britain: Bantam Press, 2006).

6. Audrey Barrick, "Modern Youth Ministry 'Unbiblical,' Ministry Leader Claims," *Christian Post Reporter*, see http://www.christianpost.com/article/20091212/modern-youth-ministry-unbiblical-ministry-leader-claims/index.html.

7. Fields, 56.

8. David L. Goetz, "Forced Out," *Leadership* (Volume XVII Number 1, Winter 1996) 42.

9. Michael Anthony, *Foundations of Ministry: An Introduction to Christian Education for a New Generation* (Wheaton, IL: Bridgepoint Books/Victor Books, 1992), 61-68. Biola University Professor of Christian Education Michael Anthony suggests four basic components essential to any ministry philosophy. Not surprisingly, they parallel those mentioned by DeJong, but they are broader and a bit more inclusive. I have added the fifth question because it is absolutely critical. It decisively shapes one's answer to each of the other four questions.

10. Aubrey Malphurs, *Ministry Nuts and Bolts* (Grand Rapids, MI: Kregel, 1997), 9-10. In fact, Malphurs suggests that Values come before Mission. I tend to favor the approach of others who suggest that strategic planning must begin with a purpose or mission statement. On the other hand, Malphurs is quite right in suggesting that core values shape a ministry's purposes. I still prefer beginning with the mission or purpose. But there is certainly some merit for those who might suggest it's a bit of a "chicken or the egg" question.

11. Management consultant Peter Drucker argues that a mission statement should be brief enough to fit on a T-shirt. Cited in Malphurs, 65.

12. Fields, 65.

13. Many of these have been taken from a listing in Malphurs, 83.

14. From Malphurs, 86; Fields, 57; the Eastern University catalogue; and the Chick-fil-a website, http://www.chick-fil-a.com/#pressroom.

15. Don't even think about adopting this mission statement for your middle-school ministry.

16. Malphurs, 25.

17. Malphurs, 167. This includes some slight amendments to Malphurs's original list.

18. The number of core values will vary. Willow Creek Community Church (Barrington, IL) is committed to ten core values. Wooddale Church (Eden Prairie, MN) has crafted a list of seven core values. Collins and Porras, in *Built to Last* (New York: Harper, 1994, p. 219) remark that the visionary companies they studied typically have from three to six core values. For a good list of values that might stimulate the imagination, consider Malphurs, 48-58, 163-177.

19. Fields, 235.

20. Adapted from Malphurs, 33.

21. Malphurs, 113. I have made some slight adaptations to Malphurs's chart.

22. Irving Stone, *Men to Match My Mountains*, (New York: Berkley Books, 1982), 104-115.

Chapter 6

1.Of course, I am not saying that adults always add the "mature" steadiness, and teenagers always add the creativity or innovation. There are clearly mature and steady teenagers, and their input will be essential, just as there are innovative and creative adults whose input adds color to the ministry (see 1 Timothy 4:12). But, commonly, in the Scripture there is a pattern of elder oversight. One of the advantages of age is experience, and one of the payoffs of experience is lessons learned. That's one of the benefits of aging. It should be added that an unfortunate by-product of those same experiences can be pride and over-caution—skewing the decision-making process too far on the side of discernment/judgment, sometimes because we fear making a bad decision, sometimes because of an over-confidence about our ability to always make the right decision.

2. Robert Moskowitz, *Creative Problem Solving Workbook*, (AMACOM, a division of American Management Associations, 1978) p 61.

3. Em Griffin, "Four Ways to Make Group Decisions," *Leadership* (Spring 1982).

4. Griffin.

5. Irving Janis, *Victims of Groupthink* (Boston: Houghton Mifflin, 1982).

Chapter 7

1. Jim Collins, *Good to Great* (New York: HarperCollins, 2001).

2. Jim Collins, "Good to Great," *Fast Company*, October 2001 (www.fastcompany.com).

3. Collins summarizes this concept with the phrase, "'Who' before 'What.'" He writes: "Most people assume that great bus drivers (read: business leaders) immediately start the journey by announcing to the people on the bus where they're going—by setting a new direction or by articulating a fresh corporate vision. In fact, leaders of companies that go from good to great start not with "where" but with "who." They start by getting the right

people on the bus, the wrong people off the bus, and the right people in the right seats. And they stick with that discipline—first the people, then the direction—no matter how dire the circumstances."

I wouldn't dispute that people are important. But I believe that "Why" and "What" *must* always come before "Who" (see chapter 4) because there are two central questions we must answer before we can determine what kind of people *are* the *right* people to get off the bus, and who are the right people on the bus: (1) Why are we on this bus to begin with? Where are we going? And why are we going there on a bus when there are other faster and more comfortable forms of transportation? (2) What is our intent for being in this bus? Don't we need to have a common sense of purpose for the trip before we could know who were the *right* people to get on the bus? No doubt, "great vision with mediocre people [will] produce mediocre results," but great people with bad or blurred vision will drive the bus off the road.

4. Karen Jones, Dave Rahn, and Merton Strommen, *Youth Ministry That Transforms* (Grand Rapids, MI: Youth Specialties/Zondervan, 2001), 272.

5. Jones, Rahn, and Strommen, 278.

6. Len Kageler, *The Youth Ministry Survival Guide: How to Thrive and Last for the Long Haul* (Grand Rapids, MI: Youth Specialties/Zondervan, 2008), 109.

7. Kenneth Mitchell, *Psychological and Theological Relationships in Multiple Staff Ministry* (Philadelphia: Westminster Press, 1966), 261-262.

8. "Despite the common perception that senior pastors look down upon youth ministers and feel the need to constantly look over their shoulders, this is not at all supported by [the] data; their relationships appear to be very healthy...but significant differences do exist between denominations and organizations...Southern Baptist youth ministers rank at the bottom of the list, scoring significantly lower than those in Episcopal churches... The good news is that regardless of age, gender, tenure and the size of the community, congregation or youth group, the level of support does not vary significantly. Youth pastors perceive high levels of interest and trust from their senior pastors and supervisors." Jones, et. al. 273-274.

9. Lyle E. Schaller, *The Multiple Staff and the Larger Church* (Nashville: Abingdon Press, 1980), 91-92. Although this study is quite old, I suspect that the data is still relatively valid for youth workers. Even though we are seeing an increase in the median age of youth workers (more youth workers are staying in youth ministry longer), the average lay-person still generally sees youth workers as young people, or older people who haven't really grown up.

10. It has been over two decades since Mark Lamport prepared an unpublished survey of 103 youth workers (1987), 27 percent of whom said that they would consider leaving (or had already left) their youth ministry position because of frustrations over staff relationships. The more recent work by Jones, Rahn, and Strommen (cited above) suggests there is still a similar correlation. Twenty minutes of conversation with any random group of youth workers will only verify this reality.

11. Marshall McLuhan, *Understanding Media: The Extensions of Man* (Cambridge, MA: MIT, 1994), 7.

12. Dr. Frank James, cited in Sue Edwards, Kelley Mathews, and Henry J. Rogers, *Mixed Ministry: Working Together as Brothers and Sisters in an Oversexed Society* (Grand Rapids, MI: Kregel, 2008), 25.

13. Edwards, Mathews, and Rogers, 27-28.

14. Edwards, Mathews, and Rogers, 105-106. All the citations for the original research on each of these issues are documented in full detail in this fine book.

15. For more practical guidelines on this topic, I recommend Jack Crabtree, *Better Safe Than Sued* (Grand Rapids: Zondervan, 2008) and Sue Edwards, Kelley Mathews, and Henry Rogers, *Mixed Ministry: Working Together as Brothers and Sisters in an Oversexed Society* (Grand Rapids: Kregel, 2008).

16. These suggestions come from a seminar presented over 20 years ago by Dr. Earl Palmer, who at the time was senior pastor of the First Presbyterian Church of Berkeley (CA) and has since retired. Dr. Palmer's words are especially relevant for youth workers because his years of ministry included service as both a senior pastor and a youth pastor.

17. Stanley Seashore, *Applying Modern Management Principles* (Ann Arbor, MI: Foundation for Research on Human Behavior, 1963), 18-36; cited in Kenneth Kilinski and Jerry Wofford, *Organization and Leadership in the Local Church* (Grand Rapids, MI: Zondervan, 1973), 96-97. (Don't you love it when books written in the early sixties describe their management principles as *Modern*?)

Chapter 8

1. Stuart Cummings-Bond, "The One-Eared Mickey Mouse," *Youthworker Journal* (Fall, 1989), 76.

2. Mark DeVries, *Family-Based Youth Ministry* (Downers Grove, IL: Inter-Varsity Press, 1994), 41.

3. DeVries, 124.

4. This close connection between a father and his teenage son or daughter is a fundamental element of what is called *attachment theory*. For a broader explanation of attachment theory, see my book *This Way to Youth Ministry* (Grand Rapids: Zondervan/Youth Specialties, 2003). For further summary of the evidence regarding father attachment, see Chap Clark, "The Changing Face of Adolescence: A Theological View of Human Development" in *Starting Right*, ed. Chap Clark, Kenda Dean, and Dave Rahn (Grand Rapids: Youth Specialties/Zondervan, 2001), 59. Clark cites research that demonstrates a positive correlation between healthy father-child attachment and "reduced risk-taking behaviors," "greater interpersonal competence," "greater self-esteem," "increased likelihood of identity formation," "greater social competence," "greater career self-efficacy," and "increased problem-solving ability." Linda Nielsen, in *Adolescence: A Contemporary View* (Philadelphia: Harcourt, Brace College Publishers, 1996), 300-322, also provides a very thorough summary of the research findings.

5. Linda Nielsen, *Adolescence: A Contemporary View* (Philadelphia: Harcourt, Brace College Publishers, 1996), 296, 302. Adolescents of both genders show problems in getting along with peers and performing well in school when they have been under-fathered or poorly fathered.

6. John Bowlby, cited in Nielsen, 323.

7. Chris Smith, *Soul Searching* (Oxford, UK: Oxford University Press, 2005), 261.

8. Because this approach suggests that the sole locus of spiritual instruction is the family, it is sometimes referred to as *hyperfamilism*. For the rationale of this position, see Audrey Barrick, "Modern Youth Ministry 'Unbiblical'" www.christianpost.com/article/20091212/modern-youth-ministry-unbiblical-ministry-leader-claims/index.html. See also Scott Brown, July 21, 2005, taken from www.visionforumministries.org/issues/uniting_church_and_family/the_sufficiency_of_Scripture_a.aspx, cited in Steve Wright, *reThink: Decide for Yourself—Is Student Ministry Working?* (Wake Forest, NC: InQuest Publishing, 2007), 88-89.

9. The scope of this book doesn't allow me to address this issue in depth, but let me say that I certainly appreciate the concern for faithfulness to Scripture. The problem is, in the context of this discussion, I don't think it's the right question to ask. I think a better

question to ask would be: Is youth ministry *helpful*? Does it help us to do what Scripture calls us to do? If it does, and there are many evidences and examples of youth ministries where that is the case, then I believe it is *biblical*. But, using that very same criteria, there are clearly youth programs that are *un*biblical, just as there is preaching that is *un*biblical, pastoral leadership that is *un*biblical, and church discipline that is *un*biblical.

10. See Mark DeVries, *Family-Based Youth Ministry* (Downers Grove, IL: Inter-Varsity Press, 1994), Steve Wright, *reThink: Decide for Yourself—Is Student Ministry Working?* (Wake Forest, NC: InQuest Publishing, 2007), Chap Clark, *Disconnected: Parenting Teens in a MySpace© World* (Grand Rapids, MI: Baker Books, 2007), and Walt Mueller, *Opie Doesn't Live Here Anymore: Where Faith, Family, and Culture Collide* (Cincinnati: Standard Publishing, 2007).

11. DeVries, 64.

12. DeVries, 66.

13. DeVries, 66, 67

14. Wright, 155.

15. DeVries, 176.

16. DeVries, 177.

17. DeVries, 177.

18. For example, the Center for Parent and Youth Understanding at cpyu.org.

19. Merton Strommen and Irene Strommen, *Five Cries of Parents* (San Francisco: Harper, 1985), 191.

20. DeVries, 183.

21. For resources and curriculum see www.homeword.com and www.parenteen.com.

22. DeVries, 177.

Chapter 9

1. Don Posterski, Marv Penner, and Chris Tompkins, *What's Happening: The State of Youth Ministry in Canada* (Scarborough, Ontario, Canada: Muskoka Woods, http://www.whatshappeningcanada.com, 2009), 47. Out of a total of 117 responses to this question, "the dislike of fund-raising was stated 35 times."

2. Paul Borthwick, "How to Design an Effective Youth Ministry Budget," *Youthworker* (Fall, 1984).

3. James D. Berkley, *Leadership Handbook of Management and Administration* (Grand Rapids, MI: Baker, 1994), 459ff.

4. Mark Tennyson, "Zero-Based Budgeting" in *Leadership Handbook of Management and Administration*, ed. James Berkley (Grand Rapids, MI: Baker, 1994), 468-469.

5. Jan Hoffman, "The Frugal Teenager: Ready or Not" in *New York Times*, October 10, 2008. cf. also, Bill Osgerby, *Youth Media* (New York: Routledge, 2004), 27-28.

6. Dennis and Marilyn Benson, *Hard Times Catalogue for Youth Ministry* (Loveland, CO: Group Books, 1982).

7. Lynn H. Pryor, "Door to Door Car Wash," *The Ideas Library on CD-Rom* (El Cajon, CA: Youth Specialties, 2002).

8. For more examples and guidelines, see Ginny Olson, Diane Elliot, and Mike Work, *Youth Ministry Management Tools* (Grand Rapids, MI: Zondervan, 2001), 107ff.

9. Berkley, 479.

Chapter 10

1. John Ordway in Stephen Ambrose, *Undaunted Courage: Meriwether Lewis, Thomas Jefferson and the Opening of the American West* (New York: Touchstone, 1996), 131.

2. Doug Fields, *Purpose-Driven Youth Ministry* (Grand Rapids, MI: Zondervan, 1998), 272.

3. This letter is genuine. Only the name and location of the church have been changed.

4. From the CORE, 2003, Session One. CORE was a one-day youth ministry training event offered in reference to the shave-athon by Youth Specialties.

5. Kenda Creasy Dean, *The Godbearing Life* (Nashville: Upper Room Books, 1998), 90.

6. Kenneth Gangel, "Four Images of Ministry," in *Leadership Handbook of Practical Theology*, ed. James D. Berkley (Grand Rapids: Baker, 1994), 269.

7. Ronald Wilson, "Letter From an Ex-Volunteer," *Leadership*, Summer 1982, p. 50-53.

8. Paul J. Loth, "How to Involve Volunteers in Church Ministry," *Christian Education Today* (Fall, 1985), p. 9. I have made some slight changes to Loth's list only to better fit the youth ministry context.

9. Fields, 274.

10. Fields, 277.

11. V.A. Hodgkinson and M.S. Weitzman, *Giving and Volunteering in the United States* (Washington, DC: Independent Sector, 1992). This data is based on a broader study of volunteerism, and not specifically youth ministry.

12. Fields, 277-282.

13. For specifics on how this plays out, see especially the "Resource Inventory" offered in *Purpose-Driven Youth Ministry* (Zondervan, 1998) p. 280.

14. Mark Senter, *Recruiting Volunteers in the Church* (Wheaton, IL: Victor Books, 1990), 24. Senter actually identifies three concerns. I have taken the liberty of adding a fourth.

15. Probably more informal than formal.

16. Cited in Senter, 23.

17. Obviously, in youth ministry, there will always be a need for a long-term commitment by some leaders. Short-term commitment simply is not the kind of soil that breeds a ministry of nurture and trust. But a wise youth leader will think of ways to use short-term leaders in such a way that their brief stints of service take some of the pressure off the long-term volunteers.

18. Senter, 142-144.

19. Andrew Stuttaford, "Lancers, Fusiliers, Rats," *National Review*, April 21, 2003, vol. LV, no. 7, p. 32.

20. Richard Foster, *Celebration of Discipline* (New York: Harper and Row, 1978), 112-113. I have reworded Foster's distinctions.

21. Merton Strommen, *Five Cries of Youth* (New York: Harper, 1979), 99. "Our analysis shows that the most powerful predictor of youth who see faith as 'very important' is participation in the life of a congregation. Contrariwise, the most powerful predictor of youth for whom faith is not important is little or no participation in the life of their congregation. In other words, dropping out of congregational life is strongly associated with a diminished interest in religious faith."

22. Fields, 295.

23. Marlene Wilson, *The Effective Management of Volunteer Programs* (Boulder, CO: Volunteer Management Associates, 1983), 122.

24. Jesus' words in Mark 9:42 make it quite clear that he takes very seriously the welfare of the young and vulnerable: "If anyone causes one of these little ones—those who believe in me—to stumble, it would be better for them if a large millstone were tied around their neck and they were thrown into the sea."

25. "Law and Disorder: An Interview with Tax and Law Expert Richard Hammar," *Christianity Today* (May, 2003, Vol. 47, No. 5), p. 48.

26. "Law and Disorder," 48-49. The whole subject of legal issues might well be a book of its own. For further reading and study on specifically the issue of volunteer leaders and legal liability issues, see these resources: Thomas F. Taylor, *Seven Deadly Lawsuits* (Abingdon, 1996); Carl F. Lansing, *Legal Defense Handbook for Christians in Ministry* (Navpress, 1993); Jack Crabtree, *Better Safe than Sued* (Zondervan, 2009); Mazur and Bullis, *Legal Guide for Day-to-Day Church Matters* (United Church Press, 1994); and especially William T. Stout and James K. Becker, *The Good Shepherd Program* (Nexus Solutions, 1996), http://www.nexus-solutions.com. Another good free resource for screening guidelines and suggestions can be found at http://www.lifeway.com/article/156788/#child, "How to Protect Your Church From Lawsuits" by Jon McLanahan.

27. In their study of 510 volunteers in some 105 non-religious human service organizations (HSO) like Big Brothers Big Sisters, Ram Cnaan and Toni Cascio found that volunteers who were required to fill out an application form for service scored higher in commitment (hours spent in service) than those who did not. (Ram A. Cnaan and Toni A. Cascio, "Performance and Commitment: Issues in Management of Volunteers in Human Service Organizations," *Journal of Social Science Research*, vol 24 (3/4), 1999, p. 23.)

Chapter 11

1. Paul Hersey and Ken Blanchard, *Management of Organizational Behavior, Fifth Edition* (Englewood Cliffs, NJ: Prentice-Hall, 1988), 174-181. I have made some minor changes in the presentation of their work.

2. Hersey and Blanchard use terms, *ability* and *willingness*.

3. Fields, 275.

4. Joseph J. Galbo, "Adolescents' Perceptions of Significant Adults: A Review of the Literature," *Adolescence*, vol. XIX, no. 76, Winter, 1984, p. 951-970.

5. Rodriguez Tome, cited in Galbo, 953.

6. Galbo, 955. In another study of sixth, eighth, and tenth graders, students from all grades mentioned adults over 40 years old (Hauck, E.F., *Adolescent Relationships with Significant Adults Other Than Parents: A Community Study*, Doctoral dissertation, Ohio State University, 1971, *Dissertation Abstracts International*, 1971, 34, 2191A-2192A, University Microfilms No. 71-27, 482, cited Galbo, 953).

7. Rodriguez Tome, cited in Galbo, 953.

8. Cnaan and Cascio, 18-19, 23.

9. Les Christie, *Unsung Heroes* (Grand Rapids, MI: Zondervan/Youth Specialties, 1987).

10. George H. Litwin and Robert A. Stringer Jr., *Motivation and Organizational Climate* (Cambridge, MA: Harvard University Press, 1968), 81-82.

11. The data does not indicate that any one specific approach for recruitment is more likely to produce more positive volunteer response in terms of satisfaction, tenure, or commitment. "That is, recruitment brings people in HSO's (Human Service Organizations), *but it does not help to explain their volunteer performance*" (Cnaan and Cascio, 22).

12. Jane Eisinger, "Leadership Gets a New Look," *Association Management* (June, 2002), 32. The data cited comes from Independent Sector's *Giving and Volunteering in the United States, 2001*.

13. David Sills, *The Volunteers* (Glencoe, IL: Free Press, 1958), p. 110-111.

14. Ed Dayton and Ted Engstrom, "How to Light a Fire Under People Without Burning Them Up," *Christian Leadership Letter*, A Ministry of World Vision, Monrovia, CA, May, 1979, p. 3.

15. Gary C. Newton, "The Motivation of the Saints and Interpersonal Competencies of Their Leaders," Unpublished paper, 1986. Cited in Senter (1990), 158.

16. Wilson, 53.

17. Cnaan and Cascio, 24-25.

18. See B. Gidron, "Prediction of Retention and Turnover Among Service Volunteer Workers," *Journal of Social Service Research*, 8, (1 / 2), 1-16, and J.C. Lammers, "Attitudes, Motives and Demographic Predictors of Volunteer Commitment and Service Duration," *Journal of Social Science Research*, 14, (3 / 4), 125-140.

19. Ambrose, 246.

Chapter 12

1. Joshua Piven and David Borgenicht, *The Worst-Case Scenario Survival Handbook* (San Francisco: Chronicle Books, 1999), 129.

2. For more on this, go back to chapter 5, "Visioneering."

3. These three statement all come from the same article: Audrey Barrick, "Modern Youth Ministry 'Unbiblical,' Ministry Leader Claims," *Christian Post Reporter*, www.christianpost.com/article/20091212/modern-youth-ministry-unbiblical-ministry-leader-claims/index.html

4. Larry Richards, *Youth Ministry: Its Renewal in the Local Church* (Grand Rapids, MI: Zondervan, 1972), 39.

5. Dennis Miller, *Changing Lives* (Shakopee, MN: CD Publishing, 1988), 188ff.

6. For a much more thorough explanation of this programming funnel, see my book, *This Way to Youth Ministry: An Introduction to the Adventure* (Grand Rapids, MI: Zondervan, 2003), 494-511.

7. Adapted from Doug Stevens, *Called to Care* (Grand Rapids, MI: Zondervan/Youth Specialties, 1985), 172.

8. John A. Fairbank and Donald M. Prue, "Developing Performance Feedback Systems," *The Leader-Manager* (Edison, NJ: John Wiley and Sons, 1984), 337.

9. William L. Johnson and Annabel M. Johnson, "Planning for University Faculty Assessment: Development of a Brief Summative-Evaluation Instrument" (Big Sandy, TX: Ambassador College, 1990), *ERIC*, ED *325* 059, 6-9.

10. Reprinted by permission from GROUP Publishing, Box 481, Loveland, CO 80539.

11. Originally published in Duffy Robbins, *Ministry of Nurture* (Grand Rapids, MI: Youth Specialties/Zondervan, 1990).

12. Jim Rayburn III, *Dance, Children, Dance* (Wheaton, IL: Tyndale House, 1984).

13. Gordon MacDonald, *Facing Turbulent Times* (Wheaton, IL: Tyndale House, 1981).

14. If you don't know of anyone in your area, see the website for Spiritual Directors International, www.sdiworld.org. But my strong recommendation is that you be very discerning about whom you choose as a spiritual director. SDI makes very little attempt at theological discernment among its members. Consequently, the range of theological commitments is widely varied from those with a deep commitment to biblical truth and orthodox theology all the way to "have-it-your-way," "you-make-the-call," new age Oprah-ism. There are some wonderful spiritual directors on this site, but be discerning.

15. Henri Nouwen, *The Genesee Diary* (New York: Bantam Doubleday Dell, 1981), 16-17.

Chapter 13

1. Paul Woods, "Surviving Church Politics," *Group* (September, 1986).

2. William H. Willimon, *Crisis and Conflict*, in Berkley, 187.

3. Marlene Wilson, *Survival Skills for Managers* (Boulder, CO: Volunteer Management Associates, 1981), 132.

4. "Straight Talk on Staff Dynamics," *Youthworker* (Fall, 1985).

5. Ron Susek, *Firestorm: Preventing and Overcoming Church Conflicts* (Grand Rapids, MI: Baker, 1999), 27.

6. Susek, 138.

7. Gary Larson, *The PreHistory of the Far Side*_(New York: Andrews and McMeel, Universal Press Syndicate, 1989), 230.

8. Wilson, 133.

9. John Godfrey Saxe, *The Blind Men and The Elephant*, http://www.wordinfo.info/words/index/info/view_unit/1/?letter=B&spage=3

10. Larry McSwain and William Treadwell, *Conflict Ministry in the Church*, cited by Willimon, 192.

11. McSwain and Treadwell, 194.

Chapter 14

1. I recommend that you check out *Decision Making and the Will of God: A Biblical Alternative to the Traditional View*, Garry Friesen, (Portland, OR: Multnomah Books, 2004); *Decision Making by the Book*, Haddon Robinson, (Discovery House Publishers, 1998); *The Will of God as a Way of Life*, Jerry Sittser (Grand Rapids, MI: Zondervan, revised ed, 2004); *Under the Unpredictable Plant: An Exploration in Vocational Holiness*, Eugene Peterson (Grand Rapids, MI: Eerdmans, 1994).

2. Frederick Buechner, *Wishful Thinking: A Theological ABC* (New York: Harper and Row, 1973), 95.

3. In *Leadership Journal's* study of Protestant pastors who were "forced out" of their positions, "pastors indicated that conflicting visions for the church was their greatest source of tension and the top reason they were terminated or forced to resign." David L. Goetz, in an article in *The Reading Eagle*, September 28, 1996, p. A6. The article adds that 53 percent of forced-out pastors failed to ask adequate questions about the church before they accepted to call. The number one issue they *did* investigate according to the survey? Money and benefits.

4. This table is my adaptation of material offered by Michael Anthony in *Introducing Christian Education*, ed. Michael Anthony (Grand Rapids, MI: Baker, 2001) p. 56-57. It originally appeared in Duffy Robbins, *This Way to Youth Ministry* (Grand Rapids, MI: Zondervan, 2002).

5. Doug Scott, "Candidating and Interviewing," in Berkley, 118.

6. Doug Scott, in Berkley, 119.

7. As of this writing, the most recent edition is *The 2010-2011 Compensation Handbook for Church Staff.* Data from this survey is also made available in shorter (and cheaper) volumes specific to various staff positions (i.e., an edition that includes only the data for youth pastors).

8. If the congregation were to sell the parsonage (depending on the strength of the local market), they could take their profit and put it into some sort of money fund, and the interest from that fund could actually generate enough income to pay for the housing allowance, and still provide the congregation some savings. Let's say, for example, the church made a $400,000 profit from sale of the ministry-owned property, and it put that money into a fund that paid out 5 percent interest. That's $20,000 a year in interest income, without ever touching the initial $400,000. That just stays in the bank. Then, they use that $20,000 to provide a housing allowance of $666 per month. On its own, that may not be enough for an adequate housing allowance (it would depend on the local real estate values), but remember, now the congregation is no longer saddled with the expenses like maintenance and property taxes, so some of those savings could be used to supplement the housing allowance.

9. See churchlawtoday.com.

Chapter 15

1. For more *Cokelore*, and lots of other urban legends, go to Snopes.com.

2. Jonathan Grenz, "Factors Influencing Vocational Changes Among Youth Ministers," *Youth Ministry Journal*, Fall, 2002, Vol. 1, no. 1, p. 73.

3. Kageler, 194. The figure of 3.7 years comes from Kageler's own unpublished study, while the 4.8 years is cited from S. Merriman (*Group Magazine*, November, 2003).

4. Paul Borthwick, *Organizing Your Youth Ministry* (El Cajon, CA: Youth Specialties/Zondervan, 1987), 49-50.

5. Grenz, 81. He added that, of this group, most were still employed in vocational ministry, and of the 29.2 percent employed by parachurch or denominational youth ministries, 84.2 percent were still involved in a youth ministry-related position. So, they're still involved in youth ministry; they just aren't youth ministers.

6. Rolf Memming, "United Methodist Clergy in Transition," in *The People(s) Called Methodist*, ed. William B. Lawrence, Dennis M. Cambell, and Russell E. Richey (Nashville: Abingdon Press, 1998). Cited in Dean R. Hoge and Jacqueline E. Wenger, *Pastors in Transition* (Grand Rapids, MI: Eerdmans, 2005), 28. It should be noted here that a vast majority of these folks (93%) were still involved in *some* form of Christian ministry, but they were no longer working in a local church.

7. Barbara Brown Zikmund, Adair T. Lummis, and Patricia Mei Yin Chang, *Clergy Women: An Uphill Calling* (Louisville, KY: Westminster John Knox Press, 1998) cited in Hoge and Wenger, 28.

8. Posterski, Penner, and Tompkins, 25, 114.

9. Grenz, 82.

10. Kageler, 188-189. See also, Grenz, 82.

11. Jones, Rahn, and Strommen, 20-21.

12. Hoge and Wenger, 29.

13. John Cionca, *Before You Move: A Guide to Making Transitions in Ministry* (Grand Rapids, MI: Kregel, 2004), 66.

14. Andre Bustanoby, "Wars You Can't Win," *Leadership Journal* (Winter 1993), 63.

15. Nouwen, 74.

16. Kageler, 145.

17. For more on this, see Len Kageler, *How to Expand Your Youth Ministry: Practical Ways to Increase Your Attendance* (Grand Rapids, MI: Zondervan, 1996), particularly his material on why your youth group might *not* be growing in attendance.

18. Cionca, 197-200.

19. Edward White, ed. *Saying Goodbye: A Time of Growth for Congregations and Pastors* (Washington, DC: Alban Institute, 1990), xi.

Chapter 16

1. Posterski, Penner, and Tompkins, 135.

2. The study involved youth workers from the following denominations: Baptist Union of Great Britain, Church of England, Salvation Army, Methodist Church, and United Reformed Church.

3. Interestingly, their study showed only one youth worker in twenty is sixty or over, compared to one of every five senior pastors.

4. I originally heard about these stages in a seminar given by Brent Bromstrup at the Youth Specialties National Youth Workers Convention.

5. For more on this, see Clark, especially his description of *the world beneath*, the private world of adolescents isolated from adults.

6. Thanks to my good friend, Paul Borthwick of Development Associates International for helping me inventory these important questions.

Epilogue

1. Watchman Nee, *The Normal Christian Worker* (Hong Kong: Church Book Room, 1965). Passage taken from on-line version. http://www.ntmu.net/NCWorker.html#1, ch 1.

Appendix A

1. As an essential complement to this chapter, I strongly recommend Paul Borthwick's excellent book, *How to Choose a Youth Pastor: The Complete Handbook on Finding, Hiring and Keeping the Best Youth Pastor for Your Church* (Nashville, TN: Thomas Nelson, 1993). There simply is no other book on this topic that even comes close to this excellent, thoughtful volume.

2. The best source for up-to-date information on fair compensation for church and ministry professionals is *The 2010-2011 Compensation Handbook for Church Staff* by Richard Hammar (Christianity Today International, 2009).

3. Kageler, *Youth Ministry Survival Guide*, 108.

4. Kageler, 111.

5. Kageler provides in his book a good example of the kinds of questions that both a youth pastor and his or her supervisor might want to consider in terms of ministry compatibility (111-112).

6. See chapter 5, "Visioneering."

7. See chapter 5 for more on the distinction between a mission statement and a vision statement. Briefly stated, a mission statement is a statement about where we want to go; a vision statement is a description of what it will look like when we get there.

8. Borthwick offers some excellent examples (*How to Choose a Youth Pastor*, 207-213).

9. Go to the Web site for the Association of Youth Ministry Educators http://www.aym-educators.org/

10. Denver Seminary, Gordon-Conwell Theological Seminary, Fuller Theological Seminary, New Orleans Baptist Theological Seminary. There are many other excellent choices. This is only a partial listing.

11. Adapted from a list from Paul Fleischmann (National Network of Youth Ministries), cited in Borthwick, 189-190.

12. Adapted from Joshua Griffin, from his blog MoreThanDodgeball.com (February 23, 2009).

13. Mike Kupferer. From http://reflectionministry.blogspot.com/2009/07/open-letter-to-youth-minister-search.html. Used with permission.

Appendix B

1. For more interview questions a search committee might ask, see Appendix A.

Share Your Thoughts

With the Author: Your comments will be forwarded to the author when you send them to *zauthor@zondervan.com.*

With Zondervan: Submit your review of this book by writing to *zreview@zondervan.com.*

Free Online Resources at

www.zondervan.com

Zondervan AuthorTracker: Be notified whenever your favorite authors publish new books, go on tour, or post an update about what's happening in their lives at www.zondervan.com/authortracker.

Daily Bible Verses and Devotions: Enrich your life with daily Bible verses or devotions that help you start every morning focused on God. Visit www.zondervan.com/newsletters.

Free Email Publications: Sign up for newsletters on Christian living, academic resources, church ministry, fiction, children's resources, and more. Visit www.zondervan.com/newsletters.

Zondervan Bible Search: Find and compare Bible passages in a variety of translations at www.zondervanbiblesearch.com.

Other Benefits: Register yourself to receive online benefits like coupons and special offers, or to participate in research.